CONTRACT LAW AND THEORY

Third Edition

TEACHER'S MANUAL

ROBERT E. SCOTT
Lewis F. Powell, Jr. Professor *and*
William L. Matheson & Robert M. Morgenthau
Distinguished Professor of Law
University of Virginia

JODY S. KRAUS
Professor of Law,
Caddell and Chapman Research Professor *and*
Professor of Philosophy
University of Virginia

ISBN#: 0820556300

Editorial Offices
744 Broad Street, Newark, NJ 07102 (973) 820-2000
201 Mission St., San Francisco, CA 94105-1831 (415) 908-3200
701 East Water Street, Charlottesville, VA 22902-7587 (804) 972-7600
www.lexis.com

(Pub.03020)

TABLE OF CONTENTS

INTRODUCTION

One of the prominent features of this casebook is that we do not try to hide the ball. Both doctrine and theory are set out in detail and with as much clarity as we can command. We do this because we have found that the level of engagement and quality of analysis improves substantially if the students have the reinforcement of the reading materials to supplement the classroom discussion. One concern a first time teacher of the materials may have, however, is whether the book steals too much of the teacher's "thunder." We would like to assure you that such is not the case. There will be plenty of opportunities to pull rabbits out of hats and to have the collective "ah ha" that we all secretly cherish. Thus, while the notes and essays are clear, one needs to remember that integrating doctrine and theory is not easy for first year law students still struggling with the basic structure of the legal system and the elements of legal analysis, even if it is there for all to see. Thus, for example, we assign the essays as part of the reading, but we teach the cases and problems as if the essays were not there. A handful of students may have the basic insights at the outset but virtually no one will be able to work through the analysis step by step without the careful Socratic dialogue for which first year law teaching is justly famous.

In an important sense, then, this is not a "teach against the casebook" book. Not that you cannot do so if you choose, but we find that you can accomplish much more by teaching *with the book*. Another concern that first-time teachers often experience is not being able to "answer" all the questions posed by casebook authors. Many of the theoretical questions do not have "answers," of course, but in the following chapters of this Manual we do provide you with the analyses that we find most convincing. We also give you "answers" to all the problems and doctrinal questions, including an indication of how the court ruled in the case from which the problem was drawn.

The casebook is designed to be used in Contracts courses of varying credit hours. The most common pattern, we have found, is four credits (that is our experience at Virginia). Some schools offer Contracts as a five credit course and a few retain the traditional six credit offering, extending over two semesters. For those teaching a six credit course, we believe it is quite feasible to cover most, if not all, of the book. But for those who teach one semester courses (whether four or five credits) some omissions are necessary. One of the reasons that we find the overview chapter so useful is that it allows you to omit entire chapters of the book while still introducing students to the complete framework of contract law rules.

For those who would value some guidance on coverage and choices for omitting materials, we can share some of our experiences (both good and bad). One of us has taught Chapter 11 (Third Party Rights) at the end of a four credit, one semester course and strongly recommends against doing it. The material is important, but it is also difficult, and, coming at the onset of first semester exams, it is too doctrinally complex for anxious first year students. We think that Chapter 11 works very well if it is taught in the spring at the conclusion of a six credit, two semester course, as a springboard to the second year courses in Commercial Law and

Corporations.

For those teaching a one semester course, then, begin by omitting Chapter 11. We also omit (either entirely or in large part) Chapters 7, 8 and 9 dealing with performance, excuse and conduct constituting breach. At Virginia, we offer a second semester elective, Contracts II, that covers performance issues in depth. Typically fewer than 50 students elect the course each year, however. With those omissions, we believe it is quite feasible to cover the first five chapters completely, as well as substantial portions of Chapter 6 (Interpretation) and Chapter 10 (Remedies). Both Chapters 6 and 10 have been structured to provide flexibility in coverage. In the case of Chapter 6, for example, one can cover (most or all) of sections A and B, which provide in-depth analyses of the parol evidence rule under both the common law and the UCC, and omit Section C on plain meaning versus contextual interpretation without impairing students' ability to deal intelligently with interpretation issues. Chapter 10 can be taught in one of several ways. One approach is to cover (most or all) of Sections A and B, which treat thoroughly all of the basic doctrinal and theoretical issues concerning contract damages and associated remedies. Thereafter, omit Section C, which is designed to provide an opportunity to work through the UCC remedial scheme as an illustration of how the various default rules fit together. Alternatively, one of us has covered Sections A1 and A2, B1, B2 and B3 and then assigned most of Section C. This worked quite well for the better students, but, coming at the end of the semester, it was a bit daunting for those who don't yet feel fully comfortable with the different techniques of common law and Code analysis.

For what it is worth, here is the course syllabus that Scott has used in a 56 class course (with some success in covering all of the assigned material).

Class	Assigned Reading
1	Chapter 1, pp. 1-14: *Bailey v. West, Part I*; Restatement (Second) of Contracts §§ 1, 2 and 4.
2-5	Chapter 1, pp. 7-34: *Bailey v. West, Part II*; *Lucy v. Zehmer*; *Leonard v. Pepsico*; *Essay: An Introduction to Theories of Contract Law*; R2d §§ 16, 18 and 20.
6	Chapter 1, pp. 34-44: *Corthell v. Summit Thread Co.*; *Joseph Martin v. Schumacher*; R2d § 33; Uniform Commercial Code §§ 2-102, 2-105(1), 2-204, 2-305.
7-8	Chapter 1, pp. 44-55: *Hamer v. Sidway*; *St. Peter v. Pioneer Theater Corp.*; R2d §§ 71, 81.
9	Chapter 1, 55-67: *Williams v. Walker-Thomas*

CHAPTER 1

AN OVERVIEW OF CONTRACT LAW

A. Introduction

Chapter One, as the title suggests, is designed to give students an overview of contract law. It provides an introduction to many of the most basic doctrines of contract law in order to provide the foundation for a more rigorous examination of these and other principles later in the course. Since contract law doctrines are interrelated and courts often rely on several doctrines in deciding cases, we have found that an introduction to the basics provides the coherence necessary to make more exacting analysis possible.

At the same time, we introduce in this chapter the outlines of the various theoretical approaches to contract law. An economic analysis focuses principally on the *effects* of a particular legal rule; it considers the consequences of a legal decision the most critical factor. We begin by asking students to think about why decisions are written down and published and why the outcomes of the cases are always binary– a winner and a loser. This leads to a discussion of the trade offs between two quite different conceptions of justice. Should the law be primarily concerned with justly regulating future transactions (that is, with the effects of its rulings) or should it be concerned with the justice of the dispute between the parties before the court. This latter perspective introduces autonomy theories of contract, which view the justification for state coercion of reluctant promisors as resting on the goal of promoting the autonomy interests of the contracting parties. We also ask students to view either of the "unitary value" theories with skepticism– perhaps a pluralist perspective best captures what the law is trying to do.

B. Sources and Functions of Contract Law

We begin with a definition of the study of contract law: the study of the legal enforcement of promises. Two questions follow from this definition. The first is the descriptive question: what promises will the state enforce? The second is a normative question: how can we justify state coercion as a means of enforcing promises? We emphasize that the answers to these questions are not purely academic, but are essential to the practicing lawyer. In order to serve their clients well, attorneys must be able to answer the first question, and doing this requires them to understand the implications of the second. If the circumstances of a case do not justify coercive state action, then the promise will not be enforced. Students need to develop a fundamental understanding of the theoretical underpinnings of contract law, therefore, in order to help them discern patterns of judicial enforcement. The book provides several tools for developing theoretical insights, and we find that explicitly pointing out the nexus between the theory and practice of contract law can help prepare students for the theoretical component of the course.

The discussion of the sources and functions of contract law beginning on page 2 is the first of these tools. Contract law serves four basic functions: sorting enforceable from unenforceable promises; providing default rules that fill the gaps in incomplete contracts; interpreting the meaning of promises made; and determining which rules should be default rules and which rules should be mandatory. This final function helps to define acceptable bargaining behavior for contracting parties because mandatory rules prohibit certain types of bargaining practices, particularly those infected with fraud or duress. The four functions can provide a framework to help students evaluate individual doctrines and theories.

This section also gives a brief introduction to the various sources of contract law, including the common law, the Restatement, and the UCC. At this point in the course, we find it helpful to explain the difference between controlling and persuasive authority and the relationship between common and statutory law. This serves as an introduction to the principle of *stare decisis* and is helpful to students as they read cases in this and other first year courses.

C. Enforcing Promises
What is a Promise?

We begin the course with this question and ask students to read §§ 1,2 and 4 of the Restatement (Second) and the first case, *Bailey v. West*. We find that there is a great deal of substantive analysis to be mined here: the nature of promise-making; the role of conduct and context; the reliance of our legal system on majoritarian or "reasonableness" intuitions; the all-or-nothing, or "binary," character of most contract law rules; and the distinction between promissory and non-promissory liability. There are also some interesting procedural questions raised in *Bailey* and spending some time with the respective roles of fact finders and appellate reviewers pays off in the long run.

Bailey v. West *(Page 5).* Before a court can decide that a promise should be enforced, it has to be clear that a promise had been made. Often this is not in dispute, but, as *Bailey* demonstrates, the question is sometimes litigated. You may want to introduce this case by asking: what is the legal authority for a possible holding that a promise had, in fact, been made to Bailey to pay for the boarding of the horse? In turn, how can one argue that Bailey made a return promise? Bailey and West never even talked to one another, so how could a contract possibly arise? Of course, §§ 1, 2, and 4 of the Restatement provide such legal authority and answer these questions. Although the court finds that no promise was made, its discussion of contracts implied in fact helps to elaborate on Restatement § 4 and underscores the fact that a contract need not consist of a written or oral promise in order to be enforceable. Conduct alone can suffice. In the court's opinion, West's conduct did not constitute a promise. Is there a credible argument to be made that it did?

The court's discussion of the elements of a contract implied in fact (an exchange of conduct promises) allows us to walk the students through Bailey's best argument:
"West, through his authorized agent, Kelly, made a promise to pay for Bascom's Folly by delivering and unloading the horse from the van at my stables. I, in turn, by my conduct in taking control of the horse promised to provide the usual and ordinary services associated with my business. Since this conduct is the normal and typical way in which I enter into engagements to care for horses in my business, the reciprocating conduct meets the definition

of "promise" in Restatement § 2, and a contract is formed through the exchange of conduct promises."

This is a pretty good argument. One of the reasons Bailey loses is that it is raised for the first time on appeal (see the key paragraph at the bottom of page 6).

The court also rejects Bailey's argument that he should recover on a quasi-contractual theory. We spend some time on the elements of quasi-contractual liability. Most students understand from their reading that, while both express contracts and contracts implied in fact are formed by legally binding promises, a quasi-contract is not a contract at all, but an imposition of liability for a benefit conferred in the absence of a promise (usually because the benefit was induced by fraud or deceit or the recipient was aware that the benefit was being conferred by mistake and did not take reasonable steps to correct it). It helps to have students work through the strategy they would use if hired to represent Bailey. It is a given that Bailey conferred a benefit. Either that benefit was induced by a promise or it was not. Thus, one can argue in the alternative: If West (through Kelly) made a promise, then Bailey wins on a theory of a contract implied in fact. If, on the other hand, West did not make a promise, then Bailey wins on a theory of quasi-contract. The argument loses, however. Why? Clearly Bailey conferred a benefit and West "appreciated" the benefit in the sense of understanding what Bailey was doing. But in this case retention was not an "unjust enrichment." Rather, Bailey was a "mere volunteer." Why? Justice Holmes' famous quote from *Day v. Caton* at the bottom of page 13 gives the answer. West had no reason to know that Bailey remained under a mistaken impression that he (West) was going to be responsible for paying the cost of boarding the horse. Bailey's belief that the benefit he was providing would be compensated by West was not induced by West's fraud, nor did West fail to take reasonable steps to correct Bailey's misimpression. In short, Bailey was a doofus.

Note 3 (Page 10). Bailey raises questions about agency relationships. Bascom's Folly was delivered to Bailey's farm by the van driver (Kelly) who had been hired either by West or West's trainer to transport the horse. Hence, it is through an agency relationship that West's alleged liability arises. We explain the basic structure and requirements of the agency relationship, and use the questions and hypothetical in Note 3 to help the students understand and explore the implications that the agency relationship has in this case. Obviously, one must assume that Kelly had apparent authority to board the horse. Is that plausible? Perhaps for a few days, but surely not for four years.

Note 5 (Page 10). Is the court's decision in *Bailey* designed to achieve justice between the two parties involved or is it meant to establish a legal rule that will guide other parties in the future? From an *ex post* perspective it is not clear that Bailey should bear the entire loss. West and his trainer must have known that Kelly would need to leave the horse somewhere, and that ownership was in dispute. We ask the students to speculate about the untold story. How did *Bascom's Folly* get to Bailey's horse farm in Rhode Island? Most plausibly because Kelly was on his way back from Queens to Boston via I 95 and had to dump the horse somewhere (perhaps in order to get back in time for the Red Sox game at Fenway Park). It would not seem unreasonable under those circumstances for Bailey to assume that he was to take care of the horse and that the owner, whoever that turned out to be, would compensate him for that care. This seems to be the rationale followed by the lower court, which did award some damages to Bailey, and yet, in the end, Bailey is made to bear the entire loss.

Perhaps, then, the court wants to establish a rule to regulate the *ex ante* behavior of parties in similar situations. We explain the difference between *ex post* and *ex ante* judicial rule making, and explore the advantages and disadvantages of each approach. What behavior adaptation does *Bailey v. West* encourage? Why would a court interested in future justice choose West's understanding of the episode over Bailey's (does it come down to comparative advantage in this case: who was in a better position to resolve the uncertainty)? Deciding this question requires the court to make an assumption about how "reasonable" people would react in this situation. The implication is that Bailey was idiosyncratic in assuming that, without more, West (through Kelly) was promising to pay for the care of the horse. But why should the idiosyncratic party have to adapt his behavior to the majority and not the other way around? One answer is that this is the least cost solution and reducing transactions costs is socially desirable in these settings.

Lucy v. Zehmer *and* **Leonard v. Pepsico** *(Pages 14 and 19).* These cases work in tandem and focus on the problem of discerning intent to promise. Section 2 of the Restatement defines a promise as "a manifestation of intention . . . that *justifies a promisee* in understanding that a commitment has been made." This focus on the understanding of the promisee, rather than the actual intention of the promisor, creates an objective standard for determining whether a representation, or manifestation, is a legal promise. *Lucy* and *Leonard* both use a reasonableness standard to make that determination. If a reasonable person would be justified in construing the representation as an earnest offer, then courts will enforce that promise. What is the purpose of adopting an objective standard, or, in other words, why is the subjective intent of the promisor less important than how a reasonable person would construe the promise? Does the answer to this question suggest that contract law is concerned about the behavioral effects of its decisions and is interested in creating incentives to encourage parties to behave in certain ways? If so, what norm explains why we would want to see the party with mistaken subjective intention conform his or her behavior to the more "reasonable" majority? Conversely, what principle justifies "reasonable" people being permitted to rely solely on their intuitions about whether a promise has been made without requiring them to inquire further?

In *Lucy,* the court carefully details the evidence that the Zehmers appeared to make a good faith offer to sell the Ferguson farm; in *Leonard,* the court goes to great lengths to show why no reasonable person would consider the Pepsi points ad a serious offer. What evidence is there to rebut these arguments? We have the class argue in favor of Zehmer using the analysis in *Leonard.* How many people sell property worth $300,000 in today's dollars in a bar on a bar receipt, after drinking all day and having summarily rejected similar offers from Lucy many times in the past? In short, "It's the context, stupid!" Most people are comfortable with the conclusion in *Leonard* that the context of the advertisement demonstrates that the offer was not serious. If that is so, why doesn't the context in *Lucy* demonstrate the same? One possible answer is that the lawyering on Zehmer's behalf seems pretty weak. Rather than focusing on the important question – did Lucy have reason to know that the Zehmers were jesting? – Zehmer's lawyer seems to have been intent on proving that Zehmer was "high as a Georgia pine" and didn't know what he was doing. Having failed to show disability, he was stuck.

[For those who are committed legal realists, one of Scott's students grew up in Dinwiddie county and came up after class to offer the following explanation for the case. Apparently the Zehmers were infamous as being the only Republicans in this rural south side Virginia county during the era of the Byrd machine and were not "well-liked." While that might explain local prejudice against the Zehmers, it doesn't explain what happened here. The Zehmers won in the Dinwiddie circuit court. They lost at the Supreme Court in Richmond where presumably no one knew anyone.]

Essay: An Introduction to Theories of Contract Law (Page 23). Because individual liberty is so strongly favored in the Western tradition, state coercion requires justification. In *Lucy*, the defendant did not wish to carry out his promise, and yet the court required him to do so. Why is state coercion justified in this instance, if it is indeed justified? In order to answer this question, one must examine the dominant theories used to justify contract as a distinct area of law. These justifications can serve as useful tools for analyzing cases throughout the course. We ask students how they would justify the court's holding using one or a combination of contractual theories.

The discussion of Charles Fried's autonomy theory serves as a good starting point for this examination because many students will already have a sense for the moral implications of making promises. For Fried, it is the making of the promise that binds the promisor with a moral obligation. The moral obligation arises because the promisor has voluntarily invoked a convention that creates in another an expectation that the promise will be carried out. By so doing, she has invited the trust and confidence of the promisee. When a promise is broken, there is a breach of trust that amounts to the violation of one's moral duty.

This theory appeals to common sense, but students should be allowed to explore its limits in the legal context. For instance, it is not self-evident why promising creates a moral duty. If all promises do indeed create moral obligations, why do courts not enforce all promises? Should they enforce all promises? If court's should enforce promises on moral grounds, shouldn't they also enforce other moral breaches? Few people would argue that marital infidelity should be criminalized, and lying only creates legal liability when one is under a legal duty to tell the truth. Finally, there would seem to be situations in which breaking a promise is justified; this would indicate that the moral obligation created by promising is not absolute. How does this affect Fried's theory, if at all?

Economic theories of contract law view the judicial enforcement of contracts as a mechanism for creating rules that provide proper incentives for future contracting parties. Legal rules should provide incentives that lower the overall costs of bargaining in order to increase the total size of the contractual pie. The rulings in *Lucy* and *Leonard* can be justified on economic grounds because they deter idiosyncratic bargaining. They force parties to conform their behavior to prevailing norms or risk losing out by entering into a bargain they didn't really intend. This lowers the total transaction costs because bargainers can safely rely on objectively reasonable manifestations; they need not take precautions to protect themselves against idiosyncratic bargainers. Economic theorists maintain that this is what most parties would want because all parties to a transaction benefit when transaction costs are lowered.

Reliance theorists argue that contracts should be enforced because entering into a bargain invites reliance on the promises made. If I enter into a contract with you, you will change your behavior because of my promise. You may incur expenses in anticipation of my performance; you may forego other bargaining opportunities, or you may simply get your hopes up. In any case, a breach on my part will result in a detriment to you. Reliance theorists posit that breaching parties should be liable for detrimental reliance because they invited the reliance in the first place.

This theory, too, has its limits. As *Note 2 on page 30* points out, in cases where there is an instant retraction, no substantial reliance exists. If Zehmer told Lucy right after the contract was signed that it was all in fun, then how could Lucy really have relied on that promise to his detriment? If the simple fact that he thought he had purchased the farm amounts to reliance, then every promise must be said to invite some reliance, and yet not every promise is enforced. How would one draw the line? How much reliance would be necessary to make a contract enforceable? Did the court rule in Lucy's favor in order to compensate him for his detrimental reliance or was there another reason? Leonard seems to have relied substantially on what he thought was a real offer. Raising $700,000 was surely no small task, and yet the court refuses to compensate him for that reliance. Was the court wrong in doing so? Is it possible that an idiosyncratic person's reliance has less social value than that of a reasonable person?

Instant retraction creates problems for economic analysis as well. Information is an economic good. Thus, an economic rationale for enforcing promises is to encourage parties to rely on the information contained in a promise so that their present plans more closely conform to a future reality. If so, the value of the lost information in the case of instant retraction is de minimus. Thus, one could argue "no harm, no foul." One distinction in the economic approach is that it focuses on "reliability" rather than "reliance" per se. Enforcing a promise, even in the extreme case of instant retraction increases the ex ante reliability of that promise. It gives the promisee the informational value of the promise sooner rather than later and thus enhances social welfare. A clear rule promotes the informational value of a promise more than would a case-by-case analysis of the quantum of reliance prior to the retraction. Moreover, a retraction rule would create the problem of "inefficient reliance." Without a clear rule – "once you have promised, you are bound" – parties have incentives to rely in order to make the promise binding, rather than to gauge their reliance on the optimal level of investment necessary to realize their future plans.

Indefinite Promises and Open Terms

This section address the question: How completely must a promise specify the assumed obligation in order to be enforceable? The traditional common law answer to this question differs from that of the UCC and the modern common law. The traditional rule is that a contract based on incomplete promises that leave out material terms is void for indefiniteness. The modern rule focuses on the underlying question of intent rather than the fact of omission itself. If the parties intend to be bound, a contract can omit basic terms like price or date and time of delivery and still be enforced. In such cases, courts turn to standards such as reasonable market value and standard industry practice in order to fill the contractual gaps. Contract law's default rules often provide guidance to courts on which standard to choose when faced with the task of filling gaps. However, not all gaps can be filled. There is a point at which contract terms are too vague or indefinite to be enforced. But how does one know when that point has been reached? One way to resolve this problem is to look at the intent of the parties, but the only evidence of that intent may be the contract itself, and it can be difficult or even impossible to clearly discern intent when the terms are indefinite or unspecified. Indeed, at least one of the parties is likely to argue that the contract cannot represent their intent because it is too vague to do so. Courts can overcome this difficulty by invoking the reasonable person standard: what would a reasonable person have intended when making this contract? But sometimes, as the *Schumacher* case shows, courts decide that the contract is so vague that no reasonable person would think he had received a promise at all.

Corthell v. Summit Thread Co. *(Page 34).* This suit was brought against the Summit Thread Company by one of its former employees. The employee, Corthell, had developed several inventions that could be used to improve Summit's products. The company offered to pay Corthell a definite sum for the completed inventions and promised to give him "reasonable recognition" in return for turning over all future inventions to Summit. Corthell subsequently turned over four inventions to the company, after which Summit terminated his employment. Corthell received no compensation for the final four inventions and sued to recover damages for breach of the contract.

The *Corthell* court states the traditional rule that a contract must be "sufficiently definite" to be enforceable, but it also points out that seemingly vague language, such as "fair price," can be definite enough to enforce. The case, then, seems to turn on the issue of whether or not the phrase in question, "reasonable recognition," can be given a more definite meaning in light of other provisions in the contract. The defendant-company argues that it cannot because the fact that it has reserved the right to set the amount of recognition means that it could pay the plaintiff nothing if it so chooses. The court disagrees. Just because the defendant has the right to set the level of recognition, the court says, does not mean that it can do whatever it wants.

Though the court rejects the company's interpretation of the level of compensation clause, the company's argument seems to be supported by the plain language of that clause. As a basis for its decision, the court looks past the plain meaning to the intent of the parties, as the contract itself stipulates: "All of the above is to be interpreted in good faith on the basis of what is reasonable and intended and not technically . . . ." The court interprets "reasonable recognition" to mean "reasonable compensation," and decides that the company's intent, as evidenced by the language of contract, was to provide reasonable compensation in return for the plaintiff's inventions. Thus, the company had bound itself to pay reasonable compensation, and to pay nothing would be manifestly unreasonable. The court was then able to use a reasonableness standard to fill the gap left by the contract's vague language regarding payment.

Joseph Martin, Jr. v Schumacher *(Page 38).* This suit arose as a result of a rent dispute between a landlord and tenant. The lease contained a renewal clause allowing the tenant to renew the lease at his discretion at a rental rate "to be agreed upon." The landlord demanded a rent increase from $650 per month to $900 for the renewal period. An appraisal of the property set the fair market rental value at $545.41. The plaintiff asked the court to set the rent at the appraiser's figure or to choose another reasonable amount. The Supreme Court granted a motion for summary judgment against the plaintiff, but the Appellate Division overruled and ordered the trial court to set a reasonable rent if the plaintiff had established the fact that the parties' intent was not to terminate in the event that no agreement could be reached. On the landlord's appeal of that decision, the Court of Appeals ruled that a mere agreement to agree is too vague to be enforceable. Had the parties decided on a formula for calculating the rent, the clause would have been clear enough, but they failed to do so, and the court refused to set the rent for them.

The fact is, however, that setting a reasonable rent would not have been a difficult task for the court. The fair market price could easily have been ascertained; the plaintiff provided an appraisal to assist the court in that task. So what message is the court trying to send by not enforcing the contract? The court argues on autonomy grounds that an agreement to agree cannot be enforced because it lacks the certainty and specificity necessary to evidence the parties' intentions. It is so vague, the court says, that it does not even "hint at a commitment to be bound by the fair market rental value" for the property. In the face of such vagueness, especially when a material term is at issue, one cannot simply impute a given intention to one of the parties because doing so would violate that party's freedom to contract.

There is a further argument in support of the holding in *Schumacher.* The common law indefiniteness rule can be seen as a kind of global "information-forcing" rule. It encourages the parties to take the extra time to specify their obligations in instances where they clearly have the comparative advantage in doing so. Encouraging parties to take precautions in spelling out their obligations reduces litigation ex post. Moreover, since the litigation process is subsidized by the state, the contracting parties otherwise have inadequate incentives to take precautions on their own. The indefiniteness rule may thus serve to encourage the parties to internalize the costs of uncertainty about the meaning of their obligations.

One interesting aspect of this case is the court's discussion of the precedent relied upon by the plaintiff: *May Metropolitan Corp. v. May Oil Burner Corp.* That case involved an agreement for the sale of oil burners that could be renewed annually with a sales quota "to be mutually agreed upon." The *May* court enforced the clause because the parties' course of dealings provided a context that gave meaning to the uncertain term. The *Schumacher* court limits this holding to contracts for the sale of goods under the UCC, but it's only reason for doing so is that the sales-of-goods setting is "more fluid." The concurring opinion in the case questions this limitation, saying that the principle should apply in other settings as well, including real estate contracts. We have the students read the relevant sections of the UCC: §§1-205(1), 2-204, and 2-305. Isn't it clear that the parties intended to make a contract and that the tenant had an option to renew? If so, isn't it clear that "there is a reasonably certain basis" for alleviating the indefiniteness of the price term, namely appraising the property's fair market value as the plaintiff did? Is there any reason why the principles expressed in these UCC sections should be limited to the sale of goods? Can one make the argument that a course of dealings, as defined by the UCC, was established over the preceding five years that would help the court determine the landlord's intent? In those five years, the rent increased in yearly increments from $500 to $650. Upon renewal, the landlord demanded an immediate increase of $250. Hence, the parties' course of dealings would seem to indicate that such an increase could not have been contemplated by either party during the original negotiations.

Note 2 (Page 41). *Schumacher* parallels an earlier case, *Walker v. Keith*. The court in *Walker* argues that "rental in an ordinary lease is a very uncomplicated item. . . . It, or a method of ascertaining it, can be easily fixed with certainty." Should ease of ascertainment be used as a standard by which court decide whether or not a term is too uncertain? Which way does that cut? If rent is uncomplicated, it's because the market will set a range of reasonable rents for a given property. A landlord can then offer a rent within that range on a take-it-or-leave-it basis, confident that the tenant will not likely find a better deal on the open market. But setting future rents may not be so simple. In fact, given the difficulties inherent in predicting future market behavior, such a term would likely be the subject of extensive dickering. Instead of setting the exact rental, the courts in both *Walker* and *Schumacher* suggest that agreeing upon a method for calculating the rent would have made the term enforceable. The parties may have assumed, however, that they would be able to agree upon a rent within the reasonable market range at the time of renewal. Why shouldn't a court honor that intention and set a reasonable rent? After all, doing so would be quite simple. If the "agreement to agree" in *Schumacher* had read "Tenant may renew this lease for an additional period of five years at annual *reasonable* rentals to be agreed upon," would it have rendered the clause enforceable?

Judge Jasen's dissent in *Schumacher* suggests that the court should set a reasonable rent if the lessee can establish an entitlement to renewal under the lease. This raises the question of why a landlord would enter into a lease that includes a renewal option. As with all long-term contracts, the chances of regretting the contract at some point in the future are high, and the prospect of renewal may become onerous. It is possible that this was the case in *Schumacher*. It is unlikely that the landlord would be able to get almost twice the appraised value from a new tenant, so why does he demand it as a condition of renewal? If he regrets entering the lease, he may be trying to force his tenant out. Another possibility is that the option gives him a holdout right. This is a commercial lease involving a small business. It might be devastating for a small but established business to change location, and the landlord could be taking advantage of that fact in order to extort an unreasonable rent. If either of these motivations is indeed the reason for the sharp rent increase, shouldn't the court follow Judge Jasen's advice and set a reasonable rent on public policy grounds, especially if the tenant had paid a premium in order to secure the renewal option? What would the implications of such a ruling be ex ante?

Which Promises Will Be Enforced?

Section 3 provides a brief introduction to contract law's enforcement doctrines. The emphasis in this section is on consideration, particularly the evolution from the benefit/detriment model of consideration to the bargain model. This approach provides some historical context for students and exposes them one of contract law's most basic problems: distinguishing between enforceable and unenforceable promises.

We have the students begin by reading § 71 of the Restatement. Consideration basically means that a bargain has taken place. It serves as evidence that the parties are acting of their own accord and that they have made an exchange that each feels is in her own best interest. Consideration also serves as evidence that the parties intended their agreement to be legally enforceable. Hence, the requirement of consideration can be justified on both autonomy and economic grounds: it shows that the parties have acted of their own volition and that they have made an exchange that (presumably) is economically beneficial to both parties and thus enhances social welfare.

One challenge that students may initially have with this material is understanding that terms such as consideration, benefit, and detriment have specific meanings within the context of contract law and that those meanings have little to do with the "plain meanings" they have hitherto ascribed to these words. It can be helpful to explain this at the outset; once students get over this initial semantic hurdle, understanding these concepts is much easier.

Hamer v. Sidway *(Page 45)*. *Hamer* involves a promise made by an uncle, William E. Story, Sr., to his nephew, William E. Story, 2nd. The elder Story promised to pay his nephew $5,000 if he would abstain from various vices until his 21st birthday. The nephew complied with the conditions and, upon fulfilling his commitment, he requested the money. They both then agreed that the uncle should keep the money in a bank account until the younger Story was prepared to handle such a large sum, but the uncle died without actually having given any of the money to his nephew. The nephew later assigned his right, which was eventually assigned to the plaintiff who sued the uncle's estate after it refused to honor the claim.

This case provides a clear explication of the original common law model of consideration: the benefit/detriment formulation. The defendant argues that the promise was without consideration because the nephew suffered no detriment as a result of his abstention. In fact, the defendant argues, the nephew benefitted as a result of his temperance. Therefore, if there was no benefit to the uncle (and no detriment to the plaintiff), then there could be no consideration to support the promise and render it enforceable. The court rejects this argument, saying that consideration does not require that one party profit from the deal; it requires only that one party give something that the other requests. In other words, it does not matter that it was "good" for the nephew to abstain from vice (surely it was); what matters is that he was induced by the uncle's promise to give up a legal right. In the legal sense, then, a party suffers a detriment when he refrains from doing something he would otherwise be entitled to do, even if doing so improves his general welfare (see *Note 4 on page 54* for further discussion of this point).

But what about the uncle? The defendant seems to assume that the uncle was not benefitted in any way by the nephew's forbearance. Is there an argument that he was? He perhaps had a strong interest in protecting the family name, or perhaps the idea of his nephew abstaining from cards and liquor brought him great personal satisfaction. The question is whether or not such "benefits" qualify as consideration. After all, one can assume that no one would make a promise in the first place without expecting some benefit from it. Hence, all promises benefit the promisor in some way, but, of course, not all promises are enforced. There seems to be an assumption at work in *Hamer* that when one party suffers a legal detriment, the other must receive a legal benefit. In other words, you can tell if the benefit qualifies as consideration by looking at the detriment.

Hamer is a good place to test the students' understanding of why we need to prove consideration in the first place. After all, the uncle made an unambiguous, morally binding promise. Why can't the plaintiff recover on that basis alone? Here is it important to see that, without consideration, this is merely a promise to make a gift and thus is unenforceable. We emphasize that gift promises carry great moral weight, especially after they have been relied on, and yet the law denies enforcement. This implies that the legal purposes are other than reinforcing notions of conventional morality or protecting reliance per se. It also helps to ask why the executor of the estate resisted the claim so vigorously. Again, isn't it clear that the uncle would have wished the money to be paid? The answer, of course, is that the executor has a fiduciary duty to the beneficiaries of the estate only to honor obligations that are legally enforceable. It is not surprising, therefore, that most of the litigation over gift promises occurs in just this setting.

St. Peter v. Pioneer Theatre Corp. *(Page 46).* The St. Peters were regulars at their local theater's "Bank Night" drawings. To enter the drawing, one had only to sign a register; buying a ticket was not required. The person whose name was drawn had to then find the theater manager within three minutes in order to claim the prize, which in this case was $275. On the night in question, the St. Peters were waiting outside the theater for the drawing when a woman (allegedly an employee of the theater) came out and told Mrs. St. Peter that her name had been drawn. But when she approached the manager, he told her that it was her husband's name that had been drawn. Just as the St. Peters approached the manager, he told them that they were one second too late to claim the prize. The St. Peters sued, alleging that they had entered into a contract with the theater and that the theater had breached by refusing to pay them the $275. The theater's motion for a directed verdict was granted for several reasons, most notably because, according to the theater, the prize was an unenforceable promise to make a gift, and that no consideration had been given by the St. Peters in return for the promise to pay $275. If consideration had been given, they argued further, then the arrangement would constitute an illegal lottery.

We spend time with the structure of the theater's argument. Their counsel presents the court with only two options: 1) either there was no consideration given and thus the promise was gratuitous and therefore unenforceable, or 2) there was consideration given and thus the transaction was an illegal lottery and therefore unenforceable. Either way the plaintiff loses. The theater bases its argument on an earlier case argued in the same court, *State v. Hundling.* The court in that case held that "Bank Nights" were not lotteries because no valuable consideration was required to enter, and the payment of valuable consideration was a necessary element of a lottery. This, the theater argued, meant that Bank Night drawings constituted mere gratuitous promises, and gratuitous promises are not enforced.

In rejecting this argument, the court invokes two concepts that will be fleshed out later in the course but warrant some explanation here. The first is the difference between a bilateral and a unilateral contract (or in the Restatement's language: a promise for a promise and a promise for a performance). While a return promise constitutes consideration in a bilateral contract, completed performance constitutes consideration in a unilateral contract. Bank nights are promises to enter into unilateral contracts. The theater promises to pay $275 in return for the promisee's act of signing the register and hanging around the theater. By completing the required performance, the St. Peters provided consideration.

The second concept invoked by the court is the adequacy doctrine, which can be found in § 79 of the Restatement. We have the students read this section and explain that courts normally allow parties to decide what constitutes adequate consideration in return for their promise. It does not matter, therefore, that the theater received nothing of monetary value from the St. Peters. The theater decided that signing the register was sufficient consideration for the promise to pay $275 and the court would not second guess that decision. Hence, the court found that consideration was given by the St. Peters. Moreover, there were good economic reasons for the theater to request the register be signed and the patron to appear within three minutes. Obviously, they wanted most people on Bank Nights to buy tickets to the movies even though they could not require that (or else it would clearly be a lottery). By requiring appearance within three minutes they created a disincentive for people to just stand outside and wait for the drawing. But they did not count on Mrs. St. Peter. Might this explain why the theater decided to litigate this case and risk the bad publicity that would result?

Still left to decide, however, was the issue of whether or not the transaction was a lottery. The court explains that the defendant is mistaken in relying upon *Hundling*. The *Hundling* court made clear that something of monetary value must be paid in order to qualify as an illegal lottery. Lotteries were illegal because they induced people to wager "their substance on a mere chance." The St. Peters did not wager "their substance," so there was no lottery, but they did give the consideration required by the theater.

Note 3 (Page 54). We make a brief reference to this note to prepare students for the additional enforcement doctrines they will encounter in the next chapter. Though one need not offer here a detailed explanation of promissory estoppel and the material benefit rule, it is helpful to tell the students that there are some promises that will be enforced even absent consideration. We also remind them that one of the lessons of *St. Peter* and *Hamer* is that gratuitous promises are not enforceable (on any theory). We remind them that they still don't know why some serious promises are enforced and others are not, but that they will have to wait until Chapter 2 to address that issue directly.

Limits on Enforcement: Unconscionability

There are instances when contract law does not enforce promises even if they are supported by consideration. Doctrines such as fraud, duress, and unconscionability provide grounds on which courts can *selectively* refuse to enforce contracts whose terms are "unreasonable" or that arise out of a bad bargaining process. As we have seen, contract law seeks to honor the autonomy of contracting parties who seek to achieve reciprocal economic gain. Hence, the bargaining process must reflect the voluntary decisions of well-informed parties who possess the capacity necessary to understand the commitments they are making. Likewise, if the terms of the agreement are unreasonably onerous to one party, such that the party is denied the "essence of the bargain," a court may set the contract aside. This section focuses on the doctrine of unconscionability, and in particular, how the doctrine of unconscionability intersects with public policy considerations.

Williams v. Walker-Thomas Furniture Co. I&II *(Pages 56 & 57).* Ms. Williams, a single mother supporting her seven children with a monthly welfare stipend of $218, entered into several installment contracts at various times with a furniture store, Walker-Thomas. The contracts contained a cross-collateral clause, which meant that every time she purchased a new item from Walker-Thomas, all of the previous purchases served as security for the new contract and could be repossessed in the event of a default. After she had paid her balance down to $164, she bought a stereo that raised her balance to $678. The store knew of her financial situation but sold her the stereo nevertheless. Ms. Williams subsequently defaulted, and Walker-Thomas repossessed many of the items she had previously purchased. She then filed suit on the grounds that the contract should not be enforced because there had been no meeting of the minds and because it was contrary to public policy.

Both the District of Columbia Court of Appeals and the US Court of Appeals for the DC Circuit find the cross-collateral clause objectionable, and students often agree. After all, Williams had paid for most of the items she had purchased before the default, and it seems unfair to take everything away under the circumstances. We find it useful to push the students a bit to think through their initial intuitions that "unfair" contracts or contracts where one of the parties has "unequal bargaining power" should be declared unconscionable. The notes following *Walker-Thomas*, particularly ***Note 2 on page 61*** and ***Note 3 on page 62***, are designed to get students to realize that *selective* non-enforcement of contract terms on purely substantive or distributional grounds is counterproductive to widely shared goals of a fair and just society. Such outcomes might vindicate the oppressed party in an individual transaction but it is likely to have deleterious effects on many others. It is for these sorts of reasons (we believe) that the overwhelming majority of courts decline to set aside contract terms on the basis of substantive unconscionability alone. Rather, courts (and the students) need to identify those cases where both procedural and substantive problems are present.

We begin this process in *Walker-Thomas* by reviewing the law of secured transactions in ***Note 1 on page 60.*** We find that students see the issues more clearly once they understand that the law requires Walker-Thomas to hold a disposition sale and that any surplus over the amount of the debt must be returned to Ms. Williams. The fact that there is generally no surplus but rather a deficiency explains why secured parties who finance consumer goods include such a clause in a contract. Given the rate of depreciation in consumer goods, without a cross-collateral clause the financing seller risks being under secured. Thus, as per Note 1, such clauses are authorized (as a general proposition) in UCC § 9-204(1). It is a separate question why installment sellers repossess when the costs of repossession exceed the value of the goods obtained and the prospects of collecting the deficiency are small. This is the familiar "lost value" problem that prompted the FTC rule restricting non-purchase money security interests in consumer goods. One reason why the seller repossesses in such a case is that the signaling value of repossession on other debtors of the seller – telling them, in effect, that this is a "tough" creditor and they should pay this debt first rather than that of more forgiving creditors – exceeds the cost of repossession. There is a debate in the literature as to whether such *in terrorem* devices are, on balance, benign or malign and whether purchase money security interests in consumer goods should be condemned on the same basis as are non-purchase money security interests under the FTC rule. For a review of the arguments, and one view of the cathedral, see Robert E. Scott, *Rethinking the Regulation of Coercive Creditor Remedies*, 89 Colum. L. Rev. 730 (1989).

The underlying problem, in any case, is poverty. People in William's position obviously pose a high risk for lenders. By including cross-collateral clauses, lenders are able to better secure themselves against the risk of default. This is particularly important in a contract for the sale of furniture and household items, which depreciate quickly. Thus, the benign justification for the clause is that allows retail stores to offer lower prices and lower interests rates to high-risk borrowers. Without such clauses, the costs of credit for such borrowers would be higher.

At this point we turn to the "procedural unconscionability" problems. Perhaps the problem is that Ms. Williams was not sufficiently aware of the risks of this credit purchase. The DC Circuit seems to think that this could be one reason for finding the cross-collateral clause unconscionable. They hold that a contract might be unconscionable if, considering the circumstances surrounding the agreement, one party lacked a "meaningful choice" and the terms are "unreasonably favorable to the other party." Perhaps Williams lacked a "meaningful choice" in the sense that the clause was buried in fine print, in a form she signed in blank, and expressed in language that is unintelligible to most people. She probably could not have purchased these items on credit without the cross-collateral clause, but was she deprived of the choice not to purchase the stereo at all?

The actual holding of the case, of course, is limited to the plaintiff's right on remand to raise the unconscionability argument even though the contract was made before the effective date of the adoption of the UCC in D.C. The case then settled. We ask students why Walker-Thomas was so stupid as to litigate this case once D.C. Legal Services brought the action rather than settling and thus avoiding the bad precedent that forced them to rewrite all their forms. (Possibly it was because D.C. Legal Services was not interested in settling until they got the holding they wanted.).

Note 2 (Page 60). Many people feel that cross-collateral clauses are unfair because they can be used to deprive people of property for which they have already "paid," at least in ordinary understanding. However, fairness is at best an amorphous concept. Another approach to the problem is to ask what are the ex post and ex ante implications of not enforcing the contract.

Ex post, the decision not to enforce obviously would once again put Ms. Williams in possession of the repossessed items, but would that be a vindication of her rights or a violation of Walker-Thomas'? If she knew that the clause was there and if she received a reduced price on the merchandise or a lower interest rate in return for accepting the clause, then it seems difficult to justify the decision not to enforce. She got what she paid for, and she knew of the risks she was assuming when she entered the contract.

And yet there are circumstances under which one could make a strong argument that not enforcing would vindicate her rights. If, as the DC Court of Appeals implies, the clause was buried or hidden, that might support an unconscionability defense. Evidence that the clause was misrepresented to her by the store would also support such a defense. Finding that the store charged her a higher interest rate despite the presence of the clause would also indicate unconscionability. Charging a higher rate would undermine the purpose of the clause, and the store would be getting more than it bargained for.

Ex ante, the effects of holding cross-collateral clauses unconscionable in general could be far-reaching. If cross-collateral clauses allow high-risk borrows to obtain credit they otherwise couldn't (or could otherwise only obtain at a higher rate of interest), then finding that they are unconscionable per se would limit the opportunities of others in Williams' situation (see *Note 4 on page 63*). Hence, even if there were good reasons not to enforce the clause in this case, it might be advisable to limit the unconscionability claim to instances where both "procedural" and "substantive" unconscionability is present. In fact, that is the test followed by the large majority of courts that have addressed unconscionability claims over the past 30 years.

Another approach would be to ask what would have happened had there been no cross-collateral clause. After default, the store could have filed suit and recovered judgment on the balance due. If the judgment were not paid, Walker-Thomas could obtain a writ of execution and the sheriff could levy on sufficient non-exempt assets to pay off the debt. Ms. Williams could then elect to file for Chapter 7 bankruptcy to discharge the debt, and whether or not she could keep the furniture would turn on the liberality of the exemption provisions in D.C. Even without the clause, therefore, she might risk the loss of assets if the debt is in default.

The real problem, then, is the way the sale was induced– a home solicitation, a contract signed in blank with fine print and unintelligible language. We point out to students that all of these deceptive practices are now barred explicitly in D.C. and virtually every other state by Retail Installment Sales legislation of the sort referred to by Judge Quinn in the lower court opinion.

Note 6 (Page 64). This Note is designed to help students understand the difference between substantive and procedural unconscionability. Though the two are theoretically distinct, in practice it is often difficult to separate them. In *Walker-Thomas*, Judge Wright says that, "[u]nconscionability has generally been recognized to include an absence of meaningful choice on the part of one of the parties together with contract terms which are unreasonably favorable to the other party." The first part of this statement describes procedural unconscionability, while the second alludes to substantive unconscionability. The absence of meaningful choice, he says, can be discerned by looking at the "circumstances surrounding the transaction," and he indicates that unequal bargaining power and hidden terms, among other things, would be evidence of procedural unconscionability. He then goes on to argue that when a party with unequal bargaining power signs a "commercially unreasonable contract without knowledge of its terms, it is hardly likely that his consent, or even an objective manifestation of his consent, was ever given to all the terms." In such cases, courts should disregard the traditional duty to read rule so that they can "consider whether the terms of the contract are so unfair that enforcement should be withheld."

Under the duty to read rule, one who enters an agreement without knowledge of its terms assumes the risk of entering a bad bargain. The purpose of the duty to read rule is to provide an incentive for parties to find out about the contractual obligations they are assuming. Hence, the duty to read seems designed to thwart substantive unconscionability. It follows, then, that

substantive unconscionability should not be the sole criterion for setting aside a contract. On the other hand, evidence of substantive unconscionability could serve to create a presumption of procedural unconscionability. Under such a construction, the defendant would then have the burden of showing the absence of any process defect.

Problem (Page 66). This problem deals with the issue of "smoking gun" unconscionability. Though such cases are rare, there are instances in which a contract term is so unreasonable that courts assume that it must have been the product of some defect in the bargaining process. In the problem, Cliff has signed up for over 40,000 hours of dance lessons. Although there is no evidence that the process was flawed, it is hard to imagine that anyone not suffering from some form of diminished capacity would consent to such a bargain. When a court simply can't believe that someone would agree to such an unreasonable term, it may refuse to enforce the contract unless the defendant sustains the burden of showing that the bargaining process was free from any impediments created by the defendant. Thus, even in "smoking gun" cases the decision not to enforce is not, strictly speaking, justified solely by a finding of substantive unconscionability, but is justified instead by the presumption of procedural unconscionability created by the unreasonable term.

D. Performance of the Obligation
Introduction to the Idiosyncratic Bargainer

In *Lucy* and *Leonard* we saw the reasonableness standard at work. In those cases, the issue was whether a reasonable person would consider the manifestation made by the defendants to be real promises. In *Lucy*, the answer was yes; in *Leonard*, it was no. The default rules of contract law provide for a presumption against unreasonable, or idiosyncratic, behavior on the part of contracting parties. Hence, Lucy was granted his request for specific performance of the real estate contract, but Leonard was denied his Harrier jet. This default presumption allows for reduced transaction costs because parties can expect the other party to behave reasonably, and the onus is on the idiosyncratic party to make his particular wishes known.

Jacob & Youngs v. Kent *(Page 67).* Jacob & Youngs, a general contracting firm, built an expensive country residence for the defendant (over $850,000 in today's dollars). Nearly a year after construction was completed, the defendants discovered that much of the pipe was manufactured by companies other than the Reading company, contrary to the contract specifications. The pipe used was of similar grade and quality, but, relying on the architect's refusal to give a certificate, the Kents refused to pay the final $3,483.46 remaining on the contract and demanded that Jacob & Youngs tear out all the non-Reading pipe and replace it at the contractor's expense. Jacob and Youngs sued to recover the remaining balance.

The defendant argued that the contract required exact compliance with the specifications (arguing, in effect, that the "perfect tender" rule should apply to this contract). Justice Cardozo rejected the argument that the contract specifications were to be literally followed in every respect and instead applied the "substantial performance" standard as is customary in construction contracts.

We find that students need to work through the substantial performance rule carefully. As Cardozo states, the rule does not mean that "substantial performance" equals full performance. Rather it means that substantial performance plus money damages equals performance sufficient to satisfy the implied condition of exchange that full performance must be tendered before the final payment is due. Here the money damages are zero since the pipe used was equal in quality and market value to Reading pipe. Generally people do not worry about the brand of pipe used as long as the quality meets contract specifications, and so, since the contractor substantially performed, the implied condition is satisfied and the Kents are obliged to perform their promise to make final payment.

The problem in construction contracts is that the general contractor must submit a bid in order to secure the project. He, in turn, must solicit bids from sub-contractors and base his bid on those. Once, the bids are locked in, the contractor risks losing money if the actual cost of the project exceeds the bid price. Hence, during the building process, contractors will substitute equivalent materials if they can get them at a lower cost. This usually poses no problems. Most people don't care what brand of wallboard or lumber or pipe is used to build their house as long as the substituted materials are of equal quality. By doing this, contractors are able to lower the cost of the project, which, presumably, will result in lower prices for the consumer. The size of the contractual pie grows, and everyone benefits.

But why shouldn't the Kents be able to opt out of the substantial performance default rule and insist on a perfect tender? It appears from the contract clause reproduced in *Note 4 on page 74* that the Kents intended to opt out of the substantial performance default rule. Why doesn't the court honor this clause as it pertains to the pipe? Cardozo recognizes the ability of parties like the Kent's to opt out ("This is not to say that the parties are not free by apt and certain words to effectuate a purpose that performance of every term shall be a condition of recovery") but it seems clear that he does not believe the standard-form language reproduced in Note 4 represented a genuine opt out. Rather, he seems of the view that the "Reading pipe" specification was a generic usage (like Kleenex or Xerox) indicating only a quality standard that the contractor had to satisfy and not a specific requirement that only Reading pipe of that quality standard could be used. (Note that the clause in Note 4 is a standard AIA boiler-plate and makes no special reference to Reading pipe.) To hold this view, Cardozo must be assuming that it is the Kents who are behaving strategically, seeking to avoid making the final payment on the house. What would motivate them to do that?

But what if Kent is the grandson of Mr. Reading, the founder of the Reading Pipe Company, and he attaches great subjective (idiosyncratic) value to Reading pipe? Indeed, there are several indications that he did attach such value to it: he asked for it specifically, he reserved the right to reject all work that did not comply with specifications, and he wanted all the pipe torn out of his new house in order to have it replaced. Is it impossible to opt out of default rules like substantial performance? Again, the question arises: shouldn't the buyer get what he asks for? Cardozo says that "[i]ntention not otherwise revealed may be presumed to hold in contemplation the reasonable and probable." Although Kent specifically wanted Reading pipe, there is no indication that he attached significant subjective value to it; there is nothing to indicate that, ex ante, he would want the entire house torn down in order to correct it. (Once again the general "right of rejection" clause does not deal specifically with Reading pipe.) One must reveal one's idiosyncratic intent in order for it to take effect.

What, then, is the best way to signal such intent? Is there an objective measure courts could look to in order to determine if idiosyncratic contract terms should be enforced? Suppose a contractor enters into two contracts to construct homes. The homes are essentially the same except that one of the buyers is a Reading pipe fanatic, and the other doesn't care what kind of pipe is used as long as the toilets flush. Is there any way a court could tell that subjective value was attached to the brand of pipe in one contract but not in the other? Aside from the language in the contract, the price should reflect the special needs of the "fanatic." If a contractor knows that the buyer is serious about accepting only Reading pipe, he will charge a higher price because he won't be able to substitute other pipes of equal quality even if they cost less. The Reading pipe fanatic will have to pay a premium to cover the potential costs involved with using only one type of pipe. Indeed, if the clause in Note 4 is taken at face value, the price for the contract would be astronomically high, or more likely no contractor would bid on the job without some appropriate modification as it exposes him to strategic fly-specking by the home owner. Hence, the question courts need to answer in such cases is not did the buyer get what he asked for, but rather did he get what he paid for? In this case, we don't have the relevant information to make that determination. Or do we? What about the fact that the architect refused to give a certificate? One way to solve this sort of information problem is for the parties to agree that a "contract referee," such as the architect, will make the determination that the buyer is getting what he paid for. If a referee is agreed to, shouldn't the referee's judgment be conclusive?

Note 1 (Page 72). We take some time to explain the difference between dependent and independent promises. The illustration in this note should be helpful, and it will also be helpful to explain these terms within the context of *Jacob & Youngs*. The question in that case is whether or not the promise to make final payment for the work was dependent upon the installation of Reading pipe. Kent, of course, argues that it is, but Cardozo disagrees. Because the purpose of the contract was to build a house that meets quality specifications, and because the contractor did so, he substantially performed his part of the bargain, and the installation of other brands of pipe was an insignificant violation. The proper measure of damages, then, is the difference between the value of Reading pipe and that of the pipe used (which is zero). Hence, the contractor earned his money despite not keeping his promise to install Reading pipe. Once the contractor substantially performed, the implied condition is satisfied and the promises are independent.

Note 3 (Page 73). The first two cases involve the sale of goods, so the perfect tender rule would apply. Both Ken and Sharon could reject the goods under that rule. In Ken's case, the application of the perfect tender rule might seem harsh given that the variation from the contract is slight, but in the sale-of-goods context, any deviation from the contract constitutes grounds for rejection. (But note that this rule is subject to some qualifications. Most important is the seller's right to cure the defect under § 2-508.)

The third case is based on *Jacob & Youngs*, and Cardozo would likely decide it the same way. However, if it could be shown that the Kants paid a higher price for the right to demand only union-made pipe, then a court might find that the promise to pay was dependent on the promise to install union-made pipe.

Note 6 (Page 76). Default rules in contract law can be justified on the grounds that they save parties the time and expense (and risk of mistakes) in dickering over every detail of the agreement. These implied terms lower overall transaction costs, and thereby increase the value of the contract.

Furthermore, because parties can opt out of them, they serve merely as a template that can be altered in almost any way the parties choose. What's more, they greatly reduce litigation costs because they give courts handy tools by which they can settle disputes over issues the parties may not have considered at the time of contracting. Without such rules, judicial decisions on such issues would be more difficult to reach, and attorneys would have a great deal of trouble predicting the outcome of many contract disputes. There is an open question, however, that is raised in the next group of cases, and in the ***Essay on page 85***. Is the creation of default rules by the state cost-effective? What are the necessary conditions that must be satisfied for the state to create default rules that suit the purposes of many parties *and* at a lower cost than the parties themselves would incur if required to specify the relevant terms individually in each contract? In short, if the justification for default rules is social welfare, then the cost to the state of creating the rules must be part of the efficiency calculus. Default rules, then, must be cost-effective and when those rules are designed to cover many different contexts and many heterogeneous parties, there is a risk that the state's efforts will not be worth the candle.

Allocating Risks

One of the purposes for exchanging promises, i.e., making executory contracts, is to exchange one set of risks for another set that is presumably less burdensome than the first. As per the example on page 76, by making hotel and kennel reservations in advance, the vacationer has shifted the risk of available supply and increasing market prices to the kennel and the cottage respectively. The vacationer has assumed a reciprocal set of risks. The vacation may be canceled or market prices might drop between the time of contract and the time the vacation begins.

An interesting question is why we see these kind of fixed-price contracts even in well-developed commercial markets; why don't the parties just wait and purchase goods or services on the spot market when they need them? Often, of course, they do just that. But sometimes, by exchanging risks of fluctuations in price and supply, parties can reduce the *total risks both parties face* because of different comparative advantages in risk bearing. One such advantage is where one party would face associated costs (i.e, fixed debt obligations that cannot be postponed) that might have severe consequences if goods were not available or prices rise to the point where fixed obligations cannot be met. In a perfect market, those risks could be hedged by insurance, etc., but executory contracting often solves an "incomplete markets" problem; that is, it provides a least-cost means of insuring against the asymmetric risks parties face in volatile markets.

But courts often have to adjudicate disputes arising out of events that neither party fully anticipated at the time of contracting. The role of contract law in such instances is to provide default rules that will justly allocate risks not specifically allocated by the contract itself. To do this, however, courts must justify forcing one party to bear a loss that it apparently did not voluntarily assume and for which it was not (explicitly) compensated by the contract. This section offers an introduction into these problems and the way in which contract law has dealt with them.

Stees v. Leonard *(Page 77)*. The defendant contracted to construct a building on a site owned and selected by the plaintiffs. Owing to soft soil conditions, not discovered until defendant began excavating for the foundation, the building collapsed at three stories. After several attempts defendant abandoned the project. The plaintiffs sued for breach of contract. The defense: 1) the plaintiffs chose the location themselves and therefore had a duty to choose a suitable lot, and 2) the plaintiffs had made an oral agreement to keep the soil drained and had failed to do so. (For procedural reasons this second argument was not available to the defendant.)

The rule articulated in *Stees* (one of us labels it the "performer's risk" rule) is that the risks associated with performance of an obligation assumed by contract are assigned by default to the performing party (absent prevention by an act of God, the law, or another party to the contract). Had the builder wanted to protect himself against the risk of soft soil, he could have done so in the contract. Courts are not entitled to remake the agreement for the parties, and so, when a risk materializes that was not allocated by the contract, the court will let it lie where it has fallen. Despite the court's stated unwillingness to "interpolate[] what the parties themselves have not stipulated," they appear to imply a promise by the builders to do whatever is necessary in order to complete the building (shore up the foundation and drain the ground), even though they had only explicitly agreed to follow the plaintiff's plans and specifications. The rule (if not the decision in this case) is justified by the assumption that, in general, a promisor will have a comparative advantage over the promisee in ascertaining and reducing the risks associated with his own performance. As between the parties, therefore, the promisor, in general, is the better risk bearer (unless the risk itself is beyond the contemplation of the parties or some other excusing circumstance is present, as in *Taylor v. Caldwell*, supra).

In *Stees,* the court does not ask whether this is the default rule that the parties would have chosen for themselves had they foreseen the risk. We have the students negotiate ex ante to see if the default is one they might agree to. Why would the promisor ever agree to bear unknown risks? The answer, of course, is that the promisee pays him to bear those risks as part of the contract price. One way to have students see this point is to use an insurance metaphor. In addition to contracting to build the structure, the defendant is also issuing an insurance policy in favor of the owner which will pay off if any of the normal risks of construction prevent full performance. In turn, the owner pays a contract price that includes not only the price of the structure but the premium for the associated insurance policy. If the risk were on the promisee, she would have to self-insure or buy insurance from Lloyd's of London. This insurance would be more expensive than the insurance offered by the promisor because the promisor has the ability to take precautions and reduce the risks to some degree. It is the same reason why home owners insurance will cost less if purchased by the owner than by a third party (assuming the insurer would even allow a third party to purchase the insurance at any price). One of us calls this the "oily rag" principle: home owners can better take precautions that reduce the costs of insuring against future risks.

Note 2 (Page 81). The *Stees* court is convinced that the contractor could have protected itself against the risk of soft soil if it had wanted to do so, but isn't it apparent that there are some risks whose occurrence is so unlikely that it isn't worth the extra cost of dickering over them? Perhaps *Paradine* is an example of that problem. Would it have been worth it to the parties to decide who would bear the costs of a marauding army displacing the tenant? To answer this question, one would have to weigh the likelihood and economic impact of the occurrence against the costs involved in dickering over it. In hindsight, it is easy to see that the tenant should have bargained for a clause that would free him from paying rent should he be chased from his home by an invading army, but at the time of negotiations such things are not always so clear. One solution, of course, is to include a general exculpatory clause – such as a *force majeure* provision – that limits the promisor's liability for all external causes over which the parties have little or no control (and thus no risk bearing advantage).

Note 3 *(Page 81)*. The doctrine established in *Spearin* (which applies by its terms only to government contracts) might have saved the builder in *Stees* had it been the law in Minnesota. The *Spearin* court held that a contractor who is bound to follow plans and specifications provided by the government is not liable if, by following those plans, performance of the contract becomes impossible. The fact that the *Stees* plaintiffs chose the building site and provided the plans and specifications to be followed would seem to absolve the contractor under this rule. The key difference between government contracts and the *Stees* contract, however, is that parties are required to accept the federal government's specifications, while contractors negotiating with private parties are free to dicker over the specs.

Note 5 *(Page 84)*. This Note introduces students to the concept of comparative advantage, which will play an important role throughout the course. The idea is that, in selecting a default rule, courts should choose the one that the broadest number of parties would most likely adopt under the circumstances. In the case of risk allocation, that rule would be the one that would place the risk on the party who best understands the magnitude (cost) of the risk and who can take steps to prevent it at the least expense. The party who has this "comparative advantage" would presumably be willing to accept the risk at the time of contracting (in return for some form of compensation, of course) because doing so would decrease the overall cost of the contract and would therefore benefit both parties.

The discussion of default rules also helps solve the problem of how courts can justify placing the cost of an unforseen contingency on a party that never explicitly agreed to bear it. As long as the parties are aware or should be aware of the default rules in advance, they can be said to implicitly accept those rules when entering into legally enforceable agreements. Just as a baseball player implicitly agrees to abide by the rules of his sport when joining a team, a contracting party agrees to abide by contract law's default rules when engaging in that activity. Unlike the baseball player, however, the contracting party can opt out of the default rules in order to protect herself against a given risk. But if she chooses not to, then she must face the possibility that a court will allocate that risk to her ex post. Hence, when deciding whether or not to dicker over a particular risk, one of the factors that must be considered is the likelihood that a court will allocate that risk to you should the issue later be litigated.

Excuse for Nonperformance

Taylor v. Caldwell *(Page 88)*. The plaintiff entered into a contract to use the defendant's music hall for the purpose of presenting a series of concerts. Before the first concert, the music hall burned down. The plaintiff sued to recover damages for the defendant's nonperformance. The court held that, where the continued existence of a thing is essential for the performance of a contractual obligation, there is an implied condition that the promisor will be excused should that thing cease to exist. This is an exception to the general "performer's risk" rule that a promisor must either perform or pay damages for nonperformance even if performance has become unexpectedly burdensome due to intervening events.

What is the basis for the implied condition found by the court? The opinion mentions impossibility, and this is one of the exceptions set forth by the *Stees* court as well. In this case, however, impossibility means only that the court is unable to provide a remedy that would make this particular music hall available. But it is not impossible to provide the plaintiff with another remedy. If it is impossible to keep your promise, you can still pay damages. Indeed, money damages, not specific performance, are the standard remedy in contract. So impossibility can't really be the reason for this exception; and if it is not, how does one reconcile this case with *Stees* and *Paradine*, in which the nonperforming promisors had to pay? Certainly the fire was a foreseeable risk against which the music hall owners could have protected themselves in the contract, and the *Stees* rule – if you promise to do it, you must do it – is a perfectly clear default rule from which they could have opted out.

As the ***Essay on page 93*** suggests, we believe that one way to explain the result in *Taylor* is as an information-forcing default rule. Because the plaintiff contracted for a particular music hall, it suggests that the plaintiff valued that particular performance more than the market value of alternative music halls. To the extent that a promisee places a special valuation on a particularized performance, the promisor needs to know how much that special performance is worth in order to determine the optimum level of ex ante precautions. By excusing performance if the specific thing is destroyed, the default encourages the promisee with special information to disclose how much that particular performance is valued as a precursor to negotiating a stipulated damages agreement with the promisor (and agreeing to pay a higher contract price in return).

We find that students see the distinction between these cases quite clearly with a hypothetical that combines *Stees* and *Taylor*. For example, you might ask what result if a performer contracts with a booking agent to arrange for a concert hall in London on the nights in question. Subsequently, the Surrey Music Hall burns down and the agent declines to perform on the grounds that the fire has reduced the available supply and thus increased the price of the remaining concert halls. Under those conditions, of course, the *Stees* rule would apply. The agent has the comparative advantage in reducing the risk of price increases, and the facts suggest that no particular hall was important to the performer. Hence the "performer's risk" default rule applies.

Note 3 (Page 92). One way to analyze the risk-allocating default rules is in terms of comparative advantage: who can bear the risk at the lowest cost? This requires one to determine 1) who was in a better position to determine the probability of the risk occurring; 2) who was in the best position to take cost-effective precautions against the risk; 3) who could best anticipate the costs of the risk; and, 4) who could best be able to reduce those costs. In *Stees*, the builder was most likely in the best position to do all of these things. Because they are builders by profession, they were probably be in a better position to decide whether or not the soil was suitable for the proposed building, and they were probably in a better position to reduce the risk by keeping the soil drained. Furthermore, the builders probably best understood the potential impact of building on wet soil, and they could reduce that impact by proposing another building design (one shorter than three-stories) or simply by keeping the soil drained. If all of the above holds true, then the builder could bear the risk at the lowest cost and the court was correct in allocating the risk to them (even though they justified their decision on different grounds).

As Note 3 points out, the owners of the music hall in *Taylor* were in the best position to surmise the probability of the risk occurring, and they could better take steps to prevent it. However, the lessee knew better what the destruction of the music hall would cost him (how much money will he lose by not holding the concerts, or how important is it that he use this particular hall) and could better take steps to reduce those potential costs by providing for an alternative location. So it is not clear from this analysis who has the comparative advantage. But the owner of the music hall will take precautions against fire in all events because the benefits that he will receive from doing so far outweigh the costs. Hence, if the court had allocated the risk to him, it would leave the plaintiff with no incentive to take precautions of his own; he would know that he could collect damages should the hall burn down. By allocating this risk to the plaintiff, it gives the performer an incentive to take precautions and therefore results in the maximum reduction of the risk, which lowers the overall costs of the contract.

E. Remedies for Nonperformance
Introduction
In the vast majority of contracts cases, courts enforce contracts not by compelling the breaching party to perform, but by requiring her to pay a specified sum of money to the nonbreaching party. Parties will sometimes specify a damage measure in the contract itself, but when that is not the case, courts face the often difficult task of calculating the proper amount of damages to award. When calculating an award, courts must consider the proper aims of damages awards in contract. What principles should courts follow in deciding how much to award and on what grounds? The quote from Holmes' decision in *Globe* helps answer this question. Like other default rules we have discussed, the default rules governing damage awards should reflect as closely as possible the terms to which most parties under the circumstances would have assented at the time of contracting.

For students who find discussions of "default rules" and "hypothetical bargains" much removed from the language of the cases, we find it useful to point out that the analytical technique that we use to think about contract problems in general and damages issues in particular is not new. We may be pouring old wine into new bottles, but, many years ago, Justice Holmes, in analyzing what the proper measure of damages for breach ought to be, stated that "the common rules have been worked out by common sense, which has established what the parties probably would have said if they had spoken about the matter." We find this point is worth emphasizing here because it is so much ignored in contemporary litigation (and scholarship). Contract damages rules are defaults and, just as with all contract defaults, that means it is appropriate (indeed, necessary) to analyze them from the ex ante perspective. Again, quoting from Holmes, damages rules "should be worked out on terms which it fairly may be presumed he (the promisor) would have assented to if they had been presented to his mind."

Either at this point in discussing *Globe*, or in the discussion of *Freund* that follows, we find it very useful to have students negotiate a damages rule ex ante, taking the respective positions of buyer and seller (or author and publisher). From this ex ante perspective the students quickly come to see that, while punitive or exemplary damages are great for the promisee ex post, they are not so wonderful ex ante because the promisee must pay for them in the contract price. On the other hand, ex post the promisor would like to have damages as small as possible, but ex ante, the promisor must agree to damages that are roughly equal to the value of the promise in order to induce the valuable return promise from the promisee (one has to "give to get"). Students come to see that some version of the substitution principle – that damages should substitute for the performance in question – is what a promisee would bargain for and pay for. This follows from the intuition that a promisee seeks to enter a contract which entails legal enforcement because the promisee wants the promise to be reliable. But on the other hand, the promisee does not want the promise to be more reliable than it is worth because she must pay for the extra protection. Looking at damages rules in terms of buying and selling insurance protection is a useful way of driving home this point: I want to insure your promise but I am not willing to pay for extra insurance beyond the value of the promise to me.

In *Globe*, the plaintiff seeks to recover the cost of sending its train cars to Louisville, but this was an expense it was willing to incur under the contract; the shipping cost is not an additional expense that plaintiff incurred as a result of the breach. Had the plaintiff wanted the defendant to cover the cost of delivering the oil, it could have bargained for that, but this requirement would have raised the price of the contract because, despite what your local pizzeria would have you believe, there is no such thing as free delivery. Hence, one can assume that it was cheaper for the plaintiff to send its own cars then to have the defendant arrange for delivery, and awarding plaintiff the cost of sending the cars would be giving it more than was bargained for. By awarding the difference between the contract price for cotton oil and the market price in Louisville, the court places the plaintiff in the position it would have been in had the contract been performed. In other words, plaintiff's expectations under the contract are met by measuring damages in this way.

Freund v. Washington Square Press *(Page 99).* Freund, an author and college professor, entered into a contract with Washington Square to publish a book he was writing. Under the terms of the contract, Washington Square was to pay him $2,000 upon receipt of the manuscript and then had 60 days in which to terminate the contract should it find the manuscript unsuitable for publication. If Washington Square did not terminate within the allotted time, it agreed to publish the book in hardcover and paperback and pay Freund royalties calculated as a percentage of the retail price. Washington Square failed to terminate the contract within the 60-day window but refused to publish the book nevertheless. Freund sued to recover damages based on 1) an alleged delay in his academic promotion as a result of the refusal to publish, 2) the loss of royalties, and 3) the cost of self-publication had Freund arranged to publish the book on his own. The lower court denied damages for items 1 and 2 but awarded damages for the cost of self-publication. The appeals court overturned the award and instead awarded him nominal damages.

This case provides a nice introduction to the issue of damages because of its clear explanation of their purpose and the limitations placed on them. Damage awards in contract are not meant to punish the breacher, but rather to make the nonbreaching party "whole" in some way. As § 344 of the Restatement (Second) makes clear, that is done by protecting one of three of the nonbreacher's "interests:" expectancy, reliance, or restitution. But recovery on any of these bases is denied unless the damages 1) are a foreseeable result of the breach, 2) can be measured with a reasonable degree of certainty, and 3) are adequately proven. Each of Freund's claims fail to overcome one of the above limitations: royalties are too speculative; the delay in promotion, if there was one, was not adequately proven, and he was promoted in spite of the breach; and the plaintiff did not actually publish the book himself, so the breach did not cause him to incur the cost of doing so. Hence, the plaintiff suffered no loss for which he could be compensated even though the court found that the defendant had indeed breached.

While this case does a nice job of stating the default rules for damage calculations, it also begs several important questions relating to the theoretical grounds upon which these rules are based. *Note 1 on page 102* addresses some of these questions. We have the students attempt to justify the default rules using economic, autonomy, and reliance theories of contract law. For instance, is contract law's preference for money damages over specific performance a vindication of the breacher's right to decide whether to perform or pay damages? In other words, would enforcement by means of specific performance violate the breacher's autonomy? Is it possible that, under an economic theory, it might be in a party's best economic interest to breach the contract and pay damages instead of performing? Under what circumstances would that be the case?

What about the uncertainty issue? It seems likely that Freund would have earned some royalties on the sale of his book, so why do the default rules bar recovery on the grounds of uncertainty? Perhaps its because royalty arrangements are themselves the result of uncertainty. Publishers agree to pay a percentage of the revenues or profits from a book because they never know in advance how many copies will sell. By paying royalties only on the books sold, they reduce their risk and thereby lower the overall cost of contracting. In other words, publishing contracts provide for royalty payments because they specifically do not want to bear all the risk that the book won't sell. Hence, it cannot be said that Washington Square would have agreed to pay damages for lost royalties at the time of contracting.

Note 3 (Page 103). As a result of Mary's breach, John must now buy wheat on the open market at double the contract price, $2. Consequently, to protect John's expectancy interest, Mary would have to pay him the difference between the contract price and the market price on the day of breach, which was $1 per bushel. But had he not entered into the contract with Mary, he would presumably have entered into a contract with another seller for about the same price as what he agreed to pay Mary. Hence, the damages would be calculated in the same way: the difference between the contract price he would have bargained for had he not contracted with Mary (presumably $1 per bushel) and the market price on the day of the breach, or $1. Thus, although the goals of the damages measures are theoretically distinct, they may result in identical damage awards.

Problems (Page 105). Under the facts in the first problem, the builder's expectancy interest would be $55,000, as measured by his expected profits of $10,000 (contract price less expected construction costs) plus costs incurred to date of $60,000 less the deposit of $15,000.

The builder's reliance interest would be the amount that he has spent in reliance on the contract, or $60,000, minus the $15,000 deposit for a total of $45,000 (plus any opportunity costs that he incurred in making this contract and not taking his second best opportunity).

Under the restitution model, the landowner would have to recompense the builder for any benefit conferred upon him under the contract. The increase in value to the land is $40,000, so that is the amount available to the builder. However, the deposit would once again be deducted, leaving the builder with a total restitution interest of $25,000.

In the second problem, the analysis turns on whether one takes an ex ante or an ex post perspective on damages questions. From an ex ante perspective, A's expectation interest is measured by the difference between the $1,000,000 expected increase in his land as a result of the well, less the payment to B to drill the well, discounted by the ex ante probability that the well would prove to be a "dry hole." In other words, viewed ex ante, A has bought the chance to increase his wealth by having B drill the well and is entitled to recover of the value of that chance if B elects to breach. Only that amount will induce the right incentives for B to invest in the contract by drilling (before we know whether the well will strike oil or not).

Under an ex post analysis (the one that most courts are drawn to since they confront the problem ex post), A's expectation interest is zero. An ex post analyst would reason that the purpose of damages based on the expectation interest is to put the nonbreacher in the same position she would have been in had the contract been fully performed. It is not meant to put the her in the position she *believed* she would have been in had the contract been fully performed. In other words, even though she expected an increase in the value of the land as a result of the drilling of the well, that expectation was based on an erroneous belief: that there was oil beneath her land. Hence, even if the contract had been fully performed, there would have been no increase in the value of her land, and no damages can be said to have resulted from the breach

Essay: Evaluating Damage Measures with the Coase Theorem (Page 105). This essay introduces students to the theory of efficient breach. This theory, based on an economic model of contract law, posits that it will sometimes be more "efficient," i.e., it will make at least one party better off and will make no one worse off, for a party to breach the contract and pay damages than to perform her part of the bargain. As Judge Posner points out, in order for a breach to be efficient, the profits from the breach must be greater than the profits to both parties from completing the contract, and the damage rule must limit the recoverable amount to the profits lost by the nonbreacher. Hence, the choice of damage rules is essential because it will determine whether or not efficiency can be achieved through breaching. If the breacher has to pay penalty damages of 20 times the contract price, and he only stands to gain 1.5 times the contract price from the breach, then an otherwise efficient breach will be deterred. In that case, it would be wiser for him to perform than to breach, even though this results in a net social loss. For Posner, then, damage rules should be designed not to prevent breaches, but to provide incentives for parties to behave efficiently.

Under Posner's theory, the damage rule is important because it can either facilitate or discourage economic efficiency. But damage rules are just default rules, and the parties can bargain around them if they so choose. So even if there is a default rule setting damages at 20 times the contract price, the party that seeks the breach could negotiate around that rule by offering to pay the other party a portion of his increased profits from the breach. Posner's response to this is that it would require an additional transaction, which would raise the cost of the contract and would therefore be less efficient than simply setting compensatory damages as the default.

But Posner, in making this argument, is relying on assumptions that simultaneously undermine that argument, assumptions developed by Ronald Coase in his essay, *The Problem of Social Cost.* Certainly bargaining around default rules increases transaction costs, but the theory of efficient breach can only hold true if one assumes that no transaction costs will arise as a result of the breach. Posner assumes that when an efficient breach occurs, the breacher will simply send a check to the nonbreacher and that will be the end of it. But if there is an information barrier or if litigation ensues, i.e., if there are transaction costs, then the efficiency of the breach is diminished or even destroyed.

Perhaps, then, the best default rule would be one that would lower expected transaction costs (both pre- and post-breach) for most of the contracting population most of the time. That is, the rule should be the one that most parties would choose if negotiating costs were low enough for them to dicker over it. By imposing this rule, most parties will not need to expend time and money negotiating a damages clause, but will simply opt to follow the default rule. Idiosyncratic parties will still be able to bargain around this rule, but they must do so at their own expense.

Choosing the default rule that most parties would themselves choose can be justified on economic grounds; indeed, the Coase Theorem itself justifies choosing rules that lower transaction costs for the majority of contracting parties. By removing transaction costs from the bargaining context, the Coase Theorem really serves to underscore their importance. Because they effect every aspect of the bargaining process, contract law can facilitate efficient bargaining by providing default rules that lower transaction costs for most parties. "Friction" cannot be removed from the bargaining process, but it can be reduced, and implementing majoritarian default rules can help achieve that. Assuming that this majoritarian approach to setting default rules is the right one, what arguments can the students make for and against the use the compensatory damages as the default rule for breach of contract damages?

Specific Performance.

One problem with compensatory damages is that courts must decide what economic position the nonbreacher would have occupied after performance of the contract. This can be a difficult question to answer, and there is always the risk that the court will over- or under- compensate the party seeking relief. One possible way to cure that problem would be to make specific performance the default remedy for breach. That way, the nonbreacher would (theoretically at least) be able to get exactly what he bargained for. Specific performance is, however, typically available only when money damages are inadequate or unavailable, which is rarely the case. In this section, we examine the specific performance remedy and suggest an explanation for contract law's preference for money damages over specific performance.

Klein v. Pepsico *(Page 113).* Pepsico entered into a contract with an airplane broker to sell him a corporate jet that he, in turn, planned to sell to Klein. Pepsico breached, and the trial court ordered specific performance of the contract. The 4th circuit reversed the order of specific performance and remanded the case for trial on the issue of damages.

This decision in a case governed by the UCC follows the Code rule that specific performance is available only when the goods to be purchased are unique or in other proper circumstances. The court found that, even though only three other comparable aircraft were available at the time, the airplane was not unique as that word is used in UCC § 2-716. Moreover, the court found that Klein's failure to cover in this case was due to rising prices not scarcity. While comment 2 suggests that inability to cover is strong evidence of "other proper circumstances," Judge Ervin holds that Klein was not "unable" to cover but merely choose not to because prices were increasing. Increasing market prices are not a basis for specific performance. Rather, the thickness of the market is the key and here there was competent testimony that other G-II's could be purchased.

Though specific performance is dealt with in greater depth in Chapter 10, this is a good opportunity to get students thinking about what variables make a good "unique." If they understand what circumstances warrant specific performance, it will be easier for them to understand why it is not generally available. Section 2-716 is a good place to start. The notes indicate that all the circumstances surrounding the contract must be taken into account when considering specific performance; but traditionally, specific performance was available at common law only when the goods were truly unique. Comment 2 mentions heirlooms and priceless works of art– things for which there is no real substitute. The sale of land is another typical situation in which specific performance is available to the buyer. We refer the students to *Lucy v. Zehmer*, in which the plaintiff-buyer was granted specific performance of a contract for the sale of land. Why is specific performance available in that situation, and why is it typically only available only to the buyer of land and not the seller?

Note 1 (Page 115). The court in *Klein* repeats the familiar rule that specific performance is available only when money damages are inadequate. This note explores the issue of adequacy by contemplating some of the expenses Klein might incur in an effort to cover. Under UCC § 2-712, once he covered on the market (even at a significantly higher price) he would be able to recover the difference between the contract price of Pepsico's G-II and the one he bought as cover. In addition, he would be able to recover the $50,000 in broker's fees as incidental damages under § 2-715(1). However, he would not be able to recover his attorney's fees and other costs of litigation, and this is where money damages fall short. But granting him specific performance wouldn't change that. In either case he would have to file suit and incur legal expenses in order to get the relief he sought. Potential litigation costs are simply a risk inherent in contracting and should be figured into the total cost of the contract at the time of negotiations.

Note 2 (Page 115). As noted earlier, § 2-716 also allows for specific performance "in other proper circumstances." Comment 2 seems to connect this to the uniqueness requirement by saying that the inability to cover is "strong evidence of 'other proper circumstances.'" In other words, if substitute goods are unavailable, then specific performance may be appropriate. Comment 3, however, expands on this by granting the right of replevin to buyers when cover is *"reasonably unavailable"* (emphasis added). *Ace Equipment*, the case cited in the Note, provides some insight into what "reasonably unavailable" might mean. In that case, Ace Equipment was granted specific performance because it could not purchase substitute goods in time to meet its third-party commitments. The issue, then, was not that they couldn't cover, but rather that they couldn't cover in time. Without the goods to be supplied by Aqua Chemicals, Ace would breach contracts it had made with other parties. The goods were not unique, but money damages would have been inadequate to prevent breaches by Ace, which would likely lead to further litigation, loss of goodwill, and noncompensable damage to Ace's business reputation.

Essay: Why isn't Specific Performance Generally Available? (Page 115). This essay seeks to provide a justification for the general rule that specific performance is only available under limited circumstances. As we have seen, damage rules create incentives for parties to behave in certain ways. One way to evaluate a given damage rule is to consider the incentives it provides to contracting parties when a contingency occurs that causes the promisor to regret having made the contract. An efficient damage rule will motivate the parties to minimize any losses that result from regret. Such a rule would be chosen by most parties at the time of contracting because mitigating the potential economic loss from ex post regret will lower the overall cost of contracting and will make both parties better off ex ante. This implies also that an optimal damage rule will motivate the regretful promisor to choose between "performing and losing" and "breaching and paying" based on which option is less costly. Ex ante the promisor knows that, should it come to regret the promise, she will be able to choose the least costly of two alternative courses of action. One option is to perform anyway (perhaps by acquiring the substitute goods on the market and tendering them to the promisee in performance of the contract). Alternatively, the promisor can elect to breach, require the promisee to salvage by covering (or reselling) on the market, and then simply pay the amount of the damage bill when it is submitted. In general, the ability to choose between these options will reduce the ex ante cost of the contract (and increase the size of the pie for both). The right of the promisee to demand specific performance eliminates this choice. The question, then, is when it is desirable to do so?

In a thick market, where fungible goods are readily available, a specific performance default rule will increase the costs of contracting because it induces an injured buyer to refuse to mitigate her losses. She knows that she can force the seller to perform. This would rob the seller of a chance to require the buyer to salvage the broken contract even if that is less costly than having the seller salvage himself. In a thick market, either party will normally be able to find cover for the contractually agreed upon goods. Hence, if the seller can cover at a lower cost than the buyer, she will simply purchase substitute goods on the open market and tender them in fulfillment of her obligation. When that fact is coupled with the fact that there are other strong incentives not to breach besides the threat of damages – loss of goodwill and damage to one's business reputation, for instance – then it seems that sellers would only breach when it is clear to them that it is cheaper for the buyer to cover. In that case, it is less expensive to "breach and pay" than "perform and lose."

If, however, the buyer can always demand specific performance, she will have no incentive to mitigate losses and cooperate with the seller should the seller breach. In fact, the seller won't ever voluntarily breach in that case because she will be forced to perform anyway. Hence, *to the extent that the breaches we see are illustrations of a benign effort by the promisor to minimize the costs of salvaging a broken contract,* money damages are preferable to specific performance under thick market conditions because damages promote mitigation by allowing the promisor to choose to breach and pay when that is the cheapest salvage option. (For those who want to take the other side and argue for the parties' right to contract for specific performance or for specific performance as the default, note the Essay in Chapter 10, page 992, *The Case for Specific Performance* that draws on Alan Schwartz's article *The Case for Specific Performance,* 89 Yale L. J. 271 (1979).)

Limitations on Compensation

In this final section of the chapter we introduce students to a sampling of the doctrines that function as limitations on compensation. Having already studied *Freund,* supra, students are generally comfortable with the notion that some recovery fails under the *certainty limitation.* And *Hadley v. Baxendale*, which follows, is a case the students take to with (too much) zeal. We find, therefore, that it is useful at this point to make specific note of the *mitigation principle*, which is discussed in the introductory text. We haven't included a mitigation case in Chapter 1 in order to keep the length of the Chapter manageable. But mitigation is another idea that comes naturally to the students and taking some time to introduce it here, perhaps with an hypothetical based on *Rockingham County v. Luten Bridge,* supra page 1050, will permit students to recognize mitigation issues when they arise in the chapters that follow.

Hadley v. Baxendale *(Page 118)*. This celebrated case established the foreseeability limitation on the recovery of consequential damages. The plaintiff ran a mill whose shaft broke, completely halting operations. The engineer needed the shaft to use as a pattern for a new one, and so the plaintiff employed a carrier, Pickford & Co., to take the shaft to Greenwich where the new shaft would be manufactured. The reporter of the case states that the employee who delivered the shaft told Pickford's clerk that the mill was stopped and that the shaft needed to be sent immediately, but, as Note 1 following the case points out, this evidence must have been rejected by the court. The delivery of the shaft was delayed, and the mill stoppage continued for several days, resulting in lost profits. The plaintiff sued to recover those profits as consequential damages resulting from the breach, but the court held that the lost profits were too remote to have been foreseeable by Pickford at the time of contracting and therefore could not be recovered.

The *Hadley* rule regarding recovery of "consequential" damages has two prongs: 1) The plaintiff can always recover (without any showing that the seller could foresee) those damages that follow naturally, i.e., in the ordinary course of events, from the breach, or that reasonably could have been considered in the contemplation of both parties at the time of contract; and, 2) The plaintiff can recover those damages that result from special circumstances to the extent that those special circumstances were communicated to the defendant. We ask the students what recovery, if any, would Hadley be entitled to under the first prong of the court's rule? (At least the fair rental value of the shaft during the period of the delay.) It is the second prong of the rule that gets the most attention, but in many cases the issue will turn on whether the damages in question resulted from "the ordinary course of events" or were a result of "special circumstances." For example, lost profits for a business entity are now generally regarded as an ordinary and not a special circumstance (although the quantum of profits may be extraordinary in a particular case) (*see* UCC § 2-715, Comment 6).

We ask the students to compare the "special circumstances" test in *Hadley* with the modern version of the rule in Restatement § 351. The key difference is the evolution from the "tacit agreement" or "communication" test in *Hadley* to the modern "reason to know" test of the Restatement and the UCC.

The justification for the *Hadley* rule is that parties should be compensated for bearing risk. When the possibility of extraordinary damages is known at the time of contracting, a risk premium can be figured into the price of the contract and appropriate precautions can be taken to prevent breach. Had Pickford known that the mill would be stopped until the new shaft arrived, it could have charged Hadley a higher price as compensation for bearing the extra risk. What's more, had they known of the risk, they would likely have taken greater precautions to ensure timely delivery of the shaft. The Hadley rule, then, is essentially an information-forcing rule: if the party with special needs does not divulge them, she will bear the risk of the loss.

Note 8 (Page 124). Many commentators have questioned the relevance of the Hadley rule in the modern commercial context. Large, highly structured firms enter into literally hundreds of contracts, many of which will involve the exchange of boilerplate forms. It is commercially impractical to think that each transaction will receive the contemplation necessary to opt out of the *Hadley* rule. Moreover, the argument goes, the rule is unnecessary because managers will average their liability out over all the transactions they enter without concern for each individual agreement. Hence, the average cost of their overall liability will be factored into the prices they charge customers in the normal course of business dealings. The question, however, is whether doing away with the foreseeability limitation would penalize "normal" customers in this context by forcing them to subsidize high risk customers?

Note 9 (Page 125). The problem is that, without an information-forcing rule and without a limitation on consequential damages, high-risk customers will have no incentive to divulge their situation, and the result will be that normal customers will have to pay a premium in order to cover the additional costs resulting from the "invisible" high-risk customers. When all the customers are pooled and there is no way distinguish between high-risk and normal customers, the other party must raise the rates that normal customers pay in order to compensate for the risk they bear that some of the parties will have extraordinarily high consequential damages. Thus, there is inefficiency in pricing: the majority of customers pay more than they should while the minority pay less then they should.

This also leads to inefficiency in the level of risk reduction. Risk reduction is efficient when the costs of avoiding a breach equal the benefits of not breaching. To take more or fewer precautions would be wasteful. However, when the consequential damages rule is unlimited and the customers are pooled, it is impossible to reach that point. There will always be too many precautions taken for some customers and too few for others. Hence, forcing information can promote efficiency by weeding out the high-risk customers and adjusting prices and precautions to account for the increased risk.

This question has been the subject of much contemporary scholarly analysis. In particular, one might want to read the articles by Ayres & Gertner, Jason Johnston and Barry Adler (all referenced in the bibliography). One conclusion that follows from the game theory analyses of *Hadley* problems is that solving asymmetric information problems with a general default rule is very difficult. That is because deciding whether there will be a "pooling" or a "separating" equilibrium in any given case is fact-specific. Thus, while economic analysts can model the optimal default for individual cases, it is virtually impossible to suggest a default that would apply across many different transaction-types. One conclusion that might follow from this is to ask whether the exercise of writing efficient default rules is one that courts in a modern, heterogeneous economy are equipped to perform. Perhaps the focus should shift from creating more default rules to providing standardized models for individual lawyers to use in tailored settings.

CHAPTER 2

ENFORCING PROMISES

A. Introduction

Pedagogy. The challenge to teaching promissory enforcement doctrine is that its key concepts – bargain and exchange as set out in R2d § 71, promissory estoppel in § 90 and unjust enrichment in § 86 – are sufficiently indeterminate that it is difficult to explain or predict when courts will find a promise worthy of enforcement and when they will not. Our pedagogical strategy is to take each case and ask why the court did or did not believe § 71, § 90 or § 86 was satisfied. Teaching consideration doctrine, promissory estoppel and the material benefit rule provides a great opportunity to put students in the position of legal counsel arguing on opposite sides of each case, using the same doctrinal language as the touchstone of their arguments. As an example, we contrast the language of R2d § 79 and R § 79, com. c, which directs courts not to inquire into the adequacy of consideration (the mere presence of *any* consideration should suffice for enforceability) with the language of § 79, com. d (reproduced in Note 1 following *Wolford* on page 149), which instructs courts not to enforce promises if the bargain is a sham or a pretense, or the value of what is exchanged for the promise is nominal. Thus, comment c instructs courts not to judge the adequacy of consideration, but comment d instructs them that nominal consideration is no consideration at all. These two comments should suffice to construct equally plausible arguments for and against the finding of consideration in almost every case, based on the mechanical application of the plain meaning of the Restatement sources. (To be sure, the distinction rests on whether *in fact* there was a bargain or rather merely a gift "dressed up" to look like a bargain. But this distinction is not apparent from the plain language meaning of § 79).

As one refines students' litigation or oral advocacy skills in the classroom, the indeterminacy of the language of the doctrine itself becomes painfully clear. Ultimately, students (and teachers) are faced with a choice between throwing up their hands and becoming either extreme legal realists (it's what the judge ate for breakfast), critical legal studies proponents (its all about power, class, or political agenda), or maintaining that judges, lawyers and the law itself, are in good faith, and that there is a (relatively) determinate law of contract enforcement that consists in the *theory* underlying the plain meaning of the enforcement doctrines, rather than in the plain meaning itself.

That's where the economic analysis of promissory enforcement comes in. The *Essay on page 152* outlines the theory we believe renders the consideration cases largely consistent. (Some exceptions apply– competing public policies, etc.) Although we include the essay in the consideration section, we generally don't spell it out in detail in class until we've gone through a similar exercise in teaching promissory estoppel– R2d § 90. Here the enforcement puzzle becomes even more confusing for students as they realize that some promises are enforced even when consideration – as defined in § 71 – is lacking. Promissory estoppel appears to offer an alternative and overlapping enforcement rationale for enforcing all promises that induce reasonable reliance, yet virtually all promises induce reasonable reliance. The cases denying enforcement under promissory estoppel can't be explained by mere bad lawyering or the absence of reliance in fact. So either the courts are making it up as they go along, and the cases are a hodge-podge of idiosyncratic judicial reactions to specific cases, or something (*theory*) lies beneath the plain meaning of § 90. We hope the essays on pp. 152, 171, and 185, along with extended notes, such as notes 6 and 7 on p. 168, will provide substantial guidance to students on how to apply what we call the "expanded bargain" theory of promissory enforcement to explain many of the promissory estoppel cases (or at the very least, to help them place those cases within a pedagogically helpful analytic framework).

After solidifying the enforcement theory underlying the consideration and promissory estoppel doctrines, the chapter then turns to pockets of enforcement doctrine that have evolved to address particular substantive areas in contract law: charitable subscriptions, preliminary negotiations, and promises to insure. Although the foundation for enforcement in these areas is the same in principle, a number of specific considerations unique to each substantive context must be brought to bear to understand these enforcement patterns. They are interesting in their own right, are often the subject of extensive and engaging scholarship (especially preliminary negotiations), feature famous cases (especially charitable subscriptions and preliminary negotiations), and make effective, independent assignments for professors interested in exploring those areas. They are, however, by no means essential to understanding the fundamentals of contract enforcement doctrine and may be skipped to make room for coverage elsewhere. Finally, the chapter ends with consideration of the material benefit rule (R2d § 86). Here, our objective is to reprise (and reinforce) the prior analysis in the context of the final contract enforcement doctrine students must master. We set out the cases and ask whether the plain meaning of § 86 can be used to predict the outcomes in these cases. (Note that "Gilmore's Puzzle" reprinted on page 232 is a useful way to make this point.) We then turn to the expanded bargain theory and ask whether it does a better job. At this point in the chapter, students are well-positioned to take the lead in the classroom application of theory to doctrine.

In general, throughout this chapter, we begin by taking the cases and doctrine on their own terms, working students through the arguments in each case, applying the doctrines enunciated in the cases and the Restatement to the facts in the case, and practicing making opposing arguments. We then set out the cases as so many data points to explain or predict. Once we've covered the consideration cases, we then turn to promissory estoppel and undertake the same exercise. When we get to the key promissory estoppel cases in section C.3 (*Feinberg* and *Hayes*), we ask students to try to distinguish these cases. Given the doctrinally persuasive arguments for and against recovery in each of the cases, it's usually straightforward to demonstrate that the language of the law alone will not suffice to enable a good lawyer to predict who will win. In a planning context, this alone should motivate an interest in whether contract theory can do better. In the litigation context, although contract theory is not necessary to marshal competent doctrinal arguments for or against enforcement (as our class exercises demonstrate), lawyers can make more effective arguments by relying on contract theory. Theory explains precedent by rendering it coherent and principled. It therefore provides courts with not only a doctrinally plausible argument, but also a coherent defense of an enforcement decision that comports overall with the objectives and principles that animate contract law.

In short, a satisfactory account of these different outcomes requires moving beyond the surface of the doctrine and turning to some consideration of the purpose for enforcement. A simple cost/benefit calculus, then, asks whether enforcement in any particular class of cases is likely on balance to do more good than harm. For us, the most persuasive answer to that question is the "expanded bargain" theory which predicts that courts in general will enforce promises made in bargaining contexts even where the bargains are incomplete or inchoate but will decline to enforce promises made in non-bargain contexts.

The *Essay on page 152* introduces the economic analysis of promissory enforcement according to which the cost and benefits of promissory enforcement are traded off in order to maximize the net beneficial reliance on promise-making activity. Notes following the cases lead students to develop and apply this analysis in the particular context of each case (*see e.g., Notes 6 and 7 on pages 168-170*). The analysis is recapitulated briefly in the economic theorists section of the *Essay on page 171* (at 173). *Notes 1 and 2 on pages 183-84* invite students to apply the theory to reconcile promissory estoppel cases. The *Essay on page 185* provides a more complete presentation of the economic theory, and contrasts it with an autonomy approach. By this point in the chapter, students should have a firm grasp of the net beneficial reliance formula for predicting promissory enforcement. Although it is sometimes difficult to apply on the facts of all of the "chestnut" cases, the theory can provide a coherent account of promissory enforcement, as we explain below.

Theory. The expanded bargain theory holds that contract law will (and should) enforce promises when doing so maximizes net beneficial reliance. It then predicts that, as a general matter, net beneficial reliance is enhanced by legal enforcement of promises made in bargain contexts (even if incomplete or inchoate) but that legal enforcement of gratuitous promises is denied because it will actually reduce the net beneficial reliance on such promises. It's crucial to emphasize that the goal is maximizing *net* beneficial reliance, not beneficial reliance per se. We explain the theory by asking students what legal sanctions would maximize beneficial reliance per se. Sanctioning promise-breaking with the death penalty or physical torture would do a fine job of maximizing the beneficial reliance of any promise made. The problem, of course, is that such Draconian measures would deter people from making promises in the first place. This is what economists call an "activity level" effect– here the underlying activity affected by legal sanctions for breaking promises is the activity of promising itself. As we say in class, in a regime of such extreme sanctions for promise-breaking, the one promise made every decade would be very reliable indeed. This should make clear that maximizing beneficial reliance per se is not a reasonable goal. Instead, promissory enforcement should take into account the effect of sanctions on both the increase in the reliability of promises and the decrease in the activity of promising. The latter includes not only the number of promises made, but their *quality* as well. The more qualified and conditioned a promise, the less beneficial reliance it makes possible. All else equal, sanctions will lead potential promisors to reduce both the quantity and quality of the promises they make. Thus, whether promise-breaking should be legally sanctioned depends on whether the loss of beneficial reliance resulting from the decrease in the quantity and quality of promises made is outweighed by the gain of beneficial reliance resulting from the increase in the reliability of the promises that are still made. Enforcement is justified, on this view, only if it increases the *net* beneficial reliance that occurs under the enforcement regime compared with the *net* beneficial reliance that occurs without the enforcement regime.

To make this last comparison, we begin by asking students whether promises can be reliable even in the absence of legal sanctions. This introduces a discussion of the *extra-legal* (non-legal) sanctions for promise-breaking, which include third-party sanctions (e.g., reputational losses in business and social communities) and first-party sanctions (internalized psychological costs for engaging in morally wrongful conduct). A few examples in Socratic dialogue demonstrate that, even in the absence of legal enforcement, most promises are reliable both because they are made in good faith and because breach would result in costly non-legal sanctions. Given that the addition of legal sanctions will have a negative activity level effect on promising, legal enforcement of promises is justified only if limited to classes of promises that are both *relatively* unreliable (in the absence of legal enforcement) and not subject to a significant negative activity level effect.

Here, we can distinguish between promises made in bargain and non-bargain contexts (so-called "reciprocal" and "non-reciprocal" contexts). A promise is made in a bargain context if the promisor and promisee are in competitive market and, typically, are dealing with one another at "arm's length." The critical feature of such contexts is that the promisee has *leverage* to insist on receiving a *legally enforceable* promise *and* the ability to induce such a promise from a reluctant promisor by increasing the value of what the promisor is to receive in exchange. (One must "give to get.") In other words, bargaining in competitive markets has a feedback effect in which legal enforcement can be "priced out." Since enforcement is "paid for" in any bargain context, there is little reason to fear an activity level effect in which future promises are over-deterred. In this context, the price of refusing to make the promise will be the loss of the promisee's reciprocal promise (to provide goods or services).

In contrast, a promise is made in a non-bargain context if the promisor and promisee are *not* in a competitive market and, typically, are *not* dealing with one another at arm's length. Intra-familial and gift promises provide the paradigm examples of classes of promises made in a non-bargain context. The critical feature of non-bargain contexts is that the promisee does *not* have leverage to insist on receiving a legally enforceable promise. If the promisee did not receive a legally enforceable promise, she would be unable to compel the other party to make it. In the extreme case, the mere request the make the promise legally enforceable might lead the promisor to withdraw the non-legally enforceable promise. In less severe cases, the promisor would simply refuse to make the promise legally enforceable upon request from the promisee. Moreover, in a non-bargain context, the promisee is usually constrained by the context from offering to "pay" the promisor to make the promise legally enforceable (say, by offering to promise something of value in return). Indeed, in many gift contexts, an offer to "pay" the promisor to make the promisee legally enforceable may itself lead the promisor to withdraw the promise.

The expanded bargain theory thus supports the claim that contract law generally enforces promises made in bargain contexts but generally declines to enforce promises made in non-bargain contexts. Note that this formulation is broader than the scope of enforcement under the traditional bargain theory of consideration in R2d § 71. That section enforces only promises that are *in fact bargained for and where mutual assent is concluded.* According to the expanded bargain theory, courts will enforce promises made in *bargain contexts*, even if the bargain is inchoate or incomplete in some respects. Conversely, the theory claims that contract law maximizes net beneficial reliance by declining to enforce promises made in non-bargain contexts. This is so for two reasons. First, in general these promises tend to be very reliable anyway because the extra-legal sanctions for their breach are very costly to the breacher. Again, our paradigm example is intra-familial promises. For example, a promise from father to son that the father will pay for his son's college tuition is, all else equal, extremely reliable. A father would be loathe to break this promise because (1) he is likely to care a great deal for his son's welfare (so the costs of breach to him include the costs of breach to his son), (2) he is likely to feel quite guilty for acting immorally, especially given that his moral duty to his son is greater than his duty to strangers (morality recognizes the increased burdens of a fiduciary duty), and (3) he would be subjected to analogous 3rd party sanctions (sanctions from other family members as well as sanctions from others in his community) for breach of promise, again, especially given that his promise was to his son. Therefore, little additional benefit in reliability is to be gained by adding the additional sanction of legal enforcement to the extensive set of existing extra-legal sanctions.

Second, by making such promises legally enforceable (absent clear expressed intent to the contrary), the law may well deter promisors, such as this father, from making these non-bargain-context promises in the first place. Just as the father is likely to keep his promise to his son, so he is also likely to view legal liability for his promise as inappropriate. Moreover, if the threat of an additional legal sanction marginally discourages this father from making a gift promise, the son lacks the means to induce it by offering an appropriate payment in return. The notion of "bargaining" for a gift promise violates many long-held cultural values. Although the son may be marginally better-off if the father's promise were legally enforceable, the father is likely to want to retain the flexibility of breaching without pain of legal sanction in the unlikely event he feels compelled to breach. Thus, if such promises were legally enforceable, and the father resolves to simply wait and make a gift rather than promising to give the gift in advance of the transfer, the son is constrained by social sanctions from inducing the gift promise from the reluctant promisor. This reflects the social fact that the father's promise is gratuitous– he is not making it in order to receive a benefit from his son, but rather to enable his son to receive a benefit.

Thus, a regime that by default enforced promises made in non-bargain contexts would not be likely to increase by much the reliability of the non-reciprocal promises made because they are already very reliable. And such a regime would likely have a significant, negative activity level effect: It would increase the costs of making promises in non-bargain contexts because most promisors, at a minimum, would have to incur the costs of opting out of the default enforcement regime by specifying that their promises are not intended to be legally enforceable. In many cases, would-be promisors in non-bargain contexts would be wary to risk legal liability and so would decline to make a promise in the first place. The result is that enforcement of promises made in non-bargain contexts is likely to decrease the quantity and quality of very reliable promises that would otherwise be made (and thus would reduce the beneficial reliance these promises make possible). And because little is to be gained by legally enforcing this class of promises, which are very reliable even without legal enforcement, the overall effect of legal enforcement of non-bargain promises would be to reduce net beneficial reliance generally. In short, in this setting, legal enforcement does more harm than good.

In contrast, promises made in bargain contexts are not as reliable as those made in non-bargain contexts. To be sure, promises made at arm's length in a competitive market are policed by significant extra-legal sanctions in the form of reputational losses. But reputation is often ineffective in large, heterogenous communities. In settings where social sanctions are low, changed market circumstances may make the promisor's performance so costly that the benefits of breach may well outweigh the social costs. In addition, promisors who make promises in bargain contexts have no independent concern for the welfare of the promisee (they have no altruism), and the moral sanctions for their breach are, arguably, less severe (because they owe no independent fiduciary or other moral duty to the promisee). Thus, there is more to be gained by enforcing promises made in bargain contexts than promises made in non-bargain contexts. But more important, the negative activity level effect of promissory enforcement in bargain contexts is insignificant. This is because, *in bargain contexts, the promisee has the ability to induce the promisor to make a legally enforceable promise.* The promisor's promise is no gift horse– it is the quid pro quo for the promisee's promise or performance (even if in bargain contexts that lack an actual bargain, the quid pro quo is implicit). It is the market price the promisor must pay for what he wants to receive in return. Thus, legal enforcement of promises made in bargain contexts is not likely to deter promisors from making promises– there will be little or no negative activity level effect on promising. By enforcing these promises, then, contract law maximizes net beneficial reliance: It makes these bargain-context promises more reliable without significantly decreasing their quantity and quality. In short, in this context, legal enforcement does more good than harm.

The Chapter's objective, thus, is to help students understand, explain, and perhaps justify contract law's promissory enforcement pattern using either the economic or autonomy approaches. The economic theory provides an explanation (and arguably a justification) for contract law's pattern of enforcing promises in bargain contexts but declining to enforce in non-bargain contexts. It is important to bear in mind, however, that this enforcement regime is to some extent a *default regime.* Promisors can, in most instances, opt out of it by expressly indicating their intent to make or not to make a legally enforceable promise. The standard economic approach to creating contract default rules argues for setting the default to favor the majority preferences in order to save net transaction (or contracting) costs. The theory, ultimately, rests on (indeed states) the presumption that most promisors in non-bargain contexts *do not want* to make legally enforceable promises, while promisors in bargain contexts do (because the promisees pay them to make their promises enforceable).

By focusing on the *presumed intent either to be or not to be legally bound,* one can show that the economic theory is simply a richer elaboration of the most common autonomy theory of promissory enforcement. According to autonomy theory, the law should (and does) enforce all promises *intended* by fully autonomous individuals to be legally enforceable. What autonomy theory lacks is a criterion for identifying presumed intent in the absence of an expressed statement of intention by the promisor. The economic approach provides the basis for such a presumption. As discussed above, those making promises that could have been bargained for likely intended those promises to be legally enforceable (because generally the promisee will wish to pay for legal enforcement). When a promise could not have been bargained for, its maker probably did not intend, or would not have intended, the promise to be legally enforceable. Though it is sometimes rough around the edges, the theory thus does a nice job of explaining why each case comes out on the side it does (or at least helps students organize their understanding of these cases and doctrines according to how well the theory sorts them).

B. The Consideration Doctrine

Consideration is the classical doctrine for distinguishing between enforceable and unenforceable promises. Traditionally, all promises not supported by consideration were deemed gratuitous and held unenforceable.

Bargain Versus Gift

Kirksey v. Kirksey *(Page 132).* The defendant, brother-in-law of the plaintiff, promised, upon learning of his brother's (the plaintiff's husband's) death, to give the plaintiff and her children a home to live in and land to cultivate if they moved 70 miles to his property in Talladega. She did so, and he initially provided what he promised. After some time, however, he forced them to leave. The plaintiff then sued. The court found that the promise was a "mere gratuity" and, as such, was not enforceable.

This case illustrates the doctrinal requirement of a bargained-for performance or return promise. The loss and inconvenience to which Ormond, J. refers is not sufficient consideration because it was not "sought by the promisor in exchange for the promise" (§ 71(b)); rather, it was a condition for the receipt of a gift.

Note 2 (Page 133). This Note gives us a chance to introduce students to a famous law school hypo and discuss the difference between an act that is the condition of a gift and an act that is the return performance sought by the promisor. The difference turns on the intent of the promisor– to give a gift or secure something in return. In *Kirksey*, the brother-in-law did not seek to secure the inconvenience suffered by his brother's widow. He sought to provide her and her children with a safe, comfortable place to live. Thus, her action in coming to Talladega was analogous to Williston's tramp walking to the clothing store. (This is the same issue raised in Chapter 1 in *St. Peter v. Pioneer Theatre, supra*).

Kirksey illustrates the traditional reluctance of common law courts to enforce gift promises not supported by consideration. When discussing this case, our objective is limited to explaining the doctrinal distinction between a conditional gift and a bargained-for exchange. We don't emphasize (at this point) that the promise is intra-familial. *Kirksey* is the first data point for our analysis of the consideration doctrine (really the third counting *Hamer* and *St. Peter* in Chapter 1). After covering more cases, we can later return to list *Kirksey* alongside the other consideration and promissory estoppel cases. With this perspective, one can show how the *Kirksey* result would be predicted by the expanded bargain theory because it is an intra-familial promise.

In re *Greene* (Page 134). In *Greene*, the trustee in bankruptcy refused to honor the plaintiff's claim against the bankrupt's estate, which she based on an alleged contract. After having an affair with the plaintiff, Greene promised to pay her a set sum per month for their joint lives, and to make other payments on her behalf. In exchange, the writing stated that the plaintiff would pay one dollar and other consideration, as well as release Greene from all claims she had against him. The court found the agreement unenforceable because unsupported by consideration. One dollar (not even paid), it said, is not enough to support a promise to pay thousands. Also, a release from claims that are not valid (the plaintiff apparently had no valid claims) was found to be insufficient to constitute consideration.

In re Greene can be used to demonstrate a number of points. First, it is clear that the promisor intended his promise to be legally enforceable. Both parties did their level best to instruct a court to treat their agreement as legally binding. Why else execute a written document under seal and recite that Trudel (plaintiff) has paid Greene one dollar plus "other good and valuable" consideration? Indeed, it is not clear what else the parties could have done to make it clearer that they intended their agreement to be legally enforceable. In the teeth of this evidence of intent, the court nonetheless states that "[t]he parties may shout consideration to the housetops, yet, unless consideration is actually present, there is not a legally enforceable contract." [136] The consideration doctrine here has taken on a life of its own. The court goes through a formal analysis of whether the various candidates for consideration actually qualify as consideration and finds in each case that they do not.

On the doctrinal merits, it's worth pointing out that the court's summary rejection of the claim that Trudel's release of claims against Greene qualifies as consideration is, at the very least, too quick. The court treats the fact that Trudel's claims were in fact specious as dispositive. But R2d § 74 provides that release from claims constitutes consideration so long as the claims are believed to be valid by the one releasing them (regardless of whether they actually are valid). The court never considers this question.

On the bargain theory of consideration, the underlying question is whether the parties' bargain was real or merely a pretense. The court considers and rejects the claim that the agreement should be enforced as a bargain to compensate Trudel for past cohabitation (and illicit intercourse). It properly rejects that defense of enforcement on the ground that past consideration is no consideration at all (past consideration cannot induce a bargain because the promisor received the benefit before making the promise). If this wasn't an agreement to compensate past benefits, was it a bargain at all? If so, about what? Certainly not the dollar, and probably not (at least not centrally) the release of Trudel's claims. The obvious candidate is discretion (non-disclosure). Quite plausibly, Greene stood to lose much if Trudel went public with their affair. He stood to gain much by keeping her happy. An enforceable promise to pay a $1000 annuity, assign and pay for a life insurance policy on his life, and to pay four years of rent for her apartment would go a long way toward keeping her happy. In addition, it's possible that he actually cared about her and wanted her to do well despite the end of their relationship (though we find few students who go for this apparently antiquated romantic suggestion). A hush-money bargain rings true to the facts. But then why not enforce it? So described, it comes close to sounding like a blackmail agreement. Perhaps the court implicitly recoiled at the prospect of using the law to promote the incentives for blackmail. There is a rich literature on the problem of explaining the prohibition against blackmail. The puzzle is that it is perfectly legal to undertake what the blackmailer threatens to do if not paid, provided he does it without threatening to do it first. Why should a threat to do what is otherwise a legal act itself be illegal? There are lots of interesting answers in scholarship by Jeff Murphy, James Lindgren, Richard McAdams, and others.

Or perhaps it wasn't the specter of blackmail per se, but a concern to preserve the substantive values of marriage that drove the court's decision– i.e., the court was loathe to reward Trudel for successfully "tempting" Greene to abandon fidelity to his wife. Viewed as a pro-marriage decision, however, the court's decision seems one-sided: It appears to punish Trudel (the ostensible home-wrecker) at the expense of rewarding Greene, the unfaithful husband (who succeeded in "tempting" Trudel to abandon her moral scruples). A feminist perspective might object to this disparate treatment of these two equally immoral actors. Viewed from the point of view of incentives, however, the court's decision might deter spousal infidelity by undermining the credibility of promises that are made to pay for silence from past partners in adultery. Future spouses considering adulterous affairs may be deterred on the margin because they have one less tool to reduce the costs of infidelity– the ability to make a legally enforceable promise to their partner in adultery once the affair ends.

In any event, the case cries out for some such policy analysis to explain why the court would refuse to follow the parties' clear intent. Any number of doctrinal arguments were, and could be, made for enforcement under the bargain theory of consideration. That the court refused to find a bargain here indicates a contravening policy concern– one that makes the goal of maximizing net beneficial reliance undesirable in this context. If the court doesn't like the bargain the parties are striking, it also doesn't want to encourage beneficial reliance on such promises. *In re* Greene therefore might be set aside as a policy exception to the general rule in favor of enforcing promises in bargain contexts. Here is a promise in (some kind of) bargain context, yet the court does not enforce it. The case also demonstrates how courts can use the consideration doctrine to achieve an underlying policy goal, even when the doctrine would ordinarily generate a different result. We leave the students with the question of why the court would refuse to follow the parties' intent. "It is said that the parties intended to make a valid agreement. It is a non sequitur to say that therefore the agreement is valid." (p. 136) As a general matter, why is this a non sequitur? If not as a general matter, then what is special about this case?

Note 1 (Page 137). There is no widely accepted theory on the question of what is sought to be accomplished by the consideration requirement. It is often thought of as a device that distinguishes enforceable from unenforceable promises on the basis of form. Professor Lon Fuller argues that it serves three functions: evidentiary, cautionary or deterrent, and channeling. As an evidentiary device, consideration provides courts with evidence of whether an agreement exists. As a cautionary device, consideration helps ensure that hasty, unreasonable or unintentional promises (e.g., jokes) will not be enforced. Finally, as a channeling device, consideration provides a framework into which parties must fit their agreements if they want their agreements to be binding– again, to insure intent to enforce is present. Unfortunately, Fuller argues, there are no "abstract" transactions (those that have the same legal effect regardless of context); the channels cut by formal transactions familiar to modern law are not sharply and simply defined.

Whether these are the correct criteria is a matter of debate. Even if they are, they are not applied on a case-by-case basis. Instead, they produce a rule. As with all rules, this one will be both under- and over-inclusive. This raises a question that appears throughout contract law and many other areas of law: If a rule is over-inclusive and under-inclusive, why have a rule at all? Why not apply the criteria directly to particular promises?

Note 2 (Page 138). The biggest puzzle of all, in our view, is why American law has never created an alternative to the seal. The demise of the seal in the United States is explained by the erosion of the form to the point where it lost all its value as *form*. But why not provide a substitute that parties can invoke when they wish their gift promises to be legally binding? Such an alternative exists with the Model Written Obligations Act, but few states have enacted it (or any substitute). We can't see the policy arguments against having available an appropriate formal mechanism for making a gift promise legally enforceable other than the reluctance to have the state subsidize this kind of private behavior. But we do enforce gifts (including deeds of gift) and testamentary dispositions, so why not a formal promise to make a gift?

Adequacy of Consideration

Batsakis v. Demotsis *and* Wolford v. Powers *(Pages 144 & 147).* In *Batsakis*, Batsakis loaned Demotsis the equivalent of $25 while the two were in war-time Greece. In return, Demotsis promised to pay Batsakis $2000 plus interest once she gained access to her funds in the U.S. Batsakis sued for payment. Demotsis argued that the agreement fails for lack of consideration because $25 is inadequate consideration for a promise to pay $2000. The court rejected this argument, holding that "mere inadequacy of consideration will not void a contract." (p. 146)

In *Wolford*, Charles Lehman promised to provide for the welfare of his friend's (Wolford) child if Wolford would name the child after Lehman. Wolford did so and Lehman executed a note in fulfillment of his promise. Lehman died and the executor of his estate refused to honor the note, claiming that there was no consideration. The court held that Lehman's promise was enforceable under the adequacy doctrine.

Following *In re* Greene, we begin by exploring why Batsakis would require Demotsis to sign a note indicating that she received the equivalent of $2,000, and why Demotsis would agree to sign such a note, when their actual agreement was that Batsakis would loan her the equivalent of $25. The answer, we argue, lies in identifying the actual bargain that they intended to strike: a $25 loan in return for a promise to pay $2,000 plus 8 percent interest per annum. If that was the real bargain, why not reflect it accurately in the writing? Recall that the parties in *In re* Greene understood, even as lay persons, that a court might refuse to enforce a promise unsupported by consideration. That belief led them to attempt to structure their deal in every way possible to achieve their goal of making Greene's promise legally enforcement (i.e., they shouted consideration to the housetops). Unfortunately for those parties, their efforts were to no avail because, arguably, their bargain ran afoul of independent policy considerations. It seems likely that the parties in *Batsakis*, and Batsakis in particular, similarly were aware that a court might refuse to enforce their real bargain because it would appear to be so lop-sided– indeed, so lop-sided that a court might suspect fraud or incapacity, or simply refuse to enforce the agreement as unconscionable or otherwise against public policy: The Batsakis-Demotsis written agreement did not specify a specific date for repayment (it specifies only that Batsakis will be repaid "at the end of the present war or even before" if he can find a way to collect from Demotsis' relatives in America). But we can get some idea of the price Batsakis demanded by assuming various payback periods. If the $25 loan were to be paid back at $2,000 in just 1 year, its effective interest rate would be exactly 7,900% (compounded annually). If it were to be paid back at $2,000 in 5 years, its effective interest rate would be just over 140% (compounded annually). Paid back over 10 years, its effective interest rate would be just about 55% (compounded annually). (Because these calculations omit the additional 8 percent annually on $2,000 which Demotsis promised to pay Batsakis, the effective interest rate for their actual loan is even higher for these periods).

Viewed in this light, Batsakis might reasonably conclude that a court would most likely not enforce his bargain. To increase the probability of enforcement, he insisted that the written agreement state that he loaned Demotsis $2,000 at 8 percent interest (rather than $25 at somewhere ranging from 50% to over 2000% interest). Since Batsakis was unwilling to loan the $25 for any less, and it was worth it to Demotsis to pay his price for $25 at that time, the parties agreed to take this measure to attempt to avoid judicial second-guessing of their agreement.

As in *In re* Greene, the parties' intent to make their agreement legally enforceable seems clear. Quite likely, without expected legal enforceability this agreement would not have been made. This then raises the question of why Batsakis could expect to receive, and Demotsis to pay, such a high effective interest rate for a loan. ***Note 2 on page 149*** goes some way towards providing this explanation. In brief, the interest rate reflects the extremely low probability of repayment under those circumstances (i.e., there was probably a high probability Demotsis would not survive the war, let alone get access to her funds in America and follow through on her promise).

The court, however, mentions none of this. It dispenses with the case by invoking the adequacy doctrine (the famous "peppercorn" theory of consideration from *Whitney v. Stearns* (1839))– the parties alone, and not the courts, shall be the judge of the adequacy of the consideration in their bargains. Since Demotsis concedes she agreed to pay $2,000 at 8% for a $25 loan, it's not within the court's province to judge whether she received adequate consideration: "Defendant got exactly what she contracted for according to her own testimony." (p. 146) R2d § 79 and R2d § 79, com. c, reprinted in ***Note 1 on page 148*** set out the adequacy doctrine and its rationale.

Wolford provides a much more direct and extended elaboration of the adequacy doctrine invoked in *Batsakis*. Here the twist is that the consideration for a promise to pay money is nonpecuniary (as it was in *Hamer, supra* Chapter 1). The issue is whether the court should substitute its own judgment in place of the Lehman's judgment of the adequacy of the benefit he received in return for promising to pay the plaintiffs $10,000. Is $10,000 too much to pay for having a child named after you? The court invokes the adequacy doctrine, which directs courts to leave valuation of consideration to the parties. Once the court is convinced there was a genuine bargain (consistent with public policy), the adequacy of the bargained consideration must be left to the parties. The case can be mined for extensive quotations defining and defending the adequacy doctrine. (Note that Lehman also received services from the Wolfords in the form of personal care when he was ill as well as carriage rides for recreation. These might be presumed gratuitous, but one could argue they implicitly were additional consideration for his promise).

The adequacy doctrine invoked in *Batsakis* and elaborated in *Wolford*, seems to provide ample doctrinal support for the *Wolford* decision, except for the R2d § 79, com. d, reprinted in **Note 1 on page 148**, which sets out the nominality doctrine, the converse of the adequacy doctrine: "Disparity in value, with or without other circumstances, sometimes indicates that the purported consideration was not in fact bargained for but was a mere formality or pretense. Such sham or 'nominal' consideration does not satisfy the requirement of § 71." So it appears that, as a doctrinal matter, the *Wolford* court could have just as plausibly invoked the nominality doctrine to invalidate Lehman's agreement. Returning to *In re* Greene, recall our point that the court there could have just as easily invoked the adequacy doctrine, rather than the nominality doctrine, to find Greene's promise enforceable. Comparing *Wolford* to *In re* Greene nicely illustrates the point and counter-point under the adequacy and nominality doctrines. This is the precise issue raised by **Problem a. on page 151**. (Indeed, one of us (Scott) assigns the first twenty pages of Chapter 2 as background and spends two days having the students take either side and argue this problem, which is taken from *Schnell v. Nell* (discussed in detail below).

So why enforce in *Batsakis* and *Wolford* but not in *In re* Greene? Doctrinally, you can argue that there is no reason to doubt, under the nominality doctrine, that the agreements in *Batsakis* and *Wolford* were truly bargained for. In both cases, the bargain is quite plausible. The *Batsakis* bargain was, in short, an extraordinary bargain because it was made under extraordinary circumstances. Under any other circumstances, it would be hard to explain why Demotsis would have agreed to pay, and Batsakis would have insisted on, such a high price. But not under the circumstances they were in. Again, *see* Note 2. (You could explore whether even under those circumstances, or even *especially* under those circumstances, Batsakis was taking unfair advantage of Demotsis. Was the agreement formed under duress?– *see* Chapter 5 for more on duress. We doubt that Batsakis was acting immorally, let alone illegally. Even at the rate he charged, one could argue the loan was charitable. But there is surely room for disagreement here). *Batsakis* then presents a fair bargain that is otherwise unobjectionable. Likewise, the *Wolford* bargain is quite plausible: An old man at the end of his life may well actually find the prospect of immortality in the naming of a friend's son worth $10,000. There is no reason to suspect the absence of a genuine quid pro quo. The same is in fact true of the bargain made in *In re* Greene. There is no reason to doubt it was a genuine bargain. The result in *In re* Greene can be explained only by a concern to promote goals outside of contract law.

Problems (Page 151). a. In *Schnell v. Nell*, the court held that the adequacy doctrine applies only to the exchange of something of indefinite value (not money) for money or for something else of indefinite value. It does not, the court held, apply to exchanges of sums of money. The court also held that consideration of one cent in exchange for a promise to pay $600 is unconscionable and thus void. In addition, the court held that where a claim is legally groundless, waiving it is not consideration. Here, the legatees had no claim arising out of the decedent's will. Finally, the court held that the love the husband had for his wife (which, in *Schnell*, was stated in the agreement as consideration for the promise) could not serve as consideration for the promise because it was past consideration, and it was no consideration for a promise to pay money to a third party.

Zachariah's promise is, at bottom, gratuitous. The apparent bargain was a mere pretense, window dressing to make a gift look like a bargain, and thus it fails under the nominality doctrine. So the drafting question at the end of the problem challenges students to make a gratuitous promise binding. In the absence of the law of the seal, Zachariah could make the promise enforceable only by requiring something valuable in return– thus effecting a genuine bargain. Alternatively, he could leave the money to these promisees in his will. But they would have to wait for his death, and he would be free to change his will at any time. Finally, he could effect a present gift, but, presumably, he does not have the money available now to make a present transfer. As in *In re* Greene, it seems clear that Zachariah intended his promise to be legally enforceable– why else sign and seal a written contract and specify that the promisees must pay $1 to Zachariah? Students should wonder why contract law is averse to enforcement of gratuitous promises where the promisor's intent to make the promise legally enforceable is clear. In our view, there is no good reason. The rule against enforcement of gratuitous promises should be a default rule (most gratuitous promisors would not want their promises to be legally enforceable). But promisors should be able to opt out of this default rule by using a device – such as the seal, or in this case, stating that the promisees paid $1 consideration – that makes clear their intent to make an enforceable gratuitous promise. (*see Note 2 on page 138*, discussing the history and policies underlying the seal and Model Written Obligations Act, both of which are designed to enable parties to make gratuitous promises enforceable and to remove doubt about the enforceability of even non-gratuitous promises).

b. In *Williams v. Carwardine*, the court held that Williams was entitled to the reward money despite the fact that she was induced to identify the murder not in order to secure the offered reward but because she had been beaten and believed she was going to die and wanted to ease her conscience. The justices held various that: "[t]he advertisement amounts to a general promise, to give a sum of money to any person who shall give information which might lead to the discovery of the offender. The plaintiff gave that information." "There was a contract with any person who performed the condition mentioned in the advertisement." "We cannot go into the plaintiff's motives."

c. In *Fiege v. Boehm*, the court held that while a promise not to prosecute a claim which is not founded in good faith does not constitute consideration, such a promise is sufficient consideration if the party forbearing had an honest intention of bringing the claim and believed it was well-founded. The court held that the mother's claim in the case before it satisfied this standard and thus was sufficient consideration, regardless of whether the promisor was the father.

C. Promissory Estoppel
Introduction

Promissory estoppel is the second of contract law's three enforcement doctrines. Even more so than the consideration doctrine, its key concepts are vague. R2d § 90 sets forth the doctrine, providing for enforcement of a promise which the promisor should expect to induce action or forbearance and which does induce such action, but only if injustice can be avoided by enforcement. In our view, *every* serious promise induces reasonable reliance of some kind. Certainly, in most cases a good lawyer can make the case that her client reasonably relied on a promise from the moment he received it. The only truly open question is the extent and kind of reliance, which the language of R2d § 90 treats as irrelevant, except, at least in principle, insofar as they affect the injustice of non-enforcement under the last clause of R2d § 90. But despite R2d § 90, com. b (reprinted in *Note 4 on page 167*), the *Essay on page 220* suggests that the "injustice" clause has been used as a public policy catch-all, rather than a vehicle for requiring any specific extent or kind of reliance as was required for enforcement under § 90 of the First Restatement (requiring reliance to be "definite and substantial").

If every promise induces reasonable reliance, including gratuitous promises, then R2d § 90 would eviscerate the point of the consideration doctrine– i.e., to exclude gratuitous promises from legal enforcement. Absent independent public policy considerations, all promises would be enforceable. The challenge of understanding R2d § 90, then, is to discern how courts *apply* it to exclude the enforcement of some promises. We treat it as just another doctrine, like the consideration doctrine, designed to separate enforceable from unenforceable promises (we draw a Ven diagram on the board consisting of a circle within the circle. The large circle includes all promises, the smaller one includes only enforceable promises. Consideration, promissory estoppel, and the material benefit rule are all devices for selecting which promises make into the inner circle). As the introduction to this chapter of the manual indicates (along with the Essays in this chapter), we believe all three enforcement doctrines, as applied, fall under the expanded bargain theory, which serves the objective of enforcing promises only if doing so will maximize net beneficial reliance. But as we teach the doctrines in this chapter successively, we treat each on its own terms, as if it is conceptually independent of the others– we take their Restatement formulations at face value before turning to any unifying theory.

The cases in this section nicely illustrate the difficulty in applying the doctrine to explain and predict the enforcement patterns we see in promissory estoppel cases. In turn, the expanded bargain theory does a nice job of reconciling otherwise these otherwise inconsistent results. The *Introduction to intrafamilial contexts on page 161* explains how the expanded bargain theory grows out of efforts to understand why the doctrine of promissory estoppel did not, as some predicted (e.g., Gilmore), swallow up contract, despite its capacious language in favor of enforcement. As Professor Stanley Henderson has shown, promises made outside of bargain contexts, it turns out, are not enforced under § 90. Section 90 is used to expand enforcement beyond the traditional confines of the consideration doctrine, but not beyond the context of exchange.

Promises Made in Intrafamilial Contexts

Haase v. Cardoza *(Page 162).* Alice Cardoza promised to pay Rose (her deceased husband's sister) $10,000 and to pay Loretta Haase (her niece) $3,000 in monthly installments. After Alice made payments for eight months, Rose asked Alice to sign a note for the balance. Alice refused and stopped making payments. Rose sued and her claim was rejected on the grounds that Alice's promise was unsupported by consideration and that Rose had failed to demonstrate any reliance to support enforcement under promissory estoppel.

As with the consideration cases covered so far, our objective here is to keep the doctrinal puzzle going, rather than to resolve it before the students have a chance to appreciate the doctrinal problem that needs to be resolved. So we begin by running through the consideration analysis under R2d § 71. Was there a bargain between Alice and Rose? What did Rose have to offer Alice? Nothing except her forgiveness. Why then would Alice make the promise? Clearly, to assuage her moral guilt by discharging a felt obligation to her husband. There was certainly no actual bargain (and just as clearly no bargain context, but we'll come back to this later). What about promissory estoppel?[1] As we've said above, we believe all credible promises induce reasonable reliance. It's possible that bad lawyering explains this case– Rose's failure to prove all the actions she took during eight months of payments in anticipation of this significant increase in her monthly income. But we doubt it. Would the case have come out differently if Rose proved that she bought a car, or went on a vacation, in reliance on the promised stream of monthly $50 payments? We don't think so. The question for the students is why? Taken at face value, wouldn't R2d § 90 allow for recovery if Rose demonstrated actions taken in reliance? If so, then once even the bad lawyers catch on, promissory estoppel will swallow up consideration and all promises will become enforceable.

So what's the key to understanding *Haase*? We ask students whether they thought Alice was sincere and credible in her promise. Answer: Of course she was – she made it when she was ill, perhaps even contemplating her own demise and reflecting on the wishes of her dead husband. Moreover, she made it on her own, with no inducement but her own conscience. What were the odds of her breaking that promise? But she *did* break her promise. What does that prove? Well, consider the circumstances. She followed through like clockwork on her promise until what happened? Rose came in and asked to sign a promissory note. That's what did it. *Why?* That's the question for students to chew on. In short, she broke her promise because she didn't intend to make a legally enforceable promise. Rose's request amounted to a request to make the promise legally enforceable. (Note that even if Alice had signed the note, the promise would still be unenforceable. Simply committing the promise to writing has no bearing on whether it is enforceable as between the parties

---

[1]Note that the court discusses promissory estoppel as a "substitute for consideration." The initial reception and understanding of promissory estoppel was inconsistent in many courts. Promissory estoppel is now – and for the most part was then – viewed as a *distinct* ground of recovery, not as an extension of the consideration doctrine. The court also discusses the enforceability of promises based on past consideration. "Past consideration" is, strictly speaking, an oxymoron. If the promisor has received value from the promisee before the promisor makes her promise, the promise could not have been made as a condition of receiving that value. To qualify as consideration, the value must be given in order to induce the promise. "Past consideration," however, sometimes refers to promises enforced under the material benefit rule, covered later in this chapter. But as such, it is a misnomer.

(unless Rose sold the note to an HDC). But this is beside the point. Clearly Rose, and more importantly Alice, *believed* that signing a promissory note would have legal significance). Why would Rose make the request, especially given that Alice had kept the promise so far and gave every indication of continuing to do so? Perhaps she feared Alice would die and her estate would discontinue the payments. Or perhaps she needed evidence of the $50 payments as additional income to qualify for credit elsewhere. In the face of her belief that signing the note would make it legally enforceable, Alice recoiled at the request. At a minimum, she didn't want to make the promise legally enforceable, but given that she then discontinued the payments, she evidently took umbrage at Rose's request.

What does this show? It shows that Rose was looking a gift horse in the mouth and that Alice viewed her as ungrateful and impudent. In Alice's view, Rose's job was to *be grateful and shut up*. (Obviously, Alice wasn't thrilled by the prospect of paying Rose in the first place, or she wouldn't have waited a year and half, and for an extended illness, to decide to pay Rose the money her husband wanted Rose to have. And even then, she doesn't make the payment outright, but chooses to make a promise for $50 monthly payments. We would imagine Alice is not too fond of Rose, or is very fond of money, or both.)

The court doesn't enforce the promise and clearly the promisor didn't intend to make an enforceable promise. Right result, right reason. So once again, would a demonstration of Rose's reliance have changed the result under R2d § 90? Not a chance. We come back to *Haase* when we line up the consideration and promissory estoppel cases under the expanded bargain theory. It's a paradigm case of non-enforcement of a non-bargain context promise– an intrafamilial promise in which, as is typical, the promisor does not intend to incur legal liability, and the promise is extremely reliable in the absence of legal sanctions. *Haase* provides a graphic and highly effective illustration of the likely negative activity level effect of enforcing promises made in non-bargain contexts. What is likely to happen? Would-be promisors will decline to make the promise, fearing undesired legal liability, thus depriving prospective promisees the benefit of relying on what would have been an extremely reliable promise. Whenever we want to remind students of the negative activity level effect of enforcing promises made in non-bargain contexts, we just remind them of Alice's reaction to Rose's request to sign a promissory note.

Ricketts v. Scothorn *(Page 164).* Ricketts gave his granddaughter, Katie Scothorn, a promissory note for $2,000 plus interest so that she would not have to work. In reliance on this promise, she quit her job. Ricketts died without having paid the note, but having expressed his desire to pay it. The executor of his estate refused to honor the note on the grounds that it was not supported by consideration. The court agreed that the promise was to make a gift, and thus was not supported by consideration. But the court held Ricketts' estate was equitably estopped from asserting the defense of lack of consideration because Scothorn had relied on Ricketts' promise: "Having intentionally influenced the plaintiff to alter her position . . . it would be grossly inequitable for the maker [of the promise], or his executor, to resist payment . . . ." (This equitable estoppel bar to asserting the defense of failure of consideration is the precursor to promissory estoppel. In class, we invite the students to read equitable estoppel in these early cases as the equivalent of promissory estoppel).[2] Thus, the court allowed Scothorn to enforce the promise.

At first blush, the case seems to be a counter-example to the claim that contract law generally does not enforce intrafamilial promises. Indeed, students naturally should have predicted that *Ricketts* would follow the *Haase* decision not to enforce the promise. But there is a critical difference between the cases. In *Ricketts*, the intrafamilial promisor died without having revoked his promise– it is his estate that is refusing to perform, not the promisor himself. (It's worth pointing out to students that, for this reason, *Ricketts* is not an example of an unreliable intrafamilial promisor. In fact, when intrafamilial promises are broken, it's typically the executor of the promisor's estate that refuses to perform – because of her fiduciary duty to the beneficiaries of the estate – not the original promisor). In *Haase*, it's the intrafamilial promisor herself (Alice Cardoza), rather than her estate, that is refusing to perform. (And of course, as we've said above, rather than demonstrating the unreliability of intrafamilial promises, *Haase* demonstrates both the high reliability of such promisors, and their aversion to making legally enforceable promises). Although most intrafamilial promisors prefer to make legally unenforceable promises (and not much is to be gained by legal enforcement given their high reliability), it seems equally clear that such promisors would want their promises to be enforceable against their estate provided they had not revoked their promises before they died.

The *Ricketts* rule – which enforces unrevoked intrafamilial promises after the promisor's death – should not have a negative activity level effect on intrafamilial promising because intrafamilial promisors will still retain their power to revoke during their lifetime (hence, Alice Cardoza is still free to revoke her promise to Rose). But just as the intrafamilial promisors of the world (such as Ricketts and Cardoza) generally wish to retain their right to revoke their promises during their lives, they would equally intend their promises to be carried out by their estate if not revoked before their death– after all, they intended to give their promisees not only the gift promised but the beneficial reliance on that promise as well.

If we return to the language of *Ricketts*, the court's ruling of the scope of the promissory estoppel recovery is broader than we have suggested above. The court states that " . . . it would be grossly inequitable to permit *the maker, or his executor*, to resist payment on the ground that the promise was given without consideration." [166] In our view, to the extent the court opines on the question of recovery from an intrafamilial promisor himself, rather than his estate, its language should be treated as *dicta*. We doubt that the *Ricketts* court would have so held had Ricketts himself refused to perform the promise. (Note that in almost every case, there are facts available to allow a court to dismiss the reliance as insignificant– for example, here, Scothorn entered employment

---

[2]The doctrine of promissory estoppel evolved out of the doctrine of equitable estoppel. Initially, courts allowed promisees to use equitable estoppel to prevent promisors from raising the defense of lack of consideration. Equitable estoppel was thus used as a "shield" against a promisor's defense to enforcement. But eventually courts allowed promisees to enforce promises directly under the doctrine of promissory estoppel (as a "sword"). In older cases, such as Ricketts, the beginnings of promissory estoppel were couched in the more familiar doctrine of equitable estoppel.

again in just over a year, before her grandfather died and with his consent). And in any event, *Haase* is the representative case on recovery against a living intrafamilial promisor: Absent special circumstances, promissory estoppel will not lie, even in the face of demonstrated substantial reliance.

Note 2 (Page 166). In the first hypothetical, Alice promises to pay *before* Rose promises to light a candle. In the second, Alice offers to promise to pay *if* Rose will promise to light a candle. The first is therefore not a bargained-for promise– Rose's promise was not a condition of receiving Alice's promise. Alice's promise is an unenforceable, gratuitous promise (no quid pro quo). The second is a bargained-for promise– Rose's promise *was* a condition of receiving Alice's promise. Alice's promise is an enforceable, non-gratuitous promise (by making it she received a quid pro quo).

Note 7 (Page 168). This note introduces the fundamentals of the theory underlying the non-enforcement of intrafamilial promises. It also raises potential limitations on that theory that can provide the basis for critical class discussion of the theory.

Problems (Page 170). *a.* First, Ortiz could argue that Aunt Mary actually executed a gift of the rugs to him (that the letter constituted constructive delivery). Assuming that argument fails, Ortiz could argue for enforcement under promissory estoppel (§ 90). There is ample evidence that he relied on Aunt Mary's promise to give him the rugs. As a doctrinal matter, the Bank could argue that Ortiz's reliance was not reasonable because it was not the kind of reliance that Aunt Mary should have expected. Since she promised to give him the rugs because he appreciated their value, she likely would not have expected him to sell them. Still, who's to say selling the rugs isn't appreciating their value? Moreover, he planned to sell only one of the rugs but planned to use the other for personal enjoyment. As useful as this kind of doctrinal exercise is, we believe, these arguments will not be controlling. Instead, enforcement will turn on whether the promise was made in a bargain context. Aunt Mary's promise is obviously an intrafamilial promise. It is thus presumptively unenforceable. The only twist here is that her promise resulted from Ortiz's initial efforts to bargain with her on price for the rugs. But despite the (atypical) bargain context that began their interaction, clearly Aunt Mary felt a bargain was inappropriate with her nephew. She intended to make a gift of the rugs and, we would argue, would not have intended her promise to be legally enforceable. Indeed, we would predict that just as Alice Cardoza recoiled at Rose's request to sign a promissory note, so Aunt Mary would have been put off by a request from Ortiz to commit her gratuitous promise to writing. One could argue, however, that Ortiz clearly felt comfortable bargaining with his Aunt in the first place, and might well have been able to persuade her to accept money for the rugs, or, if possible otherwise, to make her promise legally enforceable. But on the facts as they are, Aunt Mary likely did not intend her promise to be legally enforceable. Thus, despite his definite and substantial reliance on her promise, a court would not likely enforce this intrafamilial promise had Aunt Mary refused to perform it. But here Aunt Mary died before revoking her promise. As in *Ricketts*, although intrafamilial promises generally are not legally enforceable, once the promisor dies there is no reason not to enforce. We believe a court would enforce this intrafamilial promise under the *Ricketts* rule.

b. In *Ervin v. Ervin*, the court held that the divorced father was not required to pay for post-secondary education because there were no special circumstances (physical or mental handicap) that would require a parent to provide post-secondary education, and there was no showing of a binding agreement concerning the child's college education. The letter in which the father promised to pay for the child's college education "merely responds to an inquiry at the time by the plaintiff," which made the court doubtful that it was a promise. Even granting that it was a promise, the court ruled, there was insufficient evidence to support a finding that the plaintiff detrimentally relied on the promise. Therefore, there was no showing of injustice.

c. In *Wright v. Newman*, the court held that Wright was obligated to support the child under the doctrine of promissory estoppel. Because of Wright's promise, Newman refrained from identifying and seeking support form the natural father of the child. Had she not refrained from doing so, she might have secured an alternate source of financial support for the child, and the child might now have a natural father in his life. This detrimental reliance, the court held, is sufficient to satisfy the doctrine of promissory estoppel.

Promises Made in Employment Contexts

Feinberg v. Pfeiffer Co. *(Page 174).* The Board of Directors of Pfeiffer Co. promised to pay Feinberg, a long-time employee who had risen through the ranks to the position of Ass't Treasurer, retirement benefits beginning whenever she wanted to retire. It did not require her to retire at any specific time. She continued to work for a year and a half, and then retired. The company paid her the retirement benefits for approximately seven years, but then a new president stopped the payments on advice from the company's auditors. Feinberg sued, and the court held in her favor, ruling that Pfeiffer's promise was enforceable under promissory estoppel.

Hayes v. Plantations Steel Co. *(Page 178).* Six months before Hayes retired he announced his intention to retire. One week before the effective date of his retirement, Hayes spoke with his employer, Hugo Mainelli. Mainelli, then an officer and stockholder of Plantations, promised to "take care" of Hayes. The company made retirement payments to Hayes for three years following Hayes' retirement, after which they were discontinued by the new ownership of the company. Hayes sued and the court ruled that Plantation's promise was not supported by consideration, and was not enforceable under promissory estoppel because Plantation's promise did not induce Hayes' decision to retire and his other reliance was insufficient to ground recovery.

Feinberg and *Hayes* appear at first glance to be like cases decided differently. The opinions from each court point to differences in reliance– Hayes did not rely, according to the Rhode Island court, while Feinberg did, according to the Missouri court. But, as *Note 1 on page 183* suggests, it's not plausible to suppose that Hayes did not rely on the promise he received. The court rightly points out that Hayes announced his retirement far in advance of receiving any retirement promise. But Hayes maintains he wouldn't have retired absent that promise. It's certainly possible that Hayes would have abandoned his intention to retire, less than a week before his announced retirement date, had he not received the promise. The court rejects his claim. However, his retirement decision itself is not the only potential form of Hayes' reliance. The court also argues that his annual visits to the company to inquire about the duration of the payments demonstrates that he was not relying on the payments after retirement. But to the contrary, such visits to insure continued payments at least equally suggest he had relied substantially and was continuing to rely on the payments (as would any rational person in his place– who would not change his behavior appreciably upon receiving $5,000 annually for five years?). The existence of reliance cannot explain the different results in *Feinberg* and *Hayes* (or if it does, it's only by virtue of bad lawyering– a failure to put in evidence of reliance). As a general matter, despite judicial rhetoric to the contrary (driven by the doctrinal language of R2d § 90), the enforcement patterns under promissory estoppel cannot be accounted for by distinguishing between relying and non-relying promisees. All promisees rely to a greater or lesser extent (and most can prove it if necessary).

Rather than focusing on the difference in timing between the promises Feinberg and Hayes received and their respective retirement decisions (looking for differences in actual reliance), we believe the key to distinguishing *Feinberg* and *Hayes* is suggested in Note 2. Feinberg was still a valuable employee when the promise was made to her– indeed, the Board gave her a raise at the same time it promised to pay retirement benefits, and she continued to work for the company for over a year following the promise. The Board's likely intention in voting to give a raise and retirement benefits to Feinberg was to insure that she remain at the company. In class, we speculate that Feinberg was an underpaid, invaluable employee. She had worked at the firm for 37 years before she received the promise. She was bookkeeper, office manager, and assistant treasurer of Pfeiffer Co. She sounds less dispensable than the President and CEO. We all know people like her that in effect "run" the company in so many essential, but under-appreciated, ways. By making the promises, the company was trying to insure that as Feinberg came within a decade of retirement age, she didn't look elsewhere for employment that came with retirement benefits. She was still a marketable talent (with at least 5 or 10 years expected professional life remaining), at risk to the competition, and at a potentially devastating internal cost to the company. In effect, the company was trying to pre-empt her dissatisfaction by anticipating her concerns and intervening proactively to make a valued employee happy.

On this (concededly elaborated) set of facts are considered, it's clear that Feinberg could have marched into Max Lippman's office and demanded a legally enforceable promise of retirement benefits had she been so inclined. That she did not in fact make such a demand takes Pfeiffer's promise outside of the plain meaning interpretation of the consideration doctrine (there was no bargain-in-fact). But it does not take the promise outside of the bargain *context*. Her market leverage suggests that Pfeiffer's promise was made in a bargain context, even though it was not, strictly speaking, bargained for. In our view, it is in precisely such settings that courts turn to promissory estoppel to enforce a promise that is unenforceable under the consideration doctrine but is nonetheless made in a bargain context. Most promisors in these settings would intend to make a legally enforceable promise. If such an enforcement rule would otherwise deter such promisors from promising (the feared negative activity level effect of enforcement), the promisee in these bargain contexts can be relied upon to force the promisor to make the promise. In anticipation of that dynamic, the promisor would intend legal enforceability in the first place (i.e., to pay the promisee her market value– an enforceable promise for retirement benefits). Thus, enforcement in these cases increases net beneficial reliance.

On the contrary, Hayes was at retirement age (i.e., the age at which most individuals decide to retire). There is no evidence Hayes was a particularly valued employee at Plantation, or that he was marketable at other companies (in fact, because of his age he probably would have been unable to secure a position elsewhere). The retirement promise made to him was likely motivated out of personal sentiment, rather than the business necessity driving the promise in *Feinberg*. Indeed, there is every reason to believe that Plantations *welcomed* Hayes' retirement and intended the retirement promise as a gesture of good will (worth making not only because it is morally laudable but also because of the good will such generosity creates for the company with its remaining employees). Did Hugo Mainelli likely intend the promise to be legally enforceable? Would Hayes have been able to "bargain" for an enforceable promise? We doubt it. Mainelli's promise was not only not bargained for, just as Pfeiffer's promise was not bargained for, but unlike Pfeiffer's promise, it was not made in a bargain context.

As a counter-point, however, it bears mentioning that although Hayes was evidently an "at will" employee, nonetheless, under the Age Discrimination in Employment Act, Plantations would not have been free, at least not without fear of costly litigation, to force him to retire. A worker discharged at age sixty-five would have a potential claim for age discrimination that could embroil an employer in costly litigation and cause bad publicity. That factor suggests at least the prospect of a bargain context, even for a worker who otherwise has no market leverage: "I'll retire if you'll promise me retirement benefits. Otherwise, just try to fire me and I'll see you in court." Yet this does not seem to have been Hayes' gambit, given that he announced his intention to retire well in advance of receiving the promise. Although it might have been a factor motivating Mainelli's promise, at the time of his discussion with Hayes, Mainelli had no reason to fear Hayes would not follow through with his own plan to retire. Of course, had Mainelli, contrary to the facts, promised Hayes retirement benefits in return for Hayes' promise to retire, the promise would have been enforceable under R2d § 71 as an actual bargain. Alternatively, if Mainelli had made the promise before Hayes had announced his decision to retire, but not in an actual bargain with Hayes, and Hayes subsequently decided to retire because of the promise, the promise would have been enforceable under R2d § 90– it would have been made in a bargain context in which the promisor's motive was not to retain an employee (as in *Feinberg*), but to retire employee.

Another point worth noting is that in both of these cases the promises were kept until someone other than the original promisor became responsible for their performance. The promises to Feinberg and Hayes were probably very reliable, as long as the original people that made the promises (Lippman and Mainetti) remained in control of performance. This would suggest that the *Ricketts* rule should apply in *Hayes*– Mainelli would want to retain the right to revoke his promise as long as he is in control of performance, but wouldn't want the company to be bound if other leadership takes over. But since Mainelli was promising *on behalf of* Plantations, and not personally, in effect the original promisor in these corporate promise cases is never succeeded by another. As a legal matter, the corporation remains the original promisor throughout. Although Mainelli personally might have liked to bind the company to his promise, it probably would not have been in the company's interest to do so. Thus, it would be unreasonable to suppose it was Mainelli's intent to act on his own interests at the expense of the company's interest his office requires him to promote. In contrast, in *Feinberg* it probably was in the company's interest to bind the company in the future, so it would be reasonable to suppose that was the Board's intention when it made its promise.

Once we work with students to explain the difference in outcomes between *Feinberg* and *Hayes*, one of us returns to all the consideration and promissory estoppel cases so far considered in the course and invites students to use the expanded theory to explain their outcomes. Under the column of enforcement, we have *Hamer*, *St. Peter*, *Batsakis*, *Wolford*, *Ricketts*, and *Feinberg*. Under the column of non-enforcement, we have *In re* Greene, *Kirksey*, *Haase*, and *Hayes*. How well does the expanded bargain theory of enforcement account for these results? Take them one at a time:

Hamer: Intrafamilial promise, which is presumptively a non-bargain context. So this looks like a potential counter-example. But the uncle *actually bargained* for the nephew's behavior. It is therefore consistent with the expanded bargain theory. Recall the reasoning: We can't say the nephew's refraining from various vices was a simply condition for a gift, as in Williston's tramp case. Clearly, the nephew was induced to forgo the vices in order to satisfy the condition of the uncle's promise. This was therefore an (atypical) intrafamilial promise that was bargained for. The expanded bargain is not needed to account for the result because it is a promise made in the straightforward, actual bargain contemplated by R2d § 71. Although the expanded bargain theory does not require a promise to be the subject of an actual bargain in order to be enforceable (that's the whole point of "expanding" the bargain), it certainly enforces such promises as paradigm bargain contexts. (Note that although the case was decided under the benefit/detriment theory of the § 75 of the First Restatement, which does not expressly require a bargain, the bargain theory is necessary to account for the results under § 75 as well.)

St. Peter, *Batsakis* and *Wolford*: Again, all of these are actual bargain cases, predicted by the expanded bargain theory (and of course, by the narrower actual bargain requirement of R2d § 71). Recall that Pioneer Theater made its promise as part of an actual bargain with its patrons (if they hadn't made the promise to patrons like the St. Peters, they would have run afoul of the lottery statute).

Ricketts: An intrafamilial promise, presumptively unenforceable, but the promisor died without revoking the promise. So a net beneficial reliance calculus carves out an exception to the expanded bargain idea: Even though the promise was not made in a bargain context, enforcement in these circumstances maximizes net beneficial reliance because it will not deter these promisors from making their promises (i.e., it will not have the negative activity level affect ordinarily associated with enforcing promises in nonbargain contexts). Such promisors incur no legal liability and remain free to revoke, even though their promise is enforceable if not revoked prior to their death.

Feinberg: Paradigm case for the expanded bargain theory. No actual bargain, but the promise is enforced under promissory estoppel because the promise was made in a bargain *context*.

In re Greene: Intimate context, but not quite intrafamilial. Might presume against enforcement on the ground that promises between intimates are usually not intended to be legally enforceable. But here there is a bargain context, and intent to be bound is obvious. The expanded bargain theory predicts enforcement, but contravening public policy drives the opposite result.

Haase: Paradigm case of a nonbargain context. Theory correctly predicts nonenforcement. Demonstrates the negative activity level effect of enforcement in these contexts.

Hayes: Paradigm case for the expanded bargain theory. No bargain context but detrimental reliance (despite court's denial of detrimental reliance). Expanded bargain theory explains why promissory estoppel does not lie in these cases.

Socratic method works beautifully for running students through these cases and having them tie the theory to the doctrine. It's a nice reprise before moving on to the substantive enforcement areas below. Understanding these doctrines requires consideration of policy issues and economic considerations that do not necessarily apply to promissory enforcement questions generally. We come back to reinforce the expanded bargain theory at the end of the chapter when we discuss the material benefit rule.

Charitable Subscriptions
R2d § 90(2) reads as follows: "A charitable subscription . . . is binding under Subsection (1) without proof that the promise induced action or forbearance."

Salsbury v. Northwestern Bell Telephone Co. *(Page 189)*. Northwestern Bell promised by letter to donate money to a new college. The college failed before the first scheduled payment on the pledge, so the company did not pay. Salsbury, who was the President of the Board of Trustees of that college, sued for payment and won. The court rejected ordinary promissory estoppel as grounds for enforcement (the court didn't think reliance could be demonstrated), and admitted that enforcing under consideration was a fiction. However, the court adopted R2d § 90(2), and used it to rule in favor of the plaintiff.

Congregation Kadimah Toras-Moshe v. DeLeo *(Page 192)*. The decedent, a member of the Congregation, made oral promises to the Congregation's Rabbi to donate $25,000 to the Congregation. He died without reducing the promise to writing and his executor refused to honor it. The court refused to enforce it, finding that there was no consideration or reliance, and that even if it adopted R2d § 90 (which it did not do), the promise would still be unenforceable because a failure to enforce it would not create an injustice.

Note 1 (Page 193). In *Allegheny College v National Chautauqua County Bank,* Mary Yates Johnston pledged $5,000 to the College for a memorial fund to be named after her, the proceeds to go toward educating students preparing for the ministry. After paying part of it, she repudiated. After her death, the College sued her executor for payment. The court (Cardozo, J.) strained to find consideration and, finding it in the College's implied commitment to name the fund after Johnston, enforced the promise.

In teaching these cases, some time can be devoted to working through the possible doctrinal avenues for enforcement by analyzing the arguments for finding consideration and promissory estoppel. *Allegheny College* provides an ideal case for exploring the viability of the consideration route, as does the "mutual subscriber inducement"theory invoked in the cases cited in *Salisbury* on page 190 (*Brokaw v. McElroy, Trustees v. Noyes,* and *In re Estate of Leigh,* and *Young Men's Christian Assn. v. Caward*). Promissory estoppel can be explored in both *Salisbury* and *DeLeo*. In *Salisbury*, reliance is demonstrable– the subscription was actually assigned to a material supplier. For a demoralizing look at how courts sometimes treat distinguishing precedent as a mindless exercise in mechanics, ask students why the court dismisses this evidence of reliance: "Plaintiff relied on defendant's letter but not the form of it." (pages 190-191) What does this mean? Apparently, it means that the court had already ruled in previous cases that reliance on a particular, standard pledge form was not sufficient for enforcement, reliance in this case could justify enforcement only if based on something other than the pledge card. But it turns out that although the college sent the material supplier a copy of an unsigned pledge form reflecting the pledge Northwestern Bell made in its letter, the college did not send the actual letter. Would the court have us believe it would have enforced the promise if the college had sent the letter to the supplier? Same promise, different piece of paper, different enforcement result? Can precedent be this wooden, or is the court bending over backwards to abandon precedent and start fresh with a rule that obviates the need for these maneuvers in the future?

In *DeLeo*, we return to our mantra: Promisees always rely. No doubt bad lawyering could account for the result here. Evidently, the Congregation failed to put in sufficient evidence of its reliance. But we doubt the charitable subscription cases generally can be parsed according to whether the promisee can demonstrate reliance. The fighting issue is whether enforcement in these contexts would increase net beneficial reliance (or equivalently, whether most charitable promisors would intend to incur legal liability for their promises). The cases favoring enforcement – often cases in which courts torture doctrine to enforce these promises, such as Cardozo's opinion in *Allegheny College* – evidence a perceived policy argument in favor of enforcement. The Restatement (Second) and at least some courts treat charities as uniquely in need of legal enforceability for the promises they receive. However, as we note below (and in *Note 3 on page 196*), this position is not so clearly supportable.

A case can be made that these promises are like intrafamilial promises – motivated by loyalty, moral conviction, and altruism – and therefore should not be enforced (because there is more to lose by deterring charitable promises than to gain by increasing the reliability of charitable promises made). In addition, there is no reason to suppose that (at least large) charities require special protection from the risk of donor breach. While charities certainly rely on the promises they receive, (large) charities are uniquely suited to manage this risk by calculating the probability of breach through actuarial data based on the large number of these promises they receive. But a case can also be made that charitable promises are made in bargain contexts, despite the fact that they are gift promises. As anyone familiar with fund-raising can attest, donations are often motivated by competition for prestige among potential donors. Relatedly, (as Cardozo emphasizes) donors often receive significant nonpecuniary returns for their donations in the form of name recognition (the George Q. Donor Heart and Lung Wing). Charitable organizations may therefore have considerable leverage to induce a legally enforceable promise. However, because charitable organizations thrive on good will (and wither on bad publicity that pits them *against* their donors), it may rarely be in the interest of charitable organizations to enforce promises, even if they are enforceable. This suggests that the legal rule here is irrelevant: The context of charitable giving is so rich in informal norms that any legal norms are dwarfed in comparison. (Scott, who has had some experience in these matters, suggests that legal enforcement matters only in the case where the donor dies before the promise is performed. Action against the executor is eased by a rule of presumptive enforcement.)

Problem (Page 197). In *Coretta Scott King v. Trustees of Boston University*, the court upheld a lower court ruling that the King papers were given to the University, and therefore the University had title to them. In order for a charitable pledge or subscription to be enforceable in Massachusetts, the promise must have been supported by consideration or reliance. The court found that the bailment of Dr. King's letters to the University (in Massachusetts, bailment may be evidence of donative intent) in combination with letter from Dr. King naming the University as repository for his letters provided sufficient evidence of donative intent to submit to the jury the questions of whether there was a promise to donate the letters and whether there was consideration or reliance by the University. Since charitable subscription agreements are usually not the product of bargains, the requirement of a "meeting of the minds" is different in that context than in arm's-length commercial agreements.

Preliminary and Incomplete Negotiations

At common law, each party bore the risk of its own precontractual reliance. Such preliminary promises are not enforceable under § 71 because the exchange is still inchoate. The question is whether courts will change their minds when promissory estoppel is claimed as the basis of enforcing promises that induce precontractual reliance.

Coley v. Lang *(Page 199).* Coley and Lang signed a letter indicating that Coley would buy all of the outstanding shares of Lang's company, IAS. The letter indicated that the agreement would be "reduced to a definitive agreement binding upon all parties" by later that month. When the specified date for making the writing arrived, Coley informed Lang that, because Lang had not obtained approval for several things related to the sale, the transaction could not be accomplished within the agreed-upon time frame. Coley then abandoned the agreement. Lang sued for enforcement based on his reliance on the letter. The court rejected Coley's argument, finding that there was no reliance sufficient to support that claim.

Hoffman v. Red Owl Stores, Inc. *(Page 204).* Hoffman made numerous financial and other decisions at the recommendation of Red Owl Stores officials and in reliance on their promises that a franchise would be his at the end of the process. Hoffman and Red Owl engaged in extensive negotiations and preparations aimed at Hoffman opening a Red Owl franchise grocery store. Eventually, the deal fell apart and Hoffman sued for damages.

As a matter of doctrine, *Coley* represents the "majority" common law rule, and *Hoffman* is a celebrated exception. The supposed difference between these two cases is the there was no substantial reliance in *Coley* while there was in *Red Owl*. But, as *Note 1 on page 211* suggests (and should be obvious to students by now), it is almost never the case that a promisee did not rely on a promise. As a pedagogical exercise, it can be a useful to ask students to make the case that Lang did rely (and to respond to the court's arguments dismissing his reliance evidence). The real difference here is found in the bargaining conduct of the parties, particularly Red Owl. While the court found (as noted in Note 1) no evidence of bad faith on the part of Red Owl, the evidence suggests otherwise. The amount of money Red Owl required of Hoffman increased substantially over the course of the negotiations, with no explanation. Also, Red Owl's main representative in the negotiations urged Hoffman not to mention the partnership agreement he had with his father-in-law regarding the grocery store; later, other Red Owl officials insisted that the father-in-law's investment be a gift (Hoffman refused). Thus, it seems possible (likely?) that sometime during the negotiations Red Owl decided to take Hoffman (and his family) for a ride. On the other hand, there is no taint of bad faith in *Coley*, and that decision conforms with most other decisions on preliminary/incomplete negotiations.

The reason why promises made in preliminary/incomplete negotiations are usually not enforceable is founded in the economic analysis laid out in *Note 3 on page 213*. In short, before the major terms are agreed upon, and thus before the benefits of the deal are clear, both sides will prefer to bear risks as promisees rather than as promisors. Put another way, before they are certain that a binding agreement will produce gains that will outweigh their costs, parties prefer to be free from obligation. This means that their negotiating partner is not obligated either, but each side would rather have to adjust their reliance than be liable for their promises. Note: this argument assumes each party is risk averse, an assumption that may not be justified when one or both parties are corporations.

The difficulty with these cases, then, is determining at what point the parties are clear on the major terms. To avoid chilling negotiations, most courts rarely enforce promises made in the course of uncompleted negotiations.

Problems (Page 212). *a.* In *Mooney v. Craddock*, the court found that even though there was no mutual agreement as to all essential terms of the lease, the promissory estoppel doctrine can and should be invoked to prevent injustice to Mooney. Mooney relied heavily on the promise (indeed, he retired from the military and moved his family to Colorado from Germany), and Craddock should have expected his promise to induce this action. The court limited recovery to the actual loss sustained. The court did not address whether Craddock had grounds for a promissory estoppel claim against Mooney.

b. In *Fried v. Fisher*, the court found that this was a good candidate for promissory estoppel. Indeed, the court said "All the safeguarding features thrown around the doctrine of promissory estoppel – that the promise be one likely to induce action, that such action be of a definite and substantial character, that the circumstances be such that injustice can be avoided only by the enforcement of the promise – are here present." Fried told Fisher that Brill had taken over the lease, and that he was releasing Fisher from it. Since Fried knew why Fisher wanted to be released, this promise was likely to induce the action that Fisher took. Fisher substantially changed his position by opening another business. The court evidently believed it would be an injustice not to enforce Fried's promise.

Promises to Insure

East Providence Credit Union v. Geremia *(Page 214)*. Defendants' car loan from the plaintiff required them to carry automobile insurance. In the event that they did not, plaintiff would secure insurance, and the defendants would have to pay for it. When defendants became unable to pay their premium, plaintiff notified defendants that it would pay for the policy and add the amount to the defendants' loan. Defendants notified plaintiff that they approved of this. Plaintiff failed to make the payment and, unbeknownst to plaintiff or defendants, the policy was terminated. Subsequently, the car was destroyed. The plaintiff sued for the amount outstanding on the loan, and the defendant counter-claimed for the amount of the insurance policy. The court ruled for the defendant by holding the plaintiff's promise enforceable both because it was supported by consideration (the court believed the bank's promise to pay the insurance premiums was supported by an implied reciprocal promise from the Geremias to pay the bank interest on the money it used to pay the premiums) and because it induced reasonable, detrimental reliance rendering the promise enforceable under promissory estoppel.

Note 1 (Page 217). *Graddon v. Knight* is a good example of a court using promissory estoppel to enforce a promise to insure. The court found ample evidence to support the finding that the bank, which was financing a home being built by the Graddons, agreed to secure insurance for the home. The home was later destroyed by fire. Because the court found that the Graddons relied on the bank's agreement, it held the bank liable.

Spiegel v. Metropolitan Life Ins. Co., also excerpted in Note 1, is another example of promissory estoppel being used by courts to enforce a promise to insure. There, an agent for the insurance company repeatedly promised to arrange for the renewal of the plaintiff's husband's life insurance policy. The plaintiff's husband died after the agent had failed to renew the policy. The court held the agent liable for full amount of the policy.

Students should be suspicious of the courts' focus on reliance as the deciding factor in these cases. Comment e to § 90 (discussed in *Spiegel*) calls on courts to inquire into whether the reliance was justified and whether the promise was merely one to use reasonable efforts to procure insurance. Thus, the real question is, as with all promissory estoppel cases (indeed all enforcement cases generally), whether the promisor intended the promise to be enforceable. As *Note 3 on page 219* points out, promises to procure insurance are made in highly competitive market. When this is the case, enforcing the promise to procure insurance is not likely to have a substantial activity-level effect. The competition will force promisors to make their promises legally enforceable, lest those promisees who insist on it take their business elsewhere.

D. The Material Benefit Rule

We take the three cases in this section (together with *Boothe v. Fitzpatrick*, excerpted in *Note 3 on page 231*) as a group. One of us has the students read all the cases and then asks them to come to class prepared to solve "Gilmore's Puzzle" reprinted on page 232. The question: Is the Material

Benefit rule incoherent, as Gilmore suggests, or can it be rationalized under the expanded bargain theory or the intent to be bound theory (or any other theory)?

Past Consideration in General: Promises for Benefit Received

Mills v. Wyman *(Page 224)*. After Mills had provided care to Wyman's dying son, Wyman promised to pay Mills for his efforts. Mills subsequently sued to enforce the promise. The court refused to enforce the promise, finding that the "kindness and services toward the sick son were not bestowed at the defendant's request," and hence the subsequent promise was not supported by consideration. The case is one of the old chestnuts standing for the proposition that past consideration, including a preexisting moral obligation, is insufficient to enforce a gratuitous promise.

Promises for Non-Donative Material Benefits

Having started with the general rule of non-enforcement of promises supported only by past consideration, we now take up the most important exception: the material benefit rule.

Manwill v. Oyler *(Page 226)*. In *Manwill*, the plaintiff made payments on the defendant's behalf on a farm now occupied by the defendant and also transferred valuable grazing rights and 18 head of cattle. The defendant later orally promised to repay the plaintiff, but then reneged on that promise. The plaintiff could not maintain an action for repayment of the payments themselves because the statute of limitations on that contract action had run. Instead, the plaintiff sued on the defendant's subsequent promise to repay the loan. The plaintiff's theory of recovery was the material benefit rule. But the court rejected recovery under that doctrine on the ground that the plaintiff had not shown that he expected to be compensated for his payments (under the material benefit rule, a promise for previous benefits conferred is not enforceable unless the benefits were conferred non-gratuitously).

Webb v. McGowin I and II *(Pages 227 and 228)*. Webb was badly injured while saving McGowin's life. In recognition of this, McGowin subsequently promised to make payments to Webb for the rest of his life. He made these payments for eight years, but, after he died, his estate refused to continue them. The court held that McGowin's promise was enforceable under the material benefit rule.

In each of these cases, the opinions recognize the moral obligation to provide some compensation, but in the first two, the courts decline to enforce the promises. It should come as no surprise to the student that moral obligation does not itself create legal obligation– that would prove too much, as many believe there is at least a *prima facie* moral obligation to keep all promises.

Section 86 of R2d provides that a promise will be enforced if made in recognition of a benefit conferred on the promisor non-gratuitously and if necessary to prevent injustice. Obviously, this doctrine is vague enough to allow rulings either way on virtually any fact pattern. The real issues here, as with the other enforcement doctrines, are the context in which the promise is made and the promisor's ex ante intent.

By this point, students should be able to apply the expanded bargain theory to explain the material benefit rule. The rule enforces only those promises made to compensate for *non-gratuitously* conferred past benefits. Why is this fact relevant to an analysis of the *subsequent* promise? One answer is that the fact that the promisee expected compensation when the initial benefit was conferred is key evidence of the context in which the subsequent promise is made. If the subsequent promise is made in a bargain context, then presumably the promisee would not be reluctant to seek an enforceable promise, and the promisor will be willing to give one (in exchange for a release from social and reputational sanctons). Enforcing promises made to compensate for past benefits non-gratuitously conferred will thus not have a significant activity level effect (i.e., it will not deter promisors in these settings from making such promises in the future). Why? Because social norms and internalized moral norms, rather than the competitive market, give the prospective promisee (who confers a non-gratuitous benefit) leverage to ask the beneficiary to compensate for the windfall he received at the prospective promisee's expense. (Another way of saying this is that the promisee can "pay" for the subsequent promise by restoring the promisor's reputation as a decent person with whom one can bargain in good faith.) Strong social norms hold that, all else equal, it is wrong to profit from another's innocent mistake in conferring a benefit before the anticipated bargain has been completely nailed down, and it is laudable to promise to repay for such benefits. Thus the promisor has powerful incentives to promise to repay the benefit even if the promise is legally enforceable in order to earn the approval of the promisee and other prospective bargainers.

For example, suppose A mistakenly digs a well on B's property (believing it to be C's property, on which C requested A to dig the well). As a result, the market value of B's property increases at least by the amount of A's cost of digging the well. B promises to pay A's costs for digging the well. B's promise is enforceable under the material benefit rule. The expanded bargain theory explains the result: B will feel compelled to make a subsequent promise even if legally enforceable because in return he receives the validation of the social community. Thus, enforcing B's promise will not have a negative activity level effect on promisors in B's position and will increase the reliability of such promises. Moreover, the subsequent promise solves the problem of *valuation*-- it allows us to judge just what the benefit conferred by the promisee was worth to the promisor and thus to apply an appropriate remedy in the event of breach.

In contrast, enforcing promises made to compensate for past benefits that were gratuitously conferred *will* have a significant activity level effect (i.e., it will deter promisors in these settings from making such promises in the future). Why? For the same reasons enforcement would deter intrafamilial promises. Such promisors are unlikely to intend their promises to be legally enforceable and less likely to make them if they are. Here there are no social or moral norms to motivate the promise, and the promisee has nothing to "offer" in return. Such promises are instead motivated by a sense of charity and compassion, rather than social or moral duty. For example, A gives B a monetary gift at a time when B is struggling financially. B acknowledges the benefit (one could hardly imagine otherwise) and subsequently promises to compensate A in recognition of his gratitude. If B's promise were legally enforceable, B would not be equally likely to make it. Like Alice Cardoza, B views his promise as "above and beyond the call of duty." If B declines to make a promise (because it is legally enforceable), there is little A can do in such a context to extract one. If A requests that B make the promise legally enforceable, B will probably refuse. Moreover, B's promise, made out of sense of charity, is probably quite reliable. So little is to be gained by making it legally enforceable.

So goes the enforcement account of the material benefit rule. It's easier (though certainly not uncontroversial) in theory than when applied to the cases:

Mills: The above account would hold that since Mills took care of Wyman's son without any expectation of compensation, Wyman would not feel obliged to preserve his reputation in the marketplace by promising to repay. Or in any event, he would be unlikely to intend his promise to be legally enforceable, and social and moral norms would not give Mills the leverage to demand (or "pay" for) such a promise. To be sure, one could plausibly argue that morality *did* require Wyman to repay Mills for the cost of caring for his dying son, but morality certainly did not require him *to promise to do so*. The promise, once made, is very reliable. Legal enforcement is unlikely to do much good and, to the extent that it marginally discourages such promises, it can do harm.

On the other hand, the case for enforcement rests on the intuition that morality really gave Mills no choice but to confer the benefit, which would have been the moral responsibility of Wyman were he available. On this view, the initial benefit would be non-gratuitous Thus, Mills was really acting as an agent for Wyman, and therefore has a moral claim to compensation for his trouble. This argument would be stronger if Wyman's son were a minor, but he was an adult at the time Mills cared for him, thus lessening the claim that Wyman had a special responsibility for his care.

Manwill: The court here found the material benefit rule unsatisfied, and the promise therefore unenforceable, because there was no evidence that Manwill expected compensation for the benefit he conferred. This conclusion is puzzling. As the court noted, Manwill could not have brought a straightforward contract action because it was barred by the statute of limitations. Thus, his failure to bring a contract claim arising out of the events of 1950-54 does not establish that he conferred the benefits gratuitously. Is it just that his lawyer was inept? If we believe the benefit here was non-gratuitously conferred (it was an ordinary loan agreement where the statute of limitations had run), then we accept that, in the absence of the statute of limitations, Manwill would have not merely a moral claim, but also a valid legal claim to be repaid. In that event, like all promises to compensate for a non-gratuitously conferred past benefit, the promise here should be enforced. A promise to repay money is a classic example of a promise compelled by social and moral norms, notwithstanding procedural barriers to making out a legal obligation to repay money borrowed. Those who have been loaned money typically feel a responsibility to repay their lender, and those who do not do so are likely to be viewed with disdain by others. In this context, a recipient of such a benefit who makes a promise in recognition of the benefit is likely to intend that promise to be enforceable (and thus there would be no negative activity level effect by enforcing these kinds of promises).

But the court treats the benefit as gratuitously conferred (perhaps because of poor lawyering). If Manwill's payments were made without an expectation of repayment (which strikes us as unlikely), then he would indeed have less standing to demand a promise to repay him. Oyler would be acting out of a sense of gratitude, rather than moral obligation, and so might be less inclined to intend his promise to be legally enforceable. On this interpretation, net beneficial reliance aligns with denial of enforcement, as the general account of the material benefit rule holds above.

McGowin: Application of the material benefit rule, on its own terms, is difficult in this case. Was the benefit conferred gratuitously or non-gratuitously? Did Webb intend to risk grievous physical harm to himself in order to save McGowin without any expectation that McGowin would compensate him if he is injured? Or did Webb assume that McGowin would compensate him for any injury he sustained in saving McGowin's life? The questions seem absurd under the circumstances. Webb certainly did not confer the benefit by mistake. But on the other hand, that hardly establishes that he conferred it without an expectation of compensation. The truth is that Webb probably did what he did without any conscious thought at all, let alone after contemplating whether his intent was donative or not. His action resulted from an instantaneous decision to save another's life. Period.

This case strikes us as most analogous to *Ricketts v. Scothern,* supra. The key here is that McGowin clearly *intended* his promise to be legally enforceable. He made the payments faithfully for eight years until his death and never indicated any intention to revoke during his lifetime. Thus, while this is essentially a gratuitous context, it is one in which the imposition of legal liability will have no negative activity level effects. Just as with Mr. Ricketts, legal enforcement is no deterrence to a promisor who knows that an unrevoked gratuitous promise will be enforceable against his estate. Thus, enforcement against the estate is likely to do more good than harm . So here, the role of theory is not merely to defend the result of the doctrine as it clearly applies in the case, but to explain how the doctrine should apply to this case (which is the same role theory played, for example, in explaining when promissory estoppel should ground recovery). Strong social forces and moral norms compel one whose life is saved to compensate his benefactor, especially one injured as badly as was Webb, at least to the degree to which he is able. In light of these forces, such promisors are likely to intend their promises to be enforceable. And, in any case, McGowin never sought to revoke his promise. Enforcement in this context therefore maximizes net beneficial reliance.

Note 5 (Page 233). A final point is worth emphasizing. Note 5 raises the question of why, if some of these promises are enforceable, liability is not imposed for all non-gratuitously conferred benefits, even in the absence of a promise by the beneficiary. The reason is that, in the absence of a subsequent promise, it is difficult to determine to what extent, if any, the recipient valued the benefit. The subsequent promise reveals at least the beneficiary's minimum subjective valuation of the benefit received. Hence, courts are able to measure with a high degree of accuracy the amount of liability the promisor *intended* to assume and avoid overvaluing the benefit.

CHAPTER 3

THE BARGAIN CONTEXT

A. Introduction

In Chapter 3, we move from examining the broad issues of enforcement dealt with in Chapter 2 to a careful analysis of promises that are clearly made within the bargain context (i.e., are governed by Restatement § 71). In the simplest of terms, a contract results from a bargained for exchange when one party makes an offer and another party accepts that offer. So the question we ask in this Chapter will no longer be "is this promise enforceable?" but rather "do the words and actions of the parties constitute an offer and an acceptance?" Students learn to answer these questions by mastering the default rules governing offer and acceptance and then analyzing the ways in which courts use them to settle disputes. Though our focus may have changed, the object of our inquiry remains to discern patterns of judicial enforcement. In the end, we want students to be able to predict with some accuracy the point at which negotiations ripen into offer and acceptance.

We find it helpful at the outset to guide students through the shift in language (and focus) from the broad conception of an enforceable promise in Restatement § 71 to the more precise language of offer and acceptance. It may be useful to walk the students through this transition by tracing the progression in the Restatement from § 71 to §§ 17, 22, 24, and 26. Section 71 provides that "to constitute consideration a performance or return promise must be bargained for." Section 17(1) explains that (except as noted in subsection (2)), a contract requires a bargain in which there is a consideration *and a manifestation of mutual assent to the exchange*" (emphasis added). As § 22 states, that manifestation of mutual assent normally takes the form of an offer and an acceptance. But one can express a willingness to enter a bargain without that manifestation constituting an offer. As §§ 24 and 26 explain, a manifestation is only an offer if it justifies the other party "in understanding that his assent to that bargain is invited and will conclude it." If the recipient of a manifestation of willingness to enter into a bargain knows (or has reason to know) that a "further manifestation of assent" is required, then the expression is only an invitation to negotiate and cannot form the basis for legal liability. An offer, then, is simply a conditional promise: one that is explicitly conditioned on a particular response from the promisee. In the terms we began with in Chapter 1: "I promise to do X *if* you promise to do Y."

B. Offer and Acceptance
Subjective and Objective Tests of Mutual Assent

Restatement § 17 states that the requirements for a bargain are "a manifestation of mutual assent to the exchange and a consideration." The mode of signaling one's assent is given in § 22: an offer by one party and an acceptance by the other. This sounds uncontroversial enough, but, as we have seen in *Bailey v. West, Lucy v. Zehmer,* and *Leonard v. Pepsico,* it is not always clear whether an offer has been made or an acceptance given. When ambiguity arises and the issue is litigated, courts must apply default rules to determine whether there has been a manifestation of mutual assent. This section focuses on the two tests–the subjective and objective tests– traditionally used by common law courts to determine what constitutes offer and acceptance.

Reminding students of the circumstances of *Lucy* can help drive home the distinction between these two approaches and the implications of adopting either of them. Recall that Zehmer claimed that his acceptance of Lucy's offer was intended only as a joke. Under the subjective test, Zehmer would be free of his obligation if he could show that he really was joking; the court would honor his actual intent. But the court instead employed the (by then dominant) objective test and found that, despite Zehmer's actual intent, he had indeed accepted Lucy's offer and had thereby entered into a valid contract. It was the *manifestation* of intent that mattered, not the actual intent.

If Zehmer was honest in alleging that he was just kidding, on what basis can the court's decision be justified? Isn't the court violating his autonomy by forcing him to sell his farm when he had no intention of doing so? As we discussed in Chapter 1, one justification is that the objective test forces the party with the comparative advantage, the idiosyncratic party, to inform the other party of her actual intentions or risk losing out by making a deal she didn't intend. Forcing the idiosyncratic party to manifest her actual intent lowers the risk of contracting for the "normal" party without requiring the normal party to take special precautions against a hidden contrary intention. Furthermore, it expedites the bargaining process by allowing parties to rely on widely held conventions for manifesting intention, as the hypothetical on pages 239-240 points out. This also lowers transaction costs because the parties needn't constantly define the meaning of their words and actions unless they ascribe idiosyncratic meaning to those words and actions.

Offer

The Restatement embraces the objective test and, as such, defines offer in § 24 as "the manifestation of willingness to enter into a bargain, so made as to justify another person in understanding that his assent to that bargain is invited and will conclude it." This reflects the traditional, simple paradigm of bargaining over time with negotiations culminating in an "offer" and an "acceptance." Litigation results when the parties disagree over the "timing" question: At exactly what point was the plaintiff justified in believing that his assent would conclude the deal?

Dyno Construction Company v. McWane, Inc. *(Page 242).* Dyno won a large government contract to construct a water and sewer system for the City of Perrysburg, Ohio. Dyno had contacted McWane, a pipe manufacturer, for price quotes to use in its bid, and, after the contract was awarded to Dyno, McWane sent two faxes to Dyno with quantities and prices for the materials needed. On November 22, Dyno called McWane and told them to order the materials. Lewis, one of Dyno's owners, said he thought they had a "done deal," but McWane then sent a package to Dyno containing a purchase order and credit application. On the back of the purchase order was a clause limiting McWane's liability to repair and replacement. Lewis said he never received those forms, and, after informing McWane of that fact, McWane faxed the forms to Lewis on December 1. However, he failed to fax the back of the form containing the liability-limiting clause. Lewis signed and returned the forms, and McWane delivered the materials. Unfortunately, the materials were defective, but, pursuant to the clause limiting its liability, McWane refused to compensate Dyno for consequential damages suffered as a result of those defects. Dyno filed this suit in order to recover those damages.

The question is whether or not the price quotes faxed to Lewis before November 22 constituted an offer that Lewis then accepted during the phone call on that day. If so, then the liability-limiting clause was not part of the contract and, under UCC § 2-715, McWane would be liable for Dyno's consequential damages. The court cites authority for the proposition that price quotes generally do not constitute offers, but also notes that if a price quote is detailed enough, it may suffice. The court first employs a textualist analysis to decide that, as a matter of law, the price quote was too preliminary to qualify as an offer. None of the language in the price quote indicated that it was an offer; the word "estimate" was printed at the top, and the quote invited Lewis to "Please call." Moreover, the price quote is incomplete; a number of terms had not been agreed upon. An examination both of words used and terms not yet agreed upon suggests that the proposer anticipated further negotiations. This conclusion is then buttressed by a contextual analysis. In particular, the fact that Lewis voluntarily signed the purchase order indicates that he understood that the price quote as only a preliminary negotiation. Given the objective test, this may have been an important fact for the court as it suggests that the proposer's understanding was "manifested" to the recipient. As a consequence, the contract was not formed until Dyno returned the purchase order.

When discussing this case, we find it helpful to have students review the facts of the cases cited by the court in order to have them isolate the factors courts look to in deciding whether a particular proposal is an offer or only an invitation to negotiate. The key factors can be grouped in two broad categories: text and context. Thus, courts look both at the relative precision or vagueness of the terms, whether "magic" words such as "offer" are used and also at the sequence and extent of prior negotiations. Many students (and both of us) find a factor analysis inherently unsatisfying and imprecise. One way of rationalizing the results of the cases is to ask whether there is a normative principle that can supply a presumption to govern doubtful cases. An answer that predicts well is that efficiency considerations argue for a presumption that ambiguous proposals are treated as preliminary negotiations and not offers. Such a rule will encourage parties engaged in negotiations to take more care in formulating and presenting proposals that they intend to have effect as offers. Since the legal issue only arises in cases where the parties have not clearly manifested their intentions, a presumption against offers induces more clarity and reduces subsequent litigation costs at a relatively modest expenditure of additional negotiation efforts. Moreover, the fact that the state subsidizes the litigation process indicates that parties may not fully internalize the costs of sloppy negotiating behavior. A number of students will recognize that this is the same analysis that governed in *Bailey v. West*, supra.

Lefkowitz v. Great Minneapolis Surplus Store, Inc. *(Page 246).* Ordinarily, advertisements are considered invitations and not offers because they are not focused on a particular recipient but rather are extended to a general population of readers. Thus, in cases where the proposer looks to a return promise rather than a performance, a plausible assumption is that the proposer cares about the nature of his putative contracting partner and thus does not intend to be bound until that person is identified. Lefkowitz is an exception to that general rule and, therefore, has found its way into casebook lore. It is a fun case to teach because the behavior of both parties is difficult to rationalize at first blush.

The defendant placed two newspaper ads advertising a limited number of fur products to be sold on a first come first served basis at deeply discounted prices the following Saturday. The ads were placed a week apart. The first advertised 3 fur coats for $1 each, and estimated that they were worth "To $100.00." The second advertised 2 mink scarfs "Selling for $89.50" and 1 lapin stole "worth $139.50" all for $1 each. Lefkowitz was the first customer at the store on both Saturdays. The first time, the store refused to sell him a coat because they said house rules only permitted them to sell to women. The second week, they again refused to sell him anything because he knew about the house rules. In its defense, the store contends that a newspaper advertisement does not constitute an offer, but is instead an invitation for an offer of sale on the terms stated. The court holds that if the ad is "clear, definite, and explicit, and leaves nothing open for negotiation, it constitutes an offer . . . ." Using this test, the court upholds the trial court's ruling that the ads for the coats and the scarves were too indefinite to constitute offers because the value of those items was not stated with certainty. The ad for the stole, however, stated the exact worth of the item, and therefore constituted an offer.

But does this seem like the logical outcome of this case? It is not necessary that the value of the item be stated with certainty in order for there to be an offer; only the price at which the seller is willing to sell need be stated definitely. The uncertainty of the items' value might prevent the court from calculating money damages, but the advertisements place an estimated value on them that the court could reasonably assume represents their market value. Hence, a remedy could be provided. Furthermore, it would seem more logical for the first ad to be construed as an offer since it in no way manifested the store's intention to sell only to women (*see* Restatement § 20(2)(a)). Lefkowitz did what the store required (like the St. Peters in *St. Peter v. Pioneer Theatre*, supra, he showed up), and he should be compensated for the store's breach. But when he answered the second ad, he knew about the rule, thus making the offer inoperative under Restatement § 20(1)(b).

But why does the store litigate this case to the Supreme Court of Minnesota and face the attendant bad publicity? One plausible explanation is that Lefkowitz is a dealer known to the store who is trying to sabotage and exploit a legitimate sales promotion. If so, the store would be willing to expend significant resources in demonstrating their resolve not to be jerked around in this manner.

Problem (Page 249). A court should find that the advertisement is only an invitation to negotiate and not an offer. The key, of course, is that this is an invitation looking to an offer to enter into a bilateral contract. Thus, Christy is looking for a return promise. It is important for her, therefore, to know the identity of a potential contracting partner who will be promising to pay $3,000 in the future. She would want to assure herself that Adam was a responsible person who could deliver on his promise to pay for the car. Thus, the problem illustrates the general rule that advertisements that are not addressed to any specific person are typically not considered offers to sell.

Problem (Page 250). Just as Lefkowitz knew the second time he went to the store that the offer was not made to him (because he was a man), the issue in this hypothetical is whether the killer himself was an intended offeree. If you want to keep the money out of the killer's hands, then you would have to show that he knew, or had reason to know, that he was not the intended offeree or else provide some other justification for denying him the reward. One might, for instance, make an argument based on custom: you need not state explicitly that wanted individuals cannot collect rewards offered for their capture because everyone knows that such a condition is necessarily implied. One might also justify denying him the money on public policy grounds: what incentives would be created if we allowed criminals to collect rewards for turning themselves in?

Problem (Page 251). In *Courteen Seed,* the court held on these facts that the October 8 telegram, "I am asking . . . ," was only an invitation to negotiate and not an offer. The court used a textualist analysis in reaching that conclusion focusing on the use of the verb form "am asking" rather than the more traditional "am offering." But doesn't the context of the negotiations suggest a different inference? After all, this telegram follows three prior exchanges between the parties and is a direct response to a communication from Brown that states, "Wire firm offering naming absolutely lowest f.o.b." What else could the reply to that wire be other than an offer?

One way to approach this problem is to use the tests employed in *Dyno* and *Lefkowitz.* The communication is fairly definite in that it states an asking price, a quantity, and a method of delivery. However, the text of the communication indicates that this was an invitation rather than an offer. First, it identifies it as an "asking" price, which implies that the other party is free to offer a lower price. Second, it states that the seller already had an offer for the seed from another buyer. That is a clear indication that the seller expects the buyer to quote him a price higher than that already offered. He was looking for an offer from the buyer.

But all of this seems a bit makeweight to us. This is another example that only makes sense if you put a thumb on the scales in favor of invitations over offers when the communication in context is unclear or ambiguous. A bright line rule that looks to clarity in fixing legal liability encourages clarity in party negotiations. The moral of this story is that a clever clover buyer must be able to distinguish between an offer and an invitation for an offer; the clever buyer gets the clover.

a. Methods of Acceptance

Ever-Tite Roofing Corp. v. Green *(Page 252).* The Greens sought the services of Ever-Tite in re-roofing their home. To that end, they signed a writing that set out the terms of the contract, including the work to be done and the amount of the monthly payments. The writing constituted an offer from the Greens to Ever-Tite, which, according to the terms of the writing, could accept the offer either upon written acceptance by an authorized officer or "upon commencing performance of the work." The day after receiving a satisfactory report on the Greens' credit, Ever-Tite sent a crew to the defendants' home in order to begin the work. Upon their arrival, they found another crew working on the roof and were told by the Greens that the job had been contracted to another company. Ever-Tite sued to recover damages for the Greens' breach; the Greens argued that either the offer had lapsed or they had revoked prior to acceptance by Ever-Tite.

The trial court found that the Greens had revoked their offer before Ever-Tite commenced performance, thus terminating Ever-Tite's power of acceptance. This could be justified under either § 42 or § 43 of the Restatement. These sections set forth the requirements for the revocation of offers. Under § 42, revocation occurs when the *offeree receives from the offeror* a manifestation of an intention not to enter the contract. Section 43 allows for revocation by definite action: once the offeror takes definite action inconsistent with an intention to enter the contract and *the offeree acquires reliable information to that effect* the offer is revoked. The Greens manifested their intention not to enter a contract with Ever-Tite when Ever-Tite arrived at their home. They also took definite action inconsistent with an intention to enter a contract with Ever-Tite by contracting with another company. But under both sections, there can be no revocation until the offeree knows that the offer has been revoked. So the court must decide whether the Greens' had communicated their revocation to Ever-Tite before performance had begun.

This trial court and the appeals court disagree about the time of commencement. The trial court apparently thought that performance would not commence until the Ever-Tite crew was actually on the roof doing the work. The appeals court, however, finds that performance commenced with the loading of the trucks in Shreveport. Hence, the offer was accepted prior to the Greens' attempted revocation, and a contract was formed. (See *Note 1 on page 248* for further discussion of this point.)

This case turns on an understanding of two propositions. First, the standard rules as to permissible methods of acceptance are only defaults. The offeror is always free to opt out of the defaults and to specify an *exclusive* mode of acceptance. Second, the exclusive method of acceptance in this case–either the signature of an authorized official or "commencing performance of the work"– does not look to acceptance by performance but rather looks to one of two possible promissory acts (*see* Restatement §§ 4 and 30(1)). The promise is manifested either by the act of signing the writing or by the act of commencing performance. Ever-Tite thus accepts by a making a conduct promise to perform the re-roofing job.

But if the acceptance was promissory then wasn't Ever-Tite required under Restatement § 56 to communicate their acceptance to the Greens? Under § 50, the offeror is the master of her offer, and she can waive the notification requirement (pursuant to § 50(1) and § 56). Arguably, that was the case with this offer; notification was waived by the offeror. Waiving the default requirement of notification makes sense from Ever-Tite's perspective. After all, once they confirm that their sales person has signed up a financially responsible party, they want to bind the offeror immediately. But why would the offeror, the Greens in this case, want to dispense with notice? The answer, of course, is that they probably would not. The "offer" nominally came from the Greens but the form was prepared by Ever-Tite's attorneys and is designed to promote the interests of Ever-Tite as the offeree.

Students may wonder about the structure of this deal. Why was the writing the Greens signed constructed as an offer from them to Ever-Tite and not as an acceptance of Ever-Tite's offer to do the job? The answer is that Ever-Tite did not want to make an offer without first knowing whether the Greens' credit would be approved. By structuring the writing as an offer, Ever-Tite is able to defer acceptance (and thereby formation of the contract) until they received the credit approval. That way there is no risk of them being bound should the Greens' prove to be a bad credit risk.

Incidentally, a substantial portion of the opinion is devoted to the issue of whether or not acceptance was given within a reasonable time, pursuant to Restatement § 41. This, however, seems irrelevant. There is no time specified in the contract, so, under § 41, acceptance had to be given within a reasonable time. The work was commenced the day after the Green's credit was approved, and it would be ludicrous to argue that Ever-Tite should have commenced performance before they knew whether or not they would get paid. Acceptance was clearly given within a reasonable time, and the only real issue is when performance commenced (and whether notification of that act was required).

Ciaramella v. Reader's Digest Association, Inc. *(Page 255).* Ciaramella, a former employee of Reader's Digest Association (RDA), sued RDA for allegedly violating his rights under the ADA and ERISA. During settlement proceedings, Ciaramella's attorney requested several revisions to the settlement proposed by RDA, and, after those revisions were made, told RDA's attorney, "We have a deal." However, the settlement agreement contained a clause stating that the parties would not be bound until the settlement had been signed by both parties. Before Ciaramella signed the agreement, he sought counsel from a second attorney and decided that the settlement was unacceptable. RDA filed a motion to enforce the settlement on the grounds that it had been accepted orally. The district court agreed and granted RDA's motion. Ciaramella appealed, arguing that he had not accepted the offer because the parties did not intend to be bound until both had signed the written agreement.

Restatement § 30(2) provides for acceptance of an offer by any reasonable manner or medium, and certainly under most circumstances the oral assent proffered by Ciamarella's attorney would suffice. This, however, is a default rule around which the parties can bargain if they so choose. The court here is interested in honoring the party's intentions: they should not be bound if they intended not to be bound until the formal agreement was signed. To determine if that was indeed their intention, the court employs a four part test, asking: 1) did they expressly reserve the right not to be bound in the absence of a signed writing; 2) was there partial performance; 3) had all the terms been agreed upon; and, 4) was the agreement one that would normally be reduced to writing? Based on this multi-factor test, the court holds that the parties had opted out of the default and were looking to a "closing" as the moment when legal liability attached. The party's intention trumps the default rule, and the 2nd Circuit vacates the order enforcing the settlement.

Note 1 (Page 260). *Ciaramella* offers an opportunity to ask students why parties would wish to "delay" enforcement beyond the time when assent is manifested. In many large transactions–such as merger agreements, real estate sales, and commercial asset transfers–the principals will reach agreement on the main features of the deal–price, etc.– well before the closing. The reason that the contract is not formed until the closing is that the transaction is then handed over to the lawyers to work out the balance of the details. But often "technical" issues, such as the extent and nature of the warranties offered by the seller, will affect the price that has previously been agreed upon by the clients. If the lawyers cannot successfully bargain in the "shadow of the deal," they may have to return to the clients and seek adjustment of some of the previously agreed upon elements. Thus, in an important sense, it is not until the "private constitution" has been hammered out that the parties are prepared to risk legal liability. If this is true, then what should we make of the four factor test adopted by the 2nd Circuit? Shouldn't the express reservation of liability until closing be the single, conclusive factor? Why is part performance relevant? One answer is that it allows the court to use supplementary doctrines, such as promissory estoppel to enforce "pre-contractual reliance." At least one of us wonders whether the use of such a broad multi-factor standard rather than a bright line rule is wise in these business contexts where presumably the parties can negotiate over all issues including the protection of any pre-contractual investments.

Note 2 (Page 261). The contract in *Ever-Tite* is bilateral. It allows for a promissory acceptance by signing the writing or, in the alternative, by commencing performance. Normally it would be subject to the notification requirement in § 56, but the argument would be that the clause providing an exclusive mode of acceptance functions as a waiver of the notification requirement. In other words, the offer manifests a contrary intention.

One important difference between bilateral and unilateral contracts is that under a unilateral contract, the promisee is under no obligation to perform. The offer is not accepted until performance is completed, which means there is no contract (and hence no legal liability) until the promisee has fully performed (although as we will see, Restatement § 45 gives the offeree who begins performance an option to complete the performance). A bilateral contract, on the other hand, creates an obligation as soon as the offer is accepted. Under § 50(3), the party accepting by promise is legally bound to carry out her promise in full, and she will be held liable if she breaches. Hence, if the promisor wants an executory commitment from the promisee, then a bilateral contract will better suit her needs. If no reliable commitment is required, or if the parties are unsure about the promisee's ability to perform, then a unilateral contract would be preferable because then there is no legal liability until the performance is complete.

In *example a*, Julie's offer appears to be an invitation to enter unilateral contract, and she does not request notification of performance. Under § 50(2), Gary need only commence performance to signal his acceptance. Gary cannot enforce Julie's promise until performance is complete, but per § 45, beginning performance gives Gary a unilateral option to complete and Julie cannot revoke the offer in the interim. Per § 54, the contract is formed upon completion and Gary need not notify Julie of his acceptance.

The offer in *example b* is more ambiguous. Julie may be looking only to the performance, but, arguably, she may be inviting a promissory acceptance. Julie does ask for a promissory acceptance, but she does say that she wants it done tomorrow, which would indicate that she is looking for a promise from Gary to perform at the specified time. Under § 32, in doubtful cases Gary has the option to accept either by promising to perform (thus creating a bilateral contract) or by rendering the performance itself. Here, Gary accepts by promising to shoe Julie's horse the next day, and, by telling her directly, he has satisfied the notification requirement of § 56.

Once again, Julie's offer in *example c* is ambiguous and so, under § 32, Gary is free to accept either by promising or performing. He accepts by commencing performance, and, under § 45, Gary now has a unilateral option to complete and enforce the promise to pay $500. This is true even though under the circumstances it seems that Julie would want a promise from Gary to paint the entire garage. She wouldn't want him to be able to quite in the middle with no legal obligation to complete the job. The burden, however, is on her to specify the nature of the offer and the modes of acceptance more clearly.

In **problem d**, the Carbolic Smoke Ball Company is inviting acceptance by performance. Under § 54(1), Ms. Carlill had no duty to notify the Company of her acceptance because they did not expressly request it. The default assumption in the case of offers that invite performance is that notification is not necessary for acceptance since the offeror has indicated by the nature of the offer that having a credible commitment before performance was not important. In any case, Ms. Carlill will promptly notify the Company of her performance because she wants to collect the money, thus discharging her duty under § 54(2). Hence, her use of the smoke ball constituted acceptance and created a binding contract.

Problem e is governed by UCC § 2-206(1) which parallels Restatement § 30(2). But the Code's language is even stronger: "unless *unambiguously* otherwise indicated" (emphasis added). Nevertheless, the court in *Antonucci* held that the offer required acceptance by the dealer manifested by a signature of an authorized agent and thus explicitly defined the exclusive manner of acceptance. Like the writing in *Ever-Tite,* the document here constitutes an offer by Antonucci to buy the truck. Since the offer specified that a signature was required to make the contract binding, then, as with Ciaramella, no binding contract had been formed, and Antonucci was free to revoke his offer when the truck arrived. In the absence of this exclusive method of acceptance, ordering the truck that Antonucci had offered to buy would be a reasonable manner of acceptance and his revocation would have come too late.

b. Silence as Acceptance. We describe the relevant doctrine in the text and ask students to read it independently. It is straightforward and useful to know when we turn to the more complex issues involving the "battle of the forms" in Section C, infra.

c. The Mailbox Rule

We generally assign this section as independent reading. The only point worth noting is that, despite changes in post office regulations, the mail box rule still lives! It remains one example of the utility of a coordinated solution to a general problem. After all these years, the rule functions as a "Schelling point." Most parties understand "intuitively" that legal liability attaches upon dispatch. The permutations of the rules, which used to occupy law professors in days when Contracts was a six credit course are not relevant in the real world and probably not very interesting either.

Revocation of Offers
a. Revocation in General

In many cases, revocation is a straightforward matter: the offeror can revoke her offer at any time prior to acceptance and revocation terminates the offeree's power of acceptance. However, in the case of unilateral contracts, the issue is more problematic. Under the old common law rule, an offeree could only accept an offer for a unilateral contract by fully performing. Because no contract exists until the offer is accepted, the offeror was free to revoke his offer at any time before the performance was complete. Wormser's Brooklyn Bridge hypothetical on page 268 does a nice job of setting up the problem, but his analysis overlooks the "obvious injustice" suffered by the offeree. He argues that there is no injustice because the power to withdraw is mutual— just as the offeror can revoke the offer at any time prior to acceptance, the offeree can cease performance at any time without incurring legal liability because she has no legal duty to perform.

But the mutuality argument is flawed. While it is true that the offeree can cease performance at any time without incurring legal liability, to do so will result in a net loss to her because she will have invested time and money in her partial performance. As a practical matter, the very act of commencing performance will restrict the offeree's ability to cease performance because she would bear the total costs of the completed work. She cannot bill the offeror because he is under no obligation to pay until performance is complete. The offeror, on the other hand, suffers no loss if he revokes his offer after the offeree has commenced performance. Even if the offeree is one step away from crossing the bridge, the offeror need not pay him anything because the offer has not yet been accepted and no contract exists.

In addition to allocating uncompensated risk to the offeree, this default rule can create opportunities for strategic behavior on the offeror's part. If I enter into a unilateral contract with a farmer to plow his field for $1,000, he could revoke his offer just as I am about to begin the final pass without having to pay me for my work. He will have received a benefit at no cost to him, and I will be forced to bear the total cost of my lost time and other expenses. More likely, the offeror will threaten to revoke in order to coerce a renegotiation of the price. Hence, even though there is mutuality in the sense that neither party incurs legal liability until performance is complete, there is a moral hazard created by the offeror's power to revoke.

The effect of this rule, then, is to make offers for unilateral contracts less reliable. In the above hypothetical, I will have no incentive to accept by performing unless the farmer also promises me that he will not revoke after I have commenced performance as long as I complete it within a reasonable time. Such a promise would eliminate my risk of losing money as a result of a premature revocation, and it will deter him from executing a strategic revocation. Partial performance would function as consideration for the subsidiary promise not to revoke; it would make the offer irrevocable subject to completion of the invited performance in accordance with the offeror's terms. Indeed, this is the newer common law rule, embodied in § 45 of the Restatement. Under this rule, the offeror is still not bound to pay until performance is complete, but the offeree need not worry about suffering a loss due to the offeror's revocation as long as she completes the required performance in a timely fashion.

Obviously this is a rule that offerees would bargain for because it reduces their risk, but it is reasonable to assume that most offerors would want this rule as well. Ex ante, it will make their offers to enter unilateral contracts more reliable, and it will therefore be easier for them to find parties willing to contract with them.

b. Irrevocable Offers

Offerees can limit the offeror's power to revoke by buying an option to exercise the power of acceptance before a specified time. This concept is fairly straightforward, and the hypothetical on page 270 provides a clear example of how this works. Some offers, however, are irrevocable strictly as a result of the context in which they are made. As the next case demonstrates, bids made by subcontractors to general construction contractors can function as irrevocable offers if the general contractor can demonstrate that he has detrimentally relied on the bid.

Pavel Enterprises, Inc. v. A.S. Johnson Company, Inc. *(Page 270).* Pavel Enterprises (PEI), a general construction contractor, sought a bid for mechanical work from A.S. Johnson, a mechanical subcontractor. PEI used Johnson's bid to calculate its own bid for a contract to renovate the Maryland campus of the National Institute of Health (NIH). After the initial low bidder was disqualified, PEI was notified that it was now the low bidder and would be awarded the contract. PEI formally accepted Johnson's bid on September 1. Johnson then notified PEI that it had made an error in its bid and sought to withdraw, but PEI refused their request to withdraw. NIH formally awarded the contract to PEI on September 28, and PEI found a substitute mechanical subcontractor. They sued Johnson for the difference between their bid and the cost of the substitute contractor.

As the court notes, the process of bidding on construction contracts posses unique problems in contract law. When a general contractor calculates a bid, he uses the various bids given him by subcontractors in order to arrive at a final figure. If a subcontractor revokes his bid after the general has submitted the bid for the entire project, and if the general contractor wins the contract, the revocation will be to the general's detriment because in most cases he will have chosen the low-bidder. The general contractor is therefore unlikely to find a substitute at the same cost, but he is nonetheless still bound by his own bid. Hence, if the subcontractor is not legally bound to the general when he submits a bid, then the general bears the risk that the sub will revoke his offer, and he will be unable to cover at the same cost. This problem was addressed in two celebrated cases, *James Baird Co. v. Gimbel Bros., Inc.* and *Drennan v. Star Paving,* both of which are discussed extensively in *Pavel.*

The *Baird* and *Drennan* courts offer opposing opinions on the issue of whether or not subcontractors' bids constitute irrevocable offers. Using traditional contract theory, Learned Hand held in *Baird* that the subcontractor's bid was a normal offer to contract that was revocable until accepted by the general contractor, i.e., until after the contract had been awarded to the general. But this created an asymmetrical relationship between the subcontractor and the general: the general was effectively bound once the prime bid was submitted but the sub was free to revoke (unless, of course, the general opted out of the default by negotiating an option).

In *Drennan*, Justice Traynor uses the theory of promissory estoppel (and the doctrinal analysis of part performance of an offer to enter a unilateral contract per Restatement § 45) to create a "reliance option." By placing a bid, the subcontractor invites reliance on that bid. Hence, once the general actually acts in reliance on the bid, that reliance makes the bid irrevocable. Doctrinally this is accomplished by implying a subsidiary promise not to revoke once the bid is used by the general. Reliance on this subsidiary promise creates the option. This, however, only reverses the asymmetry, for now the subcontractor is effectively bound to the general, but the general is not bound to the subcontractor. He can still shop around for lower bids.

PEI's claim fails on both theories. Using a traditional contract model, the trial court had found that no contract had been formed because the offer had been revoked prior to acceptance. The appeals court declined to review this finding. Addressing the issue of promissory estoppel, the court finds that PEI's behavior shows that it did not actually rely on the bid. For instance, after learning that it was the low bidder, Thomas Pavel, PEI's president, went to Johnson's to facility to make sure he wanted to do business with them, and he also requested a revised bid from all the mechanical subcontractors who had previously submitted bids. Not only was PEI not relying on the bid from Johnson, it was actively shopping for lower bids. Without actual reliance, a promissory estoppel claim cannot prevail.

Note 1 (Page 278). As this note points out, it is not accurate to say that the general contractor relies on the sub-bid per se, because the bid is implicitly conditioned on the general's winning the contract and explicitly conditioned on acceptance of the bid. The sub does not say "I will do the steel work," but rather says, in effect, "I will do the steel work *if* you promise to pay me $$$$." As Hand points out, the sub-bid is an offer–a conditional promise–so it cannot be relied upon per se. Moreover, until the contract is awarded, the general is effectively foreclosed from accepting the subcontractors' bids; if he did, he would be bound to pay them whether or not he got the job. But this statement is too facile. After all, the general could accept on condition that it is awarded the prime contract. The reason that the general does not conditionally accept the sub-bid that it uses in its calculations is that the general wants to wait until after the prime contract is awarded before making a decision. Why? One reason is that the financial health of the sub may have deteriorated in the interim. Thus, the only issue in these cases is whether the context justifies a default rule that the sub-bid is irrevocable until a reasonable time after the prime contract is awarded and the general has the opportunity to evaluate its options and notify the sub of its acceptance. *Pavel* shows, however, that the general's actions after the prime contract is awarded are relevant to a finding that there was insufficient reliance by the general on the sub's promise not to revoke. The inference is that if the general uses its discretion to verify the continuing viability of the sub, the option would stick. But if, as here, the general uses its discretion to strategically shop for better bids, then the sub would retain a right to revoke. One can support such a complex rule on the grounds that it deters opportunism by the general. But the question is whether the rule in *Pavel* is too complex and fact dependent to be applied accurately by courts.

Note 2 (Page 278). As the court notes, the *Drennan* rule has enjoyed widespread acceptance, and is codified in § 87(2) of the Restatement. Like many default rules, this one has the effect of creating incentives for the parties to act in certain ways. Under normal circumstances, even if the sub bid is revocable, subcontractors will rarely, if ever, revoke their bids because, as *Note 3 on page 279* points out, there are strong extra-legal sanctions–loss of reputation and future business, etc.– that make such bids self-enforcing. Therefore, subcontractors will only revoke when they would suffer substantial financial losses that exceed any reputational costs. (Why might those costs be less than the expected losses from performance in *Baird, Pavel,* and *Drennan*?) The *Drennan* rule allocates the risk of such mistakes to the subcontractors (unless the general has "reason to know of the mistake, i.e., the bid is so low it signals a problem), and, at first blush this seems intuitively reasonable, given that the subcontractor clearly has the comparative advantage in avoiding such mistakes.

But isn't the question what rule creates the best ex ante incentives to minimize the risk of bidding errors? If so, won't the sub take cost-effective precautions owing to the extra legal sanctions even without the threat of legal liability? Perhaps, then, the *James Baird* rule encourages optimal care by both parties. Hence the *Baird* rule may be the one preferred by most parties in the construction industry, and the Schultz study cited in *Note 3* seems to confirm this. Because the *Baird* rule places the risk of a bid mistake on the general contractor, it gives him an incentive to notify subs of apparent bid mistakes. Because extra-legal sanctions already provide incentives for subs to take precautions against miscalculations, general contractors are willing to accept the risk allocated to them by the *Baird* rule.

C. Offer and Counteroffer
Introduction

Dataserv Equipment, Inc. v. Technology Finance Leasing Corp. *(Page 281).* Dataserv contacted Technology about purchasing some computer features that Dataserv was trying to sell. Technology sent a written offer to Dataserv, and Dataserv then sent a proposed form contract for Technology to sign. Technology objected to three contract provisions and sent written notice to Dataserv on October 1 that they would not sign the contract until the objectionable provisions were changed. Dataserv changed two of them accordingly, but retained the third, the "Indepth Clause," which provided that a third-party, Indepth, would install the features. A few weeks later, Dataserv offered to substitute any other third party for Indepth, but Technology refused. On November 8, Dataserv offered by phone to remove the Indepth clause all together, but Technology told them it was "too late" and there was no deal. The next day, Technology again told Dataserv by telephone that they had waited too long and the deal would not go through. Dataserv, however, continued to act as if a contract had been formed, and on November 12, they informed Technology that the features were ready for pickup and that they needed to pick them up and pay for them before November 15. Technology responded that their offer had been withdrawn, and no contract had been formed. Dataserv then sold the features to another company, but during the negotiations with Technology, the price for those features had plummeted, and Dataserv sued to recover from the Technology the difference between the price of their alleged contract and the market price.

We begin by having the students read Restatement § 39. Under § 39(1) Technology's request on October 1 to delete three of the contract provisions qualifies as a counteroffer, and the issue in the case is whether or not Dataserv rejected that counteroffer. If so, there was no contract and, consequently, no breach. The court found that Dataserv rejected the October 1 counteroffer by refusing to change the Indepth clause, and that this rejection terminated their power to accept the offer pursuant to Restatement § 36(1)(a). Therefore, their subsequent offers to change the Indepth clause constituted new offers that Technology rejected, and no contract was ever formed.

Note 1 (Page 283). Per UCC § 2-207, it is possible to both accept an offer and include proposal for new or different terms. Generally, the additional or different terms will be proposals for additions to the contract. This is an explicit attempt to adapt to the demands of a complex, modern market. But, as *Dataserv* shows, § 2-207 does not reverse the common law rule: if the reply is, in fact, a counteroffer, it is a rejection of the initial offer which can only be revived by the offeror. As for the question of whether or not it is wise for courts to establish default rules in such a market, the answer is not completely clear. From an economic perspective, courts should only be developing default rules if they can do so at less cost than the parties themselves and if they can establish default rules that reflect what the majority of parties would bargain for under the circumstances. Critics argue that modern market conditions make it impossible for courts to establish majoritarian default rules, but given the fact that parties can always bargain around default rules if they need to, there seems to be little basis for arguments that default rules severely hinder complex contract negotiations. Drafting attorneys will be familiar with the default rules and will know when special circumstances require special terms.

Furthermore, one could argue that the inefficiencies created by inapt default rules are ultimately corrected by the process of common law adjudication. This argument assumes that courts can observe the frequency with which parties opt out, and if a given default rule is clearly inapt, then eventually courts will catch on and change the rule. We have seen examples of this kind of judicial evolution already (indeed, the rules regarding counteroffers provide one such example), and though it may be slow, it does result in change. (Kraus likes this argument better than Scott does, probably because he is younger and more optimistic about the possibilities of improvement in institutional design.) Still, the debate about judicially-created default rules is likely to intensify as transactions increase in the complexity and diversity of their terms.

The Common Law View
a. The Mirror Image Rule

One problem with the mirror image rule is that it assumes a certain type of bargaining process; namely, one in which two parties sit down and hammer out an agreement by a back-and-forth process until each side agrees precisely and completely to the terms of the contract. But, of course, this is often not the case. In the real world, firms exchange forms all the time. Often they are preprinted forms with boilerplate provisions, and often those forms go unread. Because parties don't always conform to the conceptual norms implicit in the mirror image rule, they may act as if they have a contract even though they have exchanged forms with different or even contradictory provisions. At common law, when parties acted as though they had a contract without having satisfied the mirror image rule and litigation ensued, courts had to decide which offer (or counteroffer) contained the terms of the contract. In order to resolve this quandary, the common law employed the last shot doctrine.

b. The Last Shot Doctrine

The last shot doctrine provided a wonderfully simple solution to the problem described above: the terms of the contract were the terms contained in the last offer or counteroffer made before the parties commenced performance. But for all its simplicity, this rule seems highly arbitrary and allows for strategic behavior by contracting parties. If, for instance, I don't like all the terms of an offer, I could conceivably mail a counteroffer containing terms favorable to me and then commence performance immediately (say by shipping the goods to you). If you failed to read my form and also commenced performance (by accepting the goods and forwarding payment), I would have fired the last shot and my terms would prevail.

UCC Section 2-207

This section of the UCC is designed to eliminate the mirror image rule and the last shot doctrine. Because its provisions tend to create some confusion in students' minds, we find it helpful to work through its terms in some detail before beginning with the next principal case. *Note 2 on page 290* can be helpful in working through the statute. You may want to begin by pointing out that the language before the comma in paragraph 1 is a clear repudiation of the mirror image rule, and that it does not employ the language of offer and counteroffer. Instead of constituting a counteroffer and a rejection of the offer, an expression of acceptance containing additional or different terms is construed under § 2-207 simply as an acceptance. That is, despite the additional and different terms, it constitutes a valid acceptance and results in a binding contract. The language after the comma, however, creates the exception to that rule: if acceptance is *expressly* conditioned on assent to the additional or different terms, then the response *is* a counteroffer, there is no acceptance, and, hence, no contract at that point. This allows a party to effectively resurrect the rules of offer and counteroffer image rule by explicitly requiring the other party to agree to the terms upon which acceptance is conditioned.

Paragraph 2 explains what happens to the *additional* terms when acceptance is not expressly conditioned on them. Between non-merchants (you can refer students to § 2-104 for the definition of "merchant"), the terms do not automatically become part of the contract; rather, they are construed as proposals for addition to the contract. Between merchants, the terms automatically become part of the contract unless they fall under one of the exceptions set forth in subparagraphs a, b, or c. (In truth, of course, the exceptions in sub paragraphs a, b and c tend to consume the generalization itself.) Subparagraph a allows merchants to protect themselves against the inclusion of additional terms by including in the offer an express limitation on acceptance to the terms of the offer. Terms that would "materially alter" the contract are barred from automatic acceptance by subparagraph b, and Comment 4 provides examples of such terms. Subparagraph c gives merchants the power to object to the additional terms either ex ante or ex post. We ask what justifications can students provide for these three exceptions? (Note that subsection (2) does not mention "different" terms. See *Note 4 on page 292* for a discussion of this drafting omission.)

When no contract exists because acceptance is expressly conditioned on the additional or different terms, and the parties nevertheless conduct themselves as though there is a contract, paragraph 3 governs. Under paragraph three, such conduct creates a contract, the terms of which are those "on which the writings of the parties agree, together with any supplementary terms incorporated under any other provisions of [the UCC]." Paragraph 3, then, replaces the last shot doctrine. Instead of the contract consisting of the terms contained in the last form exchanged, it consists of the terms upon which both of their writings agree plus the default rules of the UCC.

Ionics, Inc. v. Elmwood Sensors, Inc. *(Page 285).* This case involves a classic battle of the forms. Ionics, a water dispenser manufacturer, contracted with Elmwood to purchase thermostats for use in its dispensers. Ionics placed multiple orders with Elmwood, and each time they sent a purchase order stating that the contract would be governed exclusively by the terms printed on the purchase order, including a provision allowing Ionics to seek any remedy available under state law. Around the time of its first order, Ionics also sent a letter informing Elmwood that they needed to indicate any objections to those terms in writing. Upon receipt of each order, Elmwood would send Ionics an acknowledgment stating that the contract was governed exclusively by the terms included in the acknowledgment, and Ionics was given ten days to object. Among the terms in the acknowledgment was one purporting to limit Elmwood's liability. Despite the fact that the forms contained opposing terms, Elmwood shipped and Ionics accepted several orders. Neither party contested the existence of a valid contract; the only issue in the case is the extent of Elmwood's liability. The resolution of this issue hinges on the court's interpretation of UCC § 2-207.

This interpretation begins with a discussion of an infamous prior decision of the First Circuit, *Roto-Lith, LTD v. F.P. Bartlett & Co.* Like *Ionics*, *Roto-Lith* involved an acknowledgment that purported to limit Bartlett's liability. The court there held that "a response which states a condition materially altering the obligation solely to the disadvantage of the offeror is an 'acceptance . . . expressly . . . conditional on assent to the additional . . . terms.'" This implies that a response proposing to alter a material term of the contract is a counteroffer even if the response does not explicitly condition acceptance on assent to the proposed terms as required by § 2-207(1). As virtually every commentator and the UCC Permanent Editorial Board subsequently pointed out, this interpretation of § 2-207 totally eviscerates its repudiation of the mirror image rule. By adopting a facially absurd reading of the statute–that express can mean implied–the court ignores the rule established in § 2-207(1) and only the exception remains.

Despite *Roto-Lith's* tortured reading of § 2-207, the court's reasoning is not completely senseless. After all, if the offeror has received a definite and seasonable acceptance from the offeree, there is no way that he will agree to proposed additional terms because those terms will always benefit the offeree. If the offeror has an acceptance in hand, then a contract has been formed, and the offeree has no power to propose new terms. Hence, the only way a proposal for different or additional terms makes sense is if acceptance is conditioned on assent to those terms. This seems to lead to the conclusion that either the statute or the offeree's behavior makes no sense. The *Roto-Lith* court chose the statute and decided to imply a condition where none was expressed.

This argument fails, however, because it rests on the faulty assumption that the parties read each other's forms. If the forms go unread, as was the case with Ionics and Elmwood, then the offeree may very well propose additional and different terms in its acceptance without expressly conditioning the acceptance on assent to them. The Code simply acknowledges the reality that sometimes people act as though they have a contract even though they haven't knowingly consented to the other party's terms. In fact, this is one of the major differences between the last shot doctrine and § 2-207. Whereas the common law operated on the assumption that the offeree assented to the terms of the last form exchanged, § 2-207, as Comment 6 makes clear, assumes that parties object to conflicting terms. As the *Ionics* court notes, this is a much more reasonable assumption. If terms conflict, there is no rational basis for the assumption that parties have agreed to them.

Completing their reversion to the common law, the *Roto-Lith* court then ruled that because Roto-Lith did not object to the clause limiting Bartlett's liability and took delivery of the goods, it accepted Bartlett's counteroffer, including the limitation on liability. In other words, the last form exchanged before performance governed. With that, § 2-207(3) was but an empty shell, and the last shot doctrine had new life in the First Circuit.

Happily, the *Ionics* court overruled *Roto-Lith* and restored § 2-207 to its apparent, intended meaning. Because Elmwood's acknowledgment contained additional and different terms, assent to which was a condition of acceptance, no contract was formed under § 2-207(1). But because the party's conduct nonetheless recognized the existence of a contract, § 2-207(3) applies. Because the court ruled only on whether or not to uphold the trial court's denial of Elmwood's motion for partial summary judgment, it does not attempt to determine exactly what the terms of the contract were. However, given the fact the parties' writings did not agree on the extent of Elmwood's liability, the UCC's default rules would govern that issue and Elmwood would be open to liability for breach of the implied warranty of merchantability (UCC § 2-314) and for Ionics' incidental and consequential damages resulting from the breach (UCC § 2-715).

D. Contract Formation in the Internet Age

Step-Saver Data Systems, Inc. v. Wyse Technology, Inc. *(Page 296).* Step-Saver contracted with The Software Link, Inc. (TSL) and Wyse Technology to purchase software and computer terminals for use in a multi-user computer system it was developing. The system failed to function properly from the outset, and when TSL and Wyse could not remedy the problems, several of Step-Saver's clients filed suit against them. The firms argued over who was responsible for the problems, and when it became clear that they could not settle the dispute amicably, Step-Saver filed suit. TSL contended that the box-top license included with their software constituted the final and complete expression of the contract's terms. This license included a term disclaiming all express and implied warranties–except the warranty that the disks contained in the box were free from defects–and absolving TSL of liability for damages suffered as a result of using the program. The issue: were the terms contained in the box-top license part of the contract, or were they proposals for additional and different terms and hence excluded under UCC §§ 2-207(2)(b) or 2-207(3)?

In order to resolve this issue, the court had to determine when and how the contract was formed. The license stipulated that opening the package would indicate acceptance of the contract. TSL, therefore, argued that the contract was formed when Step-Saver received the package, saw the terms of the box-top license, and opened it. If they wanted to reject the terms, TSL maintained, Step-Saver should have returned the package unopened within 15 days in accordance with the terms of the license. Step-Saver maintained that the contract was formed on the phone when it ordered the software, and that the box-top license contained additional and different terms that would not become part of the contract under § 2-207.

The court's analysis of § 2-207 as applied to the facts of this case is somewhat confused, but this does not effect the ultimate outcome. The court begins by stating that the conduct of the parties demonstrated the existence of a contract, which would seem to bring the contract under § 2-207(3). Hence, the terms of the contract would include the terms upon which the parties agreed–price, quantity, and shipping–and any UCC default rules necessary to fill in the gaps. The warranty disclaimers and liability limitations would therefore not be part of the contract. However, the court then engages in a long discussion about whether or not the terms in the box-top license constituted a conditional acceptance of Step-Saver's offer. At this point, the court seems no longer interested in performance, but rather in how the contract was formed. They hold that the contract was formed over the phone, and that the box-top license constituted a proposal for additional or different terms. Because the evidence indicated that TSL would have continued with the deal even if Step-Saver had not agreed to the additional or different terms, acceptance was not conditioned on those terms, i.e., they weren't deal-breakers. The terms then fall under the first clause of § 2-207(1), and in order to determine what the exact terms of the contract were, the court uses § 2-207(2). Because this was a contract between merchants, and because the warranty disclaimer and liability limitations would materially alter it, the terms were excluded under § 2-207(2)(b). Hence, under either analysis the terms could not become part of the contract, and TSL was subject to liability for breaching its express and implied warranties.

As we see when considering the next case, *Hill v. Gateway 2000, Inc.*, Judge Wisdom's decision rests on an implicit assumption regarding the structure of the transaction. He characterizes the phone call as an offer from Step-Saver to buy software from TSL. TSL is therefore the offeree, and the box-top license is an acceptance together with proposals for additional or different terms. If, however, the phone call is characterized as a solicitation for an offer from TSL, then the box-top license constitutes the offer, and opening the package would constitute the invited mode of acceptance (a promissory act as per UCC § 2-204(1) and Restatement § 30(1)). Since Step-Saver opened the package without proposing any additional or different terms, it would presumably be bound by the terms of the box-top license, § 2-207 would not apply, and Step-Saver would lose the case. This is precisely what happens in *Gateway*.

Hill v. Gateway 2000, Inc. *(Page 303).* The Hills ordered and paid for a Gateway computer over the phone. When it arrived, they found in the box a list of terms that purported to govern the purchase contract between them and Gateway. One of the terms contained in the box was an arbitration clause. The terms further stipulated that failing to return the computer within 30 days would act as an expression of acceptance by the customer. Sometime after the 30 days had lapsed, the Hills complained to Gateway about their computer. Gateway was unable to satisfy their complaints, and they filed suit alleging mail and wire fraud under RICO. Gateway sought to enforce the arbitration agreement, but the district court held that it was invalid. As in *Step-Saver*, the issue in *Gateway* is whether or not the terms included in the package were part of the contract. Contrary to Judge Wisdom, however, Judge Easterbrook held that they were.

In reaching his decision, Judge Easterbrook relied heavily on one of his previous decisions, *ProCD, Inc. v. Zeidenberg.* As **Note 1 on page 307** points out, *ProCD* also involved a dispute over whether or not the act of opening shrinkwrap licenses constituted a contract. Judge Easterbrook held that such mechanisms for signaling acceptance were valid unless they were "objectionable on grounds applicable to contracts in general." Despite the fact that silence does not normally indicate acceptance, the offeror is master of his offer and under UCC § 2-204, the offeror is free to invite acceptance "in any manner sufficient to show agreement, including conduct by both parties which recognizes the existence of a contract." Hence, a vendor can invite acceptance by conduct: if the customer uses the software and fails to return the product within the specified time period, that use plus inaction functions as an expression of acceptance. Following the logic of *ProCD*, Judge Easterbrook held that the contract was formed when the Hills, after using the computer, failed to return the computer within 30 days. The arbitration clause, therefore, was a valid term in the contract.

Note, however, that this analysis only works when Gateway is construed as the offeror. In response to the Hill's arguments based on § 2-207, Easterbrook says that § 2-207 doesn't apply because there was only one form. To be sure, there is only one form, but nothing in § 2-207 so limits its scope. Easterbrook's better argument is that Gateway made the first "offer" by means of the terms in the box, and the Hills accepted it without proposing any additional or different terms, so § 2-207 can't apply because there simply are no additional or different terms. Under this view, everything turns on the characterization of the initial phone call. Is it merely an invitation to negotiate or is it an offer? If the Hill's phone call is construed as an offer to buy a computer rather than as a solicitation for an offer from Gateway, then Gateway would have expressed its acceptance of the Hill's offer by taking their money and shipping the computer. In that case, the packaged terms would be considered additional and different terms, and an analysis under § 2-207 would be appropriate. If acceptance was conditioned on assent to additional or different terms, the conduct of the parties would bring the contract under § 2-207(3) and the additional and different terms would not be part of the contract. If not, then § 2-207(2) would apply and those terms would be construed as a proposal for additional terms because the Hills are not merchants. Since the *proposals* were not accepted by the Hills the contract would be formed without the arbitration clause (*see Note 1 on page 307* for further discussion of this point).

Note 1 (Page 307). Neither Judge Wisdom nor Judge Easterbrook provides any justification for structuring the transactions as they do. One way to decide which party should be deemed the offeror and which the offeree is to consider the ex ante effects of each decision. Judge Easterbrook is concerned about the commercial impracticability of forcing companies to read all the terms of the contract to customers over the phone. This would increase transaction costs and, as Easterbrook points out, it would be rather annoying. Professor James J. White, for instance, argues in his article *Autistic Contracts* that arrangements such as these should be enforced because the reduction in transaction costs that they create more than offsets "the costs imposed on dissenting offerees" (*see Note 3 on page 309*) It seems, therefore, that absent assumptions about market failure or persistent cognitive errors by consumers, the standard market practice suggests that most parties–firms and consumers–in similar circumstances would prefer the rule that box-top licenses are offers, the acceptance of which could be expressed simply by opening the package and retaining the merchandise. This is a good time, we believe, to get students to think through and express the various market failure arguments in support of Judge Wisdom's contrary rule.

Note 2 (Page 308) and Note 4 (Page 310). The 2001 proposed amendments to Article 2, including the proposed changes to § 2-207, were voted down by NCCUSL during the summer of 2001 largely because of the continuing disagreement over this very issue. For those who have not focused on the on-going controversy and debate, the following is a concise history of the events leading up to the rejection of the Article 2 amendments. It is taken from an article by Scott, *The Rise and Fall of Article 2,* that appeared in a symposium issue of the Louisiana Law Review, 62 La. L. Rev. 1109 (2002).

Article 2 needs revision. This uncontested fact has been self-evident for two decades. This is not to say that Article 2 has functioned inadequately as a framework for cataloguing judicial decisions in sales contract disputes. Indeed, a number of contemporary scholars believe that the statute has performed well in directing courts how best to fill the gaps in incomplete contracts and to police unconscionable bargains.[1] But whatever one's views on these questions, it is clear that the information revolution threatens to leave Article 2 in an increasingly small backwater of commercial transactions. If the statute is to retain its primacy as a source of legal defaults that both facilitate and regulate commercial sales transactions, it must be adapted to technological and economic developments that have created entirely new markets in information technology. The original scope provision of Article 2 – covering all transactions in goods – seems inadequate, even with its subsequent common law gloss, to answer fundamental jurisdictional questions.[2] Does or should Article 2 govern information contracting? If not, what is the domain of Article 2 as distinct from the domain of alternative statutory or common law rules governing software licensing transactions?

In 1987, the Permanent Editorial Board for the Uniform Commercial Code set out to resolve these and other questions under the auspices of a study committee. The study committee concluded that Article 2 was not an adequate legal framework for addressing the many unique issues raised by software licensing transactions. In 1991, acting upon the report and recommendation of the study committee, the ALI and NCCUSL appointed a drafting committee to begin work on a comprehensive revision of Article 2, that, among other things, would bring within the scope of Article 2 the provisions on lease transactions that were then embodied in Article 2A, and would also include provisions to address the unique

---

[1] The Code's defenders far out number its critics, even among those who are dismayed by the failure of the current revision process. The comments of Professor Melvin Eisenberg in the ALI members web site forum sum up this majority view: "I should add that if the result [of the current deadlock] is no revision of Article 2, that's not the worst thing in the world. Article 2 works well now, and whatever serious drafting flaws it had have by and large been fixed up by the courts. Of course a minor tuneup would probably be desirable, but it's not imperative, and very little will be lost by sticking with Article 2 as it stands." Posting of Melvin Eisenberg, 10/19/01.

[2] UCC § 2-102 provides that "this Article applies to transactions in goods." Goods, in turn, are defined in §1-104 as "all things movable at the time of identification to the contract." Thus, Article 2 by its terms declines to resolve the issue of jurisdiction over "mixed" transactions, such as transactions involving both a sale of goods and the provision of services. Many courts have settled on two tests to provide more clarity to scope disputes. The "divisibility" test asks whether the transaction can be separated into its goods and non-goods components. If so, then Article 2 applies to the portion of the contract dealing with goods and other relevant state law (typically the common law of contracts) applies to the non-goods components. Where the goods portion of a transaction cannot be separated functionally, most courts apply a "predominant feature" test that asks which component of the mixed transaction–goods or non-goods–predominates. The predominant component determines which legal regime applies. *See e.g., Valley Farmers' Elevator v. Lindsay Bros. Co. v. Martin Steel Corp.*, 398 NW 2d 553 (Minn 1987); *but see Elkins Manor Assoc. v. Eleanor Concrete Works, Inc.* 396 S.E. 2d 463 (WVa 1990) (declining to use the predominant feature test because the "test is too subjective to provide any basis for rational analysis").

The original scope provision was unchanged in the version of the 2001 Amendments to Article 2 that was adopted by the ALI membership in May, 2001. All attempts to draft a clearer and more definitive scope provision that drew lines between the coverage of Article 2 and the coverage of other law dealing with information and software transactions fell victim to interest group competition. Lobbying by the representatives of the software and information industries was successful in persuading the Article 2 drafting committee at the NCCUSL annual meeting on August 13, 2001 to change its position and recommend a new scope provision negotiated and drafted that day. As noted above, the new provision survived a motion to delete, but a motion necessary to obtain NCCUSL approval of the entire package failed.

characteristics of software licensing transactions. The Article 2 Drafting Committee worked for several years on this "hub and spoke" scheme for incorporating all relevant transactions within the Article 2 umbrella. But the effort was abandoned when key insiders concluded that the differences between the products, their markets and practices made the draft unworkable.[3] The ALI and NCCUSL then decided to return leases to its own statute (Article 2A) and also to draft a separate UCC Article 2B for computer information contracts. Separate drafting committees were thus appointed for each of Article 2, Article 2A and Article 2B and the drafting work proceeded on parallel, but separate, tracks.

The first public indication that the private legislative coalition that had supported the UCC project for fifty years was beginning to unravel surfaced in 1999 when proposed Article 2B was brought forward by the drafting committee for final approval by the ALI and NCCUSL. The ALI declined to approve Article 2B on the ground that the drafting process, dominated by the software and information industry, had produced a "seller-friendly" statute. NCCUSL, on the other hand, decided to go forward with the project on its own, reissuing the statute as the Uniform Computer Information Transactions Act (UCITA). The controversy over UCITA centers on the provisions of the statute dealing with contract formation in standardized retail transactions. UCITA endorses current market practices in which consumers signify advance acceptance of subsequently disclosed terms.[4] Subsequently, UCITA has been adopted in Virginia and Maryland, but has encountered stiff opposition from consumer interests in other jurisdictions.[5]

---

[3] Speidel, *View from the Trenches*, supra note – at 612-13.

[4] The subsequently disclosed terms typically have provisions by which sellers or licensors seek to limit their warranty liability and/or limit the buyer/licensee's remedies for "bugs" or defects in software or other "smart" goods. Thus, at bottom, the issue has to do with the extension of Article 2 warranty liability to software and computer information providers and the mechanisms by which that liability can be shifted (in whole or in part). *See* Jean Braucher, *Uniform Computer Information Transactions Act (UCITA): Objections from the Consumer Perspective*, 5 No. 6 GLCY Law 2 (2000); James C. McKay. Jr., *UCITA and the Consumer: A Response to Professor Braucher*, 5 No. 8 GLCY Law 9 (2000); Michael L. Rustad, *Making UCITA More Consumer-Friendly*, 18 J. Marshall J. Computer & Info. L. 547 (1999).

[5] In an effort to respond to some of these concerns, the NCCUSL Standby Committee issued a report in December 2001 detailing recommendations concerning proposed amendments to UCITA that it planned to make to NCCUSL at its summer 2002 meeting. On January 30, 2002 an ABA Working Group appointed by the ABA Board of Governors filed a report on UCITA, concluding that it would be desirable to have a uniform law that set forth legal rules governing licensing in computer transactions. But the working group also raised a number of critical concerns both with the alleged lack of clarity of UCITA's terms and with the policy judgments implicit in specific provisions, particularly those governing scope and contract formation in retail transactions. See AMERICAN BAR ASSOCIATION WORKING GROUP REPORT ON THE UNIFORM COMPUTER INFORMATION TRANSACTIONS ACT, January 31, 2002. According to the dissenting member of the working group, the disagreements within the ABA are a reflection of interest group competition between the computer information industry on the one hand and representatives of large firm licensees (and their lawyers) on the other: "The key policy issue that confronts the Board of Governors in reviewing the Working Group's report is whether narrow parochial interest groups that have failed to win policy or political arguments in the...drafting process will have a second chance to defeat...a NCCUSL approved statute." See Minority Report of Donald Cohn at 6.
    Contrast the current interest group clash over UCITA with the original efforts by Llewellyn to enact Article

The split between the ALI and NCCUSL broke into the open in the summer of 1999 when revised Articles 2 and 2A were brought forward for final approval. Revised Articles 2 and 2A were approved by the ALI in May 1999 but, after encountering severe opposition from industry interests, the leadership of NCCUSL suddenly withdrew the drafts from consideration during its annual meeting two months later.[6] This action, in turn, prompted the Reporter and Associate Reporter for the Revised Article 2 to resign.[7] In an attempt to patch the tattered alliance together, ALI and NCCUSL agreed on a newly reconstituted drafting committee covering both articles, which was directed to focus on "non-controversial," technical amendments to the existing statute.[8] Two years later, the new committee brought forward the Proposed 2001 Amendments to Article 2, which were approved (subject to several minor amendments) by the ALI in May 2001. Despite the uncertainties surrounding the jurisdiction of Article 2, UCITA, or the common law over transactions in information products, especially "smart goods" that contain and are often controlled by computer programs, the drafting committee decided to retain Article 2's original, open-ended scope provision.[9] That decision was primarily a pragmatic acceptance of the status quo since intense interest group competition was able to block the more precise, bright-line alternatives suggested by either side.

---

2. Interest group competition of this sort did not emerge, as Llewellyn recognized, because "the same parties and the same types of party can tomorrow be occupying each the other end of similar disputes." In short, since parties to commercial sales transactions are both buyers and sellers, there is no reason to believe that one group or class is distributionally disadvantaged over the other. That symmetry of effects is clearly not present in the battle between the large firm licensors of computer information and their licensees.

Thus, the UCITA project is a further example of the effects of interest group competition in the private legislative process. The Schwartz/Scott model would predict continuing deadlock within the three key private legislative groups—the ABA, the ALI and NCCUSL—over the enactment of a statutory scheme governing computer information transactions. Much as with the Article 2 revisions, the debate over UCITA centers of the question of the appropriate domain of freedom of contract in mass market license transactions. In the words of dissenting member Cohn, "UCITA is and has always been intended as a commercial statute. Some interest groups have attempted to change UCITA into a national uniform consumer protection statute. The problem...is a desire on the part of various interest groups to require UCITA to include mandatory, non-waivable provisions to protect their constituents, even large companies that do not need this type of protection. The underlying current in the opposition to UCITA is a desire for more mandatory provisions and not less. More restrictions on freedom of contract and not less." Id. at 8-9.

[6] There are differing explanations for the sudden decision by the NCCUSL leadership to withdraw the July, 1999 draft. The Reporter of the Article 2 drafting committee believes that the action followed a threat by the so-called "strong" sellers (i.e., General Electric and the Automobile Manufacturer's Association) to oppose the draft, if approved, in every state legislature. *See* Speidel, *View from the Trenches,* supra note – at 611, 617-618.

[7] *Id.*

[8] *Id.* at 615-17. As reported by the Director of the ALI to its members, the drafting committee was asked "to preserve the substantive gains in the [earlier] version while restoring some of the language of the original Article 2 with which lawyers and business people are comfortable." Letter from Lance Liebman, ALI Director, to the Members of the ALI, September 17, 1999.

[9] *See* UCC § 2-102 and note – supra.

Following the ALI vote, the software and information interests continued to lobby NCCUSL for changes in the scope provision. Their interests were to prevent validation in the new Article 2 of judicial decisions that applied (directly or by analogy) "buyer-friendly" provisions of Article 2 to transactions in information and, concomitantly, to have the Article 2 amendments acknowledge the existence and applicability of UCITA.[10] At the NCCUSL annual meeting in August, the drafting committee agreed on new scope language that, while not referring to UCITA, parallels to some extent the structure and substance of the UCITA scope provision. Brought to the floor, the new scope provision survived a motion to delete by a vote of 60 to 98. NCCUSL also effectively reversed the ALI floor amendments to the statute of frauds and liquidated damages provisions. Finally, a motion to approve the new Article 2 failed by a vote of 53 to 89,[11] an action subsequently described as the "right and left ganging up to defeat the middle."

The open split between the ALI and NCCUSL is merely a symptom of the intense interest group competition that has emerged during the Article 2 revision process. Retail manufacturing interests (the so-called "strong" sellers), opposed to provisions that extended warranty liability for economic loss to remote sellers, were able successfully to block the adoption of the initial revisions to Article 2. In turn, consumer interests (including large firm licensees) opposed to the "seller-friendly" provisions in the proposed Article 2B, were able to separate the computer information article from the rest of the UCC project. From there the battleground moved to rival efforts to either secure or block the further enactment of UCITA. This included the tug-of-war over efforts to acknowledge UCITA in the scope provisions of the revised Article 2. Thus, in the effort to bring forward the seemingly uncontroversial 2001 Amendments to Article 2, each side was able to block approval of the other's proposals but unable to secure approval of its own. The resulting deadlock confirms the predictions of the Schwartz/Scott model that private legislatures are strongly biased toward the status quo whenever their proposals encounter substantial interest group competition.[12]

It seems unlikely, therefore, that Article 2 will be revised so as to deal directly with any of the unique problems presented by the new technology. Whatever happens in the future, non-Code legal regimes will be called upon to resolve the increasingly intense normative debate over the domain of free contract in retail computer information transactions as well as to specify the default rules to fill gaps in commercial information transactions. We are left with three questions: First, what happened in the intervening fifty years to change a reformer dominated process, with little interest group involvement, to a process dominated by competing interest groups? Second, why has the resulting deadlock generated so little interest beyond the affected interest groups and the academic reformers who are active participants in the private legislative process? Third, assuming the causes of deadlock and indifference can be identified, what adverse effects on contracting are the likely consequences?

---

[10] Liebman, *Introduction*, supra note — at 1.

[11] *Id* at 2.

[12] Schwartz & Scott, *Political Economy*, supra note — at 633-37.

CHAPTER 4

CONTRACTUAL RELATIONSHIPS AND CONDUCT

A. An Introduction to Relational Contracts

As the introduction to the Chapter makes clear, we now shift the focus from the relatively simple contracts that are implicitly assumed to be the norm in the rules governing offer and acceptance to the problems of writing, enforcing and interpreting complex, relational contracts. We use this transition to emphasize that the focus will shift from litigation to planning, negotiating and drafting. In one sense, the shift is from reliance on contract law and its default rules to reliance on the skills of the individual lawyer. In order for a lawyer to draft appropriate "constitutions" for the little society that consists of a promisor and a promisee, it is first important to know what it is that the parties are trying to accomplish in their relationship and what are the problems with which they must cope.

While temporal extension per se is not the litmus test of a "relational" contract, it does serve as a useful heuristic to introduce students to the central problems raised in this Chapter. We begin by assuming explicitly a contract that extends over two time periods (T1 and T2). The assumption then introduces the twin problems of uncertainty and complexity. Because the performance of the contract calls for an investment by one or both parties and because the optimal investment cannot be determined until the second period (T2), the constraints of uncertainty and complexity mean that the parties cannot at reasonable cost prescribe an outcome for all the possible states of the world that may occur in T2. Since many of the defaults that we have studied thus far are premised on the notion that the parties can bargain around them to determinate alternatives, the question now becomes: what to do in this more complex environment?

The place to begin is with a goal or objective. What are the parties trying to achieve collectively? A relatively straight forward answer is that the two parties want to maximize the value of the contractual relationship so as to increase the size of their individual shares. We then need to think about the sociology of relationships. Can they achieve this result without writing a complex contract? One possible solution is to write a simple contract in T1 that looks to present investments in the contract and then anticipate renegotiation in T2 in order to adjust to future conditions. For example, suppose that Promoter agrees to market and promote a concert tour and live CD album (to be sold only at the live concerts) for Performer at a fixed fee. (Scott likes to use Barry Goody and Smokey Robinson, respectively, but younger teachers will no doubt have examples more familiar to this generation of law students). Because Performer is relatively unknown, only skillful marketing will be likely to stimulate demand for Performer's original musical style. The parties understand that Promoter's actual costs may vary from those anticipated at the time of contract– e.g., costs of travel, bookings of concert halls, etc. may rise (or fall) unexpectedly, and that the value Performer places on these activities might change– e.g., demand may fall (or rise) for Performer's music. But they both agree informally that when and if this happens they will sit down and try to renegotiate the contract. Before they conclude this agreement, however, they call their lawyer and ask: Do you see any problems?

We ask the students this question in order to make some key points. The answer is: it depends. Assume, for example, that the Promoter's costs rise as does the demand for concert tickets and for the accompanying CD. Since demand has increased, Performer could "afford" to pay Promoter a higher fee, covering the increased costs, and still make more profit from sales of tickets and albums than she anticipated at the time the contract was signed. Promoter wants Performer to agree to a higher fee, one that would maintain Performer's expected profit on the contract and also cover the increased costs of marketing and promotion. Will Performer agree to the new arrangement? If these parties have a long term relationship, with a past and a future as well as a present, a renegotiation in which Performer agrees to cover some or all of the cost increase may well be the best way of coping with an uncertain future. The parties desire to maintain a relationship of trust and mutual gain will constrain the Performer's motivation to behave strategically upon renegotiation and demand a bigger share of the gains from the contract. Alternatively, if the parties interact in a relatively homogeneous industry or "contracting group," their desire to maintain a reputation for fairness and honesty will similarly constrain strategic behavior. In each of these cases, social sanctions – either the self-sanctions of guilt or third-party sanctions of shaming, loss of reputation and future business, etc.– will suffice.

But now, we ask, what happens if the parties have not dealt with each other before and don't anticipate the value of future dealings? Under these circumstances renegotiation is likely to fail. The Performer will have no incentive to bail the Promoter out. In turn, the Promoter, anticipating this problem is likely to take ex ante precautions– such as reducing the level of his marketing and promotion efforts as costs rise, say, by booking less expensive but also less accessible halls, reducing marketing expenditures, etc. This is the moral hazard problem facing the parties as they write their initial contract. If Promoter bears the full cost of its investment, but can only recover a fixed portion of the benefits (the promotion fee), he is motivated to shirk his obligation whenever underlying conditions change adversely.

We invite the students to suggest one solution to this problem. Why can't the parities agree that each will bear its own risks and Performer will observe Promoter's marketing and promotion efforts to insure that they meet the predetermined contract requirements? If the quality of the promotion is below contract specs, then Performer can withhold the fee, recover damages, etc. This question invites the students to think about the problem of hidden information. Such a contract will work only if the key information – the Promoter's efforts in investing in quality promotion – are both observable by the Performer and verifiable to a court.

Assume now that Performer is unable to verify Promoter's level of efforts. Here the discussion can go any number of ways. But an important insight is that now the parties need help in structuring a relationship in which the party with discretion–the Promoter who can determine (more or less without constraint) the level of effort he will put into building the machine– has the incentive to reach the parties' collective goal (which we assume is to maximize the expected value of the contract). The hidden action problem may require a different approach to defining Promoter's obligations in the contract, perhaps a best efforts clause, for example. It also requires a different pricing arrangement– perhaps a percentage of the gross (or net profits?) in order to cope with the information asymmetries. But these solutions, as we will see, have their own problems that must be addressed in turn. We don't use this initial discussion to provide "answers" to the hypothetical contractual relationship, but rather to have students begin to appreciate the kinds of concerns they must begin to address in the materials that follow.

B. Indefinite Contractual Agreements

Because relational contracts necessarily involve some indefiniteness, it is important for students to understand how courts have traditionally handled vague or incomplete contract terms before we address some of the issues peculiar to relational contracts. The first two principal cases in this chapter review some of the issues relating to indefiniteness raised by *Corthell* and *Schumacher* in Chapter 1. They serve to further demonstrate the shift from the common law rule that a contract in which material terms that are left incomplete or indefinite is not legally binding to the rule found in UCC § 2-204(3) that a binding contract can be formed even though material terms are left open (*see Note 2 on page 321* for further discussion of this shift).

Koufman v. International Business Machines Corporation *(Page 315).* IBM sought an outside investor willing to purchase a specific tract of land and construct a building on it using plans provided by IBM. The investor would then lease the building to IBM. Koufman, a potential investor, submitted a proposal on a form provided by IBM. It contained the estimated costs of the land and the building and the length of the lease, and it stated that responsibility for taxes and insurance would be negotiated by the parties at a later time. Initially, Koufman was the successful bidder, but when it became clear to IBM that construction costs would be higher than initially estimated, IBM asked Koufman to cut his costs. This led to differences between the parties, and, a short time later, IBM notified Koufman that they would not go forward with the deal because Koufman was not honoring the terms of his proposal. Koufman then filed suit against IBM for breach of contract.

The court holds that no contract ever arose between the parties, and, therefore, no breach was possible. Relying on the traditional common law rule, the court finds that the terms embodied in the proposal were too incomplete and indefinite. For instance, IBM had requested that prospective investors provide four different types of proposals. Though Koufman had done so, IBM's acceptance of his proposal failed to specify which of the four it was accepting. It also failed to assign responsibility for taxes and insurance. These omissions preclude the court from enforcing the agreement because the court is unable to determine exactly what IBM agreed to do. The implicit justification for this holding, and for the common law rule general, is that the court should honor the intent – and thereby the autonomy – of the parties by not forcing them to shoulder responsibility for failing to do something to which they never agreed. When the contract is too vague to evidence the parties' intent, the court cannot rewrite the contract because it would run the risk of imposing unintended (and, by definition, uncompensated) risk on the parties.

Paloukos v. Intermountain Chevrolet Co. *(Page 318).* Gus Paloukos filled out a form with the intention of ordering a pickup truck from Intermountain. The form specified the model, some of the accessories, the engine size, the type of transmission, and the purchase price of the truck. It left open the color (green or yellow), and at the top was printed the caption "WORK SHEET–This is NOT a Purchase Order." Intermountain's sales manager approved the sale, but they did not have the truck in stock. Paloukos paid a $120 deposit and was told that the truck would be ordered. Five months later, Intermountain informed Paloukos that the truck would not be delivered and returned his deposit. Paloukos sued for specific performance. The trial court granted Intermountain's motion of summary judgement, finding that the contract left too many terms open. The appellate court reversed and remanded for trial on the issue on contract formation.

The *Paloukos* court rests its decision on UCC § 2-204. As the comment to that section makes clear, it is designed to honor the parties' intent to enter a binding agreement. If a contract sufficiently demonstrates that intent, open or indefinite terms will not prevent enforcement, provided there is an adequate basis for measuring damages. The standard, as set forth in § 2-204(1), is whether or not the manner in which the contract was made is "sufficient to show agreement." In many cases, then, arguing that a contract is unenforceable for vagueness will be to no avail. Gaps in the contract – even the omission of material terms – will be filled using default rules supplied by the UCC. The court lists the evidence indicating that the parties intended to be bound: the form provided the sale price; the sale was approved by the sales manager; Paloukos was told that the truck would be ordered; and, perhaps most convincing, Paloukos put down a deposit on the truck. These facts, the court finds, could be sufficient to show agreement under   § 2-204(1). If so, then § 2-204(3) requires the court to enforce the contract assuming there is a sufficient basis for providing a remedy for breach. The UCC's default rules would fill in any gaps. Hence, there is a material question of fact as to whether or not a contract was formed, which makes summary judgment inappropriate.

Note 1 (Page 320). This Note asks whether or not the parties in *Koufman* and *Paloukos* intended to enter a contract. In *Koufman*, it is clear that IBM intended to contract with someone to build and lease the building, but is there evidence that it did not intend for a binding contract to arise out of its acceptance of Koufman's proposal? When IBM wrote to Koufman to cancel their agreement with him, they cited his failure to carry out the terms of his proposal as the reason for the cancellation. If there had been a contract, this would amount to a claim of breach, and IBM would presumably have had grounds to sue. But IBM didn't sue, and although there are many conceivable reasons why, one is that they didn't consider this a breach because they did not intend to be bound at that point.

Of course, under the common law bright-line rule governing indefiniteness, the question of intent was addressed indirectly, by looking at the extent to which material terms were left unspecified by the parties. If the court finds that the terms are sufficiently complete and definite, it would infer from that the intent to contract; if not, the court would infer that the parties did not intend to be bound. The UCC shifts from a bright-line rule (which suffers from the problem common to all such rules of being both under- and over-inclusive) to a broad standard. Under the UCC standard, a court is asked to focus on the underlying question of intent directly, and thus can infer that intent despite the existence of open or indefinite terms. That, of course, is just what the *Paloukos* court did. We ask the students to focus on the problems with standards– they are difficult to apply accurately in particular cases and thus the cases lack transparency.

Beyond the issue of whether the standard of "intent" can be discerned accurately by courts, there is the additional question of whether UCC § 2-204(3) is only a default rule. The *Paloukos* court does not, for example, address the relevance of the disclaimer on the top of the form stating that the form constituted a work sheet and not a purchase order. It is reasonable to assume that Intermountain knew ex ante of the possibility that the factory would not be able to deliver the truck and that the disclaimer was designed to protect them in case such a contingency arose and they were unable to perform. However, the court cites convincing evidence that the conduct of the parties was sufficient to show an agreement, thus modifying the apparent meaning of the disclaimer. The fact that consideration (the $120 deposit) was given in exchange for the promise to deliver the truck is perhaps the most persuasive evidence of Intermountain's intent to be bound. What could Intermountain have done to protect itself against the risk of production shortages? Assume the form had provided: "The parties do not intend to be legally bound by this work order. There will be no binding contract until a formal agreement is signed." Would the result be different? Or is course of performance under UCC § 2-208 always going to trump the plain meaning of such writings?

As was noted earlier, the justification for the common law rule was that it honored the intent of the parties. That is also the justification for the UCC § 2-204: it honors the parties' intent to be bound. The difference, then, is not the purpose of the rule but the choice of *rule form*. In defense of the common law rule, one might argue that the UCC violates the parties' autonomy by forcing them to accept terms to which they did not agree. Recall, however, that when parties enter contracts, they implicitly agree to abide by the existing default rules of contract law. Hence, they agree to accept the UCC's gap fillers should they choose not to opt out of them. Since both these rules can be justified on the same basis and because they both function as default rules, the truly relevant question is which rule allows the parties to contract at less cost. Because the common law forces parties to come to an agreement on most (if not all) material terms, it will potentially increase negotiation costs. Under the UCC, however, the parties will be bound to terms that are supplied by the state. Since neither party is likely to have dickered over these terms, and since many of the UCC supplied defaults are broad standards rather than clear specifications, it is likely that litigation costs are higher under the Code rule. Moreover, since the content of the Code's standard is provided by courts ex post, while the content of a bright line rule is specified ex ante, it is harder to opt out of the Code's rule with the same level of confidence (*see, e.g., Intermountain*). On the other hand, it is not clear that the common law courts understood the indefiniteness rule as a default. Could the parties in *IBM,* for example, have stated on the writing "We intend to be bound"? Would that work to make an otherwise vague deal enforceable? In short, it is hard to know which rule form is most likely to reduce transaction costs.

Output, Requirements, and Exclusive Dealings Arrangements
a. Output and Requirements Contracts.
Although the UCC allows parties to leave many material terms open or indefinite, the quantity term is one term that must be supplied even under the Code's liberal rules. For obvious reasons, there is no default rule for quantity. Without some specific agreement about quantity both parties would be fearful of a hold-up problem. In relational contracts, however, it is inherently difficult to specify quantities over the life of the contract, especially for goods or services traded in volatile markets where both supply and demand fluctuate over time. To address this problem, the UCC, following the lead of many common law courts, specifically endorses certain contracts where the quantity of goods

ordered or supplied is subject to one party's discretion. The Code, then, purports to constrain the discretion of either the buyer under a requirements contract or the seller under an output contract. One of the key questions in this section is to define precisely the nature of those constraints and to determine the extent to which they are effective in preventing strategic behavior by the party with discretion. UCC § 2-306(1) sets out the standards by which the parties' discretion in output and requirements contracts are measured: 1) good faith and 2) no quantity "unreasonably disproportionate" to prior experience or estimates. We begin by having the students study this section and by giving a brief introduction to some basic principles of these types of relational contracts.

In a requirements contract, the buyer agrees to forego her right to buy from other sellers. The seller, on the other hand, is free to sell to other buyers, provided she first satisfies buyer's demand under the contract. Theoretically at least, both parties will benefit under this arrangement because the buyer has a sure and steady supply of the goods it needs, and the seller is assured of a regular buyer for its products. However, changes in the market can cause either party to regret the contract and can create incentives for strategic behavior. Say, for instance, A agrees to sell B all the cotton she needs for her textile mill for the next 3 years at a price of $.30 per pound. As long as this price is roughly equivalent to the market price of cotton, the parties should be fine. If, however, the price falls below $.30, B (who can't buy from anyone else) will regret the contract and may reduce her demand in order to cut losses. She may feel compelled to do this because her competitors are buying cotton at the lower market price and can therefore offer their textiles at a lower price. A, in turn, will not reap the gains she expected under the contract because she is not able to sell as much cotton to B at the above-market price. This is not a total disaster to A because she can sell to other buyers on the open market when B cuts demand. But even though this market check provides some protection for A, it is only a partial check against B's strategic behavior because A must sell the excess cotton at the market price, which is below the contract price.

On the other hand, if the market price rises above $.30, B may increase her demand in order to take advantage of the savings that the contract price provides over the market price. Because the seller is obligated to satisfy the buyer's requirements before selling on the open market at the higher price, there is no market control to protect her. She must instead rely on some sort of contractual mechanism to protect her against over-demand. Such mechanism may consist of either quantity or price controls, or a mixture of both. Quantity controls include the good faith requirement of UCC 2-306(1), which, as Comment 2 points out, is meant to prevent bad-faith fluctuations in demand. Other controls, also set forth in § 2-306(1) include the use of stated estimates and comparisons to prior output or requirements. Price controls, on the other hand, are designed to preclude strategic behavior by defining the contract price as the market price. That is, instead of setting a fixed price, the contract may specify that the contract price will be the market price as determined by the use of a mutually acceptable price index. An example of this type of price indexing will be seen in *Eastern Air Lines*, the next principal case.

Output contracts – contracts in which the buyer agrees to purchase everything the seller produces – present similar opportunities for strategic behavior. In output contracts, the buyer can only buy from other sellers after she has purchased all of the seller's output. Hence, an increase in the market price above the contract price will lead to under-supply: the seller will decrease production in order to cut the losses it will suffer from selling below the market price. Once again, there is a market check to protect the buyer, but since she will be purchasing any additional goods she needs at the higher market price, this is only a partial check. Conversely, a decline in the market price below the contract price will result in over-supply: the seller will produce more in order to take advantage of the extra profits it earns by selling above the market price. Like the seller in requirements contracts, the buyer in an output contract needs contractual protection against this situation because she is obligated to buy all of the seller's output before she can purchase goods on the open market at a lower price. She, too, can look to the quantity controls of § 2-306(1) for protection against over- and under-supply, and to price indexing as a way of preventing discrepancies between the market price and the contract price.

The following two principal cases demonstrate what can happen when price and/or quantity controls fail to protect parties in relational contracts adequately.

Eastern Air Lines v. Gulf Oil Corp. *(Page 326).* Eastern and Gulf had a long-term contract, in which Eastern promised to buy all the aviation fuel it required from Gulf in those cities where Gulf had fueling stations. In order to keep the contract price for the fuel roughly equivalent to the market price, they settled on a price indicator: the price of West Texas Sour crude oil as reported in Platt's Oilgram. Apparently, this served them well for decades, but a complicated combination of global events thwarted their plans.

When OPEC embargoed oil against the US, the supply of foreign oil dwindled. Normally, this would lead to an increase in the production and price of domestic oil, but domestic oil had long been subject to government price controls, which prevented the necessary increases. In order to stimulate domestic oil production, the government introduced a two-tiered price control, which worked in the following manner: A production benchmark – the number of barrels produced in May, 1972 – was chosen for each well and that number of barrels was deemed "old" oil. Any barrels produced above that number were deemed "new" oil. New oil was not subject to price controls, and for every barrel of new oil produced, one barrel of old oil was released from the price controls and could be sold at market price. This system had the desired effect: oil production increased and, as it did, so did the price of crude oil not subject to government controls. The problem for Gulf was that Platt's did not publish the market price of the deregulated oil, it only published the price of the old oil at the controlled price.

Deregulation, then, caused Gulf's production costs to rise because it had to pay market price for much of its crude oil, but the contract price could not reflect the increase because Platt's only published the controlled price. Gulf, therefore, presented Eastern with an ultimatum: agree to a price increase or you'll be cut off in 15 days. Eastern filed suit alleging breach and was granted a preliminary injunction to force Gulf to perform according to the contract terms. Gulf argued that the contract was void for vagueness, but the court held this to be an enforceable requirements contract. The problem was not that the contract is too vague, but rather that external forces caused the price control to malfunction. As long as the price control functioned properly, the contract price *was* the market price and both parties benefitted. When the price control ceased to reflect the market price, Gulf began losing money.

Gulf also argued that Eastern exploited the malfunctioning of the price control and thus violated of the good faith requirement of § 2-206(1). They claimed that Eastern took advantage of the below-market price by "fuel-freighting"– demanding more fuel than they required from Gulf fueling stations in order to avoid buying more expensive fuel in cities where Gulf did not operate. The court rejected the argument, finding that course of dealing (UCC § 1-205(1)), course of performance (UCC § 2-208(1)), and usage of trade (UCC § 2-205(2)) indicated that fuel freighting was an accepted practice both between the parties and in the industry as a whole. Thus, Eastern was not acting in bad faith even if they were freighting fuel because Gulf knew or should have known of the practice at the time of contracting and they acquiesced to it throughout the course of their dealings with Eastern. While this is a good argument that fuel freighting per se does not constitute bad faith behavior, Eastern might have countered that engaging in fuel freighting specifically to take advantage of the low contract price does. Evidence of increases in fuel freighting since deregulation would indicate that Eastern was trying to reap a windfall at Gulf's expense and that Eastern had indeed acted in bad faith.

Empire Gas Corporation v. American Bakeries Company *(Page 332).* In order to cut costs, American Bakeries contemplated converting their fleet of vehicles from gasoline to propane. Empire Gas sold propane converters, and American agreed to buy from them "approximately three thousand . . . [conversion] units, more or less depending upon requirements of Buyer . . . ." American further agreed to buy propane fuel exclusively from Empire at all locations where Empire provided that service. American, however, never purchased any converters. Empire brought suit for breach of contract, seeking lost profits on both the converters and the fuel sales. American argued that this was a requirements contract, and such an arrangement is essentially a buyer's option contract. It gives the buyer the right to buy as much as it needs, but it also gives the buyer the right to buy nothing if it so chooses.

Judge Posner accepted the characterization of the contract as a requirements contract (is it really?). The issue for him is whether extreme under-demand – in this case no demand – constitutes a breach of a requirements contract, and he first tried to arrive at an answer through a close reading of § 2-306(1). Because the contract contained an estimate of the number of units American would buy, Empire argued that American's failure to purchase any units at all violates the second clause of § 2-306(1). Posner, however, disagreed. He read the "unreasonably disproportionate" clause not as establishing an independent legal standard, but instead only as elaborating and explaining the term "good faith." Furthermore, he argued, the clause applied only to cases of over-demand and is irrelevant when under-demand is at issue. This argument is bolstered by the fact that the last word in the paragraph is "demanded"; this indicates, according to Posner, that the drafters meant the "stated estimate" clause to provide sellers protection against buyers whose demands unreasonably exceeded the stated estimate in order to take advantage of high market prices by reselling goods bought at the lower contract price. Besides, in cases of under-demand, the seller can protect itself by finding other buyers; it doesn't need the statute to protect against strategic behavior by the requirements buyer.

But this is not the end of the case. Even if American did not violate the "stated estimate" clause itself, it may still have been acting in bad faith if it didn't have a "legitimate business reason" for its zero demand. If a buyer can simply refuse to purchase anything without offering any reason, then a requirements contract really is nothing but an option contract, and the seller bears all the risk of under-demand. But the seller has a right to expect that the buyer will purchase an amount somewhere near the estimate unless the buyer has a valid business reason to vary her demand. When the buyer demands far less than the estimate without a valid business reason, the seller's reliance becomes detrimental, and the buyer is in breach. Posner doesn't have to answer the really tough questions raised by this approach: what constitutes a valid business purpose and exactly how low can demand go before breach occurs? Zero is presumptively a bad faith quantity, but what if American had ordered 500 units? Since they ordered nothing and because they gave no definite reason at all for their actions, Posner finds their behavior prima facie bad faith.

A straightforward and textually accurate reading of § 2-306(1) would provide a more sensible approach to this problem. As noted, Posner interprets the "stated estimate" clause as an explanation of good faith, not as a separate legal standard. This reading is compromised by the fact that the clause begins with the word "except," which sets it apart from "good faith." The "stated estimate" clause is, then, a separate legal standard and may allow for a breach even if a variation occurs in good faith. That is, one party might have a valid business purpose for varying her demand, but if that variation deviates unreasonably from the stated estimate, it still amounts to breach. Comment 3 makes this clear: if there is an estimate, then disproportionate demand is a breach; it does not say anything about this applying only to cases of over-demand. Furthermore, it doesn't matter that § 2-306(1) and comment 3 refer to the amount "demanded"; obviously a buyer can demand less just as she can demand more. Hence, there seems to be no reason to apply this clause only in cases of over-demand. The simpler approach, and the one more faithful to the language of the Code would be to treat § 2-306(1) as solving two problems. The first is the enforcement question. If the parties want to conclude a requirements contract they will have entered into a legally enforceable obligation. The Code thus uses "good faith" as the premise for granting enforcement. (Note that Victor Goldberg has recently written an article in which he argues that the introduction of "good faith" is a red herring that causes mischief when courts try take the standard seriously. It would be better, he argues, to just declare such option contracts enforceable without an explicit requirement of "good faith." (*see* Victor Goldberg, *Discretion in Long-Term Open Quantity Contracts: Reining in Good Faith,* 35 U.C. Davis L. Rev. 319 (2002).)

The second problem is providing a default rule for variable quantity contracts. This is the function of the "unreasonably disproportionate" clause. The clause establishes prior experience or the parties' estimate as a center or "target" quantity around which some variation is allowed. Though the question of how much variation conforms to the default term is still subject to dispute, the default works to the extent that the parties (and the courts) have a clear starting point from which to measure any deviation, and that starting point reflects the ex ante intent of the parties.

Note 2 (Page 340). Good faith is a standard that is necessarily subject to varying interpretations. In each case, relevant facts will need to be weighed in order to determine whether or not a party is acting in good faith. One question we ask students is whether a court can make accurate determinations ex post as to whether the party with discretion is acting strategically. In *problem a,* the doctrinal issue is the extent to which the baker's business would suffer as a result of the contract. The bakery, of course, bears much of the risk that the contract price would prove too low (after all, they negotiated it), but a court is unlikely to force them to perform if, as in variable 1, there is a good chance that its losses would result in bankruptcy. According to Comment 2 to § 2-306, "good faith variations from prior requirements are permitted even when the variation may be such as to result in discontinuance. A shut-down by a requirements buyer for lack of orders might be permissible when a shut-down merely to curtail losses would not." While this refers to requirements buyers, presumably it can also be applied to output sellers. If the seller shuts down because continuation would result in bankruptcy, then the action clearly would be in good faith.

In variables 2 and 3, however, the shut down seems to be an effort to curtail losses (especially in the last example). This raises the question of whether the bakery has agreed to bear the risk of cost increases that exceed the contract price in an output contract. If the answer is yes, as the comments to the Code seem to contemplate, then the seller may be in breach if it shuts down. Such was the holding in *Feld v. Henry S. Levy & Sons,* cited in the Note. In *Feld,* the court was influenced by several factors: 1) the bakery could terminate the contract upon six months' notice so its losses could be confined, and 2) the crumb contract was only a small part of the bakery's operation. While the first factor may suggest that the parties assigned the risk of cost increases to the seller, it is harder to see why the second factor carries much weight. In any case, if the bakery is responding to exogenous market factors, then it is not acting strategically *unless* the bakery was "paid" in the contract price to take the risk. UCC § 2-306 creates a default rule based on the notion of a target created by contract estimates or prior experience that assigns cost increase risks to the seller up to the amount of the target. But cases such as *Feld* (and perhaps Posner's opinion in *Empire Gas)* attempt to use the "good faith" requirement as the mechanism for assigning risk rather than as the means of checking strategic behavior. We doubt that "good faith" is up to the former task. Wouldn't it be better, we suggest, if the default were that the output or requirements contract was an enforceable option contract and the parties could bargain explicitly to shift more risk to the party with discretion if they so choose?

Because only the price changes in **problem b**, the outcome would likely be the same in all three variables. Again, under the *Feld rule,* the bakery bears the risk (up to some unspecified quantity) that the contract price is too low, and if the bakery can survive and even thrive (variable 3) despite the losses, then it is unlikely that the *Feld* court would release them from the contract.

In **problem c**, the action of the bakery is for a valid business reason and, as per *Empire Gas,* would presumptively constitute good faith: it has purchased better equipment to reduce waste and thereby increase profits. However, if the new equipment causes a large enough variation from the stated estimate, then under § 2-306(1), the bakery may be in breach despite its good faith.

Note 5 (Page 343). This problem is designed to have the students appreciate the limitations of requirements contracts in solving contracting problems in retail contexts where marketing efforts are required. Requirements contracts work well in accommodating fluctuating quantities in long term supply contracts– such as in *Eastern Airlines.* In that setting, a requirements contract can "smooth the bumps" and assure the requirements buyer of a reliable source of supply and a hedge against low probability but high impact factors such as the need to cover fixed financing costs in times of low demand. But in many licensing and distribution contracts, the "buyer" will have important responsibilities in marketing the seller's goods. Thus, the problem with both of these clauses is that it's not clear precisely what are Deacon's contractual obligations. It is likely that the first clause would be interpreted as an enforceable requirements contract governed by UCC § 2-306. But the second clause may be vulnerable to the claim that the obligation is illusory since Deacon can return the entire quantity "for any reason." If so, the contract may be unenforceable as lacking mutuality of obligation. But beyond that, under the second clause there is nothing to indicate how much effort Deacon needs to expend in marketing them, and if something better comes along (like the chance to publish a law review article), he is apparently at liberty to cease distribution all together and return the unsold summaries for the purchase price. He bears none of the risk that the outlines won't sell or that he might regret the contract and turn his efforts elsewhere.

The first clause poses similar problems. If the language of that clause does create a valid requirements contracts, Deacon would be bound by the good faith requirement of § 2-306(1). But it is unclear exactly what that would mean in this context. How many outlines would Deacon have to buy in order to satisfy that requirement and under what circumstances? How would Stanley know if he wasn't acting in good faith? Normally, a drastic change in demand signals bad faith behavior in requirements contracts, but there isn't a record of past sales to use as a touchstone in making such a determination. Stanley might try to get him to agree to an estimate of the number of outlines he will order during the year, but Deacon would probably decline to do so because he has no basis for making such an estimate. Perhaps the best approach to this problem is to ask what both parties are trying to accomplish. Stanley wants to provide incentives for Deacon to market the outlines as aggressively as possible so that he can sell as many outlines as possible. Deacon wants to maximize his profits while minimizing the risk that he will be stuck with a bunch of unsold outlines. If Stanley were to agree to deal exclusively with Deacon, and if Deacon were to agree to use his best efforts in distributing the outlines, that would motivate Deacon to put forth as much effort as is commercially reasonable to sell the outlines without him worrying about having an office full of them at the end of the year. In addition, Stanley would have a standard by which to measure and monitor Deacon's performance, which would reduce the risk that Deacon will shirk his contractual obligations.

b. Exclusive Dealings Contracts

Wood v. Lucy, Lady Duff-Gordon *(Page 347).* Lucy, Lady Duff-Gordon, "a creator of fashions," entered into a contract with Wood, under which Wood would have the exclusive right to place Lucy's endorsement on other designer's products and to market her own designs for a period of at least one year. Wood sued, alleging that Lucy had breached the contract by endorsing products without his knowledge and withholding the profits due him. Lucy alleged in turn that the contract was not supported by consideration because Wood never bound himself to do anything to promote her endorsements and designs. Cardozo holds that a promise to use reasonable efforts is implied in exclusive dealings contracts. Otherwise, he says, the licensor is at the mercy of the distributor since she has given up the right to market her own endorsements during the period of the contract. It would be unreasonable to assume that the licensor would agree to do this without receiving a return obligation by the licensee to expend efforts in marketing the endorsements.

Why does Cardozo do this? The answer is related to issues raised in the "Stanley Law Summaries" in the *Problem on page 343*. Wood has been given the exclusive right to market Lucy's endorsement and designs. By foregoing the opportunity to work with other marketers, Lucy hopes to provide an incentive for him to put more effort into marketing her products. He knows that no one else can profit from his efforts, so he will fully internalize the benefits of his labor. But Lucy is at a disadvantage. Wood has other products to promote – indeed, the court notes that his business is designed to do just that – so Lucy needs some assurance that he will promote her products even if he has others that generate more profit. In other words, she wants him to assume some of the risk that her products won't sell as well as the parties expect ex ante. The implied promise to use "reasonable efforts" – or "best efforts," the term adopted under UCC § 2-306(2) – performs this function. If Wood commits to use reasonable efforts in marketing her products, he has assumed a legal responsibility, the violation of which would amount to breach. Without that implied promise, Lucy would be right in arguing that Wood had not really promised to do anything, and his promise would not be supported by consideration.

There are several tough questions raised by this analysis, however. First, is it clear that Cardozo had to imply either "best efforts" or "reasonable efforts" in order to determine that the contract was enforceable by Wood? That is, perhaps the default should simply be that the exclusive licensor has an enforceable contract right – in the nature of an option – to market the goods as market conditions dictate. After all, Wood has a natural incentive to maximize joint profits since the contract calls for him to receive one half of the profits from any endorsement. Thus, what exactly does "best efforts" or "reasonable efforts" add to Wood's incentives in this case? Second, we puzzle out loud (without resolution) whether there is any difference between "reasonable efforts" in Wood and "best efforts" in UCC § 2-306? We then ask the students to turn to the next principal case, *Bloor v. Falstaff Brewing Co.,* for possible answers to these and related questions.

Bloor v. Falstaff Brewing Corp. *(Page 348).* Ballantine, a struggling brewery, sold its brands, trademarks, and other property to Falstaff. In addition to the flat sale price of the property, Ballantine was entitled to royalties of fifty cents on each barrel of Ballantine brands sold for a period of six years. The contract stipulated that Falstaff would use its "best efforts" to promote Ballantine brands, and it also contained a liquidated damages clause that would be triggered by a substantial discontinuance of the distribution of Ballantine products. Ballantine alleged that Falstaff violated the best efforts clause. This breach, Ballantine claimed, led to a substantial discontinuance of distribution and entitled them to recover liquidated damages. The question that the court must address is: What exactly must a company do in order to fulfill its best efforts obligations? As with good faith, the meaning of best efforts is not self-evident. It is a standard open to broad interpretation by courts and litigants. This case provides an example of how courts interpret such terms and thereby give them meaning.

In the beginning, Falstaff spent a lot of money on advertising and promoting Ballantine brands, but during the first three years of the contract, Falstaff lost $22 million on Ballantine products. Because the company as whole was not doing well, control of the company changed hands. The new management cut advertising costs (including slashing the advertising budget for Ballantine from $1 million per year to $115,000). Falstaff also closed some distribution centers, serviced fewer accounts, and ceased some illegal practices it was engaging in to promote its beers. This turned the company around and made it profitable again, but sales of the Ballantine brand (the company actually put the same generic beer used in Falstaff brands in Ballantine labels as per the custom of the trade) nevertheless fell sharply while comparable brands were increasing their sales.

The trial court found that Falstaff had violated the best efforts obligation. Falstaff argued on appeal that the trial judge's opinion would compel them to continue promoting Ballantine at the same level regardless of the size of the resulting losses. The appellate court disagreed with this contention; Falstaff need not bankrupt itself in order to fulfill its obligations. However, once Falstaff had recovered financially, it did have an obligation to take steps to reverse or at least halt the decline of Ballantine sales. But the terms of the contract create a disincentive for doing so: Falstaff is unable to internalize all the benefits of its efforts to promote Ballantine because it must pay a royalty on every barrel sold. As a result, Falstaff did not promote Ballantine as aggressively as it did its own brands. The best efforts clause, however, required Falstaff to put more effort into selling Ballantine than its own brands. They purchased a product and part of the purchase price was the promise to use their best efforts in promoting that product. Falstaff need not bankrupt itself over Ballantine, but incurring losses does not excuse them from their obligation. Instead of promoting Ballantine, it made operational changes that allowed sales of the Ballantine label to plummet in order to bolster the bottom line of the company as a whole. This showed a total disregard for Ballantine's sales and amounted to violation of the best efforts clause.

Bloor is an important case because of the quality of the opinions by the trial and appellate courts and it has generated a great deal of commentary (*see e.g.*, **Essay: Optimal Output in Relational Contracts on page 355**). As Vic Goldberg has pointed out (*see Note 4 on page 359*), the case on its facts is not a classic exclusive dealings distribution contract. Rather the best efforts clause supports an asset sale whose price is uncertain at the time of contracting. But, in any event, the case has come to stand as an exemplar of the kind of efforts required when parties undertake a best efforts obligation. Several things can be emphasized in class. First, this best efforts clause was not implied as a default via UCC § 2-306. Rather the best efforts obligation was explicitly and expressly assumed by Falstaff. Indeed, our experience is that such best efforts clauses are ubiquitous in distribution contracts. This raises the question: Why do contracting parties write best efforts contracts given that best efforts invokes an obligation that can be defined in theory but is very difficult, if not impossible, to verify in litigation? One answer is that when parties do write best efforts contracts, the best efforts clause is supported by other contract terms designed to align the incentives of the party with discretion (the distributor) so that it is motivated to maximize the contractual pie. Net profit sharing arrangements, as per *Wood,* accomplish this objective, but, as the celebrated entertainment cases (Art Buchwald, Jim Garner, Fess Parker, Natalie Wood, Robert Wagner, etc.) demonstrate, net profit compensation is often impossible for the licensor/author/performer to verify and thus is subject to cost padding, cost shifting, etc. As a result, many parties use volume-based royalties as per *Bloor.* But once the compensation is based on net sales volume rather than net profits, the distributor's incentives are skewed: there is a moral hazard caused by the fact that the distributor bears all costs for increased efforts (Ballantine was not obliged to share the marketing costs, etc.) but must share the corresponding benefits (by paying the royalty) with the licensor. Predictably, this produces inadequate efforts. Thus, one reason for the best efforts clause is to try, insofar as the parties (or their lawyers) are able, to deter strategic behavior by the party with discretion when the incentives cannot be perfectly aligned by a combination of contract terms.

Problems (Page 360). Hypothetical a is designed for students to see that a contract that is optimal ex ante may become suboptimal ex post. Under those circumstances, the party who bears the risk (Charlie) will be motivated to renegotiate so as to minimize ex post losses. In other words, joint maximization is an ex ante concept; it does not relieve contracting parties of the risk of ex post disappointment. In *hypothetical b,* the joint maximization model would require Red to consider Doug's welfare when deciding whether or not to reset his supplement. Thus, in theory, it would require Red to reprint the supplement even if doing so would result in a loss of profits to the company so long as the joint profits from the venture are positive. One solution: Instead of resetting Doug's supplement, Red need only assign the royalties from the additional sales of Archie's supplement to Doug. Doug would then not lose out on royalties, and Red would not have to risk incurring losses.

Note 6 (Page 360). In *Van Valkenburgh, Nooger & Neville, Inc. v. Hayden Publishing Co.,* the plaintiff held a copyright to a series of books on electronics. The publisher tried to convince the plaintiff to reduce its 15% royalty on future editions, and when the plaintiff rejected the proposal, the publisher contracted with another author to produce a series of books with nearly identical content and organization. The new author, however, only received a 3% royalty. The publisher then tried to sell these books to customers who had previously ordered the plaintiff's books. The court found that the actions of the publisher were so clearly harmful to the plaintiff that it breached its "covenant to promote the author's work."

Why did this amount to breach? Consider the counter-argument presented at the end of the Note. If another publisher were to market the work of the second author, the plaintiff would still be competing against his work. Publishers often market multiple books on the same subject; indeed, Lexis publishes other contracts casebooks, but that does not mean that it has breached its duty to use best efforts in promoting this book. Hence, as long as the publisher in *Van Valkenburg* continues to promote the first author's work honestly, it should not be precluded from promoting the work of the second author.

Is there a problem with this argument in the *Van Valkenburgh* context? Perhaps. The argument rests on the assumption that the books would be competing against one another either way, and so the market would decide which book would enjoy greater success. However, if the publisher has artificially altered the competitive royalty rate, then the market would be manipulated in favor of the second author. Such market manipulation would arise if the publisher were able to get the second author to accept the lower royalty rate by promising a higher sales volume than other publishers could offer, and it could make that promise solely because it knew it was going to sacrifice the interests of the first author. Intentionally sacrificing the interests of their contracting partner would clearly not reflect the publisher's best efforts.

On the other hand, if the second author would have accepted the lower rate from other publishers, i.e., if that were the current market rate, and if the lower royalty rate weren't the sole reason that the publisher was promoting the second book in the same market as the first, then the publisher could still market both books without violating the best efforts clause. The first author, in that case, would be acting to his own detriment by insisting on a royalty rate in excess of what the market would bear.

c. Reducing Conflicts of Interest by Contract
1. Termination Clauses

Wagenseller v. Scottsdale Memorial Hospital *(Page 362).* Catherine Wagenseller was hired by the hospital as an "at-will" employee. She was recruited by Kay Smith, who also supervised her after she began work. Wagenseller received favorable performance evaluations from Smith and was twice promoted. But three months after her second promotion, she was terminated.

Wagenseller claimed that her termination was the result of personal differences that developed between her and Smith during an eight-day rafting trip. Wagenseller declined to participate with Smith in activities such as public urination, defecation, heavy drinking, and "grouping up" with other rafters. She claimed that her refusal to participate effected a noticeably negative change in their relationship and that she was fired because of it. Wagenseller's complaint alleged that she was fired for reasons that contravened public policy and that she could recover damages based on both tort and contract theories. The hospital argued that it could fire an at-will employee for no cause or even for "bad cause," that is, for reasons that contravene public policy. The court agreed that at-will employees can be fired for no cause, but holds that employees may not be fired for bad cause.

The court provides a nicely detailed history of "at will" employment contracts in England and the United States. One of the primary justifications for allowing employers to discharge employees without cause is that it gives management freedom to exercise business judgement without the fear of frivolous lawsuits. As *Note 2 on page 375* points out, it would be difficult and legally perilous for companies to have to justify every dismissal as being for good cause. Many courts have, however, decided that limits should be placed on managerial discretion. The public policy exception represents one of these limitations. Intuitively this makes sense: public policy is expressed through statutory, judge-made, or constitutional laws, and the law should not protect employers who try to coerce workers into violating the law. Theoretically at least, this rule does not constrain true business judgment because firings that contravene public policy are, by definition, not in the employer's best interest. But this argument begs the question of whether or not such a rule is truly necessary. There are powerful extra-legal sanctions that protect workers from being fired for bad cause. *Note 2 on page 375* develops the argument that the need to turn a profit and to compete for quality labor prevents employers from abusing their discretion in at will employment contracts. We ask the students: What arguments can you make that extra legal sanctions are insufficient in this context, and thus necessitate a legal rule that limits and/or regulates at will terminations?

Consumers International, Inc. v. Sysco Corporation *(Page 369).* Consumer International (CI) entered into a distribution agreement whereby Sysco would supply CI with 80% of the food service products that CI needed to distribute to its retail customers. The contract contained a clause allowing either party to terminate the contract upon sixty-days' notice. Two months after the contract was formed, Sysco exercised that clause and terminated the contract. They gave no reason for doing so. CI argues that the implied covenant of good faith and fair dealing contained in every contract barred Sysco from terminating the contract without good cause. The court rejects this claim.

The court points out that good faith means "that neither party do anything that will injure the rights of the other to receive the benefits of their agreement." Acting in bad faith requires, therefore, that one party somehow prevent the other from receiving the benefits of the bargain. In order for a plaintiff to show bad faith on the employer's part, she must first show that the benefit denied her was one she had a right to expect under the terms of the contract. That is obviously not the case with this contract; it explicitly stated that either party could terminate simply by providing sixty-days' notice. There is no indication that termination must be supported by good cause. Hence, good faith and good cause are not equivalent.

Note 1 (Page 374). Why would CI agree to the termination clause in question? This Note offers one explanation: the termination clause is a "performance bond" that CI gives Sysco. It assures Sysco that it will have a way out of the contract if CI does not perform satisfactorily. But such a clause can place a company in a catch-22. Sysco might not agree to the contract without the termination clause, but once CI accepts the clause, Sysco can terminate whether CI has performed well or not. Can one infer from this that, contrary to the court's opinion, CI did not have equal bargaining power and should be protected against the whims of their much-larger contracting partner?

Note 6 (Page 377). You would begin by arguing that the whistle-blower was acting in the public interest and therefore should be protected against retaliatory dismissal by the employer who was acting against public interest. If there were a law imposing liability for using stolen animals in research, it would support your argument. Since he was trying to prevent behavior on the part of his employer that has explicitly been deemed contrary to public policy, there would be a stronger legal argument that a public policy exception should be made in cases such as this.

2. Covenants Not to Compete

Gagliardi Bros. Inc. v. Caputo *(Page 377).* Caputo worked for nine years as a controller for Gagliardi Bros., a manufacturer of portion-controlled sandwich meats. During that time he attended board meetings and was made aware of several innovations that Gagliardi was developing to improve the taste, production, and packaging of its products. After the company was denied a patent for its Steak-umms product, it required Caputo and other employees to sign a covenant not to enter the portion-controlled meat business or to accept employment with another company in that business for one year following a termination of employment. This covenant applied to all employers within 100 miles of Gagliardi's place of business. At the time the covenant was signed, Caputo was given a raise, and he received subsequent salary increases as well. Had he not signed the covenant, his employment would have been terminated. About six years later, Caputo was fired. Soon after he quit working for Galiardi, he took a job with one of their competitors, Devault Packing Company. Gagliardi then sued Caputo, claiming that he had violated the covenant not to compete and seeking enforcement of the covenant by injunction.

The *Gagliardi* court sets out four requirements for a valid covenant not to compete: 1) it must be related to a contract of employment; 2) it must be supported by adequate consideration; 3) it must be reasonably limited in time and geographic territory; and, 4) it must be necessary for the protection of the employer. The court holds that Caputo's covenant fails on all four counts. First, it is not ancillary to the employment contract because it was executed after Caputo began his employment, and there was no change in his status as a result of the covenant. Second, there was no consideration given in return for his promise not to compete. The increase in salary, the court says, was not consideration for the promise, but was merely "one of a series of increases received by him" on a regular basis. Furthermore, there was no promise of employment for a definite term. Mere continuation of employment does not qualify as valid consideration for a covenant not to compete. Third, although one year was not excessive per se, the court holds that it was excessive in the sense that it bore no relation to the protection of Gagliardi. The geographic limitation, according to the court, no longer made sense because Gagliardi's marketing region had expanded well beyond that area. Hence, Caputo could have taken employment with a company far outside the restricted area and he still would have been competing with Gagliardi. Finally, the covenant was not necessary to protect Gagliardi as evidenced by the fact that Gagliardi no longer required employees to sign such a covenant and its business had grown considerably nevertheless. Also, even though Caputo had knowledge regarding some of Gagliardi's trade secrets, he did not have the technical knowledge necessary to help his new employer take advantage of those secrets. He was a controller, not an engineer.

One approach to this case is to ask the students whether the criteria used by the court make sense, and if so, whether the court apply them properly. The court seems to conflate the first two factors, arguing that the covenant was not ancillary to the contract because there was neither a benefit given to Caputo nor was there a change in his status. Basically, then, the court is saying that the covenant is not ancillary to an employment contract because no consideration was given. While there is a strong argument that the promise was not supported by consideration, the covenant clearly relates to his employment contract and therefore seems to satisfy the first criterion. The court also combines the final two factors. The temporal restriction is found unreasonable because it does not stand in a reasonable relationship to Gagliardi's need for protection. But can a court really make that determination? If an employer feels that it needs to enforce covenants not to compete for what would normally be a reasonable period of time in order to adequately protect itself, does a court have the capacity to second guess that decision? And if consideration is given in return for the promise, on what grounds could a court decide not enforce it? Furthermore, the court here finds that Gagliardi had grown after Caputo left, so it doesn't need protection against him. But what if Gagliardi grew in spite of Caputo? That is, perhaps it would have grown even more had Caputo not joined its competitor. Wouldn't that indicate a need for Gagliardi to protect itself against Caputo?

Note 1 (Page 382). Courts must often reconcile competing interests. Employers need to be able to fire workers without cause because, as was discussed in the previous section, requiring them to show good cause in every case would result in a loss of managerial discretion and would force them to develop costly and cumbersome procedures for documenting and justifying terminations. However, courts also recognize the need to protect workers by allowing them to find gainful employment when they are terminated. Covenants not to compete, therefore, are strictly construed to ensure that workers are not unreasonably restricted from finding new jobs.

C. Modification of Existing Agreements
We end the chapter on contractual relationships with a section on contract modification

because the analysis thus far points to one clear implication of such contracts: unless the parties write highly complex contracts, there will be many circumstances where a contract is efficient ex ante but inefficient ex post. One strategy that many contracting parties pursue, therefore, is to write a relatively simple contract (i.e., a contract that does not condition the parties obligations on all possible future states of the world) and then rely on subsequent adjustments or modification of the contract through renegotiation in order to accommodate unspecified contingencies. Since this is a very common strategy for many contracting parties, it is not surprising that contract law has developed legal rules designed to regulate the modification process. The pros and cons of the various rules are thus a key part of the discussion. The section also introduces students to the trade off between bright line rules and broad standards: The common law "pre-existing duty" rule is the paradigmatic bright line rule and the UCC in § 2-209 offers the other extreme.

Alaska Packers' Ass'n v. Domenico *(Page 384).* In March, 1900, the plaintiffs entered into a contract by which they agreed to travel to Alaska to work on fishing vessels. They were to be paid a salary of $50 for the season plus two cents for each salmon they helped catch. The salary was later raised to $60 for the season. On May 22nd of that year, a few days after the men had begun fishing, they stopped work and demanded that their salaries be raised to $100. Otherwise, they said, they would stop work altogether and return to San Francisco. Because they could find no other men, the company's superintendent in Alaska agreed to the increase. When they returned from Alaska, the fishermen demanded their $100 salaries, but the company told them that the May 22nd contract was invalid, and they would only be paid the $60 previously agreed upon. The fishermen sued to have the May 22nd contract enforced.

The court is mainly concerned with whether consideration was given in return for the promise to pay $100. The fishermen, of course, would argue that their labor was consideration for the promise, but the common law's pre-existing duty rule dooms that argument. Under that rule, an existing contract cannot be modified unless "fresh" consideration is given in return for the modification. The fishermen were already bound by contract to perform certain duties, and their promise to perform those duties provided consideration for the promise to pay $60. The pre-existing duty rule precludes them from demanding more money for duties they were already bound to perform without offering some sort of additional consideration in return. Because the court finds that no fresh consideration was given, the contract is unenforceable.

UCC § 2-209 abandons the pre-existing duty rule by allowing modifications without fresh consideration. However, in order to be valid, the demand for modification must be made in good faith, which means that there must there must be a legitimate commercial reason for the demand. (*see* Comment 2). The problem is deciding what constitutes a legitimate commercial reason. We approach this issue by asking: Under what circumstances would a party agree (without coercion) to a renegotiation demand when it inevitably means that she will be getting less than she originally bargained for? The answer is that when a modification would ultimately be less costly than breach, it makes sense to modify. The fishermen in *Alaska Packers* were impecunious; the company would not have been able to collect expectation damages from them. In addition, they would have to pay their own attorneys fees to litigate the case. Paying higher salaries may therefore have been less expensive in the long run than suing for breach. This means, however, that the party demanding the modification (the fishermen in this case) must genuinely regret the agreement and be truly willing to breach without it. If the fishermen would perform either way, the modification demand is merely an attempt to extort money from the other party. This would be a bad faith demand (and is the equivalent of economic duress; *see Austin v. Loral*, page 410, infra) and should not be enforced.

Ralston Purina Co. v. McNabb *(Page 388).* McNabb, a farmer, promised under two separate contracts to deliver 8,000 bushels of soybeans to Purina by November 30, 1972. Severe storms and flooding damaged much of McNabb's crop, and he was unable to deliver all 8,000 bushels by the deadline. Purina sent letters to him in November, December, January, and February, each of which offered a one month extension on the contracts. By the end of February, McNabb still owed Purina 3,771.47 bushels of soybeans. Because the crop damage was widespread, the market price of soybeans had risen dramatically. Purina had to cover the contract by buying beans at the market price, which was well above the contract price, and Purina sought to recover the difference between the market price on March 8th (the end of the final extension period) and the contract price. McNabb, however, contended that he had breached the contract on November 30th, the original performance date. The deliveries he made after the date of performance, therefore, were "new sales," and the checks from Purina, which reflected the contract price instead of the current market price, were simply the method they had chosen to collect damages for the breach. In other words, he contended that they had arrived at an unspoken settlement agreement.

The question for the court, then, is whether or not there was an immediate breach on November 30th or repeated modifications (extending the time for performance) followed by a breach in March. If the breach occurred in November, McNabb would only be liable for the difference between the November 30 market price and the contract price, and Purina's additional "losses" would not be recoverable under the doctrine of avoidable consequences. The court held that McNabb by his conduct accepted Purina's offers to modify the delivery date, but the modifications were made in bad faith and are, therefore, unenforceable. Purina knew or should have known that McNabb would not be able to fulfill his obligations because of the weather conditions, and they knew that there would be a sharp increase in the price of soybeans. Hence, they offered the extensions to maximize damages by postponing the inevitable breach until the prices had in fact increased. The damages are therefore calculated as of November 30th.

The court, however, misunderstands how the market functions. No one knows for sure what the market will do in the future. Had Purina known what the court assumes it knew, it would have bought all the soybeans available in November and then sold them after the price had increased. The fact is that any information affecting a commodity's market price is immediately impounded by the market and reflected in the price. Furthermore, even if they had known that the price would rise, they wouldn't get to pocket the damages from McNabb because they would still have to cover the contract at the market price. By making bad faith extensions, they would only be exacerbating McNabb's damages, not benefitting themselves. It is far more plausible that Purina offered the extensions for a legitimate commercial reason. Crop damage was widespread, and 90% of its soybean contracts were unfulfilled, but Purina needed to maintain their supply in order to meet production demands. They offered extensions to keep the soybeans coming, and, indeed, 98% of the contracts were eventually filled.

Note 6 (Page 394). Under UCC § 2-209, the decisive factor in determining whether a modification is enforceable is whether or not it was made in good faith. What would be the result in *Alaska Packers* if it had been decided under § 2-209 instead of the pre-existing duty rule? The facts presented in Debora Threedy's article cited in *Note 4 on page 393* provide strong evidence that the fishermen's demand was made in good faith. They no doubt accepted their original salary with the understanding that they would be able to earn quite a bit more from the two-cent-per-fish bonus. If substandard equipment threatened to reduce substantially the amount they could earn from their efforts, or if they would have had to work much harder in order to earn the same amount, then it makes sense that they would refuse to work without being paid a higher salary in order to compensate for the de facto reduction in their bonuses. Such facts might even provide them with a change-of-circumstances defense. Hence, the modification demand would have been made in good faith, and the fishermen would have prevailed under § 2-209.

We have already presented an argument that the modifications offered by Purina were in good faith, but what about Jordan's demand in the hypothetical in *Note 3 on page 391*? (As an aside, Jordan has since been traded.) Here the answer seems to hinge on whether or not Jordan genuinely regrets his contract. If he really could return to the NFL and earn more than he was earning playing baseball, then he might be willing to breach if his modification demand were denied. However, if he has little chance of earning more money in the NFL, it is unlikely that he would breach the contract, forego the millions he was already making playing baseball, and be liable for damages as a result of his breach. In that case, he would merely be trying to extort more money from the baseball club, and the modification would be unenforceable under § 2-209.

CHAPTER 5

REGULATING THE BARGAINING PROCESS

A. Introduction

Promises are legally enforceable only if they are made voluntarily by informed, competent adults. Various contract doctrines have evolved to insure that only such promises will be enforced. Thus, the duress doctrine renders unenforceable any promise that is not sufficiently voluntary. The fraud doctrines of willful and negligent misrepresentation, fraudulent concealment, and nondisclosure provide defenses to enforcing any promise made by an insufficiently informed promisor (recall, however, that the duty to read doctrine enforces promises made by uninformed parties who, through no fault of the other party, fail to read their agreement). And the capacity doctrines of infancy and mental illness prevent the enforcement of promises made by incompetent promisors. But even promises that meet this high standard will not be enforceable if they contravene public policy. Promises to engage in illegal and immoral conduct are typically not enforceable. Even when the illegality and immorality doctrines do not apply directly, bargains that grossly offend social norms are sometimes struck down under the unconscionability doctrine. The unconscionability doctrine also serves as a general safety net to protect parties from procedurally defective bargains not otherwise screened out under the duress, fraud, and incapacity doctrines. Finally, under the statute of frauds some promises are not enforceable unless they are in writing, even though they otherwise satisfy all of the enforcement doctrines mentioned above.

Pedagogy. With this chapter we conclude our treatment of the elements of traditional contract doctrine that are thought to constitute the "core" of twentieth-century American contract law. Thus, typically, users of the book will cover most of the material in chapters one through five in a standard first year course (as our sample syllabus in the introduction to this manual illustrates). But it is fair to say that most professors begin to pick and choose sections more carefully when they get to the material in this chapter. This chapter spans a full 200 pages and covers no less than 28 cases. It is certainly possible to familiarize students with the basics of this chapter without covering every section and every case in each section. Some of the previous chapters develop fundamental themes over the course of the entire chapter, and so are less amenable to selective assignments. But we have designed this chapter to have stand-alone sections that teach well independently of one another. In addition, the introductory and note materials allow students to read some of these sections on their own, without the assistance of class coverage. Thus, many of the sections in this chapter are ideally suited for "read independently" assignments.

We hasten to add, however, that "read independently" assignments may cause first-year students, who are often insecure and risk averse, to react with fear. No matter how accessible and intuitive the materials, first-years don't like being told that they will be responsible for material not covered in class. It may help to take time to read the notes carefully and delete the more advanced notes from any "read independently" assignment. Some of the notes reinforce and test basic doctrinal understanding. Others press students to evaluate and form theoretical analyses of the cases and doctrines. The former will alleviate insecurity and are suitable for including in "read independently" assignments. The latter will heighten anxiety if not accompanied by in-class coverage– because they are designed to help structure in-class discussion of the theoretical issues underlying these doctrines, they sometimes raise questions students have difficulty answering (with confidence) on their own.

Another reason this chapter is friendly to selective assignments is that it is unified only by virtue of the very general themes of autonomy and joint welfare maximization. Each of these doctrines, save some of the public policy doctrines, are designed to insure that the only legally enforceable promises are ones made by autonomous actors who, presumably, are exchanging promises so as to enhance their joint welfare. But each aspect of autonomy (and welfare maximization) to which the doctrines are directed raise relatively distinct doctrinal and theoretical questions. As a result, there is very little mutual dependence between sections, or even subsections, within the chapter. Thus, one can skip sections in the first half of the chapter without fear that sections assigned from the second half of the chapter will build on, and make essential reference to, the doctrines covered in the first half. (To unify the chapter for the student reading most of all of it, however, we do make *nonessential* cross-references between some sections).

Having emphasized the pedagogical flexibility of this chapter, we should mention that many professors and students regard the material in this chapter as very enjoyable to cover. Unlike the many contract doctrines that have no precedent outside of law, and thus trigger few relevant intuitions (e.g., we have yet to encounter students with strong feelings – other than confusion – about the proper application of the parol evidence rule), the doctrines in this chapter tap into very familiar and basic concepts for every student. What is the difference between the threat of the gunman and the threat of economic ruin from fierce but legal competition? Should a builder be excused from performance because the buyers have threatened that, if forced to go through with the agreement, they would resell the house to an "undesirable purchaser" and thereby ruin the economic viability of the builder's surrounding development? Should three whaling ships be able to extract a bargain for whale oil at pennies on the dollar from another whaling ship that has run aground 5000 miles from the nearest port of safety? Should under-age promisors be excused from performance even if the promisor believed they were adults as a result of the promisor's credible lies? Similarly, should a promisor be excused from performance because of mental illness even when the illness could not be detected by a reasonable person? Should a buyer be freed from a real estate purchase agreement because the seller failed to disclose that the house was widely regarded as haunted, or that the house had been the site of multiple murders? Should surrogate motherhood contracts be struck down as against public policy? Would doing so vindicate or contravene women's rights? These are just some of the many engaging and challenging questions that make for lively and memorable class discussions.

We confess, however, that as entertaining as these class sessions can be, we have over the years tended to confine such sessions to a relatively limited portion of our courses. This is so in part because some of the issues raised in this chapter are not amenable to the kind of systematic analysis that underlies much of contract law. The hard work, often at issue in these more interesting cases, is deciding about the unclear, borderline cases, in which intuitions as well as policy considerations point in opposing directions. In short, throughout this chapter, reasonable people can disagree about the precise structure of these doctrines and their appropriate application in the cases. There are no relatively uncontroversial resolutions of these problems. There is just the brute fact that the lines must be drawn and any line drawn will be subject to reasonable opposition.

In our experience, an undue exposure to perennial questions that do not admit of systematic resolution has two negative consequences for the success of a contracts course. First, it breeds insecurity for first-year students who tend to crave resolution– if not at the end of each class, at least by the end of the course. While we can clarify the basic contours of these doctrine, we cannot give students any "take home" points that carry the day on the close questions raised by the borderline, cutting edge cases. The students end up with the lesson that there are a "thousand points of light" or "many views of the Cathedral." This is, of course, the reality about many difficult questions of law, so there is no doubt that students benefit from exposure to such issues. And a competent understanding of these doctrines amounts to a competent understanding of the basics, plus familiarity with the various conflicting theoretical approaches to them. Second, teaching some of the more open-textured issues in this chapter – the best example is Baby M – undermines one of our fundamental pedagogical objectives. In our experience, students are already far too inclined to believe that all interesting questions boil down to competing plausible intuitions, that almost any position can be reasonably supported, or that every argument is equally valid or invalid (that the very idea of more or less persuasive positions is somehow bankrupt). For us, the challenge of contracts– and the first-semester in general– is to teach students that the law is neither as wooden and clear as a dictionary definition, nor as malleable and indeterminate as a lump of clay. The life of the law consists in structured legal argument. Even if, at the end of the day, more than one argument can be sustained, the lesson for the first year is that most arguments cannot be. There are many right and wrong answers in the law, and some legal arguments are better or worse than others. Our aim is to provide students with the tools for understanding what makes legal arguments better and worse, both in light of our view of the right legal answer, as well as what other legal actors will find most persuasive.

Finally, with no clear pedagogical objective other than to appreciate the many different points of view on an issue, something of a classroom vacuum is created. In such contexts, it is very easy to appear not to treat all opinions with fairness and equanimity. Managing such discussions requires a particular kind of interpersonal and group-conversational skill that some professors have in more abundance than others. In short, we have sometimes found ourselves out of our depth– in the midst of the "Oprah Winfrey" show, except without Oprah. And again, even if the interpersonal aspect of such class sessions goes well, the average first-year student will tolerate only a limited number of open-ended sessions. At the very least, professors should bend over backwards to make clear at least some set of points that students understand the professor wants them to take away from these discussions.

All of this applies most directly to cases such as *Baby M*, and of course does not apply at all to the statute of frauds. Other doctrines implicate some of these concerns but not others. For example, it is certainly possible to discuss the duress, fraud, and incapacity doctrines without students becoming emotionally invested. We suggest professors read through the materials in this chapter and assign those topics of most interest to them. Often, interests stem from scholarship in the field written by, or familiar to, the professor teaching the course. In our experience, professors experiment teaching various sections of this chapter and, depending on their interests, settle on some to assign in class, some to assign for independent reading, and some to skip altogether.

B. Duress

The duress doctrine draws the line between involuntary, and therefore unenforceable, bargains and mere "hard bargains"– voluntary bargains that otherwise fully exploit the market advantage of the promisee. R2d § 174 defines the clearest case for duress: physical compulsion. But the doctrine extends well beyond actual physical compulsion. R2d § 175 defines the conditions under which a threat constitutes duress. Subsection (1) requires the party's manifestation of assent (the duress doctrine is defined in terms of the objective theory of promise in R2 § 2) to be induced by an improper threat that leaves the party no reasonable alternative. Thus, it has three elements: (1) an improper threat, (2) inducement of the promise, and (3) no reasonable alternative. As to element (1), R2d 176 defines an improper threat. The first subsection defines an improper threat independently of the fairness of the terms of the bargain. These are so clearly improper threats that courts need not inquire into whether the threat affected the nature of the bargain. Subsections (1)(a) - (1)(c) are relatively easy to apply. They constitute threats to commit acts that are either legally impermissible or constitute an abuse of process. Subsection (1)(d) deals with the "hold up" problem. It requires courts to determine whether a threat made *under a contract* (as opposed to during the bargaining process) constitutes a breach of the duty of good faith and fair dealing.

Subsection (2) defines the conditions under which a threat will be found improper only if the resulting bargain is unfair. It is not clear what this means, but ignoring the "unfairness" precondition for the moment, subsection (2)(a) appears to provide an objective test for a bad motive: If the threatened act would harm the recipient of the threat but would not significantly benefit the party making the threat, then it appears the promisee is making it for the sole purpose of extracting an advantageous bargain, rather than bargaining to refrain from doing something he otherwise would have good reason to do.

Wolf v. Marlton Corp. *(Page 404).* In this case, the plaintiffs, the Wolfs, entered into an agreement to pay for the house to be built by the defendant, Marlton. Following marital difficulties, the Wolfs came to regret the contract. The contract provided for a $2,450 deposit, which the Wolfs had paid, and another payment for that amount upon the "closing in" of the house (when it has four walls and a roof). The case at trial is framed as an action by the Wolfs to recover their initial deposit. Marlton defends by claiming that the Wolfs breached by failing to pay the second payment due upon the closing in of the house. The Wolfs concede they did not make the payment but deny they received notice from Marlton that the house was closed in and therefore that the payment was due. Marlton responds that the agreement did not require notice. The trial court holds that the contract contained an implied term requiring notice and that the Wolfs did not receive notice. It rules the Wolfs are entitled to a full refund of their initial deposit.

On appeal, the court holds that notice was required but also received through notice to the Wolfs' attorney. The court, however, dismisses the issue of notice as irrelevant because the record indicates that the Wolfs informed Marlton of their willingness to make the second payment as required by the agreement, but Marlton refused to accept the payment. Marlton's real defense, therefore, is that the Wolfs made an improper threat, constituting duress, that prevented it from accepting the Wolfs' payment. According to Martin Field, Marlton's president, the Wolfs' attorney told him that if Marlton enforced the agreement against the Wolfs, the Wolfs would deliberately resell the house to an "undesirable purchaser." A sale to an undesirable purchaser could depress the values of the other properties Marlton owned in that area. Marlton claims that the threat constituted duress and thus constituted a breach, entitling it to retain the Wolfs' initial deposit. (It's worth noting that the parties tried unsuccessfully to settle their dispute, but the Wolfs would agree to pay no more than $500 while Marlton insisted on $1000. Both parties apparently estimated their expected costs of litigation would be less than $500, or at least Marlton believed the expected benefits of winning and setting a favorable precedent were worth somewhere between $500 and $1000).

The court rules that, if the threat alleged was made (the trial court referred to it as a "so-called" threat, which leads the Superior Court to wonder whether the trial court unequivocally believed Field's testimony), and Field both believed the Wolfs would carry it out and feared the result would harm Marlton, the threat constitutes duress. It therefore remands on these three issues.

We begin discussion of this case by first confronting the pink elephant ignored in the courtroom: Precisely what did the Wolfs mean, and Field understand, by the term "undesirable purchaser?" Neither the record of the case nor our additional but very limited efforts to research the question provide a certain answer. But all those who have considered the question have surmised the obvious. The threat was probably to sell to a racial, ethnic, or religious minority. This raises the interesting question of whether the court's decision was, or should have been, affected by its view of the morality of the threatened act. The twist here is that, by contemporary lights, the act of selling a house to a minority, especially in a neighborhood where owners collude to exclude them, would presumably be viewed as morally commendable. Why then would a threat to do something morally commendable itself be impermissible in contract law? As it turns out, we think the court's reasoning provides a perfectly coherent doctrinal explanation for this result, though we believe that today a court would at the very least pause to condemn the very practice the Wolfs were threatening to violate (the practice of discriminating against minorities in real estate sales). We note, however, that one could argue that the court is aiding and abetting housing discrimination indirectly by excusing Marlton. By holding that a threat *not* to discriminate against minorities in a resale (really the threat was more than this— it was to affirmatively seek out a minority buyer) was grounds for holding the Wolfs in breach and freeing Marlton from the contract, the court appears implicitly to condone and support the practice of discrimination against minorities.

Although we come back to it at the end of the class discussion, we temporarily set this issue aside by asking students to suppose that the "undesirable purchaser" to whom the Wolfs were threatening to resell their property was a "Megan's Law" case— a convicted sex offender who has served his term. One could argue that such persons have an equal legal and moral right to be free from discrimination in real estate sales. But at least the argument for discrimination in such cases is on firmer ground than the argument for discriminating against minorities. The premise of Megan's law is that serious social science instruments have demonstrated that some sex offenders pose a serious risk of recidivism. That increased risk, proponents argue, justifies the requirement that the public be given various levels of notice (depending on the degree of risk) of the existence of such individuals in their community so that they can take reasonable precautions. In any event, once we substitute a convicted sex offender for a minority, students are more inclined to focus on the negative effect of the threatened resale on Marlton's business rather than the negative effect of the practice of discrimination against minorities. This allows us to direct attention to the duress analysis at the core of the case.

The court relies on a set of precedents that nicely lay out the elements of the duress defense. *Kroop* extends duress to cases of *threats* of physical coercion (threatening to cut the painting contractor's head off if he comes onto the premises constitutes duress). *Rubenstein* extends duress to cases where the threat is something other than to do physical harm. *Rubenstein* also introduces the state of mind test. It's not what's threatened, but what state of mind the threat induces that counts. But *Rubenstein* also notes that the threat must be wrongful as well– it's not enough that it has a coercive effect. The Williston quotation (*Contracts* § 1606) locates the difference between a hard bargain and an impermissible threat as turning on the wrongfulness of the threat, underscoring *Rubenstein's* point that state of mind alone will not suffice to determine duress. *Miller* shows that a threat can be wrongful even if not illegal– a morally wrongful threat will do for duress. You might think the moral wrongfulness of a threat is determined by the wrongfulness of the action threatened. But *Hochman* shows a threat can be wrongful if *either* the act threatened is wrongful or the threat is made for an immoral ("outrageous") *purpose*. Thus, the *Wolf* court holds that the Wolfs subjected Marlton to duress if the threat was morally wrongful (because made for an immoral purpose) and overcame Field's will. Thus, if the threat alleged was made "for the sole purpose of injuring the builder's business" (p. 409), it is a wrongful threat.

This last point is the key to explaining why the court's analysis does not turn on the moral status of the act threatened– selling to an "undesirable purchaser." Even assuming that selling to an undesirable purchaser would be morally commendable (dropping the sex offender hypo and substituting the likely reference to minorities by that phrase), under the *Hochman* test the threat can be wrongful solely because it is made for a morally wrongful *purpose* ("malicious and unconscionable"; "for the sole purpose of injuring the builder's business").

The most plausible classification of this case under the Restatement's schema is R2d § 176(1(d) "the threat is a breach of the duty of good faith and fair dealing under a contract with the recipient"– viz. to escape liability under a valid agreement. The result can also be analyzed under § 176(2)(a) (putting aside for the moment the question of whether the resulting exchange was or was not on fair terms)– "the threatened act would harm the recipient and would not significantly benefit the party making the threat" since the *purpose* of the act is to injure Marlton's business, and the act was of no benefit to the Wolfs (they are not seeking to combat redlining, for example).

We save most of our theoretical analysis for the next two cases in this section, *Austin v. Loral* and *Post v. Jones*. But one could point out the relatively obvious autonomy and efficiency grounds for prohibiting threats made for the sole purpose of gaining release from contractual liability. They are designed purely to effect *ex post* redistributions of the contractual surplus, to reallocate risks already assigned and paid for by the parties. Giving them effect only undermines the parties' purpose in making the contract in the first place– to exchange reliable promises backed by the right of compensation. Thus, one can ask students whether, at the time of contracting, the Wolfs would have been willing to pay for the right to make such threats down the road. If such threats were permissible, the value of the contract would be severely reduced for Marlton. Its expected gain would reflect the risk that the Wolfs could use credible threats to harm Marlton in order to renegotiate a more favorable distribution for the Wolfs. At a minimum, Marlton would have charged much more for the house. At the extreme, the contract would be so unreliable that Marlton would have no reason to agree to it. Moreover, the Wolfs would then have an incentive to invest their time and energy in identifying effective threats solely for purposes of redistributing the agreed division of the contractual surplus. That activity would be wasteful because it is socially unproductive. Finally, because such threats are designed to undermine the agreed assignment of rights and risks under the contract, they contravene the autonomy goals served by contract. In short, such threats are efforts to subvert the parties commitments and thereby undermine the means for securing moral responsibility and for pursuing one's conception of the good by bargaining for reliable commitments that assist planning.

Austin Instrument v. Loral Corp. *(Page 410).* Austin was under contract to supply specialty parts to Loral as a subcontract for Loral's contract to supply radars to the Navy. During the time period that the contract covered, Loral won another government contract. Austin submitted a bid to provide parts under this new contract, but was told by Loral that it would be awarded the subcontract on only those parts for which it was the lowest bidder. Austin then informed Loral that unless Loral agreed to a price increase on the first contract (both retroactive on the parts already delivered and prospective on the parts to be delivered) and awarded Austin the subcontract for all of the parts required under the second contract, Austin would breach the first contract. Loral searched among its "approved vendors" list for other vendors from whom it could obtain the parts Austin had not yet delivered under the first contract. The only vendor that was able to estimate a time for performance stated that it could *commence* delivery in early October, but Loral needed parts to make its September and October delivery deadlines under its agreement with the government. Loral then agreed to Austin's demands.

After Austin had performed under both contracts, Loral sued Austin claiming it was entitled to recover the price increases under the first contract because it agreed to those increases under duress. (Note that Loral did not contest the validity of the second contract it awarded to Austin, even though the same threat that Loral claims induced it to agree to the price increase under the first contract also presumably induced it to agree to award Austin the second contract on all parts, whether or not Austin was the lowest bidder). The trial court rejected Loral's claim on the ground that it failed to prove it could not have obtained from other vendors the parts it needed to fulfill its contract with the Navy. The Appellate Division affirmed, but the Court of Appeals overturned the lower court ruling.

The Court of Appeals found economic duress existed if one party makes a wrongful threat to withhold goods due under a contract, the threatened party has no alternative supply, and the ordinary remedy for breach of contract would not be adequate. The bulk of the decision is devoted to the Court's explanation of its rejection of the trail court's conclusion that Loral failed to prove it lacked an alternative supply. But the more interesting questions are why Austin's threat was wrongful and why ordinary damages must be inadequate. Though the decision provides little analysis of these elements, they lie at the heart of the court's holding.

Pedagogy. Under R2d § 176(1)(d), a threat is improper if it is a breach of the duty of good faith and fair dealing under a contract with the recipient. Under R2d § 176(2)(a), a threat is improper if the resulting exchange is not on fair terms and the threatened act would harm the recipient and would not significantly benefit the party making the threat. So the question here is whether Austin's threat violates its duty of good faith under its contract with Loral, or alternatively, whether the renegotiated price is "not on fair terms" and Austin's breach would not significantly have benefitted it but would have harmed Loral.

Answering both of these questions requires the same analysis we used in Chapter 4, Section C to understand when courts would deem a modification to be in good faith and therefore enforceable under U.C.C. § 2-209 without additional consideration. A party does not necessarily act in bad faith when it informs its contractual partner that it no longer intends to perform. Indeed, both the common law and Code allow parties to anticipatorily repudiate agreements in order to trigger their partner's duty to mitigate (*see generally* Chapter 8). Similarly, the threatened act of breach is not itself morally wrong. Indeed, under the simple theory of efficient breach, the promisee fares no worse than if performance had occurred, and the promisor fares better. In our view, Austin's threat should constitute duress under precisely the same conditions that U.C.C. § 2-209 would find a modification in bad faith: When the promisor's motive is solely to extract a redistribution of the contractual surplus, rather than to avoid a performance that costs the promisor more than it benefits the promisee. The hypothetical test is whether the promisor would have refused to perform if the promisee had refused to modify the agreement (this test assumes there is no reputational benefit from refusing to perform by making subsequent threats more credible). If the promisor would have refused to perform without the modification, then presumably it is better-off paying damages than incurring the costs of performance.

Why then wouldn't the promisee simply sue and recover its damages rather than agreeing to a less profitable contract in order to induce the promisor to perform? The answer is that the promisee expects to be under-compensated either because the promisor is judgment-proof, the promisee's damages are difficult to prove (e.g., speculative), or contract damages are systematically under-compensatory (because of the American Attorney's Fee rule and statutory pre-judgment interest rates that are often below the market rate). It's also possible that promisees sometimes prefer to accommodate promisors in order to cultivate long-term contractual relationships. In these cases, the promisee is compensated for losses it sustains under the modified agreement by offsetting returns from benefits the promisor will provide to the promisee in the future (e.g., in the form of reduced future contract prices, enhanced flexibility favoring the promisee, and the like).

Ultimately, the question is whether *ex ante* the promisor would have wanted the power to agree to the modification in question. If the modification results from an attempt merely to reallocate the initial distribution of the contractual surplus, the promisor would not want the power to make the modification. These modifications are sought and made in bad faith. But if the modification results from an attempt to make performance preferable to breach for the promisor, then the promisee would want the power to make the modification. Without that power, the promisor would breach and the promisee would be worse off (for the reasons stated above).

Carrying this analysis over to *Austin*, the question is whether Austin would have performed if Loral lacked the power to make the modification Austin demanded. Or equivalently, would Loral have wanted the power to make such a modification or not? The classic example of a good faith modification occurs when exogenous events change the cost of performance to the promisor (e.g., in *Alaska Packers, supra page 384*, it is possible that the conditions for fishing were so much worse than the sailors had anticipated that performance was no longer worth the contract price). But here, the record provides no evidence of exogenous events that have changed the cost of performance to Austin. Instead, Austin appears to be taking advantage of Loral's contract-specific investment in Austin's performance in order to extract a re-division of the contractual surplus. This is the classic example of a bad faith modification. For the same reason, under a duress analysis courts should strike down such bad faith modifications on the ground that the promisee agreed to the modification under duress (i.e., the promisor's threat not to perform constituted duress). But on this analysis, courts should not strike down modifications that are made in good faith– when the promisor would breach rather perform under the original terms of the agreement.

Given the preceding analysis, if a promisee agrees to a modification even though damages would be fully compensatory, it might seem reasonable to infer that the promisee wants the modification to be enforced. This appears to be the intuition behind the requirement that a threat not to perform cannot constitute duress unless damages could not be expected to fully compensate the promisee. Simply put, if the promisee would not have been harmed by refusing the proposed modification and suing for damages if the promisor carried through on his threat of breach, the promisee's acceptance of the modification would appear to be uncoerced (and perhaps motivated by his long-term interests in accommodating his contractual partners rather than the avoidance of the threatened breach). Thus, in *Austin*, the court finds the prospect of Loral's reputational losses, which would result from its breaching its government contract, justified Loral in accepting Austin's modification and later disaffirming it after Austin had performed. Had Loral refused to accept Austin's modified terms and Austin carried through on its threat of breach (recall that Austin's threat was credible– Austin in fact had already breached by ceasing delivery after it proposed the modification and while Loral was searching for potential alternative suppliers), Loral would have had to breach its contract with the government by delivering late. As a result, its reputation with the government would have suffered. That element of its damages would be difficult to measure and therefore subject to under-compensation (again, even when there is no doubt the promisee suffered a particular kind of harm, courts generally will not attempt to compensate for that harm if doing so requires the court to speculate about the extent of that harm outside of fairly narrow objective parameters).

Unfortunately, there are two serious problems with this approach to the duress defense to modifications. First, the inadequacy-of-damages element presumes that expected damages are ordinarily fully compensatory, and only in special instances tend to be under-compensatory. For example, when the promisee's damages include speculative elements such as reputational losses, lost future profits, and opportunity costs that are difficult to value. But as we explained above, promisees will *always* expect to be under-compensated for breach damages in contract because damages are *systematically* under-compensatory. Second, even if we take the inadequacy-of damages element as courts interpret it (engaging in the fiction that expected damages are ordinarily fully compensatory), the resulting rule is both over- and under-inclusive: It has the perverse effect of allowing the duress defense in cases in which the promisor would be better off (*ex ante*) without it, and excluding the duress defense in cases in which the promisor would be better off with it (*ex ante*).[1]

The inadequacy-of-damages element of the duress defense invoked in *Austin* makes the basic mistake of taking the *ex post* perspective on duress. Of course, once Loral's gambit pays off by inducing Austin's performance, Loral has everything to gain and nothing to lose by disaffirming the modification. But the real question is what rule provides Austin the proper *ex ante* incentives. Having learned its lesson from the *Austin* court, next time round Austin would know the modification would not be enforced as long as Loral's losses from breach would include speculative components. Would this rule provide Austin with the appropriate incentives? The court's view seems to be that Loral most needs the duress defense when damages would be especially under-compensatory. Yet if Austin's threat of breach is non-strategic, this is precisely the circumstance under which Loral would benefit most by *having* the power to make a binding modification (and thus lacking the power to invoke the duress defense). Of course, if Austin's threat is purely strategic (which it appears to be in the actual case), then Loral is better off *not having* the power to make a binding modification (and thus having the power to invoke the duress defense). Although the court gets the result right in this case, it relies on the wrong rule in doing so. The bottom line is that the availability of the duress defense should turn not on whether damages are especially likely to be under-compensatory (indeed, damages are always expected to be under-compensatory), but rather on whether or not the promisor's threat of breach is strategic. The inadequacy-of-damages element is relevant only to the extent that it reliably operates as a screen for strategic behavior (and we doubt that it serves this function very well).

Post v. Jones *(Page 413).* The plaintiff's whaling ship (the *Richmond*) ran aground near Behring's Straits in the Arctic ocean just two to three weeks before ice would make the waters unnavigable and five thousand miles from the nearest port of safety (the Sandwich Islands). The defendants, operators of other whaling ships (the *Frith*, the *Panama*, and the *Junior*), agreed to salvage the oil and save the men, but required that the oil be auctioned off. At this auction (held on

---

[1]It allows the duress defense when breach would impose speculative harms on promisees, even though promisees in these circumstances would benefit from making enforceable modifications (i.e., when exogenous events have made breach preferable to performance for the promisor). And it denies the duress defense when breach would not impose speculative harms on promisees, even though promisees in these circumstances would benefit if they lacked the power to make enforceable modifications (i.e., when no exogenous event has caused the promisor to prefer breach over performance, so the promisor would make a purely strategic threat to breach only if the promisee has the power to modify their agreement).

the boats), the defendants purchased the oil at very low cost. The owners of the *Richmond* claimed this sale was made under duress, and the court agreed, holding that the defendants had taken advantage of their position to force an unreasonable bargain.

Post is one of the few 19th century duress cases that still exerts influence today. It provides a vivid context for exploring the relationship between markets, efficiency, and duress. Our first objective is to contrast an *ex post* with an *ex ante* perspective on this case. *Ex post*, it is tempting to focus exclusively on whether the bargain extracted conforms to some *a priori* notions of fairness. The most natural benchmark for a fair bargain is the value the owners of the *Richmond* would have received for its oil (and whale bones and ship's tackle) in a robust market in the same circumstances. Thus, the test might be what price the *Frith*, *Panama*, and *Junior* would have had to pay for the *Richmond's* cargo had the demand exceeded the supply at the wreckage site. That is, suppose that the *Frith*, *Panama*, and *Junior* were empty of cargo, so that none of them would be filled even if it took on board all of the *Richmond's* cargo. In this circumstance, a genuine auction for the oil (without collusion) would produce a price reflective of its value to those ships. The actual auction held seems unfair because it was held in the absence of a competitive market for the oil– because each could take its complete fill without diminishing the others' ability to do the same, the *Frith*, *Panama*, and *Junior* (the only potential buyers) were not required to compete for the *Richmond's* cargo. (Economists would say that the *Post* case is one of a time-sensitive, bilateral monopoly). Clearly, the actual value of the whale oil to these ships exceeded the price they paid. Its actual value would reflect the saved costs of the additional whaling that would have been necessary had the ships not taken on the *Richmond's* oil, in addition to the value of eliminating the risk of failing to harvest more whales and/or succumbing to injury or disaster at sea during the additional days each ship would have spent whaling at sea. In short, the value of whale oil harvested by the *Richmond* equals the sum of expected costs associated with harvesting that amount of whale oil at the time the *Frith*, *Panama*, and *Junior* came across the grounded *Richmond*.

The *ex ante* perspective on *Post*, however, asks how the rule resolving the case will affect the incentives of ships in the future. The rule will affect the incentives for salvage: the incentives for ships like the *Frith*, *Panama*, and *Junior* to search for and salvage cargo from ships like the *Richmond*. But it will also affect the incentives for taking precautions: the incentives for ships like the *Richmond* to avoid running aground. If the price for salvage is not discounted at all (i.e., the salvager has to pay full market price upon salvaging), at best ships will be indifferent between acquiring their cargo through whaling or through salvage. At worst, they will prefer whaling to salvaging. From an efficiency perspective, this result is undesirable because fails to induce waste avoidance. Once whale oil has been harvested, it is inefficient to let the oil waste and for other ships to incur the costs of harvesting an equivalent amount of oil (because it both depletes total natural resources and occasions avoidable costs– the expected costs of the whaling that could have been avoided by salvage).

On the other hand, discounting the price of salvage too steeply will inefficiently distort the market for salvage and the incentives for precautions. Too much effort will be devoted to salvaging (too many tugs at sea) and too many precautions will be taken against wrecking a ship (too many *Richmonds* running aground). In short, competitive market prices assure optimal incentives for investing in salvage and in taking precautions to avoid calamity at sea. When prices are set by a court or by statute, instead of by competitive markets, the socially optimal incentives may be distorted. In theory, the price should be just low enough to make salvage mildly preferable to whaling, but no lower. Operationalizing that goal into a real legal rule, however, is easier said than done.

C. Fraud
Willful and Negligent Misrepresentation

Spiess v. Brandt *(Page 426)*. In this case, the plaintiffs bought a resort from the defendants but sought to rescind the contract because of allegedly fraudulent misrepresentations by the defendants. The trial court ruled for the plaintiffs on the ground that the defendants knowingly made false statements regarding both the past profits and the future profitability of their property. The Supreme Court found that the defendants' statement that "they were making good money out of the resort" was a material, fraudulent misrepresentation, that the plaintiffs relied on this misrepresentation, and that their reliance was reasonable. It was reasonable because the falsity of the claim was not obvious, the plaintiffs' efforts to investigate were thwarted by the defendants, and the plaintiffs were young and inexperienced. Although the court held that the defendants' knew that they were misrepresenting their past profits (and that such an inference could be drawn from the fact that they persistently refused to allow the plaintiffs to inspect their books), the court held that their false statement of past profits would constitute a fraudulent misrepresentation whether made knowingly or not– a bad motive is not a necessary element of fraud.

Justice Peterson dissents on the ground that plaintiffs did not rely on the misrepresentation because they had already made an offer for $90,000 *before* the defendants made the misrepresentation. After the misrepresentation, the parties agreed on a purchase price of $95,000, less than six percent over the original offer and insufficient, in J. Peterson's view, to ground a claim of fraud. Further, Justice Peterson argues that the plaintiffs were young but not inexperienced.

Justice Gallagher's dissent agrees with Justice Peterson that an agreement cannot be rescinded for a fraudulent misrepresentation made after an initial offer for substantially all of the ultimate purchase price. Justice Gallagher also appears to deny that the Spiess' reliance was reasonable by noting that once the Brandts failed to produce the books to confirm their statements of past profitability, "there was nothing to prevent the plaintiffs from refusing to proceed with the transaction." (p. 432) Justice Gallagher agrees with Justice Peterson that the Spiess were not inexperienced and asserts the transaction was at arm's length. Finally, Justice Gallagher appears to deny that the Brandts' statement of past profitability was false. Instead, the alleged past losses "may be largely explained by the extensive capital expenditures made by [the Brandts] in improving the resort." (p. 433)

Danann Realty Corp v. Harris *(Page 433)*. The plaintiff purchased a lease from the defendant. The contract contained a clause stating that the defendant did not make any representations about the property, and that the plaintiff both agreed to take the property "as is" and had not relied on any statement or representation made by the defendant. However, upon discovering problems with the property, the plaintiff brought suit, alleging that the defendant made fraudulent representations about the operating expenses for the property and that the plaintiff relied on those representations. The majority held for the defendant on the ground that the plaintiff was estopped from alleging fraud because he had in the contract expressly "acknowledg[ed] that no such representations have been made, and . . . that neither party rel[ied] upon any statement or representation, not embodied in [the] contract, made by the other party" (p. 434).

The court first distinguished this case from one in which the plaintiff signs an omnibus clause stipulating that the seller made no representations and the buyer did not rely on any representations. The specificity of the disclaimer and the commercial sophistication of the parties in this case rendered the disclaimer enforceable. The court also distinguished a contrary line of cases allowing plaintiffs to claim fraud in the teeth of similar disclaimer clauses on the ground that the facts misrepresented in those cases "were matters peculiarly within the defendant's knowledge." (p. 435) In contrast, when the plaintiff, as in this case, could have discovered the falsity of the misrepresentations by the exercise of ordinary care, such clauses will be enforced. Any other rule, according to the court, would undermine the ability of businessmen "dealing at arm's length to agree that the buyer is not buying in reliance on any representations of the seller as to a particular fact." (p. 436) Finally, because the plaintiff itself represented in the contract that it was not relying on specific representations not in the written agreement, by bringing the fraud claim the plaintiff then concedes it deliberately misrepresented its intentions in the contract. Thus, the court claims that permitting the plaintiff to bring the fraud claim would be to condone *plaintiff's* express misrepresentation.

Justice Fuld in dissent argues first that a seller cannot insulate itself against a claim of fraud by fraudulently inducing its buyer to sign an agreement in which the buyer in effect waives its right to claim fraud (typically, by stating that it has not relied on any representations not in the writing and that seller has not made any representations not in the writing). Second, he argues, citing *Bates v. Southgate*, that even a *knowing* (and presumably therefore *nonfraudulently* induced) express agreement that no representations have been made should not be enforced if material misrepresentations were made and in fact induced a party to enter into the agreement. Third, he claims that the disclaimer in this case is general rather than particular because it subsumes every conceivable misrepresentation. Moreover, whether particular or general, he argues that the principle underlying the precedents that refuse to enforce such clauses applies to both particular and general disclaimers. Fourth, Justice Fuld argues that the only legitimate purpose such clauses might serve is to save an innocent party the expense and annoyance of disproving an allegation of fraud in court. But, he argues, the value of saving an innocent seller the costs of defending against fraud is outweighed by the right of judicial redress for genuine victims of fraud. Indeed, Justice Fuld argues, even the unscrupulous person "should have his day in court." (p. 439) Finally, Justice Fuld maintains that because the plaintiff's representations that the seller had not made any representations "were false to defendant's knowledge," the defendant could not have relied on the plaintiff's (mis)representations. Thus, under principles of equity, the plaintiff is not estopped from alleging a fraudulent misrepresentation against the seller. Equitable estoppel is meant to protect an innocent party's reliance on another's misrepresentations; it is not meant to protect a fraudulent party's reliance on a clause designed to allow it to commit fraud with impunity.

***Pedagogy and Theory on* Spiess *and* Dannan.** *Spiess* provides a nice, if brief, introduction to the doctrinal distinctions between fraudulent misrepresentation, fraudulent concealment, and the duty to disclose, even though the Supreme Court's ruling considers only the first of these claims. Among the statements the trial court considered, only the one considered by the Supreme Court could, standing alone, in principle support an action for fraudulent misrepresentation. Statements that amount to predictions about future value are rarely actionable unless based on statements about past material facts. Even then, it is the latter that form that basis for liability. The rule here mirrors the common law and Code decisional law on express warranties according to which statements regarding future performance do not become a "basis of the bargain" but are "mere opinion or commendation" (i.e., "puffery"). *See e.g.,* U.C.C. § 2-313. The *Spiess* court seizes on statements about past profits made by the Brandts that the court concludes were known to be false when made, thereby placing them squarely within the fraudulent misrepresentation doctrine. Similarly, in *Dannan*, the court considered whether to reverse the trial court's grant of a motion to dismiss based on an allegation of material misrepresentation of past profits and operating expenses. Thus, neither case reaches the question of whether a party had a duty to disclose. And neither focuses centrally on the doctrine of fraudulent concealment (although the court seems at times to treat the Brandts as if they fraudulently concealed evidence of the falsity of their representations by denying the Spiess' access to their books).

The issues in these cases, therefore, concern the doctrine and policy of the most straightforward of fraud doctrines– fraudulent and material misrepresentation. As a general matter, liability for knowing fraud is not difficult to justify. Both economic and autonomy theories have little difficulty explaining and justifying this doctrine. No useful purpose is served by allowing people to lie to induce others to contract with them. A rule permitting lies would undermine confidence that transactions transfer resources to higher valued uses, increase the costs of entering into such agreements, and create incentives to engage in socially wasteful activities designed to facilitate and effectuate lying. On many autonomy theories, lying directly violates the recipient's autonomy by violating their trust (see Charles Fried's *Contract as Promise*). However, a stringent libertarian might argue that while lying may be morally wrong, an autonomous individual must take responsibility for verifying and relying on the representations of others. In other words, caveat emptor might be consistent with some brands of autonomy.

When we discuss these cases, we begin by discussing the courts' analyses of the various elements in a fraud recovery. In *Spiess*, one could begin by considering whether the alleged misrepresentation was in fact false. Consider ***Note 1(b) on Page 441***, in which we raise Justice Peterson's claim that the Brandts' representation might well have been true, despite the claim that accounting records show net losses in 1946. In this era of Enron and WorldCom accounting scandals, it bears emphasizing that the truth about profits is not always clear-cut, and at the very least, is a matter of accounting conventions and practices rather than undebatable and transparent truths. Justice Peterson's claim here appears to be that the Brandts' representations were false only if the property's 1946 revenues that were reinvested in the property are treated as "expenses." If they are expenses, they are costs of running the business in that year and must be netted out of revenues to determine whether a profit was made. But if the same reinvested revenues were classified as "capital improvements," the year would have shown an accounting profit. Same facts on the ground, different accounting conventions, different result on fraud. For this reason, many parties avoid pricing contracts based on profits. But if the truth of value statements in sales contexts turns on the extent of alleged profits, there is no avoiding resting liability for fraud on the sometimes uncertain conventions of accounting practices.

The most pressing issue these cases present, however, is not whether a misrepresentation occurred, let alone the more basic question of whether the law ought to prohibit lying that induces agreement, but the conditions under which a party can avoid a contract based on a fraudulent misrepresentation. The more interesting questions concern the precise contours of the fraud doctrines. Although it is possible to cover this material without a deep foray into the R2d, it may be worthwhile to review some of the relevant provisions. R2d § 164 sets out the conditions under which misrepresentation makes a contract voidable, § 159 defines misrepresentation, and § 162 distinguishes between fraudulent and material misrepresentations. Section 164 makes a contract voidable by a party that receives *either* a fraudulent (knowing) misrepresentation *or* a material misrepresentation (not necessarily knowing, but one that would be expected to induce reliance by a reasonable person and/or by the recipient). In either case,   § 164 requires that the misrepresentation actually induce the recipient's manifestation of assent. Three points are thus worth emphasizing. First, the Restatement (Second) allows a party to void a contract even if the misrepresentation is unknowing and thus "innocent." Although the Restatement (Second) states the rule unequivocally, the case law is far from clear that there is liability in fraud for innocent misrepresentation. (And, as we discuss below, such misrepresentations may nonetheless give rise to *warranty* liability). Second, fraudulent or "knowing" misrepresentation ("knowing" is used here to stand for the states of mind described in § 162(1)(a), (b), and (c)) makes a contract voidable even if it would *not* be expected to induce reliance by either a reasonable person or the recipient– that is, even if it is *not* material as defined under § 162(2). Finally, there is no liability for misrepresentation of any sort unless it *in fact* induces reliance (§164). This last point – the reliance requirement – provides the principal focus for our central analysis of *Spiess* and *Dannan*, although the materiality requirement also comes into play.

The misrepresentation doctrine requires that the recipient *justifiably rely* on the misrepresentation in order to avoid the contract. The court in *Spiess* notes that the Spiess went through with the deal without insisting that the Brandts follow through on their request to verify past profits by examining the books. One might argue the Spiess did not intend to rely on the Brandts' representation because they asked to see the Brandts' books to verify the representation. But given that they went through with the purchase without receiving access to the books, the argument is stronger that they relied on the statements than it would have been had they been allowed to conduct their own inspection. But is it "justifiable" to rely on such a representation as the basis for purchasing an expensive commercial property and to conclude the sale without ever examining the books? Here § 169(a) provides a response: "To the extent that an assertion is one of opinion only, the recipient is not justified in relying on it unless the recipient stands in a relationship of trust and confidence. . . ." It follows that, if the misrepresentation is one of fact, even if not one on which reasonable people would rely without investigation, the special relationship of trust and confidence between the Speiss and Brandts answers that objection. Finally, one could argue, with both dissents, that the Spiess did not rely on the misrepresentations because they had already made an initial offer (for $90,000, $5000 less than the ultimate purchase price) before they received the misrepresentation of past profits. The court is inclined to find reliance because of the perceived disparity in maturity and experience between the Spiess and the Brandts.

Conceding the disparity exists, despite the dissents' claim to the contrary, it makes sense that reliance on a fraudulent misrepresentation should be easier to prove when inexperienced parties deal with experienced ones. The former will more naturally be inclined to seek and rely on representations from the latter. Again, fraudulent misrepresentation parallels warranty doctrine in which courts are most likely to construe as warranties statements made by experienced parties to inexperienced parties. Both doctrines appropriately presume that the same statements would be intended and interpreted differently by experienced and inexperienced parties.

If we set aside the fact that the Spiess made a substantial offer before receiving the misrepresentation, it's instructive to ask whether the Spiess would have been able to satisfy the reliance requirement had the Brandts made the same (mis)representation to the Spiess but allowed the Spiess to examine their books to verify the Brandts' claims. This fact alone would seem to diminish the Spiess' actual reliance claim. R2d § 167, com. b provides some help:

> The extent of a party's investigation also bears on the question of causation. If he relies solely on his investigation and not on the misrepresentation, he is not entitled to relief. One who makes an investigation will often be taken to rely on it alone as to all facts disclosed to him in the course of it. On the other hand, if the fact is not one that the investigation disclosed or would have been likely to disclose, the recipient may still be relying on the misrepresentation as well as on the investigation. Particularly when the investigation produces results that tend to confirm the misrepresentation but are still somewhat inconclusive, it may be found that the recipient relied on both and that he attached importance to the truth of the misrepresentation.

If the Spiess had confirmed the Brandts' statements, then courts will be inclined to presume the Spiess relied exclusively on their own investigation, notwithstanding the Brandts' statements. If the statement turns out to have been an intentional (fraudulent) misrepresentation, the Spiess would nevertheless be unable to rescind because they could not satisfy the actual reliance requirement. We wonder whether this rule makes sense. Why require actual reliance to avoid a contract on the basis of fraudulent misrepresentation? On some moral theories, perhaps the rule "no harm, no foul" applies (just as we treat attempts as lesser offenses than completed crimes). But there seems to be an equally powerful moral intuition that moral luck – whether or not the lie happened to cause harm – ought not make a difference in how we treat the wrongdoer. From an economic perspective, there seems to be little reason to withhold disincentives for engaging in intentional misrepresentation. Why not deter it by providing even a non-relying recipient the option of rescission if the recipient can prove the other party lied? Or put as a doctrinal proposal, why not conclusively presume reliance for intentional misrepresentation (and thus make it irrelevant whether the recipient conducted its own investigation)?

But even if the Spiess could not prove actual reliance to recover in fraud, they might follow *CBS v. Ziff-Davis Publishing*, described and reproduced in part in *Note 1(a) on page 440*. In that case, ZD made false representations to CBS, but CBS conducted its own investigation and concluded the representations were *false*. But CBS nonetheless went through with the transactions. The court in *Ziff-Davis* held that the false representations amounted to express warranties, which, with respect to sales of goods, become part of an agreement (i.e., are treated as a "basis of the bargain") even if the buyer cannot prove it relied on them. (Consider UCC § 2-313, com. 3: "In actual practice affirmations of fact made by the seller about the goods during a bargain are regarded as part of the description of those goods; *hence, no particular reliance on such statements need be shown in order to weave them into the fabric of the agreement*. Rather, any fact which is to take such affirmations, once made, out of the agreement requires clear affirmative proof.") Thus, *Ziff-Davis* illustrates that even if a party does not rely on a misrepresentation by assenting based on the belief that it is true, and so cannot recover for fraud, that party may nonetheless recover on a breach of warranty theory. For such claims, the reliance requirement is automatically satisfied for *any* representation a party makes that fairly can be described as part of the bargain– i.e., a promise that the representation is true. Even if the recipient disbelieves and attempts to disprove the representation *before* entering into the agreement, the recipient relies on the representation, for purposes of a warranty action, simply by entering the agreement. The representation is treated as a warranty *guaranteeing* the existence of the fact represented. Thus, the representation induces agreement not by convincing the recipient that the representation is true but by promising in effect to indemnify the recipient against any losses caused if the representation turns out to be false.[2]

The *Ziff-Davis* result is relatively easy to reach because CBS *disbelieved* ZD's statement after it conducting its own investigation and went through with the deal anyway. That strongly suggests reliance on the statement as a warranty. But what if CBS had investigated and *confirmed* ZD's statement? Would that make it more difficult to treat ZD's statement as a warranty? Although the question of whether a warranty exists is theoretically independent of whether a party relied on it, we suspect that the court would be more inclined to treat the statement as a warranty if CBS clearly relied on it (as in the real case) than if it was less clear that CBS relied on it (as in the present hypothetical). But if CBS's investigation was less than conclusive, the court would again presume reliance (recall R2d 167, com. b above). In any event, once it becomes plausible to suppose a statement amounts to a warranty, the reliance requirement is at least doctrinally less important. But if a warranty claim cannot be made out, we are left with the fraud actions which require actual reliance, which courts will be less inclined to presume than in the warranty context.

Ziff-Davis raises the distinction between reliance on a fraudulent misrepresentation, in which the recipient is induced to assent because it believes the truth of the statement asserted, and reliance on a warranty, in which the recipient needn't believe the truth of the statement asserted, but is

---

[2]Because a breach of warranty action is premised on the claim that the agreement containing the warranty is valid, it supports a damages award rather than rescission. Because a fraud action is premised on the claim that the agreement is invalid because induced by fraud, it grounds rescission, sometimes coupled with a restitutionary award, rather than damages. Although some courts have not let such doctrinal and conceptual logic prevent them from awarding damages in a rescission action, most require that the recipient of misrepresentations choose to disaffirm the contract and seek rescission, or to affirm the contract and seek damages, effectively transforming the misrepresentation into a warranty.

induced to assent based on the belief that the statement constitutes a promise (i.e., a guarantee) to indemnify the recipient from harm if the statement turns out to be false. *Dannan* raises another complexity in the reliance requirement: Does A's affirmative representation at the time of agreement that it neither received nor relied on any representations from B estop A from bringing a fraudulent misrepresentation action to avoid the contract, even if it can prove that it in fact received and relied on a fraudulent misrepresentation from A? The majority answers "yes;" the dissent answers "no."

There appears to be a doctrinal anomaly presented when courts are asked to enforce these clauses in the teeth of clear proof of intentional fraud and actual reliance. The nub of the problem is that the buyer's fraud claim can be barred only by application of the principle of equitable estoppel (i.e., on the ground that the buyer claiming the fraud is bound by its previous representation that it did not receive or rely on a representation by the seller). Yet if the buyer can prove that it did receive and rely on seller's representation, contrary to its own representation, then by estopping the buyer from bringing the fraud claim equity has the effect of allowing the seller to perpetrate fraud– the very evil equity seeks to prevent. On the other hand, by allowing the fraud claim to proceed, the court is also holding the buyer harmless for its *own* fraudulent misrepresentation (namely, that it did not receive and rely on a misrepresentation when, by its own admission, at the time it made that representation it knew it to be false). This apparent anomaly might be solved along the lines suggested by the dissent: The seller can hardly be heard to complain that it relied on buyer's representation. First, it certainly can't claim to have relied on the truth of the buyer's representation, since by hypothesis, it knew the representation was false at the time the buyer made it. Second, the equity clean-hands doctrine would preclude it from relying on the representation in a warranty sense (the sense in which CBS relied on Ziff-Davis' representation): Equity can't enforce a clause in order to protect a party that relied on the clause to insulate it from liability from fraud, even though it knew the representation was false. (We have no similar misgiving when CBS relies on ZD's representation as a warranty even though CBS disbelieves it because CBS is not using the warranty to perpetrate a fraud).

Despite the dissent's persuasive interpretation of equity doctrine, as a policy matter, we believe such clauses should be enforced when included in agreements between commercially sophisticated parties. Even the dissent acknowledges the legitimate purposes such clauses serve, as the court in *Ganley* recognized: "It may be desirable in dealing with unscrupulous persons to have this clause as a shield against wrongful charges of fraud." (p. 438) The suppressed premise in the dissent's equity argument against enforcing the *Dannan* clause is that the equity of enforcement should be determined *ex post*– from the point of view taken after the contract is formed and a controversy comes to court. But from an *ex ante* perspective, it's hard to see why sophisticated parties should be barred from agreeing to hold each other harmless for fraudulent misrepresentations. The point of the such agreements is not to encourage fraud, but to reduce the expected costs of adjudicating and enforcing the agreement. Given that both parties are on notice before they enter into the agreement that they have waived their right to bring a fraud claim against each other, what autonomy or economic grounds are there for objecting to the clause, even if one party can prove that it relied on the fraudulent misrepresentation of the other? Both parties have voluntarily increased their risk of fraud in exchange for a greater contractual value. Imposing the consequences of their agreement in taking such a risk is consistent with recognizing their autonomy. And of course, efficiency supports enforcement of terms believed by both parties to maximize the joint value of their contract ex ante. Here, even though such an agreement would lead the parties to take greater precautions against fraud, they presumably believe that the additional costs of those precautions would be outweighed by the reduction in the expected costs of enforcing their agreement.

Unfortunately, equitable principles have evolved from the ex post perspective in adjudication and so leave little room for enforcing these clauses. The majority in *Dannan*, however, manages to stave off the force of the ex post perspective of equity the dissent presents by insisting on the priority of the ex ante perspective: "to hold otherwise would be to say that it is impossible for two businessmen dealing at arm's length to agree that the buyer is not buying in reliance on any representations of the seller as to a particular fact." (p. 436)

Notes 1 and 2 (Pages 440-442). Notes 1 and 2 provide a series of questions that raise some of the core issues discussed above.

Problems (Page 444). a. In *Kinkade v. Markus*, the court held that the petition for rescission should be granted. The statements by Kinkade that there was "*plenty* of water and it is *good* water" was a knowingly false representation upon which the Markus' relied. The fact about which the representation was made was material since the Markus' intended to raise livestock and grow a garden.

b. In *Gardner v. Meiling*, the appeals court reversed the trial court's grant of rescission. The court held that the purchaser was not entitled to rescission based on the claim of fraudulent representation about the income of the tavern because there was no reliance on this representation (the representation was made after the contract arose). Also, the court rejected the purchaser's claim of fraudulent representation as to valuable good will because there was insufficient evidence that such a claim was made. The evidence offered by the purchaser only went to the fact of a bad reputation, and not that the seller made a representation as to reputation. Finally, the court rejected the purchaser's plea for rescission based on unilateral mistake as to the value of the tavern because there was no indication that the seller knew that the purchaser might have erred in his valuation of the business.

Duty to Read

Merit Music Service v. Sonneborn *(Page 446)*. The plaintiff loaned the defendants money as part of an contract in which the plaintiff agreed to install games in the defendants' bar and the defendants agreed to pay a guaranteed minimum from those machines for a period of years. The defendants claimed that they did not agree to the guarantee term because they hadn't read the final version of the agreement they before signing it. In holding for the plaintiffs, the court said that a party to an agreement is not excused from enforcement of it by virtue of not having read the document.

Birmingham Television Corp. v. Water Works *(Page 452)*. The plaintiff bailed property with the defendant, a storage company. The property was damaged and the plaintiff sued. The defendant asserted that the bailment agreement contained a nine month time limit on bringing damage claims under the agreement. The lower court ruled in favor of the bailee on summary judgment. The Alabama Supreme Court reversed the lower court, holding that "a genuine issue of fact exists as to whether the terms on the reverse side of the warehouse receipt were accepted by the appellant-bailor and thereby became a part of the contract of bailment." (p. 455) The court approved the standard in *Kravitz* according to which "the bailor, unless his attention is called to the fact that such conditions are intended as a part of the contract, is not charged with notice, where he has no actual knowledge, of provisions limiting liability which appear upon something not apparently related to the contract itself, or given to the bailor ostensibly for some other purpose." (p. 456)

Pedagogy. The rationale for the duty to read doctrine, set out from the perspective of both autonomy and efficiency theory in *Note 1 on page 457* is relatively straightforward. The presumption in favor of enforcement is strongest, of course, when applied to commercially sophisticated parties and weakest when applied to unsophisticated, non-commercial parties, especially ordinary consumers. Since the transaction in *Merit Music* was arm's length between merchants who had done multiple transactions with one another in the past and were represented by counsel, the court has little trouble holding the borrower to the terms of the written contract it signed. In *Birmingham Television*, the bailor is an ordinary consumer. The standard for applying the duty to read doctrine is appropriately much higher. As the cases move toward the consumer end of transactions, exceptions to the duty to read doctrine often overlap with concerns more familiar to the procedural unconscionability doctrine. Indeed, the *Birmingham Television* court is concerned with whether the bailor had reasonable notice that the bailment stub he received contained *any* contract terms on it, let alone limiting the bailee's liability. The tension between the duty to read doctrine and the substantive unconscionability doctrine is easily resolved in favor of the latter. The point of the duty to read doctrine is that individuals can and should be expected to read agreements before they sign them. However, if a reasonable person would not know of the existence of the terms because of their placement in the writing, or as in *Birmingham Television*, would not be expected to know even that their agreement was evidenced by *any* writing at all, no purpose would be served by treating them as if they had read and understood such terms. In short, the duty to read doctrine is not intended to facilitate fraud, but rather to facilitate transactions between reasonable people.

In fact, we suggest in *Note 6 on page 459* that the duty to read doctrine is probably best understood as an application of the standard objective theory of contract discussed in *Bailey, Lucy,* and *Leonard, supra* Chapter 1, and in R2d §§ 1 and 2. If a reasonable person would believe that a party's signature indicates that party's manifestation of intent to promise the terms specified in the writing signed, then that party will be deemed to have made that promise, whether or not that party in fact intended the promise manifested. A reasonable person would believe, of course, that a commercially sophisticated party would either read and understand all the terms of any agreement she signs, or intend to be bound by those terms even though she had not read or understood them. The same cannot always be said, however, for ordinary consumers, particularly when they sign standard form contracts that contain extensive legalistic language expressing unfamiliar concepts. In those instances, a case can be made that the content of these agreements should not be determined solely by the content of the writing, but that courts must police the content to insure that commercially sophisticated parties (typically repeat-player sellers who write the standard forms) do not take advantage of the common and cost-justified practice among consumers of neither reading nor understanding the majority of the terms written in standard form contracts. Again, the reasonableness standard from the objective theory grounds this result: If the reasonable, sophisticated seller would not expect consumers to read and understand all the terms of the writing the seller requires them to sign, then the fact that consumers sign cannot straightforwardedly be taken as a manifestation of their intent to agree to those terms. Instead, a reasonable seller would anticipate that consumers believe the terms they are signing conform to ordinary expectations.

Thus, courts enforce against consumers only reasonable terms in standard form contracts, not ones that fly in the face of ordinary expectations because they are atypically disadvantageous to the consumer. In some commercial buyer cases, the same argument could be made, but the standard for demonstrating the unreasonableness of the terms is much higher. Merchants wishing to bind consumers to atypical and/or particularly complex or unfamiliar terms therefore must do so by setting the terms out separately, explaining them, and having them signed separately from the general agreement. In other words, the duty to read doctrine just parallels the procedural unconscionability doctrine when it refuses to treat signatories as having read and understood, or having otherwise expressed an intention to be bound by, terms in a writing they signed.

For an analysis of more specific duty to read problems, **Notes 3 and 5 on pages 458-459** present the issues of language and illiteracy.

Disclosure and Concealment
In this final section on fraud, we move to far less firm doctrinal and theoretical terrain. Here the question is not how to define the conditions under which false statements will void an agreement, but rather if and when a failure to disclose will void an agreement (or if the agreement is affirmed, ground a claim to damages). We can begin with the distinction between non-disclosure and affirmative concealment. R2d §160 ("When Action Is Equivalent to an Assertion (Concealment)") states that "[a]ction intended or known to be likely to prevent another from learning a fact is equivalent to an assertion that the fact does not exist." R2d § 161, com. a explains that "[l]ike concealment, non-disclosure of a fact may be equivalent to a misrepresentation. Concealment necessarily involves an element of non-disclosure, but it is the act of preventing another from learning of a fact that is significant and this act is always equivalent to a misrepresentation (§ 160)." Because concealment requires affirmative action to prevent another from discovering a material fact, it is relatively easy to justify its prohibition. Most normative theories will justify rules discouraging expenditures of resources that serve only to suppress the flow of material information between contractual parties necessary to insure that transfers are mutually beneficial. Allowing such concealment would begin an "arms race" between contractual partners that would greatly increase the costs of transactions (and thereby waste resources toward a socially undesirable end– misinformation). For every measure of concealment permitted the seller, the buyer would have to take additional precautions in the form of more extensive inspections designed to counter strategic concealment. Sellers in turn would take more extensive concealment measures to undermine advanced inspections, and so forth. (Even the relatively austere, libertarian principles of caveat emptor only free the seller of any duty to assist the buyer in evaluating the sale– they do not permit

the seller to engage in undisclosed affirmative efforts to prevent the buyer's discovery of relevant information.)

As a normative matter, then, fraudulent concealment is a relatively easy case. But justifying the rules against non-disclosure is more difficult. Consider the rule governing nondisclosure: R2d § 161 (When Non-Disclosure Is Equivalent to an Assertion):

A person's non-disclosure of a fact known to him is equivalent to an assertion that the fact does not exist in the following cases only:

(a) where he knows that disclosure of the fact is necessary to prevent some previous assertion from being a misrepresentation or from being fraudulent or material.

(b) where he knows that disclosure of the fact would correct a mistake of the other party as to a basic assumption on which that party is making the contract and if non-disclosure of the fact amounts to a failure to act in good faith and in accordance with reasonable standards of fair dealing.

(c) where he knows that disclosure of the fact would correct a mistake of the other party as to the contents or effect of a writing, evidencing or embodying an agreement in whole or in part.

(d) where the other person is entitled to know the fact because of a relation of trust and confidence between them.

Section 161(a), (c), and (d) are relatively straightforward. Section 161(a) closes a loophole that would otherwise allow a party to effect a fraudulent or material misrepresentation under R2d § 164 by allowing a party not to correct a previous statement that the party believed to be true when made but subsequently learns is false. Under § 161(a), failing to disavow such statements is tantamount to making them while knowing them to be false. Section 161(c) establishes the categorical rule that there is an affirmative duty to correct a party who is mistaken about the content or effect of a writing. There is never a good reason for one party knowingly to take advantage of another party's mistaken belief about the content of the agreement they are forming. (Note, this does not mean that a party has an affirmative duty to insure their contracting partner has read and understood their written agreement. The duty to read doctrine still holds. However, if one party *knows* the other is making an incorrect assumption about the terms of their agreement, it has an affirmative duty to inform its partner of the mistake). Finally, § 161(d) states the standard and sensible rule that parties in a fiduciary relationship owe a special, affirmative duty to disclose facts when necessary to promote the interests they are legally bound to promote. Thus, while ordinary individuals have no duty to disclose information relevant to assessing the value of real estate (as *L & N Grove* confirms), Realtors have an obligation to disclose such information to their clients.

The locus of the doctrinal and theoretical debate is found in § 161(b). That section requires affirmative disclosure of any fact if failure to disclose that fact constitutes a failure to act in good faith and according to reasonable standards of fair dealing. Section 161, com. a makes clear that this section is not intended to create a general, affirmative disclosure obligation:

> Nondisclosure without concealment is equivalent to a misrepresentation only in special situations. A party making a contract is not expected to tell all that he knows to the other party, even if he knows that the other party lacks knowledge on some aspects of the transaction. His nondisclosure, as such, has no legal effect except in the situations enumerated in this Section. He may not, of course, tell half-truths and his assertion of only some of the facts without the inclusion of such additional matters as he knows or believes to be necessary to prevent it from being misleading is itself a misrepresentation.

Thus, the central challenge of the disclosure doctrine is to distinguish, under § 161(b), between cases in which good faith and reasonable standards of fair dealing require disclosure and those in which they do not.

Obde v. Schlemeyer *(Page 461).* The plaintiffs bought a termite-infested house from the defendants. They did not discover the infestation until after purchasing the house, perhaps in part because the defendants purchased a treatment from a pest control company that removed all visible signs from termites. According to the court, the defendants knew or should have known that this treatment might not have been successful in eradicating the termites. The court found that the defendants had a duty to disclose this information because it was manifestly dangerous and so latent as to not be readily discoverable by reasonable inspection.

We use *Obde* first to introduce the subtleties of distinguishing between fraudulent concealment and non-disclosure, and then to introduce an incentives-based theory of disclosure. The plaintiffs and the court view *Obde* as a case of fraudulent concealment, ostensibly because the effect of Senske's partial termite treatment was to eradicate all visible signs of termites: "[A]t the time of the sale . . ., the condition was clearly latent– not readily observable upon reasonable inspection. . . . [A]ll superficial or surface evidence of the condition had been removed by reason of the efforts of Senske, the pest control specialist." (p. 463) But what are the necessary elements in fraudulent concealment? Recall that R2d § 160 holds that "[a]ction intended or known to be likely to prevent another from learning a fact is equivalent to an assertion that the fact does not exist." Clearly, if the Schlemeyers hired Senske for the purpose of making discovery of termites more difficult for prospective buyers such as the *Obdes*, they engaged in concealment. But the court makes no explicit finding on whether the Schlemeyers intended the partial treatment of the termite problem to prevent future buyers from discovering the problem. Of course, even if that was not their intent, it is reasonable to hold that they knew (or should have known) that the partial treatment would have that effect.

But the Restatement doesn't tell us *when* such knowledge is to be determined. Suppose the Schlemeyers could have proved that they hadn't decided to sell their house until many months after Senske's termite treatment, and that they decided on partial treatment because they could not afford the full treatment and were willing to take the chance that the termites would return. Does the fact that their decision to undertake partial treatment of the termite problem was made prior to the contemplation of the sale of their home insulate them from the concealment charge? Or does the partial treatment constitute concealment because once they decided to sell, they knew or should have known that their past conduct, though innocently motivated when undertaken, would prevent prospective buyers from discovering the problem if it still existed? If so, then it would appear that when selling a used car, the owner would have a duty to disclose all prior maintenance on the vehicle that fell short of the maximum recommended repair, and yet would decrease the likelihood of prospective buyers discovering the problem requiring the repair.

This rule strikes us as improbable because it extends far beyond the easy justification for prohibiting concealment. If the point is to discourage parties from making affirmative investments in preventing the discovery of material information, there is no reason to deter parties from making investments not intended to prevent the discovery of such information. Indeed, the mere fact that a seller taking action knows that the action might prevent a prospective buyer from discovering a material fact should trigger the concealment rule only if the seller takes the action after it has decided to sell. Even though the action might have been taken for an innocent reason, the legal rule might reasonably presume an intent to deceive when the seller had already decided to sell and knew or should have known the action would have the effect of preventing prospective buyers from discovering material information. But the same inference would not be justified if the conduct was undertaken before a decision to sell had been made. A rule that treats such conduct as concealment even though undertaken independently of a sale context is over-inclusive and thus over-deters desirable conduct. Thus, if the Schlemeyers made their decision to undertake limited extermination efforts before they had decided to sell their house, that partial treatment should not be deemed to constitute concealment. If they have a duty to disclose the prior termite condition and their partial treatment of it, it should be on the independent ground that non-disclosure of the condition is affirmatively required of all sellers, quite apart from whether partial remediation measures have been taken in the past, rather than on the ground that the Schlemeyers concealed the termites.

Thus, there are two grounds for requiring disclosure. The first is that a party has engaged in concealment, which triggers an affirmative duty to disclose the facts concealed. The second is that a party is under an affirmative duty to disclosure certain facts under R2d §161(b). In our view, *Obde* is decided properly under the first ground only if we read the court as holding (implicitly) that the partial treatment was undertaken after the decision to sell was made.

Although the court explicitly holds the Schlemeyers liable based on fraudulent concealment ("Obdes were entitled to recover damages against the Schlemeyers upon the theory of fraudulent concealment"(p. 464)), the opinion's reasoning vacillates on whether the Schlemeyers are required to disclose the termite condition because they undertook the partial treatment measure, which constituted concealment, or because sellers are generally under the affirmative duty to disclose conditions such as termite infestation, which are difficult for prospective buyers to discover but are known to the sellers. At times, the court appears to be arguing for a general duty to disclose so-called latent conditions, not because the seller affirmatively concealed them, but because they are *in effect* "concealed" from the buyer (i.e., latent, but not as a result of seller's conduct) but known to the seller.

This seems to be the rule in *Perkins*: "Where there are concealed defects in demised premises, dangerous to the property, health or life of the tenant, which defects are known to the landlord when the lease is made, but unknown to the tenant, and which a careful examination on his part would not disclose, it is the landlord's duty to disclose them to the tenant before leasing, and his failure to do so amounts to a fraud." (p. 463) Clearly, *Perkins* sets out a simple rule requiring disclosure of latent defects known to the seller, and is not a fraudulent concealment rule requiring disclosure only if the defect becomes difficult to discover as a result of seller's affirmative efforts to conceal. The *Perkins* court's reference to "concealed defects" is a reference to latent defects, not defects concealed by affirmative efforts of the landlord. Similarly, the court cites the Keeton article for the proposition that "if either party to a contract of sale conceals or suppresses a material fact which he is in good faith bound to disclose then his silence is fraudulent." (p. 463) As Keeton uses the word, a party "conceals" when it fails to disclose what it is bound to disclose by good faith. (Note also the court's statement in *Reed v. King*: "'Concealment' is a term of art which includes mere nondisclosure when a party has a duty to disclose." (p. 465) But R2d § 160 uses concealment to refer to activity by a party that *generates* its duty to disclose. That is, Keeton's rule presumes that disclosure is required under the good faith standard, and describes failure to disclose as concealment, while R2d § 160 uses conduct constituting concealment as an independent ground for deciding that disclosure is required.

Thus, while *Obde* could be justified, consistent with the court's own statement of the holding, as a fraudulent concealment case under R2d § 160, the factual predicate for concealment in *Obde* is at best ambiguous in the decision as written (because the partial extermination measures might have taken place before the Schlemeyers decided to sell.) Alternatively, much of the court's reasoning seems instead to support a general duty to disclosure latent defects. While the case is easy to justify assuming real fraudulent concealment, it is much more difficult to justify as a general disclosure case.

If we assume the case is decided on the ground that sellers have a general duty to disclose termite conditions, it raises the question of how to interpret R2d § 161(b). Dean Kronman's classic article on mistake and non-disclosure discussed in ***Note 4 on page 476*** sets out an incentives-based approach to determining when disclosure should be required outside of concealment cases. Kronman argues that disclosure of material facts should be required unless disclosure would undermine the incentives for individuals to invest in acquiring the information at issue. Thus, his theory holds that only casually acquired – as opposed to deliberately acquired information – must be disclosed. Kronman uses the classic non-disclosure case of *Laidlaw v. Organ* to illustrate his theory. In *Laidlaw*, Girault (a merchant for Laidlaw & Co.) agreed to sell a large quantity of tobacco to Organ. On the date of the sale, Organ stumbled upon news (on a leaflet) that the War of 1812 had ended, and thus the market for U.S. tobacco was now much larger. Girault asked if there was any news that would enhance the price of tobacco, and Organ apparently did not respond. Girault went ahead with the sale, which was for less than half the market price. The court held that there was no duty to disclose here.

Unfortunately, *Laidlaw* provides a less-than-ideal illustration of Kronman's theory because the buyer (Organ), who was not required to disclose to his seller (Girault) the fact that the Treaty of Ghent had been signed, appears to have acquired his information casually (from a randomly distributed handbill– although Kronman conjectures he might have received the information from a network of valuable commercial "friendships"). Kronman handles this inconvenient fact by arguing that the disclosure rule must proceed by classifying case types, not particular cases. Here, Organ was a professional buyer of tobacco and thus should be presumed to deliberately invest in acquiring all information relevant to such purchases (e.g., market value of tobacco). That he happened upon the information in this particular case should change the rule that professional buyers of tobacco need not disclose information relevant to the quality and worth of tobacco. Otherwise, they would invest below the socially optimal level in acquiring that information.

Kroman's non-disclosure rule is, however, too narrow. As Trebilcock has persuasively argued, the general rationale of "bringing the information to market" justifies a more robust protection of market information. Consider the **Problems on page 475. Problem b** presents a case for non-disclosure. Here John has private information about market valuations and, if we are interested in having that information brought to the market, John's property rights in the information must be protected. Assume, however, that John's information was casually acquired. If John is under a duty to disclose the pipe's value because the information was not the product of a deliberate investment, he may well decline to offer to purchase any pipes from Mary, since he has nothing to gain by bringing the fact to Mary's attention. The pipe will remain underpriced and as a result is less likely to be transferred to its highest valued user. For example, an uninformed buyer might throw it away, while an informed buyer might place it in a museum collection. This result is consistent with Restatement §161(b) because, as *Illustration 7* suggests, market value conditions are not a mistake as to a "basic assumption" that requires correction under §161. (See comment b to §152: no mistake where the issue concerns endogenous factors).

On the other hand, consider **Problem c.** Here the issue is intentionally muddied by the fact that Mark waits for the owner to leave and the inexperienced clerk to take over before he buys the pipe. We think Mark should not be able to get away with this untoward behavior. The dominating issue is the duty to correct the pricing mistake of the clerk in order to reduce the costs of transacting by encouraging "double precautions at the margin;" that is, Mark has the comparative advantage (or "last clear chance") to prevent a loss owing to a mistake of fact. By encouraging him to do so, as well as encouraging the store owner to take reasonable precautions as well, the total costs from such mistakes can be reduced. Note that Mark does not have to disclose the private market information he possesses, merely the mistake itself (the pipe is in the wrong bin).

From an examination of the cases, it is tempting to advance a general rule allowing buyer non-disclosure but requiring seller disclosure in all cases. But in truth the disclosure analysis is symmetrical as between buyers and sellers. To advance both objectives, we would defend the principle that neither sellers nor buyers are required to disclose private information about market valuations unless, of course, they are in violation of the securities laws (see **Problem d**). By allowing parties to benefit from all information they possess, whether deliberately or casually acquired, this rule insures that all information that would affect price will be produced and disseminated into the market. On the other hand, the rule of Restatement § 161(b), requiring parties to correct latent material mistakes known to them and unknown to the other reduces unnecessary precaution costs that would result under a non-disclosure rule. The duty in this case is to correct the mistake, or risk being unable to profit from the transaction. It is *not* a duty to disclose the underlying private information on which the duty rests. This later point is consistent with the rules governing rescission for unilateral mistake under Restatement (Second) § 152. (See Chapter 8, infra).

The principle objection to such a regime is that it permits bad faith claims of rescission by parties alleging nondisclosure of material facts, when the real objective is to escape liability for independent reasons. To reduce strategic abuse of a disclosure rule such as §161(b), parties alleging mistake should have to bear the burden of proving that the other party knew of the mistake but failed to disclose it. To bear that burden, buyers may well require sellers to sign particularized disclosure statements (as is common in real estate transactions). If so, the default rule doesn't matter: With or without a rule requiring seller disclosure, the parties will bargain for express, particularized disclosure (either to overcome a rule that permits seller nondisclosure or to assist buyers in bearing the burden of proof under a rule that requires seller disclosure).

Thus, in *Obde*, we would argue the Schlemeyers should have an affirmative duty to disclose even if they are held not to have fraudulently concealed the termite condition. As owners of the house, they already have an efficient incentive to acquire and act on information in order to preserve and enhance the value of the house. That is, even if the Schlemeyers are required to disclose known termite problems, this will not deter them from paying for termite inspections (if they don't inspect, they risk losing the value of their asset). Moreover, a rule allowing nondisclosure in *Obde* will encourage buyers to conduct potentially redundant, and therefore wasteful, inspections. Alternatively, because, all else equal, owners have the comparative advantage in determining the value of their assets, buyers will bargain around a default rule allowing seller nondisclosure by requiring their sellers to sign general disclosure statements (as most states require in home purchases). Thus, the majoritarian default rule should save the parties costs of negotiating to the most preferred rule by directly requiring seller disclosure. Of course, if the parties would negotiate a particularized disclosure agreement in either case, the rule doesn't matter.

Reed v. King *(Page 464)*. The plaintiff purchased from the defendant a house in which gruesome murders had taken place. The defendant asked a neighbor to not disclose this fact to the buyer, but that issue is dismissed by the court as irrelevant because the complaint failed to allege that this request caused the buyer's ignorance of the house's history. The court held that there is an independent duty to disclose in this case and that the plaintiff can recover if she can show that the fact of the murders materially affects the value of the house.

It is worth noting, as the court reminds us, that in California the rule of caveat emptor had been long dead before this case was decided. *Footnote 11 on page 466* makes clear that California places a robust duty of disclosure on real estate sellers. *Reed* raises a novel question in California only because reputation is not ordinarily a material fact in real estate transactions. Unsurprisingly, this California court has little trouble imagining that it can be. Still, we believe that any court would concede that reputation can be material to market value generally, and certainly no less in real estate than elsewhere. The real question is not whether this fact is potentially material (although we agree that if it is not there is clearly no duty to disclose it), but whether the seller should have a duty to disclose it if it is material. The court's analysis here is, at a minimum, incomplete.

The court's opinion holds that any fact affecting the value of the house is material, but appears to concede that the seller must disclose only those material facts that buyer's reasonable inquiry would not reveal: "Murder is not such a common occurrence that *buyers* should be charged with anticipating and discovering this disquieting possibility. Accordingly, the fact is not one for which a duty of inquiry and discovery can sensibly be imposed upon the buyer." (p. 467) The trouble with this reasoning is that the murders could have affected market value only if they are relatively widely known to have taken place in that house. If they are, then why would this fact not be revealed by a reasonable inquiry? Shouldn't a reasonable inquiry turn up most, if not all, factors substantially contributing to a property's (known, current) market value? The court's mistake is to focus on the frequency of murders in houses generally (which one could be forgiven from anticipating), rather than on the fact that, assuming they are material, the murders, though unusual, could have affected the market value of the house only if they are generally known to have occurred in the house. Wouldn't a reasonable inquiry by the buyer be expected to discover either the current market valuation of a house, and/or the major factors contributing to the current market value of a house? Again, we believe a general disclosure rule in real estate transactions can be justified in principle on the ground that sellers in general have a comparative advantage over buyers in discovering relevant information, and will not be deterred from doing so by a disclosure rule. But the point here is that on the *court's* implicit view that sellers need not disclose facts that would be revealed by a reasonable inquiry, it's difficult to see why the seller should have the duty to disclose.

Note 2 (Page 473). In *Stambovsky v. Ackley*, the plaintiff bought from the defendant a house that was famous for being haunted. This fame was the result of the seller's promotion of the house as haunted. The plaintiff did not know of this reputation, but, upon finding out, sued for rescission. The court found in favor of the plaintiff. The case is fun to teach, if for no other reason, because the judge exercises absolutely no self-restraint in celebrating the fanciful facts of the case in what otherwise must be a very dry docket. On the merits, the case is a close analogue to *Reed*, although it might serve as a case for testing whether *Reed* depends on reasoning unique to California courts, or holds sway even in a state, such as New York, which is otherwise committed to caveat emptor in real estate transactions. *Stambovsky* considers the same question *Reed* considers, but the facts press the issue further: Is having a reputation for being haunted, as opposed to having been the site of multiple murders, material to the value of a house? *Stambovsky* answers in the affirmative for roughly the same reasons.

But on the question of whether the seller is under a duty to disclose a material fact, the reasoning of the cases differs. Recall that in *Reed* the court dismissed as causally irrelevant the fact that the seller asked a neighbor not to reveal the fact of the murders to the buyer. The duty to disclose was not predicated on any actions of the seller that contributed to buyer's ignorance of the material fact. In contrast, the court in *Stambovsky* emphasizes the fact that the seller intentionally created the house's reputation for being haunted. To be sure, creating a material fact is not equivalent to affirmatively concealing it, but the court in *Stambovsky* evidently believes the case for disclosure is stronger because the seller intentionally created the house's reputation for being haunted. The court seems to embrace an argument for disclosure by estoppel:

Defendant seller deliberately fostered the public belief that her home was possessed. Having undertaken to inform the public-at-large, to whom she has no legal relationship, about the supernatural occurrences on her property, she may be said to owe no less a duty to her contract vendee. . . . Where . . . the seller not only takes unfair advantage of the buyer's ignorance but has created and perpetuated a condition about which he is unlikely to even inquire, enforcement of the contract . . . is offensive to the court's sense of equity." (p. 475)

But as we argued in *Reed*, the fact that information was widely known – indeed, so widely known as to affect the market price of the house – argues against a duty to disclose because a reasonable inquiry should have turned up at least the market value of the house, even if it didn't turn up the rumor that it was haunted. In any case, it's difficult to see why seller's creating the rumor should affect the disclosure rule one way or the other.

L&N Grove v. Chapman *(Page 468)*. The plaintiff, Chapman, sold land to the defendants, referred to by the court as Curtis (the last name of husband and wife purchasers), that later became worth considerably more than the purchase price because of Disney's interest in buying it for a parking lot. The court finds that, at the time of the purchase, the defendant speculated that this would happen but did not share that information with the plaintiff. The court held that there was no duty to disclose this speculation. First, the information was mere speculation and based on publicly available information. Second, it would have been unreasonable for Chapman to rely on any representation or lack thereof by Curtis because they were both in the real estate business.

In broad outline, *Chapman* appears to be a good illustration of Dean Kronman's claim that parties need not disclose information deliberately acquired. Students often wonder, though, whether investing in information forecasts about the future value of real estate furthers allocative efficiency, or instead affects only distribution. That is, they wonder what benefit there is in letting Curtis reap the rewards of Disney's decision rather than Chapman– either way, they argue, the land will be put to its highest valued use, namely as a parking lot for Disney World. The question misses the mark because allocative efficiency is always advanced by impounding the potential future value of uses of land into its current price. To illustrate, had Curtis not purchased Chapman's land for $47,500 (at 150% of its then-market value), Chapman may have made costly and extensive investments in the soil to improve its use as grove. But those investments may not have been worthwhile if Chapman had properly taken into account the probability that Disney would have a superior use for the land in five years. Curtis' purchase avoids Chapman's potential waste. In short, uninformed decision-makers will inevitably make inefficient decisions about their assets. Allowing Curtis to benefit from superior information insures not only that assets will be put to their highest valued uses, but that investments in the assets value will be optimal. Note that this rationale for nondisclosure obtains even if Curtis acquired the information casually. The point is to insure that accurate information (including probabilities) is impounded in the market price of assets, in addition to providing efficient incentives to invest in information acquisition.

Unfortunately, the actual decision in *Chapman* provides little support for this reasoning. We can begin by clarifying that *Chapman* is not a trustee case (R2d 161(d)) because the court finds that Chapman was aware that Curtis was acting in his own capacity as principal rather than as Chapman's (seller's) broker. Instead, the court's decision rests largely on the premises that Chapman was equally sophisticated about Florida real estate and that Curtis did not have inside information but purchased the land as a speculation based on publicly available information. Both of these facts are relevant to an incentives-based disclosure regime, but they make the efficiency case for disclosure relatively *stronger*, not weaker. If Chapman was unaware of the true value of his real estate because he was not a real estate professional, or if Curtis had actual knowledge (insider or not) that the land would be purchased by Disney World for use as a parking lot, it would have been even more likely that investment decisions regarding the land would be more efficient if Curtis made them rather than Chapman. That is, the greater the difference in asset-specific knowledge between the parties, the weaker the case for disclosure: There is good reason to believe the asset will be put to a more efficient use in the hands of the buyer rather than the seller. The lesser the difference in asset-specific knowledge between the parties, the stronger the case for disclosure: There is little reason to believe the asset will be put to a more efficient use in the hands of the buyer rather than the seller.

The court's decision, however, evidently does not rest on this efficiency rationale. The court implicitly believes that the parties' equal sophistication and knowledge cut in favor of disclosure because the disclosure rules should promote so-called fairness goals such as "a level playing field" and "no unfair advantage-taking." The playing field would not be level if Curtis were sophisticated and Chapman naive. In that case, the *Chapman* court presumably would treat their relationship as quasi-fiduciary. Similarly, if Curtis had access to "inside information" that was not publicly available, he would be taking unfair advantage of Chapman. We find these notions uncompelling only because once the disclosure regime is announced, the resulting bargains reflect these risks. Sellers would be on notice that buyers need not disclose material facts, even if the seller has the information because of its relative experience or access to inside information. They would therefore take appropriate precautions, such as hiring consultants to evaluate the worth of their property (which would presumably be socially desirable) or taking contractual precautions by requiring buyers to sign disclosure statements. Of course, inexperienced sellers that are not only factually ignorant but *legally* ignorant would need more protection. Hence, if Chapman were legally naive, and labored under the misimpression that Curtis had a duty of disclosure in this case, the default rule might require disclosure in the absence of agreement to the contrary in order to force legally sophisticated parties such as Curtis to disclose the legal rule to legally naive parties. But *Chapman* is not such a case because Chapman was as legally sophisticated as Curtis.

Problems (Page 475). a. Under a strict reading of §161(b) the buyers should be allowed to back out of the deal. The sellers failed to correct a mistake as to a basic assumption. Since they knew it was important to the buyers, they had a duty to disclose it. Imposing upon them a duty to disclose will not decrease homeowner activity in the acquisition of this information since it requires no effort from them. However, there are problems with this analysis. First, it requires the sellers to understand the buyers' idiosyncrasies. While in this case that does not seem too difficult (once Andrea made her statement about peace and quiet, it would not be difficult for the sellers to imagine the fraternity house being undesirable to them), it does not function well as a rule. The holder of such preferences is in the best position to judge what will disturb them. When a buyer has idiosyncratic preferences and the thing that disturbs those preferences can be discovered through a reasonable inspection, the burden ought to be on the buyer to make that inspection.

b. As we stated above, Mary should not be able to rescind and recover the pipes. John's ability to identify the value of the pipe comes from an investment of resources (years of studying and trading in pipes). Forcing John to disclose his belief about the value of the pipe will diminish his incentive (and that of others like him) to develop the expertise necessary for making such determinations. Had Mary asked John for an estimate on the value of the pipes, he would not be permitted to lie, but he would, of course, have no obligation to respond at all (*see Laidlaw v. Organ*, in *Note 4 on page 476*).

c. As we have argued above, the efficiency values of optimal mistake avoidance trumps the nondisclosure rule in this case. Mark has a duty to disclose the pricing error but not the underlying private market information. To be sure, a rule requiring Mark to disclose the true value will undermine his incentive to buy the pipe or even inform the seller that it is mispriced. But a rule requiring him to alert the clerk to the mistake ("This pipe is worth more than $25.") allows him to still buy the pipe at a price that permits him a profit on the information.

d. The Bozkie example raises the thorny problem of disclosure in the context of securities sales. Here common law agency principles and the securities laws trump the common law of contract. Trading on insider information is currently illegal. Thus, Boskie is subject to suit by the SEC or by the Fund. Boskie is also liable to his principal under common law agency theory for misdealing. Note that many legal scholars have argued that allowing individuals to profit from insider information would improve the efficiency of markets. The classic defense of this position is Henry Manne's. Teachers familiar with the contours of this debate can use this hypothetical to analyze disclosure rules in this complex context. Otherwise, we recommend noting the issue and moving on.

e. In *In re Estate of Evasew*, the court held that the appraiser had and breached a duty of confidentiality (or trust) and that his actions constituted fraud. The court espoused certain rules that apply where a fiduciary, confidential, or unequal relationship exists. As a general rule, the court stated, fraud is not presumed and the burden of establishing it is on the party who alleges it. However, that rule is relaxed when such a relationship exists between parties to a contract, and where one has dominant influence over the other. There, if the superior party obtains a benefit, equity raises a presumption against validity. When a fiduciary seeks to profit by a transaction with the one who hired him, he has the burden of showing that he communicated to her the fact of his interest in the transaction and all the information that it was important for her to know. The facts of this case indicate that he did not do so, and therefore he obtained his advantage fraudulently. (*Id.* at 103-104)

Note 4 (Page 476). We discuss Dean Kronman's theory above in our analysis of *Obde*.

D. Capacity to Contract
The Infancy Doctrine

Kiefer v. Fred Howe Motors, Inc. *(Page 482).* Kiefer, a minor, purchased a car from Fred Howe Motors and later disaffirmed the contract. Fred Howe argued that there should be an exception to the infancy doctrine for minors who are emancipated, under which Kiefer, who was married, would fall. Also, Fred Howe argued that Kiefer did not effectively disaffirm the contract, and that he misrepresented his age and so should be liable in tort. The court rejected all of these arguments. The court asserted that there is no logical support for the emancipation exception argument. It found ample evidence of disaffirmance in Kiefer's testimony and in his attorney's letter to Fred Howe. Finally, the court found that the evidence supported the trial court's finding that Kiefer did not orally represent his age; the court also held that in signing a statement that said his age was 21 or over, Kiefer did not intend to deceive Fred Howe, and that Fred Howe was not justified in relying on that statement.

Halbman v. Lemke *(Page 486).* Halbman, a minor, bought a car from Lemke. The car soon experienced mechanical difficulty and Halbman disaffirmed the contract and demanded the return of the money he had paid. Since the value of the car had depreciated, Lemke argued that Halbman should have to compensate him for that depreciation. The court rejected Lemke's argument and limited recovery according to the rule requiring a disaffirming minor to return any consideration still in his possession. The court argues that requiring more than a return of consideration would effectively bind the minor to a contract that he is legally privileged to avoid.

Shields v. Gross *(Page 491).* Brooke Shields wished to disaffirm a contract entered into on her behalf by her mother when she was a minor. The contract allowed the company with whom it was made to publish the pictures taken of her pursuant to the contract in virtually any way it wished (see footnote 1). This case centered around the interpretation of a state statute. Holding that the legislature, in that statute, eliminated a minor's common law right to disaffirm a contract consented to by her parent or guardian, the court rejected Shields' claim of disaffirmance.

The dissent viewed the case as pitting the interest of protecting children against a concern for trade or commercialism. Viewing it, and the statute around which the case turned, in that light, the dissent argued that the legislature cannot be thought of as intending to elevate the interests of business above the interest of protecting children.

As *Halbman* and *Kiefer* illustrate, and as **Note 1 on page 497** points out, the infancy doctrine is marked by a very bright-line rule (the ability to draw an accurate line is questioned in **Note 8 on page 500**). The benefits of bright-line rules are clarity, predictability and low-cost administration. The costs are over- and under-inclusiveness. Given the prominent role of minors in today's economy, it is questionable whether the cost-benefit analysis still comes out in favor of a bright-line rule.

The policy issue in *Shields* – whether a minor should be able to disaffirm a contract entered into on her behalf by her guardian – is discussed in **Note 2 on page 497** from a theoretical perspective. It seems clear that both the economic and autonomy theories support the majority's position that such contracts should not be subject to disaffirmance.

Note 7 on page 499 focuses on the timing of disaffirmance and ratification, and in so doing presents two cases, one of which features NBA star Kobe Bryant. In that case, Bryant, then a high school student and a minor, signed an agreement with a sports memorabilia company. He later wished to disaffirm the contract, but the court found that he had ratified it, based on two facts: He deposited a check from the company after he turned 18, and he performed some of his contractual obligations after turning 18.

In the first case in this note, *Bobby Floars Toyota v. Smith*, a court rejected a claim of disaffirmance by Charles Smith, who made 10 monthly of payments on a car loan after his 18th birthday. The incentives this ruling creates are questionable. If making the payments is the key to ratification, but simply driving the car would not constitute ratification, then those in situation similar to Smith have an incentive to default on their payments, but no incentive to return the car.

Mental Illness

Faber v. Sweet Style Manufacturing Corp. *(Page 502)*. Faber entered into a contract with the defendant during a manic phase of a manic-depressive psychosis. After establishing that a contract can be rescinded upon a showing of incompetence without more, provided the other party can be restored to the *status quo ante*, the court considered whether Faber qualified as incompetent. The law no longer requires a total lack of understanding of the contract terms, said the court; rather, it recognizes stages of incompetence, and will rescind a contract if there is a connection between the "delusions" and the making of the contract that compels the conclusion that the party's action were induced by his insanity. This is essentially a but-for test. In evaluating it, the court focused mostly on the objective behavioral evidence, and found for the plaintiff. According to the court, the rapidity with which the plaintiff performed numerous serious acts, about which most people would be more contemplative and deliberate, and the fact that he complained to his doctor about his wife needing help because she was preventing him from doing these things, provided sufficient evidence to conclude that he was incompetent. Therefore, the court granted rescission.

Williamson v. Matthews *(Page 506)*. Williamson agreed to sell her house to the Matthews for substantially less than its market value. The court granted her claim for rescission based on the combination of numerous factors, which together showed that she was operating under diminished capacity. There was evidence that she was drunk at the time of contracting, that she had a past of aberrant behavior, she complained to an attorney only hours after the transaction, and her will was weakened by the possibility of foreclosure by her mortgagee. These factors, when combined with the gross inadequacy of consideration, void the contract.

Uribe v. Olson *(Page 509)*. The defendant, as conservator of her mother's estate, sought to escape a contract for the sale of land her mother entered into by asserting that her mother did not have the requisite capacity to enter into it. The court ruled against the defendant, first asserting that even those who ordinarily lack capacity can have periods of lucidity. Contracts entered into during those intervals are enforceable. Second, the court found that the circumstances of the sale – the defendant's mother answered questions correctly, participated in the listing of the property, negotiated the purchase price over several months, and made the offer that was finally accepted – demonstrated the mother's lucidity. Also important to the court was the fact that the defendant's mother read the agreement before signing it.

Note 1 (Page 511). This Note provides useful questions for guiding the discussion of these cases. The difficulty with this doctrine lies in the absence of a bright-line rule. The definition of incapacity is elusive, the question of whether the other contracting party has to have had reason to know of the incapacity is a difficult one, and there are often other factors that seem to influence the decisions.

An underlying principle can be found to justify and reconcile the results in these cases, which are seemingly inconsistent. That principle is akin to the comparative advantage criterion in *Bailey v. West, supra* Chapter 1. In the first two cases, *Faber* and *Williamson*, the allegedly incompetent persons acted alone when they entered into the agreements. In contrast, the allegedly incompetent person in *Uribe* was joined in the transaction by her stable daughter. In the first two cases, then, the party with the comparative advantage in determining if the person in question was competent was the other party. In the third case, the person with that advantage was the daughter. It would be wasteful for the other party to expend resources determining if her contracting partner was competent if the contracting partner was joined in the transaction by a party who has such intimate knowledge of the person in question.

This principle also explains the holding in *St. John's Episcopal Hosp. v. McAdoo*, which is excerpted in *Note 2 on page 512*. In that case, the defendant sought to avoid liability for his estranged wife's medical bills after signing a form by which he agreed to assume liability for them. The court found that the term in the form imposing liability on him would not have been expected by the ordinary person reading it in an emergency room. Further, the court asserted without saying so, that the hospital had a comparative advantage in determining his competency and mitigating its effects. Hospitals know, said the court, that those who bring loved ones to an emergency room will have a decreased capacity to comprehend what they read. Since the hospital authors the form, it can and should do so in a way that makes it easy for those in such difficult emotional states to understand what they are being asked to sign. In this way, the court is requiring the party who can predict and mitigate against incompetency at least cost to do so. This promotes autonomy and efficiency.

E. Public Policy Limitations

The public policy limitations – the doctrines of illegality and immorality – at first seem to offend the autonomy and economic theories of contract law. A voluntary, informed agreement between fully autonomous actors has thus far been our unqualified goal. However, such agreements can cause costs to society that outweigh the benefits to the contracting parties (externalities). Autonomy theory as well argues against enforcing agreements that harm third parties. But these arguments prove too much– if (net) negative externalities invalidated any agreement that created them, virtually all agreements would be invalid. Thus, the public policy limitations focus only on two kinds of externalities: illegal and immoral activities.

Illegality

Watts v. Malatesta *(Page 520)*. Watts sued to recover money lost on bets he made with Malatesta, a bookmaker. The claim was based on a New York statute that prohibited gambling. The majority interpreted the statute as prohibiting professional gambling but allowing recovery of losses by a casual gambler against a professional one. The court considered the plaintiff a casual gambler and the defendant a professional, and so allowed the plaintiff to recover his losses but dismissed the defendant's counterclaim for his losses (money paid out to the plaintiff from winning bets; an amount that exceeded the plaintiff's losses). The majority rejects the dissent's claim that the professional gambler also has a cause of action under the statute, saying that such a construction would mean that a criminal act would give rise to a cause of action. The court also dismisses the dissent's claim that the plaintiff's losses should be offset against his winnings because, as the court earlier concluded, the defendant has no cause of action at all.

The dissent argues that the statute, intending to prevent all gambling, provided a cause of action for recovering money lost on any and all bets. The dissent also claims that the statute could not be reasonably construed as permitting someone to recover his losses without offsetting his winnings, because that would promote gambling (making it a "sure thing"). Finally, the dissent insists that since the plaintiff's losses grew out of the same transaction as his winnings, the winnings amount to a repayment of the losses.

As *Note 3 on page 529* suggests (but the majority fails to argue), the dissent's argument that the majority's holding makes gambling a "sure thing" for the casual gambler fails to take account of the affect on the professional gambler. If the casual gambler is guaranteed to win, then the professional gambler taking the bet is guaranteed to lose. Knowing this, the professional gambler is unlikely to take any bets.

Giants v. Chargers *(Page 524)*. College football star Flowers signed a contract with the Giants before he was to play in the Sugar Bowl, which would be the last game of his college career. Knowing that signing such a contract would disqualify him from playing in the Sugar Bowl, Flowers agreed to the Giants' proposal that he sign the contract but that it be kept secret and not become binding until after the game. A few days later, Flowers contacted the Giants requesting that he be allowed to withdraw from the contract. The Giants refused and took steps (the contract became effective when and if approved by the Commissioner) to make the contract binding before the agreed-upon date. Flowers later entered into a contract (discussed before, but formalized after, the game) with the Chargers. The Giants sued in equity to obtain performance of its contract with Flowers. The trial court ruled that the early submission of the contract to the Commissioner did not make it binding, and Flowers retained a right to cancel, which he had exercised. The appeals court ruled that the Giants' complaint would not be heard in equity because they did not come to the court with clean hands. Therefore, the court affirmed the judgment of the lower court, but struck those parts of the trial court's decision that reached the merits of the claim.

The questions in *Notes 1 and 2 on page 528* are useful guides for reviewing and analyzing these cases. *Note 3 on page 529* explores the prospective regulation issue. The first consideration is courts' effectiveness in bringing about the behavior they desire– as mentioned above, the dissent in *Watts* failed to recognize all of the incentives created by the majority's decision. The second consideration is the tension between prospective regulation and dispute resolution. In cases involving illegality, courts face a special problem when enforcing a contract made for illegal purposes would deter future illegal conduct. In those cases, courts decline to enforce the contracts so as not to condone illegal behavior, and leave the prevention of future illegal conduct (that would have been deterred by enforcing the contract) to those charged with executing laws. The difficult question is whether preserving the "judicial ermine" is worth the costs of a decision that does not deter future illegal conduct.

Immorality

Roddy-Eden v. Berle *(Page 530)*. The plaintiff in this case sued for damages as a result of defendant's alleged breach of his promise to publish under his name a book written by the plaintiff. Under the agreement, they were to share the profits. The court dismissed the complaint because it was a contract to perpetrate a fraud on the public and as such was void as against public policy. The court also asserted that were there no impact on parties outside the agreement, it would still be void for having its genesis in fraud and deceit and violating the standards of proper conduct. Finally, the court pointed out that since the copy of the contract attached by the plaintiff to her complaint did not impose an obligation on the defendant to publish the book (but merely gave him permission to do so), the facts were insufficient to support recovery.

Hewitt v. Hewitt *(Page 532)*. The plaintiff and defendant had held themselves out as having been married for 15 years (Mrs. Hewitt did not realize they were not married until her divorce petition was dismissed), during which time they lived together and had children. At the dissolution of their relationship, plaintiff sought an equal share of all of defendant's assets. She advanced multiple theories, but they were all rejected by the court on the grounds that supporting her claim would undermine the state's interest in promoting marriage. The court identified this interest as dating back to a statute outlawing common law marriages and continuing in the recently-passed Illinois Marriage and Dissolution of Marriage Act. Allowing plaintiff to recover as though she and defendant had been married (which a California court allowed in *Marvin v. Marvin*, a case of similar facts discussed in the opinion) would create an alternative to marriage that was potentially more attractive than marriage. Whether such a break from the traditional policy of the state should be made was a question involving complex considerations of public policy and was rightly within the province of the legislature.

The tension between prospective regulation and dispute resolution is addressed in *Note 1 on page 539*. In *Hewitt*, the court treats as immoral a relationship that was merely lacking legal formality and did not stray for societal norms. This, then, is an example of the over-inclusiveness problem that comes with a bright-line rule; or, put another way, the court is willing to sacrifice some desirable conduct in order to prevent a greater amount of undesirable conduct. In the context of the immorality doctrine, this raises the problem of judging what conduct is and is not desirable. Judges are probably ill-equipped to make this determination; indeed, it is a controversial question whether any part of the state has the authority to make this determination, especially when reasonable people disagree. This problem is addressed in *Note 3 on page 539*.

The second part of Note 1 presents an interesting argument that Roddy-Eden could have made in *Berle*. As in *Wood v. Lucy, Lady-Duff Gordon*, *supra* Chapter 4, Roddy-Eden could have argued that Berle was the exclusive dealer of her book and as such had a best efforts obligation to promote it. Indeed, Roddy-Eden could have argued, that is the only reasonable interpretation of the contract because that is the only way to find consideration for it. Another argument available to Roddy-Eden might have been that there was an unwritten but agreed upon term that obligated Berle to publish the book, or an intended meaning of the written terms that was more expansive than the appellate court considered. This would raise the interpretive issues discussed in Chapter 6.

Note 2 (Page 539). This Note asks why courts won't allow sex to be consideration for a bargain, and why the *Hewitt* court refused to follow the trend of other jurisdictions in enforcing contracts between unmarried cohabitants so long as there is some other consideration. Sex as consideration is a familiar public policy problem. On one view, it violates autonomy and efficiency principles to invalidate such bargains. However, some argue that allowing such bargains leads to diminished autonomy for women, in particular, because of the objectification and gender roles that those actions perpetuate. The objectification of women and perpetuation of certain gender roles can also be thought of as negative externalities that outweigh the value of the bargain.

Note 4 on page 540 contains an excerpt of *Glasgo v. Glasgo*, a case similar to *Hewitt*. The *Glasgo* court had strong words for the *Hewitt* court, denouncing that decision as doing more to discredit the legal system than strengthen marriage. Denying otherwise obtainable recovery to a party simply because illegal (query: does the court mean immoral?; does it see a difference?) sexual relationships are posited as consideration (presumably, the court does not think sex is, or at least doesn't think it is the only, consideration) is "unfair, unjust, and unduly harsh."

In one sense, the *Glasgo* opinion is a compromise between *Hewitt* and *Marvin*, a California case in which the court recognized a separate contract for homemaking services apart from the illegal contract founded on sex. The *Glasgo* court made an effort to point out that the relationship before it was in no way meretricious or illicit, and so this was not a question of finding a creative way to validate a contract for sex (as the *Hewitt* court regarded the *Marvin* decision). Rather, the *Glasgo* court insisted it was merely recognizing the inequity in denying recovery to Mrs. Glasgo on the mere basis of the absence of a legal formality.

On the other hand, it's hard to imagine the *Glasgo* court not resolving the *Hewitt* and *Marvin* facts the same way. In that sense, *Glasgo* is not much of a compromise. Futher, comparing the three decisions is somewhat complicated by the fact that *Glasgo* is focused solely on *ex post* considerations, while *Hewitt* and *Marvin* are decided with an eye to prospective regulation.

In re Baby M *(Page 542)*. Mr. Stern signed a surrogacy agreement with Mrs. and Mr. Whitehead under which Mrs. Whitehead agreed to be a surrogate mother, through artificial insemination, for Mr. Stern. Upon the birth of the child, Mr. and Mrs. Whitehead were required to take all necessary steps to terminate their parental rights (for Mr. Whitehead, this was only rebutting the presumption of fatherhood). It was understood that Mrs. Stern would then adopt the child, but she was not a party to the contract. She was, however, named as the sole guardian of the child in the event of Mr. Stern's death. The contract called for a payment of $10,000 to Mr. and Mrs. Whitehead, upon delivery of the child. Also, Mr. Stern paid $7,500 to the Infertility Center of New York (ICNY) for services related to the arrangement with Mrs. and Mr. Whitehead. Mrs. and Mr. Whitehead came to regret the contract and attempted to keep the child. Mr. Stern filed suit for specific performance. The trial court found for Mr. Stern, and the Supreme Court of New Jersey reversed in part and affirmed in part.

The court held that the contract violated the law and public policy of New Jersey. New Jersey law prohibits the use of money in connection with adoptions and requires proof of parental unfitness or abandonment before termination of parental rights is ordered. The $10,000 payment, while ostensibly for services and not for adoption, was viewed by the court as a payment for adoption. Evidence of this, the court asserted, was the fact that only $1,000 would be payable under the contract if the child were stillborn, even though all "services" would have been performed. Also, the court thought the payment to ICNY was clearly in connection with an adoption. According to the court, the evils inherent in "baby bartering" were clear. The child is sold without regard to the fitness of the parents, the natural mother does not receive counseling, the monetary incentive may make the decision less voluntary, and the adoptive parents may not be fully informed of the natural parents' medical history.

Since there was no evidence of intentional abandonment or substantial neglect, and since in private placement adoption, consent and voluntariness are not a factor in terminating parental rights, Mrs. Whitehead's parental rights could not be terminated.

The court found the surrogacy contract void as against public policy because it guarantees permanent separation from one of the child's natural parents. New Jersey policy has long been that, to the extent possible, children should remain with their natural parents. Also, the mother is irrevocably committed before she knows the strength of her bond with the child. In that sense, the court says, she can't make a totally voluntary, informed decision. The lack of information about the natural mother's medical and psychological history leaves the natural father and adoptive mother with less than what public policy requires. Worst of all, the court said, the surrogacy contract fails take account of the child's best interests.

Notes 1 and 2 (Page 551). These Notes walk through the arguments made by the court and the problems with those arguments. Regarding the illegality grounds, the fact that Mr. Stern was the natural father should not matter. The court is bothered by the problems inherent in private adoption. Those are not necessarily diminished when the natural father is involved in the adoption, since, with in vitro fertilization, the biological father could be anyone who donated to a sperm bank. Further, it doesn't matter whether the legislature had surrogacy contracts in mind when it enacted this statutory scheme– if they meant to outlaw the activity that is at the basis of the surrogacy contract (the adoption), the statute should apply to that contract.

F. Unconscionability

Despite its historical roots, the unconscionability doctrine has been defined imprecisely at best and often not at all. It is most often a question of procedure, but can also be substantive. UCC § 2-302 and its Comments fail to shed much light on the definition. However, it survives today, at least in theory, as a counterweight to the principle of liberty of contract, invalidating those clauses that, as the UCC puts it, "are so one-sided as to be unconscionable under the circumstances existing at the time of the making of the contract."

Seabrook v. Commuter Housing Co. (*Page 554*). The plaintiff sued to recover one month's rent and a security deposit that his lessor refused to return. The lease under which the plaintiff paid and defendant held this money was for premises that were under construction at the time of the lease signing. A clause in the lease provided that if the premises were not ready at the start date of the lease, the lease period would begin at the first date the premises were available. The lease also released the lessor of any liability for failure to deliver the premises on the beginning date of the lease. Plaintiff claimed that these clauses, viewed in light of the way in which they were presented (small type hidden in the middle of the lease) and the superior bargaining position of the lessor, were unenforceable because unconscionable. The court agreed with these arguments and ordered the return of the plaintiff's payments.

Henningsen v. Bloomfield Motors, Inc. *(Page 558)*. Henningsen purchased a car from Bloomfield, and in the contract of sale was a clause that limited Bloomfield's and Chrysler's liability for defect to replacement of the parts. Acknowledging the basic rule in the law that one is bound by what one signs, the court regarded itself as having an overriding duty to prevent the injustice that would be done by strictly applying that rule here. According to the court, there is a tremendous imbalance in bargaining power between car makers and consumers. Consumers are forced to agree to such liability-limiting clauses because they need cars and all auto makers insist on these clauses. There can be no negotiation, the court asserted, and the buyer is forced to accept a clause that is sharply against its interests. Thus, the court found this clause unenforceable because unconscionable.

Notes 1 and 3 (Pages 562 and 563) These Notes discuss substantive v. procedural unconscionability. *Seabrook* is mainly a procedural unconscionability case, while *Henningsen* might be either. *Seabrook* left room for the possibility of enforcing the clauses in question there, but not under the circumstances of that case. The *Henningsen* court doesn't leave much room for the warranty disclaimer, declaring that an "instinctively felt sense of justice cries out against such a sharp bargain." This suggests that it views the clause itself as unconscionable. But it also suggests the process was unconscionable in its discussion of "the gross inequality of bargaining position" occupied by the consumer in the automobile industry. Since the warranty disclaimer clause is in every contract, the court views the consumer's consent as less than voluntary.

Note 2 (Page 562) This Note presents some of the theoretical arguments pertaining to procedural unconscionability. The problem with the *Seabrook* opinion from a theoretical perspective is that the factors that led the court to invalidate the clause (see Note 2) had possible purposes other than taking advantage of the lessee's legal ignorance. There is at least a plausible alternative explanation for the lease being long (there were numerous necessary terms) and in fine print (conserve space), the terms being in technical language (essential to achieving the desired meaning of the term), the lessor allowing the lessee to sign it knowing he had not read the terms (respect for his autonomy) or received legal counseling (time delay, expense, respect for his autonomy), and the lessor having superior legal knowledge (that is essential to the lessor's business).

The remaining factor on which the court grounded its decision – that the commodity leased was scarce – should not be a ground at all. A painting by Monet is a scarce commodity, but why should that fact require the seller to insure that the buyer understands the terms of a contract for its sale? It also seems clear that this fact would not make the clause substantively unconscionable. The court indicates that it does not view the clause as unconscionable when it says that it does not seek to abridge the right to contract. The parties are free, the court is saying, to include this clause in their contract so long as the bargaining process is fair.

Note 5 (Page 565). This Note addresses the theoretical underpinnings of substantive unconscionability. In short, if there are undesirable spill over effects from an agreement (negative externalities) and the inherent dignity of persons is compromised by the agreement, the economic and autonomy theories call for invalidating it. Otherwise, these theories reject substantive unconscionability on the ground that it interferes with the principle of freedom of contract.

Note 7 on page 566 discusses contract provisions that limit liability for negligence. In general, these terms are enforced unless the bargaining process was unconscionable or the terms violate public policy. This holds for cases involving corporations and consumers, as well as two corporations.

The problem in *Note 8 on page 568* presents a clause relieving the USTA of all liability of any injuries suffered by participants in the Junior Indoor Championship. Christy Nielson, a promising junior player, entered the tournament and her father signed the form on her behalf. She suffered a disabling knee injury while performing calisthenics, which expert testimony will establish was clearly inappropriate for teenagers, at the direction of a tournament instructor. The question is whether the USTA will be liable for her injury. In order to invalidate this clause she has to argue that it was forced upon her, and therefore that it was the result of procedural unconscionability. This argument was recognized in *Mutual Marine* (see Note 7) and *Galligan* (see Note 7), and was at least implicit in *Ciofalo* (the court pointed out that the contract did not involve employment or a good or service so essential that she had no choice but to assent to the terms) (see Note 7). She can argue that playing in this tournament was essential to her career (employment), and since there was no possibility of negotiating over this clause, she was forced to accept it. The USTA will argue that this tournament cannot be rightly described as relating to employment since it is a junior (presumably amateur) tournament, and she has not yet established a career in tennis. These arguments are largely factual, and if they are resolved in her favor, the court will probably find liability (especially given her sympathetic position). If the voluntariness of her agreement to this provision truly was compromised, then the economic and autonomy theories argue for invalidating the clause.

G. Statute of Frauds

McIntosh v. Murphy *(Page 570)*. Murphy offered McIntosh a job as assistant sales manager of a car dealership in Hawaii, but they never executed a written agreement. Murphy moved from California to Hawaii and began working for Murphy. After a couple of months, Murphy fired McIntosh on the grounds that he was unable to close deals or train salesmen. McIntosh sued and Murphy defended by claiming that the employment was terminable at will and that, if it was not, it was unenforceable under the statute of frauds because not performable within one year. The trial court found that it was performable within one year because acceptance was by commencement of performance (which made the contract performable within exactly one year) or, in the alternative, acceptance was made on a weekend and those days did not count for the timing issue. The jury found that the contract was for just cause and that there was no just cause for firing McIntosh. The Hawaii Supreme Court did not discuss the merits of the court's rulings since it decided the case on the doctrine of equitable estoppel.

The court finds in favor of the plaintiff under equitable estoppel because the plaintiff's reliance on the defendant's promise – moving from California to Hawaii – was foreseeable by the defendant and injustice can be avoided only by enforcing the contract. The court said that it was clear that a contract existed and whether it was at-will was a question for the jury. The judgment was affirmed.

The dissent points out (rightly) that the majority is begging the question by holding that injustice can be avoided only by enforcement. An injustice will have been done in this case only if the contract was for one year. But that is a disputed issue. Thus, the majority's resolution of the statute of frauds issue requires the resolution of a substantive issue that can only be reached after the statute of frauds issue has been decided. The dissent also argues that, even if it was a one-year contract, the court should not enforce it based on equity because doing so would be to undermine the statute.

Mercer v. Roberts *(Page 575)*. The plaintiff was hired by the defendant to open an office for the defendant's company in Texas and bring it to maturity, which both sides agreed would take three to five years. The plaintiff and defendant agreed to bonus pay as a percentage of the profits generated by the plaintiff. Then, the defendant unilaterally altered the bonus calculation, and the plaintiff quit and sued. The defendant claimed that the agreement was not performable within a year and so unenforceable under the statute of frauds (it was not in writing). The court ruled that the agreement was not enforceable. Under Texas law, the statute of frauds does not apply if the contract can theoretically be performed within a year. If not time is specified in the contract, a reasonable time will be implied given the context– in this case, a reasonable time is three to five years. Since that is greater than one year, the statute of frauds applies. The court does not allow the part performance exception because the precedent in Texas against doing so is strong (the court cites *Collins v McCombs*, in which the part performance exception was denied on facts even more sympathetic to the plaintiff).

The dissent argues that this is a series of one-year contracts so the statute of frauds doesn't apply. This is not a plausible interpretation of the agreement since both parties would have preferred a longer term agreement. The dissent also argues for an equitable exception to the statute of frauds. As mentioned above, precedent in Texas would not allow this.

Schwedes v. Romain *(Page 580)*. The plaintiff agreed to buy land from the defendant, and after an agreement was reached, the defendant took the land off the market, and the plaintiff secured financing. The plaintiff's offer to send payment before the closing was rebuffed as unnecessary by the defendant's lawyer, who also told them it was unnecessary for them to attend the closing. Before the deal closed, the defendant sold the land to another party. The plaintiff sued for breach, and the defendant claimed that since the agreement was for the sale of land and there was no writing, the agreement was unenforceable under the statute of frauds. The plaintiff argued part performance. The court rejected the part performance argument by distinguishing part performance from acting in contemplation of performance. What Schwedes did, according to the court, was the latter. Acts like obtaining financing, which are not part of one's obligation, do not constitute part performance even if they are necessary for performance.

Note 1 (Page 584). This Note is designed to keep the standards-rule issue in front of students. They should recognize that when both approaches are taken to one issue, there is an inevitable ebb and flow. We contrast *McIntosh* and *Mercer,* and the tensions between formalism and functionalism within each case, to demonstrate how rules and standards evolve from each other. The statute of frauds demonstrates the dynamic so eloquently articulated in Carol Rose's article, "Crystals and Mud in Property Law." Courts (and legislatures) begin with clear rules, which are cost-justified because of the gains from clarity, predictability and ease of adjudication. But they are just as predictably over- and under-inclusive. Even if that trade-off is justified ex ante, many courts take the ex post perspective in adjudication. They are therefore unwilling to implement the rule regime when doing so in a particular case *undermines*, rather than advances, the very policy objective the rule was designed to advance. Exceptions are therefore created, and the what began as clear rules evolves into muddy standards. Eventually, the resulting decrease in clarity and predictability coupled with the increased cost of adjudication drive courts (or legislatures) to reject the standard (or to narrow or eliminate the evolved exceptions to the rule), and a new, clear rule emerges, only to begin the process of decay again. The evil, of course, is the ex post perspective, which undermines sensible attempts to maximize the gains, and minimize the costs, of a particular legal regime. But the norms of adjudication, and particular the ancient norms underlying principles of equity – which evolved precisely to mitigate perceived injustices under the formal application of legal rules – are permanently ingrained in the American judicial psyche (and doctrine). The pattern of rules and standards revealed by the statute of frauds cases illustrates that this dynamic, and the ex post perspective, is alive and well in contract law.

Note 2 (Page 584). How does the statute of frauds hold up under the dominant contract theories? The series of questions in this Note are meant to encourage students to question the justification for the statute of frauds. At first take, the statute of frauds seems counter to both the autonomy and economic theories. But, as the last question suggests, they support it on a deeper level. In order for contracts to be enforceable, we must have a system of courts. In order for those courts to be available to all, irrespective of wealth, society subsidizes the costs of adjudication. As a result, parties do not fully internalize the actual costs of adjudication, and so they design contracts that exploit this externality: Because they do not fully internalize the expected costs of adjudication, they have inefficiently low incentives to invest in contract measures designed to decrease the probability and cost of adjudication. Thus, they will, all else equal, be less inclined to expend resources in writing down agreements, even if doing so would reduce the likelihood and costs of adjudicating their agreement. The standard economic rationale for the statute of frauds, therefore, argues that the law should require parties' agreements to meet a minimum standard of provability at the time of formation in order to be eligible for enforcement. The statute of frauds is a crude tool for insuring minimal investment in reducing adjudication costs by requiring agreements to be evidenced by a writing. It is therefore justified as a rough measure to compensate for the decrease in parties' incentive to reduce adjudication costs created by the state subsidy of adjudication costs.

Note 4 (Page 586). Here we ask if a request for admission during discovery is a proper device for overcoming the statute. Under U.C.C. § 2-201(3)(b) it is, but only for the quantity admitted. If the policy justification for the statute is providing evidence that will reduce the cost of adjudication, then the U.C.C. approach should be applied to the common law. If the justification is that the statute serves a cautionary or channeling function, then it should not. Since the latter justifications are problematic (they are over- and under-inclusive), and the former is preferred, the U.C.C. approach should be used in the common law.

Monetti v. Anchor Hocking *(Page 586)*. The plaintiff formed an agreement with the defendant for the defendant to be the sole U.S. distributor of the plaintiff's products and to turn over tangible and intangible assets (from plaintiff's wholly owned subsidiary, which had been the distributor of its products). There were two writings related to the agreement that an agent of the defendant signed. The first contained all of the plaintiff's terms and two more, but was written before the agreement was reached. The second was included in an internal memo written by one of defendant's employees, which contained all of the terms except one, and was referred to by defendant's agent as representing the "summary agreement." The court, in a highly pedagogical opinion, discusses both the UCC (2-201) and the common law statute of frauds. It introduces the predominant purpose test for determining which statute to apply, and points out that such a test is problematic. The court suggests that the UCC may be applied to part of a mixed contract, and the common law to the remainder. However, since the outcome of the case is the same under both the UCC and the common law, the court does not have to choose which to use.

Under the common law, the partial performance exception removes the contract from the statute of frauds (after the meeting establishing their agreement, Monetti began transferring assets and trade secrets to Anchor Hocking). Under the UCC, the second writing satisfies the statute of frauds (the first writing does not, says the court, because the "has been" language requires that the signed writing not be made before the agreement was reached) because the UCC does not contain all of the material terms (the second writing did not include the term that the plaintiff would hand over assets).

Note 1 on page 593 presents a thorough analysis of the choice of law issue in mixed contract cases. *Note 2 on page 594* presents the question of whether the distinction Judge Posner draws in *Monetti* between disallowing oral evidence of the existence of a contract and allowing oral evidence of the identity of a party once it is established that a writing satisfies the statute is tenable. Since the best justification for the statute is ensuring that, for certain contracts, there will be a writing (and therefore the cost of adjudicating the question of whether a contract exists will be reduced) the distinction is tenable. The first case is exactly what the statute is meant to prevent (the time and expense associated with proving the existence of a contract when there is no writing). In the second case, the goal of the statute is satisfied by the existence of the writing, and the question of the identity of the parties is a separate issue, like many other unrelated issues.

Note 4 (Page 595). The UCC's definition of "signature" is broad enough to allow a typed letter to qualify as a signed letter simply by virtue of the typer's "intent to authenticate."

Note 5 (Page 595). Butler will be unsuccessful in relying on the statute of frauds to escape enforcement. This is a contract for the sale of goods so the UCC applies. Section 2-201(1) requires that there be a writing sufficient to indicate that a contract has been made and signed by the party against whom enforcement is sought. Her writing indicates her disagreement on the quantity she originally agreed to buy, but in doing so admits that there was an agreement. Thus, it is sufficient to indicate that an agreement has been made. She may argue that the disagreement over the quantity between her writing and Safety's renders neither effective as an indication that an agreement has been made. The court will reject this argument, relying on the second sentence of 2-201(1), which says that a writing is not insufficient because it incorrectly states a term. The quantity term, however, will be limited to 75, which is the amount recognized in her writing, and not 100.

Note 6 (Page 596). The fact that many bargainers continue to ignore the requirements of the statute is not evidence that it is out of step with business practices and should be abolished. An explanation for why more agreements aren't recorded is that when one's confidence in one's contracting partner is high and perceived risk of breach is low, a writing may not be necessary. Contracting partners will choose not to make a record that satisfies the statute when they estimate a very low probability of breach.

The requirement of the statute simply shifts the calculation that the parties must make. Since the statute has been in existence throughout recent history (particularly, the rise of industrialism and commercialism), it has always been incorporated into parties' calculations (thus, there has been no increase the number of contracts recorded). Without the statute, the potential harm from not having a writing is not as high as it is with the statute. Therefore, if the risk of litigation is held constant but the statute is abolished, fewer agreements will be recorded. For a more in depth discussion of the impact of the statute in the modern commercial context, see **Note 7 on page 596**.

CHAPTER 6

IDENTIFYING AND INTERPRETING THE TERMS OF AN AGREEMENT

A. Introduction

Pedagogy. This chapter begins with an extensive introductory essay. We strongly recommend assigning this essay to first-year students, irrespective of how much of the remainder of the chapter a professor intends to assign. Although this chapter is designed to permit selective assignments of discrete sections while omitting coverage elsewhere in the chapter, each section presupposes familiarity with the concepts and doctrines introduced in the introductory essay. To be sure, the essay standing by itself provides no case-specific context to understand the doctrines it presents. For a more thorough grasp of this material, students must work through at least some of the case materials in the chapter as well. But it is possible to teach the basic doctrine and theory of the chapter by combining the introductory essay with selected portions of one or both major parts of the chapter. That said, because the chapter is pared down to relatively few, illustrative, and often classic, cases on contractual interpretation, it is certainly possible to teach the entire chapter in a one-semester first-year course without sacrificing too much coverage elsewhere. As our essays later in the chapter should make clear, the theory in this area is very much at issue in current scholarship, and the resulting debates can be quite engaging, even for first-year students. We should note, however, that the doctrinal and theoretical complexity of this area require considerable pedagogic efforts before students are well-positioned to participate intelligently in these theoretical debates. But because this material could not be more central to corporate transactional or litigation practices, students seem to appreciate the practical relevance of working through the details. And we hope our chapter demonstrates how those details turn quite directly on what position one takes on the theoretical debates underlying the different doctrinal approaches to contractual interpretation.

Although we identify some case-specific pedagogic strategies below, the pedagogical approach in this chapter is largely "hard-wired": The introductory essay provides the doctrinal background for understanding and evaluating the cases. Note that individual cases are often poor devices for teaching the doctrine in this area. Because the doctrinal complexity often confounds courts, opinions often conflate conceptually distinct questions, misunderstand one or more aspects of a doctrine, or represent only one side of a debate in a contested arena. We hope the cases as a unit provide a more balanced and coherent basis for working through the interpretive doctrines. Our introductory essay is intended to free both professors and students from the necessity of learning the doctrine, as an original matter, through study of the cases. Instead, we hope the introductory essay equips students with a firm doctrinal grounding sufficient to allow them to evaluate critically the court's doctrinal analyses.

The theoretical perspectives underlying our approach to these materials is set out, we hope clearly and succinctly, in introductory essays beginning each subsection, the case-specific notes following each case, and most extensively, in the essay entitled *The Goals of Contractual Interpretation on page 676*, and the introductory essay to section C.2., *Objectivisim and Contextualism in the UCC on page 680*. Thus, we advise first-time teachers to read the introductory essay and these last two essays before working through the case materials. Then, armed with these perspectives on the doctrine and theory of interpretation, work through the case materials with an eye toward applying them consistently across interpretive doctrines and contexts. For the students, success in this difficult area requires means doctrinal mastery. We hope the interstitial material in this chapter allows professors and students to achieve this (though we concede teaching doctrinal competence in this area is no mean feat). In the final analysis, the lasting doctrinal debates in this area, both in principle and practice, turn directly on the deeper theoretical debates we discuss.

Identifying the Terms of an Agreement: The Common Law and the Code

The key to understanding the common law and Code parol evidence cases is to distinguish between *three* kinds of writings. The first is an unintegrated writing. All written and non-written evidence of the terms of the agreement are admissible when the writing in evidence is determined to be unintegrated. The second is a partially integrated writing. A partially integrated writing provides the *final statement* of the terms of the agreement evidenced by the writing, but not the complete and exclusive statement of *all* the terms of the agreement. Non-written evidence of additional terms is admissible, but only if the proffered terms do not contradict the terms evidenced by the writing. The third is a fully integrated writing. A fully integrated writing provides not only the final statement of the terms evidenced by the writing, but also the *complete and exclusive* statement of all the terms of the agreement. No evidence other than the fully integrated writing itself is admissible to prove the existence of any express term of the agreement. (Terms not evidenced by the fully integrated writing are provided by the common law or Code default rules. Even fully integrated agreements contain the implied terms imputed into all contracts by contract default rules.)

In order to understand the cases, the concept of full integration must itself be divided into two distinct categories. The first might be labeled *per se merger*. This is the conclusion a court reaches when the parties have *explicitly* stated that their writing is both final and exclusive of any other terms, usually by including a *merger clause* in the agreement. In addition, there is a distinct category of *implicitly* fully integrated writings (that is, writings that do not contain any merger clause or its equivalent). In this category fall writings that are *fully integrated when compared to a particular proffered term* or what we will call "*term-specific merger*." This is the doctrinal effect of the common law's "natural omission" test (and the UCC's "certain inclusion" test) for full integration. Although the courts do not specifically distinguish a finding of per se merger from a finding of term-specific merger, the distinction is implicit in the natural omission and certain inclusion tests.

We can best describe term-specific merger by distinguishing the natural omission and certain inclusion tests of integration from the other methods of determining whether an agreement is fully integrated. Whether an agreement is fully integrated, in theory, turns entirely on the intent of the parties. By far, the best evidence of full integration is a written merger clause. Although the presence of such a clause in a writing is not dispositive, absent a showing that the clause itself was induced by fraud, it provides a strong presumption of full integration. Absent a merger clause, the old common law test for full integration was the "four corners" test (not to be confused with the "four corners" test for ambiguity under the common law plain meaning rule– see page 607, note 9). Looking at the writing alone, courts determine whether the parties intended to integrate their entire agreement into the writing. The completeness and detail of the written terms would suggest whether the parties intended a full integration. However, as our essay explains (see page 605), there is no reason to restrict the evidence admissible on the question of full integration to the four corners of the writing in question. Such a restriction simply presumes because of the *form of the agreement* that the parties intended to fully integrate their agreement, when the very question at issue is whether the parties intended to fully integrate their agreement in the writing. Thus, courts now generally determine full integration, in the absence of merger clause, by examining the writing *and* any other evidence of the parties' agreement. This non-written evidence includes not only evidence of additional or different terms, but evidence about how the parties' negotiations proceeded, their prior relationships, and the like. All this is relevant to determining whether the parties intended to fully integrate their agreement in the writing. Once a court determines that the parties did intend a full integration, all evidence of the agreement's terms other than the writing is excluded (even if it is evidence of additional consistent terms).

This finding of full integration requires a generalized inquiry into the parties intent to integrate. Such an inquiry can be difficult to undertake in the absence of any explicit statement of intention. The common law evolved a context-specific, and thus more manageable, inquiry to focus a court's inquiry into the parties intent to fully integrate in the absence of a merger clause. The natural omission test allows a court to limit its inquiry to the only question it must decide in order to adjudicate the case before it: whether the parties intended to exclude evidence of a particular term not in their writing, *even though that term does not contradict a term in their writing*. The courts determine a term-specific merger by asking whether the parties naturally would have omitted the proffered term from the writing. If they would have, the writing is not fully integrated with respect to that term, and the proffered evidence is admissible. If they would not have, then the writing is fully integrated with respect to that term and the proffered evidence must be excluded.

Courts uniformly consider the question of full integration only if they have first, at least implicitly, determined that the writing is at least partially integrated (and therefore cannot be contradicted by evidence of additional, inconsistent terms). Courts can then proceed directly to a determination of whether the parties' writing is per se fully integrated (say, by looking for a merger clause), or, in the absence of such clause, courts can instead invoke the natural omission or certain inclusion tests to ask whether the writing is fully integrated with respect to the proffered term. With respect to that particular term, the effect of finding a term-specific merger is, of course, precisely the same as if the court had determined the writing was per se fully integrated: Evidence of even consistent additional terms is not admissible.

Interpreting the Terms of An Agreement: The Common Law and the Code
(see the discussion of plain meaning and contextual analysis in this manual, infra.)

B. Identifying the Terms of Agreement
The Common Law Parol Evidence Rule
Mitchell v. Lath *(Page 613)*. Mitchell agreed to buy land from Lath after Lath agreed to remove an icehouse from adjacent land (Lath owned the icehouse but, apparently, not the land).

After the deal was executed and Mitchell occupied the property, Lath refused to remove the icehouse. Mitchell sued and Lath defended by claiming that the parol evidence rule barred admission of evidence that Lath promised to remove the icehouse (that promise, apparently, had been clearly established at trial). The court (Andrews, J.) agreed, arguing that the conditions for allowing proof of an oral agreement collateral to a written agreement were not satisfied. Justice Andrews held that while that icehouse promise was "collateral," it arguably contradicted the terms in the writing, and in any event was not one that the parties would have naturally ("ordinarily") omitted from the writing. As such, evidence of that agreement is excluded by the parties' subsequent written land sale agreement. In effect, Justice Andrews treats the icehouse agreement as one made in the course of negotiating the land sale agreement and concludes that had the parties intended the icehouse agreement to be binding, they would have included it in their final written sales agreement. Because the final written sales agreement did not include the prior, oral icehouse agreement, the parol evidence rule precludes admission of evidence of the icehouse agreement.

In dissent, Justice Lehman argues that the icehouse promise was collateral, did not contradict the land sale agreement, and, contrary to the majority, constituted a promise that the parties naturally would have omitted from the writing. He agrees that the writing was complete and contained the whole of the contract for the sale of the land. However, he argues, even a complete written agreement does not operate under the parol evidence rule to exclude evidence of prior oral agreements *outside of its scope*. Justice Lehman argues that even though the icehouse agreement was a condition to the land sale agreement, the icehouse agreement nonetheless falls outside the scope of the land sale agreement. Thus, evidence of the icehouse agreement is permissible under the parol evidence rule notwithstanding the existence of the written land sale agreement for which it constituted a condition.

Note 1 (Page 622). This Note analyzes the Andrews-Lehman debate in terms of the chapter's overall framework for understanding contractual interpretation, and the parol evidence rule in particular. As a matter of pedagogy, the case is made much easier to teach once students understand the collateral agreement doctrine. Although we provide one account of the collateral agreement doctrine in the introduction to this chapter, the refined account offered here improves on that and lays the foundation for a clearer explication of the case law invoking the collateral agreement doctrine. The first prong of the collateral agreement doctrine requires the oral agreement to be "collateral" or related to the agreement evidenced by the writing. Of course, if the oral agreement is completely unrelated to the writing, the parol evidence rule does not bar evidence of it. For example, if the writing evidences a land sale, and the alleged oral agreement is for the purchase of flour, proof of the oral agreement is admissible even if the writing is fully integrated. That the parties to both agreements are the same is insufficient to bring the oral agreement under the parol evidence rule. However, the party seeking to bar evidence of the oral agreement will almost always allege that the oral agreement *is* related (i.e., collateral) to the agreement evidenced by the writing. In this example, that party would allege, perhaps, that the flour agreement was, at one point in prior negotiations, a condition to the land sale, but that the parties eventually excluded that oral agreement from their final written agreement. Therefore, the parties intended their writing to exclude evidence of the oral agreement. For this reason, we believe the first requirement of the collateral agreement doctrine – that the agreement be collateral in form – will be trivially satisfied for every alleged oral agreement.

The second element of the collateral agreement doctrine provides that evidence of an oral collateral agreement is not admissible if it is inconsistent with the terms in the writing. The consistency of proffered terms with written terms is relevant only if the writing is partially integrated: If the writing is unintegrated, inconsistent terms are admissible; if the writing is fully integrated, even consistent terms are not admissible. Therefore, this second element of the collateral agreement doctrine presupposes that the writing is partially integrated. We conclude that the collateral agreement doctrine itself therefore applies only if the court has determined that the written agreement is at least partially integrated (by using a four corners analysis, for example).

The third element of the collateral agreement doctrine is the natural omission test. If the parties naturally would have omitted the agreement from their writing (even though they intended it to be included in their agreement), then the evidence of the agreement is not admissible, *even if the oral agreement is consistent with the terms in the writing.* As we have explained above, the natural omission test determines whether the writing is fully integrated with respect to a particular proffered term (That is, the contract is both *final and exclusive* with respect to that particular term.)

In sum, the collateral agreement doctrine applies to evidence of oral agreements (or oral terms) that are alleged to be related to a written agreement that is at least partially integrated. Evidence of the alleged oral agreement is inadmissible (1) if the alleged oral agreement is inconsistent with terms in the writing, or (2) even if the alleged oral agreement is consistent with the terms of the writing, if the writing is fully integrated with respect to the alleged oral term or agreement (under the natural omission test).

In *Mitchell*, Justices Andrews and Lehman agree that the collateral agreement doctrine applies. They both therefore agree that the alleged oral icehouse agreement is collateral to the land sale agreement. They also implicitly agree that the written land sale agreement is at least partially integrated. Justice Andrews first contemplates, but falls short of embracing, the claim that the oral icehouse agreement contradicts the written agreement: "Are they to do more? Or is such a claim inconsistent with these precise provisions? It could not be shown that the plaintiff was to pay $500 additional. Is it also implied that the defendants are not to do anything unexpressed in the writing: "That we need not decide." *(page 614)* Judge Lehman finds no such inconsistency: "The assertion of such further obligation is not inconsistent with the written contract, unless the written contract contains a provision, express or implied, that the defendants are not to do anything not expressed in the writing. Concededly there is no such express provision in the contract, and such a provision may be implied, if at all, only if the asserted additional obligation is 'so clearly connected with the principal transaction as to be part and parcel of it,' and is not 'one that the parties would not ordinarily be expected to embody in the writing.' " *(page 615)* Thus, Judge Lehman believes that the oral agreement would be inconsistent with the written agreement only if the written agreement is fully integrated with respect to the oral agreement. But this analysis conflates partial integration with term-specific merger. If the agreement is fully integrated with respect to the oral agreement, evidence of the oral agreement is inadmissible *even if the oral agreement would not contradict the written agreement.* A term-specific merger has the same effect as a per se merger on the admissibility of the term with respect to which the written agreement is integrated.

The problem here derives from Judge Andrew's account of the condition under which the oral agreement would contradict the written agreement. He claims the oral agreement would contradict the writing if the writing is interpreted as containing an implied term that "the defendants are not to do anything unexpressed in the writing." Such an implied term amounts to an implied merger clause, and so would exclude evidence of any additional agreement, *whether or not that additional agreement would contradict the terms of the writing.* In other words, Judge Andrews' claim that the oral agreement contradicts the writing is really the claim that the agreement is per se fully integrated. Perhaps Judge Andrews believes that evidence of any additional term is inadmissible in a fully integrated agreement only because such evidence would contradict the express or implied merger clause of the written agreement. Although it may be axiomatic that additional oral terms would contradict any writing containing an express merger clause, the merger clause per se precludes evidence of additional terms, quite apart from whether those terms contradict the written agreement. Thus, Judge Lehman is correct to claim that Judge Andrews' claim of inconsistency reduces to the claim that the writing is fully integrated with respect to the ice house agreement. Judge Andrews has no argument to demonstrate that the ice house agreement would contradict any written term of the parties' agreement. The claim that it would contradict an implied merger clause is a confused way of claiming that the agreement is fully integrated with respect to the oral agreement.

Thus, the dispute between Judge Andrews and Judge Lehman reduces to the quite reasonable disagreement on whether the natural omission test is satisfied in this case (and thus whether the agreement is fully integrated with respect to the ice house agreement). Was the icehouse agreement merely a part of prior negotiations that did not survive in the parties' final agreement? If so, the parties intended their writing to be fully integrated with respect to the ice house agreement. Or did the parties intend to be bound by the ice house agreement even though they did not include it in their writing? If so, the writing is not fully integrated with respect to the ice house agreement. No manner of doctrinal maneuvering can avoid the need to determine the parties' contractual intent. The result is that reasonable people can disagree across a range of cases presenting the question of whether or to what extent the parties to a written agreement intended to integrate their agreement. Perhaps the most powerful objective tool that may be available for resolving this problem is to determine whether the selling price changed between the time when the promise to remove the icehouse was made and when the writing was drafted and signed.

As a lawyering lesson, the case provides a powerful illustration of how drafting can make a difference. We ask our students what measures they could have recommended to either the Mitchill's or the Lath's to insure that their view of the validity of the icehouse agreement prevailed in court. The Mitchill's lawyer should recommend inclusion of the icehouse agreement into the written land sale agreement; the Lath's lawyer should recommend inclusion of an express merger clause into the land sale agreement, together with an express statement that the scope of the agreement subsumes any conditions or inducements to enter into the agreement (of course, in retrospect it would have been desirable explicitly to deny the icehouse deal in the writing, but perhaps only Monday morning quarter-backing would make the utility of such a precise clause foreseeable even to an experienced attorney).

Masterson v. Sine *(Page 617)*. Dallas Masterson and his wife, Rebecca, conveyed land to Medora (Dallas' sister) and Lu Sine (Medora's husband and Dallas' brother-in-law). The grant deed included a reservation effectively granting the Mastersons an option to buy back the land within 10 years for the same consideration. Dallas Masterson then became bankrupt, and the trustee in bankruptcy ("Masterson") sued for the right to exercise the option. The Sines proffered oral evidence that the option was non-assignable, and Masterson argued that oral evidence was inadmissible because the writing was fully integrated. The court (Traynor, J.) held the evidence admissible because it would be natural, according to the court, for the parties to omit the non-assignability clause from the grant deed for two reasons. First, the court argues, the parties didn't understand the advantage of including it in the writing (the implications for bankruptcy and the parol evidence rule). Second, they didn't see a need to include it. Both parties had the same incentive for the option to be non-assignable– they wanted to keep the land in the family. The only reason they mentioned the option at all in the deed was to give required notice of the option to third parties.

The dissent (Burke, J.) first claims that the agreement is fully integrated and therefore precludes oral evidence of the non-assignability term. Alternatively, the dissent argues that the agreement is at least partially integrated and therefore precludes oral evidence of the non-assignability term because that term conflicts with the "absolute" language of the written option. That language is absolute for two reasons. First, (implicit in Burke's argument), under the plain meaning rule it does not expressly limit assignability. Second, California statutes provide a default rule according to which options are assignable absent an agreement otherwise.

Note 2 (Page 623). This Note begins by rehearsing Justice Traynor's opinion. As part of that exercise, we focus on Justice Traynor's analysis under the natural omission test for term-specific merger. It asks students to identify Justice Traynor's explanation for why the parties might naturally have omitted the non-assignability term from the reservation in the deed. Justice Traynor's answer is that the parties might well have included the non-assignability clause in a separate oral agreement because the written reservation of a simple option in the deed was sufficient to preserve the grantee's option against third party transferees of the property. Since the only point of the non-assignability clause was to insure the property remained in the family, and one of the grantors (Medora) was the sister of one of the grantees (Dallas), the grantors would not have felt a need to commit this restriction to the writing: They knew the grantees (Dallas and Rebecca Masterson) had orally agreed that the option should not be assignable and would not attempt to assign it. Neither party had the legal sophistication to anticipate the usefulness of writing the term down to protect the property from a bankruptcy trustee. They would have had to have understood both the laws of bankruptcy and the potential for a writing to exclude oral evidence under the parol evidence rule. Thus, Justice Traynor concludes the written agreement is not fully integrated with respect to the oral non-assignability term. He therefore admits the oral evidence that the parties agreed to make the option non-assignable.

The Note then explores the structure and soundness of Justice Burke's dissent. The dissent can be framed as an argument, based on the parol evidence rule, that precludes evidence to establish that the oral non-assignability term is an additional term in the agreement. Thus framed, the dissent's argument falls under our chapter's first rubric of "identifying the terms of agreement." But as we demonstrate below, Justice Burke's argument for prohibiting evidence of a non-assignability term ultimately rests on his claim that the written option term must be interpreted as assignable. Thus framed, the dissent's argument falls under our chapter's second rubric of "interpreting the terms of agreement."

Justice Burke's argument begins by implicitly assuming that the grant deed is partially integrated. If the agreement is not integrated at all, the parol evidence rule provides no bar to admission of any evidence. If it is partially integrated, however, the parol evidence rule bars evidence of contradictory additional terms. Justice Traynor applies the natural omission test and rejects the claim that the writing is fully integrated with respect to the non-assignability term. Justice Burke does not, however, dispute Justice Traynor's analysis of the natural omission test. Instead, his argument is that evidence of the non-assignability of the written option is barred by the parol evidence rule because it would contradict the written option term in the agreement. The premise of Justice Burke's argument, therefore, is that the writing is merely partially integrated. Justice Traynor never directly responds to Justice Burke's claim. As we explain below, Justice Traynor only responds briefly, though indirectly, to one of Justice Burke's arguments supporting his claim that the oral non-assignability term contradicts the written option term.

Justice Burke offers two arguments to demonstrate that the oral non-assignability term contradicts the written option term. The first is that, under California statutes, written options must be interpreted by default as assignable– that is, unless the parties agree otherwise, options will be interpreted as assignable under California law. Justice Burke then adds the claim that under California law an option is assignable unless the parties agree otherwise *in writing*: "California statutes expressly declare that [an option] is assignable, and *only if I add language in writing* showing my intent to withhold or restrict the right of assignment may the grant be so limited." (See Note 2, second paragraph). Here Justice Burke interprets California's default rule for interpreting whether an option is assignable as containing a statute of frauds for opting out of the default rule. But while the California statutes expressly declare that an option is assignable unless the parties agree otherwise, they do not require that the parties are able to opt out of that interpretation only by doing so *in writing*. That is, the statutes do not expressly provide a statute of frauds for opting out of the California default interpretation of option terms. Thus, Justice Traynor correctly argues that, as reproduced in Note 2, "[t]he fact that there is a written memorandum, however, does not necessarily preclude parol evidence rebutting a term that the law would otherwise presume." (*page 619*) Justice Traynor's point is that California law establishes a default rule for interpreting options, written or not, but does not prohibit opting out of the default rule orally rather than in writing. The Calfornia statutes, therefore, do not establish that the written option term must be interpreted as assignable.

Justice Burke's second argument is that because the language of the written option is "absolute," the option itself must be interpreted as unqualified. The claim seems to be that the absence of qualifying language compels the interpretation of the option as unqualified. But even under the plain meaning rule, the fact that the written option contains no qualifying language can no more establish that the obligation it expresses is *not* qualified than it can establish that the obligation it expresses *is* qualified. Justice Burke's argument presumes that a written option that fails to contain qualifying language should be interpreted as unqualified. But Justice Burke's interpretive default rule is no less arbitrary than its opposite: a written option that fails to contain language stating that the option is *not* qualified should be interpreted as qualified. Given that the written option fails to state whether it is qualified or not, neither interpretation can dominate the other. Even the plain meaning rule, which Justice Burke presumably accepts, cannot generate an interpretation based on written language alone when that language has more than one possible interpretation. Ambiguous terms have no plain meaning.

In response, Justice Burke could fall back to his first argument, that California law compels options to be interpreted by default as assignable unless the parties agree otherwise. But as we (and Justice Traynor) explained above, this merely raises the question of whether the parties opted out of that default rule by agreeing otherwise. The evidence of the oral non-assignability agreement is proffered precisely to support the claim that the parties in fact did opt out of the California default interpretive rule for options. Since those statutes do not expressly require parties to opt out in writing, the oral evidence can hardly be construed as inconsistent with the written option term. Rather, the evidence is being offered to assist in the interpretation of the written option term. The claim that the oral non-assignability term would contradict the written option term begs the question against the Sines.

At bottom, Burke's claim can be supported only by arguing that the California statutes themselves must be interpreted as *implicitly* creating a statute of frauds for opting out of the default interpretation of written option terms. Although implying additional requirements into statutes raises serious questions about statutory interpretation, we can at least understand the policy argument that would support this reconstructed version of Burke's argument. The justification for implying the statute of frauds for such opt outs is that it is necessary to provide adequate notice to third parties who count such options among the assets available to them should their debtors default. When lenders verify that their prospective debtors own an option, they would have no way of verifying their prospective debtors' claim to own an unqualified option. Even though the written option recorded with the deed contains no qualifying language, they could not assume that the option is assignable. In *Masterson*, had Masterson's creditors known that his option might be non-assignable even though it is recorded without qualifying language, they might not have advanced credit to him (or if they would have, it would have been at a higher interest rate). Thus, a statute of frauds requiring qualifications of options to be in writing would allow debtors to make verifiable claims to ownership of unqualified options, and therefore lower their cost of credit. This policy argument, however, is at best buried deeply below the otherwise uncompelling doctrinal argument Burke advances.

Note 3 (Page 624). Here we present the recurring issue of prospective regulation versus dispute resolution. While a rule that denies parties the benefit of their bargain appears to violate the Kantian maxim to treat others as ends in themselves and not as means to some other end, a deeper analysis shows favoring prospective regulation to be less morally problematic. First, when a rule is well-established, parties should be expected to consider it when fashioning their agreements. If a party chooses not to include a term in a writing, she does so knowing that evidence of that term might not be admissible in litigation. Therefore, a prohibition against admitting such evidence respects the bargain into which she entered. Also, if the reason for the rule is valid (i.e., if people really do commit agreements to writing to reduce the chance of later misinterpretation of their obligations), enforcing the rule is an end to which she would subscribe, at least ex ante.

Note 4 (Page 624). This Note contains definitions of the parol evidence rule by three noted scholars. A careful reading will reveal that their differences amount to more than merely different ways of saying the same thing. Wigmore does not require any level of integration, while Corbin requires a complete and accurate integration and Williston requires just integration. Wigmore makes all utterances immaterial, while Corbin only prohibits evidence of antecedent understandings and negotiations. Finally, while both Corbin and Williston allow for at least the natural omission doctrine, Wigmore leaves no room for it. They do, however, have much in common. They embody the same basic idea that when there is a writing, it is to be privileged over, and might completely prohibit, extrinsic evidence. None of them addresses the issue of interpreting the terms, which is properly left out of a definition of parol evidence rule itself.

The UCC Parol Evidence Rule: The "Certain Inclusion" Test for Integration and the Consistency Test for Admitting Extrinsic Evidence

Hunt Foods v. Doliner (*Page 626*). Hunt bought an option to buy Doliner's stock in Eastern Can Company when the two agreed to take a break from their negotiations over the sale of the stock. The written agreement for the purchase of the option made no mention of any conditions on the option. Hunt attempted to exercise the option, and Doliner refused to sell, arguing that the option could be exercised only if he sought other bids for the stock. Hunt argued that the parol evidence rule made evidence of the condition on the option inadmissible. The court analyzed the issue under § 2-202. First, it found that the proffered condition was "clearly 'additional'" because it was not set out in the writing. The court then analyzed whether the condition was consistent with the writing. To be inconsistent, the term must contradict or negate a term of the writing. But the court held that a term or condition that merely lessens the effect of a written term does not thereby contradict or negate it. Finally, the court found that the parties would not have certainly included the condition in the writing had they agreed to it. According to the court, this standard, as set out in UCC § 2-202, com. 3, requires only that it is possible, but not necessarily plausible, that the parties agreed to the term but did not include it in their writing. Therefore, according to the court, evidence of this additional term is admissible.

Note 1 (Page 628). This note considers *Masterson* and *Hunt Foods*. We ask the students how Justice Burke might object to the reasoning in *Hunt Foods*. Whereas *Hunt Foods* treats the question solely as one of the parol evidence rule, Justice Burke's argument reveals that the parol evidence rule cannot be applied without first interpreting the meaning of the option term. Just as Justice Burke concluded that the option term in *Masterson* was unconditional because it contained no express condition, so too he presumably would conclude that the option in *Hunt Foods* is unconditional.   Justice Burke's argument implicitly relies on a plain meaning interpretation according to which options stated in absolute, unqualified terms have as their plain meaning that they are unconditional. Evidence of an additional term rendering the option conditional would therefore contradict the plain meaning of the written term. The court in *Hunt Foods* therefore implicitly rejects such a plain meaning interpretation of the option term.

We also point out that the question of whether the proffered evidence is consistent with the writing does not arise until the court has first determined that the agreement is partially integrated. The court here never expressly finds the agreement to be partially integrated. Instead, the court claims that, under UCC § 2-202, com. 3, the parties would not have certainly included the condition in their writing, and therefore concludes the writing is not fully integrated with respect to the condition. Ideally, the *Hunt Foods* court would first have found expressly that the parties intended the written option term as their final expression of that term before turning to the question of whether the condition contradicts that term. (If the court did not believe the agreement was partially integrated, then there would be no need to exclude the evidence of the condition even if it did contradict the written option term).

Once the court (implicitly) determined that the written option term was the final expression of the option term, the question then becomes whether the proffered evidence of the condition contradicts that term. This is where the *Hunt Foods* court introduces a novel interpretive principle: "To be inconsistent the term must contradict or negate a term of the writing . . . . [A] term or condition which has a lesser effect is provable." Thus, even if the appropriate interpretation of the written option term is that it is unconditional, evidence that the parties agreed the option would be conditional does not contradict the written option term because it merely "lessens" the effect of the option. Presumably, the *Hunt Foods* court would bar only evidence of a term that literally negates the written option (i.e., evidence that the parties agreed that Hunt Foods would have no option to purchase from Doliner). Such a lax interpretive maxim threatens to undermine the purpose of partial integration. If the parties intend the written option to be the final expression of the option term, and it is clear that the proper interpretation of that option is that it is unconditional, then allowing evidence that the option is conditional undermines the point of the parties' agreement that the written option term is a final expression. We try to make this point by asking whether evidence that an agreement's quantity term is "one dozen horses" contradicts a final written quantity term of "two dozen horses." *Hunt Foods* appears to answer "no"– it simply "lessens" the effect of the written quantity term. We hope the absurdity of this result speaks for itself (but of course it does not– *see Columbia Nitrogen on page 683*).

We then turn to the *Hunt Foods* interpretation of the Code's "certain inclusion" test. Here, our point is that this interpretation makes a term-specific merger practically irrelevant. In order to exclude evidence of an additional term on grounds that the agreement is fully integrated with respect to that term, the *Hunt Foods* court requires a determination that it would have been *impossible*, not merely *implausible*, for the parties to have intended that term to be part of their agreement but failed to put it in their writing. Such a lax interpretive standard for term-specific merger virtually eviscerates its purpose: to protect the agreement from ex post attacks based on alleged additional terms that significantly change the allocation of contractual benefits and burdens reflected in the final written terms of the agreement.

Why does the *Hunt Foods* court embrace such unappealing analyses of the consistency test and certain inclusion tests? We believe that the court simply did not believe that Doliner would have agreed to grant Hunt Foods an unconditional option. After all, Doliner wished to adjourn negotiations without consummating the agreement. Granting an unconditional option would allow Hunt Foods unilaterally to decide to consummate the agreement. The mystery the court does not address, however, is why Doliner would have agreed to sign a written option that failed to state that it was conditional on Doliner shopping Hunt Foods' bid. According to the record, Doliner asked his attorney why the option language failed to state the condition, and his attorney responded that Hunt Foods "insisted" that the written option not state any conditions. Under these circumstances, why would Doliner comply with Hunt Food's demand?

We imagine two scenarios in which Doliner valued a break in the negotiations. In the good faith scenario, he is not yet satisfied with all the elements of the agreement, anticipates he will be able to work them out in negotiations, but has a pressing demand that requires him to adjourn negotiations for several weeks. In the bad faith scenario, Doliner wants the adjournment because he plans to shop Hunt Foods' bid. Either way, Hunt Foods would be understandably worried that Doliner might shop their bid, so they insist on an option to protect them in the event Doliner does so. But they understand that an option conditional on proving that Doliner shopped their bid would be of little value in court because they would have difficulty carrying their burden of proof. Doliner could simply reconvene negotiations, terminate negotiations on ostensibly independent grounds, and then consummate his deal with the other bidder to whom he had secretly shopped Hunt Foods' bid during the adjournment. Even if Hunt Foods believed they could "observe" Doliner's bad faith (they could find out through "sources" if he shopped their bid), they knew they could not readily "verify" (i.e. prove) his bid-shopping to a court. Hence, they agreed *informally* not to exercise their option unless Doliner shopped their bid. But they insisted *formally* on a legally unrestricted option. Doliner would agree to these terms if either (1) he had no intention of shopping their bid (i.e., he was acting in good faith) and trusted Hunt Foods to abide by their informal agreement (either because they are principled or because reputational incentives would lead them to do so), or (2) he planned to shop their bid and then render the option useless by using precisely the gambit in evidence in this litigation: claiming that the option was in fact conditional and requiring Hunt Foods to prove the condition is met (knowing that they would be unable to bear that burden of proof). Hunt Foods then exercises the option either because Doliner in fact did shop their bid (they observed that fact even if they couldn't verify it to a court) or because they acted in bad faith by taking advantage of their legally unrestricted option and breaching their informal agreement.

Either way, we believe the court would have been wise to find the written option fully integrated and therefore to rule inadmissible the evidence of an oral condition on the option. Given that Doliner knowingly signed the written option without requiring the condition to be stated in the writing, we believe it probable that both parties intended to regulate their relationship with a dual regime of legal and non-legal norms. The difficulty of proving bid-shopping forced Doliner to grant an unrestricted option to Hunt Foods (as their demand made clear) or lose their bid entirely (or forgo adjournment and continue negotiations). Hunt Foods made clear that the price for adjournment was an unrestricted, written option (why else would they refuse to put the restriction in writing and why else would Doliner agree?).

Thus, the court can readily reconcile enforcement of the unrestricted written option with their belief that Doliner would have wished to grant only a conditional option. Given the limits of proof and the availability of informal norms, Doliner would have been quite reasonable to grant the legally unconditional option as the price for adjourning negotiations without Hunt Foods withdrawing their offer. On this account, Doliner knowingly took the risk that Hunt Foods would breach their informal agreement, or observe him shopping their bid, and exercise their unrestricted option. He preferred this risk to losing Hunt Foods' bid or continuing negotiation without an adjournment. By correctly identifying Doliner's motives, but failing to understand why Hunt Foods would not be willing to accept a restricted option (and why Doliner would be willing to sign an unrestricted option), the court undermines the ability of parties in the future to regulate their relationship with a combination of formal and informal norms.

Note 2 (Page 628). The court in *Snyder v. Herbert Greenbaum* explicitly rejected the reasoning on the standard for inconsistency in *Hunt Foods*. The court concluded in *Snyder* that unconditional, unilateral rescission was a term the parties "certainly" would have included in the final written agreement. It reasoned that "inconsistent" means the absence of reasonable harmony in terms of the language and respective obligations of the parties, and not the more narrower "negate or contradict requirement" from *Hunt Foods*.

Merger Clauses

UAW-GM Human Resource Center v. KSL *(Page 631).* The plaintiff signed an agreement with a corporation subsequently purchased by the defendant. The plaintiff claimed that the defendant's predecessor in interest agreed orally that the hotel provided (the contract was for a convention) would be staffed by union workers. The agreement contained a merger clause, which the defendant claimed made the agreement fully integrated, and thus evidence of the alleged oral agreement inadmissible. The court, after a lengthy analysis of persuasive authority, agreed with the defendant. It held that when there is a merger clause (not obtained through fraud, etc.) it becomes part of the agreement and, like any other term, must be respected. Therefore, parol evidence cannot be admitted on the issue of integration– the parties settled that matter with the merger clause. The court argued that admitting parol evidence on this question would make an agreement with a merger clause no different than one without such a clause. By including a merger clause, the parties clearly indicated that the agreement is integrated and thus removed that as a threshold issue. Since the agreement was fully integrated, the evidence of a prior or contemporaneous oral agreement is not admissible.

Finally, the court addressed the plaintiff's claim of fraud arising out of the failure of the defendant's predecessor in interest to inform the plaintiff of the impending sale of the hotel at the time of the oral agreement regarding unionized workers at the hotel. The court argues that only fraud inducing the agreement to the merger clause itself would vitiate the merger clause. Any oral representations made by the defendant would constitute fraud only if the plaintiff reasonably relied on them. But the presence of the merger clause in the writing makes reliance on any previous representations or agreements unreasonable. Since the court finds no fraud inducing the merger clause itself, it finds the clause enforceable and thus prohibits evidence of prior oral agreements.

The dissent argues that a written merger clause does not, and cannot, on its own conclusively demonstrate that the parties intended their writing to be the complete and exclusive statement of all the terms of their agreement: It is always possible that the parties did not assent to the merger clause itself. The dissent relies on the premise, established in R2d § 209, com. b, that "[w]ritten contracts, signed by both parties, may include an explicit declaration that there are no other agreements between the parties, but such a declaration may not be conclusive." Further, the dissent argues that oral evidence must be admissible to prove that the parties did not assent to the merger clause. "The oral admissions of the plaintiff that the agreement included matters not contained in the writing may be proved to show that it was not assented to as a complete integration, however complete it may look on its face." (642, citing Corbin, Contracts, § 582). "The fact that a written document contains one of these express provisions does not prove that the document itself was ever assented to or ever became operative as a contract." (643, quoting Corbin, § 578). The dissent claims that oral evidence is therefore always admissible to demonstrate that the parties did not agree to an integration clause included in the writing. Thus, oral evidence that the parties intended the agreement to include an oral term would be admissible to demonstrate that the parties did not intend to agree on the merger clause despite their knowledge that the writing they signed included such a clause. The dissent then implicitly responds to the majority's claim that plaintiff's reliance on oral representations was not reasonable given the existence of the merger clause: According to the dissent, the reliance was reasonable if the plaintiffs did not assent to the merger clause. Finally, the dissent asserts that if the parties intended their agreement to contain terms not in their writing, then the claim made by the merger clause is false. That the parties asserted that fact by including the merger clause is not sufficient to establish that fact as true. Contrary evidence should be admissible to prove it is false.

Note 2 (Page 645). Note 2 prompts students to analyze the dispute in this case. The "easy" question is whether oral evidence is admissible to demonstrate that one party did not in fact consent to the merger clause. The clearest, and least controversial, example would be fraud in the execution: The party asserting the contract (excusably) did not even know the writing it signed contained a merger clause (e.g., a blind person who was told by their contracting partner that the contract did not contain a merger clause). Alternatively, oral evidence would be admissible to demonstrate that the clause was inserted due to a scrivener's error (e.g., the secretary charged with typing the final agreement accidentally typed in a clause from a prior, rejected draft). Even the majority would concede that the integration clause cannot prevent the introduction of oral evidence for these purposes. It's also easy to identify the critical flaw in the majority's reasoning in Note 2(A). As we explain, that the proffered oral evidence contradicts the merger clause has no bearing on whether it is admissible. The evidence is being offered to prove that the parties did not consent to the merger clause, not to prove that the clause doesn't mean what it says. The court's second argument is equally unpersuasive. The merger clause bars introduction of oral evidence only if it was agreed to by the parties. That the clause, if agreed to, would bar admission of oral evidence of additional terms has no bearing on whether oral evidence should be admissible to prove that the parties did not agree to the clause itself.

The harder question is whether evidence of prior oral representations or agreements should be admissible to prove that the parties could not have meant what the integration clause in their agreement asserts– namely, that the writing contains all the terms of their agreement. Since the merger clause bars evidence of additional terms only if the parties intended it to, why shouldn't courts admit evidence that the parties intended their agreement to include terms not included in the writing, solely for purposes of determining whether the parties actually meant what the merger clause says? In principle, evidence that demonstrates the parties failed to agree to any clause is and should be admissible to prove that fact. The question here, however, is whether evidence that the parties at one time considered or agreed to a term not included in a subsequent writing is relevant to determining whether they in fact agreed on the merger clause that they included in their writing. Since the sole purpose of a merger clause is to exclude such evidence, the fact that there is evidence that the parties had previously considered or agreed to a term not included in the subsequent writing provides no reason to doubt the parties agreed to the merger clause. It is precisely under these conditions that parties benefit from clarifying their final agreement by creating a writing and deeming it to constitute the complete and exclusive statement of all the terms of their writing. In creating such a writing, they choose to preserve or eliminate prior agreements or understandings through their decision of whether to incorporate those agreements or understandings in the final writing. Thus, evidence that the parties had previous agreements or understandings not included in the writing provides no reason to doubt that the parties did not intend to be bound by the merger clause they included in their writing. Given that they knowingly included a merger clause in their agreement, there is a strong presumption that they meant to be bound by it. That presumption might be overcome by compelling evidence that they did not intend to be bound by it, such as evidence that *both* parties misunderstood the effect or meaning of the clause (for example, because counsel gave them an incorrect explanation of the clause's significance). But evidence that the parties had prior agreements or understandings provides no reason to doubt that the parties intended to be bound by a merger clause they knowingly included in their agreement (and that they therefore understood that prior agreements not included in their integrated agreement would not be provable). Yet the dissent's argument for admitting evidence of the parties' prior oral understanding is based exclusively on the potential that evidence has for demonstrating that the parties did not agree to the merger clause they knowingly included in their written agreement. In our view, because such evidence has no bearing on that question, there is no reason to doubt that the parties intended to be bound by the plain meaning of the merger clause which they knowingly included in their agreement. Thus, because the merger clause should be enforced, the evidence of the prior oral agreement should be barred.

Note 4 (Page 647) The *Seibel* a court invalidated a merger clause because it was hidden on the back of a form agreement and not conspicuous. The questions in the Note suggest that the court's true motivation is something other than forcing seller's to make merger clauses conspicuous. Even if the clause appeared conspicuously on the contract, the court could have invalidated it by, for one example, ruling that it was an attempt to disclaim a warranty and as such was invalid against an express warranty made in the same agreement (UCC 2-316). The court was more likely motivated by a desire to prevent what it saw as injustice. One way to judge whether the merger clause in this contract should have been upheld is to look at the price paid for the good. If the price was lower with the merger clause than without, then that clause ought to be enforced and evidence of the warranty term should not be admitted (this method will be particularly effective if the warranty was the only oral agreement not included in the writing).

C. Interpretation of the Terms of an Agreement
Objectivism and Contextualism in Common Law Interpretation

When a term is ambiguous, there is no difference between the contextualist and objectivist (plain meaning) approaches. Consider the "Peerless" case. There, the parties' agreement centered on the cargo of a ship called the "Peerless" that sailed out of Bombay. As it turned out, there were two such ships, each departing and arriving at the same ports on different dates. Contextualist and objectivist approaches will yield the same result. Since the term in question is ambiguous, the objectivist approach allows for contextual evidence to resolve the ambiguity.

The tension between contextualism and objectivism, therefore, arises only when a term has an unambiguous plain meaning (assuming that's possible) when contextual evidence supports the claim that the parties attached a different meaning to the term.

In re Soper's Estate *(Page 651).* Ira Soper left his wife, disappeared from his home town and assumed a new identity in Minneapolis. There, going by the name of John Young, he married again, not telling anyone of the wife he had left behind. In Minneapolis, he entered into a business partnership that provided a death benefit to his "wife" upon his death. When he died, the insurance company paid the benefit to Mrs. Young. Some time later, Mrs. Soper learned of these events and sued to recover the payment on the grounds that as Mr. Soper's only legal wife, she was the legal beneficiary of Mr. Soper's stock and life insurance plan. She argued that Mrs. Young should not be allowed to introduce extrinsic evidence that the parties intended the term "wife" to refer to Mrs. Young because the term "wife" is not ambiguous. The court, quoting several sources that advocated a more contextualist approach, found that the seemingly unambiguous term became "susceptible of construction" because "ambiguity appears when attempt is made to operate the contract."

The dissent holds firm to the plain meaning rule. The reasoning is straightforward: Mrs. Soper was the only legal wife of the decedent. There is no way to construe the word "wife" to mean anything other than the only wife the decedent had.

Note 1 *(Page 655).* This Note walks students through the arguments supporting the dissent and then the majority opinions. In re *Soper's Estate* provides the ideal context for discussing the implications of the tension between (ex post) dispute resolution and (ex ante) prospective regulation for contract interpretation. If the only goal of contractual interpretation were to discern the subjective intent of the parties to the case being adjudicated, there is no question that the majority is correct. Despite the ostensible plain meaning of the term "wife," according to which it would necessarily refer to Mrs. Soper, it is equally clear that the parties intended that term to refer to Ms. Young. The only justification for ignoring their clear intent draws on policy concerns relevant only from the perspective of prospective regulation: The state's interest in preserving the integrity of the (plain) meaning of the English language. The reason the court should ignore the parties' subjective intent and enforce only the objective meaning of the term "wife" is to preserve the reliability of the meaning of terms with plain meaning for the benefit of future parties. The practice of enforcing plain meaning, even in the teeth of decisive evidence that such meaning varies from the parties' intended meaning, allows future parties to rely on the use and understanding of the plain meaning of terms without fear that a court will, ex post (at the time of adjudication) interpret such terms contrary to their plain meaning. Such a system will provide parties with incentives to use the plain meaning of terms to express their subjective intent. From both the autonomy and efficiency perpspectives on contracting, the preservation of a reliable linguistic system for communicating contractual intent is desirable. It lowers the cost of contracting by lowering the costs of expressing intention and lowering the probability of misinterpretation by contractual partners and courts. It therefore reduces the costs of engaging in autonomous and mutually beneficial exchanges of promises relative to a system that allows courts to ignore the plain meaning of terms. Of course, this analysis presupposes that plain meaning is relatively straight forward for parties and courts to discern, and that many terms have a plain meaning, one that is, by hypothesis, context independent. Although the term "wife" presents perhaps the best example of a term with a plain meaning, most terms are susceptible to multiple interpretations. In short, a plain meaning regime won't do much good if the meaning of most terms is ambiguous and therefore context dependent.

Pacific Gas & Electric v. Thomas Drayage & Rigging *(Page 656)*. The defendant in this case agreed to assume liability, among other things, for damage to property that occurs in the course of work the defendant contracted to do for the plaintiff. During the course of that work, damage was done to the plaintiff's property. The defendant proffered evidence that the clause under which it assumed liability was intended only to apply to the property of third parties. The trial court rejected the evidence based on the plain meaning rule. The California Supreme Court reversed, with Justice Traynor writing the opinion. The court reasoned that, because words do not have perfect, plain meanings, the question of whether contextual evidence of meaning should be admitted turns on whether it is relevant to prove a meaning to which the language of the instrument is reasonably susceptible.

Trident Center v. Connecticut General Life Ins. Co. *(Page 660)*. The parties, both sophisticated businesses with counsel, negotiated an extensive contract for a loan from the defendant to the plaintiff. One clause of the contract stated that "maker shall not have the right to prepay the principal amount hereof in whole or in part" for the first 12 years of the loan. The plaintiff argued nonetheless that it had the right to prepayment in the first 12 years provided it paid a ten percent penalty. This claim was based on a second clause of the contract which provides that "in the event of a prepayment resulting from a default . . . the prepayment fee will be ten percent." Plaintiff's first argument (a within-the-four-corners argument) was that the second clause makes the meaning of the first ambiguous, and therefore justifies admitting extrinsic evidence to resolve the ambiguity. The court rejected this ambiguity argument "out of hand" because it would result in an interpretation of the first clause that rendered it meaningless: the default clause (with the ten percent penalty language) would swallow up the clause prohibiting prepayment.

The plaintiff argued in the alternative that, under the rule in California (established by *Pacific Gas*), extrinsic evidence is always admissible to interpret the meaning of contract terms (because no words have plain meanings). The court criticized this argument and the decision on which it was based. It argued that the California Supreme Court's decision in *Pacific Gas* "casts a long shadow of uncertainty over all transactions" governed by California law, and "chips away at the foundation of our legal system." Under *Pacific Gas*, parties in California can never draft a contract that is "proof to parol evidence." Further, the court wondered how, if words have no plain meaning, lower courts could be expected to follow the mandate of higher courts; or, how the state could justify imprisoning people for violating statutes that consist of "mere words . . . ." Nevertheless, the court was compelled to follow the holding in *Pacific Gas*, and held that the plaintiff should be allowed to introduce its proffered evidence of the meaning of the clause.

Pedagogy. *Pacific Gas* and *Trident Center* provide the ideal context for illustrating the centrality of the plain-meaning debate in the context of standard commercial transactions. (Although In re *Soper's Estate* provides the purist illustration of the tension between plain and contextual meaning, its facts are virtually *sui generis*. Not so in *Pacific Gas* and *Trident Center*). The plain meaning debate is personified in the likes of Justice Traynor and Judge Kozinski, two of the most articulate and forceful judges of our time. It is possible to describe the central difference between them in compact form: In adjudicating disputes, Justice Traynor takes the ex post perspective while Judge Kozinski takes the ex ante perspective. Justice Traynor is surely right that there is nothing that prevents the parties from meaning anything by the terms they use. And Judge Kozinski is also surely correct that the parol evidence rule is designed to insulate a written contract from the risk that prior written or oral statements made during negotiations will be used to interpret the content of the terms of the parties' agreement.

Unfortunately, as we have seen, the Second Restatement's parol evidence rule itself has no bearing on the standards judges should use to interpret the meaning of the terms of an agreement. While the parol evidence rule, for example, bars the introduction of prior oral statements as evidence of the terms of an integrated agreement, parties can largely undermine the purpose of this rule by reintroducing precisely the same oral statements as evidence of the meaning of the agreement's integrated terms. Indeed, any proffered evidence of the terms of an agreement can also be recast as proffered evidence of the meaning of a term in an agreement. For this reason, Judge Kozinski presumably would, in principle, favor the First Restatement's approach of using integration to trigger a more objective standard of interpretation– if the parties intended their writting to be the complete and exclusive statement of terms of their agreement, their purpose would be defeated by allowing in extrinsic evidence of the meaning of the terms in their agreement that have a (relatively) plain meaning. But that is most certainly not the law in California. Notwithstanding even full integration, courts must allow the contextual evidence of the meaning of contractual terms, providing the terms are "reasonably susceptible" to the alleged meaning.

Which brings us to a final point: Given Judge Kozinkski's hostility toward the California rule layed out in *Pacific Gas*, why didn't he simply declare that the "no prepayment" clause was not "reasonably susceptible" to plaintiff's interpretation? *Pacific Gas* clearly endorses the reasonable susceptibility standard. Judge Kozinski could have applied it in good faith without relying on an express, plain meaning argument. Perhaps in his zeal to reject the rationale underlying the *Pacific Gas* rule, Judge Kozinski failed to take advantage of the clear doctrinal avenues available under *Pacific Gas* to avoid precisely the result he ultimately allows. Indeed, one could ask, as we do in *Note 2 below,* why Judge Kozinski felt compelled to write the opinion he did, given that he believes the *Pacific Gas* precedent clearly compels reversal. Is Judge Kozinski hoping his opinion will have more persuasive authority as unabashed *dicta* in a case than as an opinion in a law review article?

Note 1 (Page 663). This Note explores the strength of the court's position in *Pacific Gas*, and points out that the problem Justice Traynor sees in the plain meaning rule (judges determining meaning) persists under his approach. In determining if a term is "reasonably susceptible" to a proffered meaning, the court must start with its view of the plain meaning. Otherwise, there is no starting point and any meaning must be considered reasonable.

Note 2 (Page 664). Note 2 points out that the court in *Trident Center* has to resort to the context of the whole writing (looking to other clauses in the writing) to buttress its argument that the meaning of the clause prohibiting prepayment is plain. But if the plainness of the meaning of one clause within a writing turns on the meaning of another within the writing, why should we doubt that whether the meaning of a clause within a writing is plain turns on evidence outside of the writing. Once the context camel's nose is in the tent, doesn't the whole camel come in?

Note 4 (Page 666). The "New Textualist" approach to statutory interpretation – led by Justice Antonin Scalia – calls for consideration of the words of statutes only in interpreting their meaning, and rejects the use of legislative history, etc. This approach closely resembles the plain meaning rule, and the criticism of the new textualist approach parallel those of the plain meaning rule. For example, not consulting legislative history, etc. leaves courts with insufficient context for arriving at the proper interpretation of the statute. Similarly, ignoring the negotiations of the parties or the course of performance, etc. can leave courts without a critical tool for determining the meaning of a term. On the other hand, the new textualist approach doesn't appear to allow for consulting context even when a term is ambiguous; because the plain meaning rule does allow for extrinsic evidence in such situation, it's not susceptible to all of the arguments against the new textualist approach.

Frigaliment v. International Sales Corp. *(Page 670).* The plaintiff sued the defendant for selling it "fowl" (lower grade chicken) instead of "broiler" (higher grade chicken). The defendant argued that the term "chicken" in the contract included all types of chickens, while the plaintiff contended it meant only broiler chicken. The court found that the meaning of "chicken" was ambiguous. It looked first to the rest of the writing to determine what meaning should be applied. There, it found some evidence to support defendant's contention in the reference to government regulations of chicken, in which that term has many meanings (including fowl). The court also looked elsewhere for evidence of the meaning of the term. The plaintiff's only evidence that the word "chicken" meant broiler was that the agreement used the English word "chicken" instead of the German word "Huhn" (the rest of the agreement was in German). This is evidence of the more narrow meaning, argued the plaintiff, because Huhn means all types of chickens. The defendant should have understood this distinction because its agents spoke German. The court rejected this argument on the force of evidence that the plaintiff's agent said any type of chickens would do.

The court also rejected the plaintiff's usage of trade argument. First, it said that when one party is not a member of the trade circle (it apparently believed the defendant was not), the usage must be very generally known in the community ("chicken"-implies-broiler-only did not meet this standard– the witness whose testimony was supposed to show this specified broiler in his own contracts) or actual knowledge of it by that party must be proven (which was not in this case). Finally (the court walked through more arguments, but this is the most persuasive), the court found that the price paid by the plaintiff was too far below the market price for broilers for the plaintiff to be justified in understanding the contract as guaranteeing broilers.

Note 1 (Page 675). One major problem with is that Judge Friendly framed the case as a question of whether the plaintiff had carried its burden of proving which of the two plausible meanings the parties intended. Yet it is doubtful that this case would have been decided in favor of the buyer if the seller was the party suing for breach.

At bottom, the case presents the question of whether the plain meaning of a term must be determined relative to some circumscribed community of speakers. Here we have a contest between two meanings, one broad and one narrow. It is tempting to argue that the broad, or inclusive, meaning of "chicken" is the term's plain meaning, and the narrow, more specialized meaning is not plain at all. But as the Corbin excerpt in *Note 2 on page 675* suggests, context determines which meaning appears plain and which does not. Narrow, specialized meanings that may be plain to farmers and industry members may not be to lay persons and judges. It may therefore be necessary to admit contextual evidence to determine whether a term has a plain meaning in a given context. A strict interpretation of plain meaning, however, would not countenance the idea of context-sensitive plain meaning. Either a term has a (unique) plain meaning or it does not. If it has more than one meaning, it is ambiguous and thus has no plain meaning. Corbin's discussion, however, supports the notion that meaning can be plain only relative to a given context. At its limit, however, this view suggests that a meaning can be plain between the parties (the narrowest of contexts), even though it conflicts with other meanings that are plain in a larger context (e.g., what most people, expert or not, take the term to mean). Thus, once one concedes that meaning can be plain only relative to a given population of speakers, the plain meaning regime threatens to reduce to a full-blown contextualist approach. To prevent such a reduction, defenders of a plain meaning regime either would have to deny that plain meaning is relative to context, or defend a particular standard for determining the unique context relative to which all plain meaning is to be determined.

Essay: The Goals of Contractual Interpretation (Page 676). This essay discusses the goals of contractual interpretation. We use this scholarly debate to frame our analysis of all the interpretation cases considered above. The Essay first takes students through the economic and autonomy theories of contract law, and how they support the objective theory of contract law. It then points out the tension between the need for prospective regulation and the desire to not violate the Kantian maxim. This tension is part of the debate between the contextualist and objectivist approaches to interpretation, which is laid out in the end of the Essay. Ultimately, that debate turns on the resolution of this tension, the plausibility of the claims that some terms have a plain meaning, and which regime minimizes the expected costs of contracting. The objectivist approach minimizes costs by lowering the probability of contractual misinterpretation; the contextualist approach minimizes costs by reducing the cost of specifying the terms of the contract. Which yields the lowest net total costs is an unresolved empirical question.

Objectivism and Contextualism in the UCC

Section 2-202 of the UCC essentially clarifies and codifies the contextualist approach of the Restatement (Second). It rejects the plain meaning rule and the ambiguity requirement for admitting extrinsic evidence of meaning, and states that even fully integrated agreements may be explained or supplemented by usage of trade, course of dealing, or course of performance. This introduces a greater possibility for judicial misinterpretation of the terms of an agreement by providing multiple meanings from which a court must choose. It also introduces the possibility that a court will use that extrinsic evidence as evidence of the meaning of a term when it is actually a series of one-time waivers that both parties understood were optional (but one party later insists were not when performance under the original contract terms is not in that party's interest). The justification for § 2-202, then, turns on the assumption that the reduction in the cost of articulating the terms of the agreement more than makes up for the increased possibility of misinterpretation.

Columbia Nitrogen v. Royster *(Page 683).* In this case, Columbia Nitrogen agreed to buy phosphate from Royster. That agreement was put in writing, and the writing contained a quantity term (minimum of 31,000 tons a year for three years), a price escalator term, and a clause that said the contract was not subject to interpretation based on prior oral agreements. The market price fell well below the contract price and Columbia Nitrogen bought significantly less than the stated quantity (less than one-tenth of the amount, according to the *Southern Concrete* court). In defending against Royster's suit for breach, Columbia Nitrogen sought to introduce usage of trade and course of dealing evidence to explain that the minimum quantity term allowed it to buy significantly less than the amount stated. The court ruled that the evidence was admissible.

The court rejected Royster's argument that the writing is fully integrated and stated that even if it is fully integrated, § 2-202 allows extrinsic evidence that is reasonably consistent with the written terms. The court also rejected Royster's argument that the integration clause prohibits the use of extrinsic evidence on the ground it did not meet the "carefully negated" standard of § 2-202, com. 2. The clause only mentioned prior oral agreements, which, the court argued, does not include usage of trade, course of dealing, and course of performance. Finally, the court considered whether the extrinsic evidence contradicted the terms of the agreement, and found that a 90% deviation was acceptable in the trade and given the course of dealing. The court was led to this conclusion by the failure of the contract to articulate the consequences of ordering less than the quantity stated. Also, it was silent about adjusting prices and quantities to reflect a declining market, which, the court said, calls for recourse to usage of trade and course of dealing to supplement and explain the contract. The court also found significance in the use of the words "products supplied" instead of "products purchased" in referring to the minimum tonnages and additional quantities. According to the court, this description is consistent with the proffered evidence. Finally, the court argued that the decision by the parties to not include a liquidated damages clause for the quantity purchased under the minimum after having considered it was evidence that falling below the minimum would not be considered a breach by the parties.

One problem with the court's reasoning that is worth noting here is that a more persuasive interpretation of the significance of liquidated damages clause negotiations implies the exact opposite of what the court asserted– that is, that falling under the quantity stated would constitute a breach. The parties' decision to reject a liquidated damages clause for such a failure hardly supports the conclusion that the parties decided such a failure would not constitute a breach. Rather, the more plausible conclusion is that the parties decided to rely on expectation damages, the contract default rule, in the event the buyer fails to order the minimum quantity required under the contract.

Southern Concrete v. Mableton Contractors *(Page 687)*. In this case, Southern agreed to sell Mableton "approximately 70,000" cubic yards of concrete. The writing stated that no conditions which were not incorporated in the writing would be recognized. Mableton ended up buying only 12,000 cubic yards. In defense of Southern's suit for breach, Mableton proffered extrinsic evidence of the meaning of the quantity term and of an additional term, both of which would support such a variation. The court rejected their arguments on the ground that evidence that 12,000 was a permissible amount under the contract contradicted the quantity term of approximately 70,000.

Mableton provided two distinct doctrinal argument for allowing the extrinsic evidence. Under the first, the extrinsic evidence was offered to prove that the term "70,000 cubic yards of concrete" meant approximately 70,000 cubic yards of concrete, and that the variance allowable under that approximation was consistent with a purchase of only 12,000 cubic yards of concrete. The court rejected this argument on the ground that the extrinsic evidence was proffered to prove a meaning that contradicted the meaning of the term "70,000 cubic yards of concrete." Under the second, Mableton offered the extrinsic evidence to prove that the parties' agreement contained an additional, non-written, term– namely, that the price term called for renegotiation and constituted merely an estimate, rather than a precise requirement. The court rejected this argument on the grounds that (1) the agreement was at least partially integrated and such evidence would therefore be impermissible because it would contradict the meaning of the written price term, or (2) the agreement was fully integrated and therefore precluded the introduction of evidence of additional terms. Rejecting *Schiovone & Sons*, the court implied that the parties were seeking to avoid the inconsistency requirement for meaning evidence by introducing the same evidence in support of an additional term. Either way, the court argued, the evidence was impermissible because inconsistent with the plain meaning of the written quantity term.

Pedagogy. One of us works students through the doctrinal manuevers in each case carefully, requiring students to present and assess each argument. Here it is particularly instructive to note that while the *Southern Concrete* court clearly rejects the basic reasoning of the *Columbia Nitrogen* decision, it nonetheless takes great pains to distinguish that case on several factual grounds (some plausibly relevant, some not; see pages 689-90). Clearly, even if it could not have distinguished the case, the *Southern Concrete* court would have rejected *Columbia Nitrogen* because it failed to recognize the existence of a core plain meaning of some terms. It is instructive to point out to students that courts will go to great lengths to avoid directly rejecting a relevant precedent. The lawyering lesson here is that even when presented with a court sympathetic to the underlying policy goals supporting your client's favored outcome, courts are far more likely to be receptive to that argument if they are presented with "doctrinal permission" to reject contrary precedent as inapplicable.

The warring theoretical perspectives in these cases are clear on the face of the decisions (just as they were between Justice Traynor in *Pacific Gas* and Judge Kozinski in *Trident Center*). The fighting issue is whether any terms can have such a thing as a core plain meaning, and whether the parol evidence rule and the common law and Code standards for admitting extrinsic evidence of meaning can be made coherent and defensible if there is not. In our view, all interpretive rules presuppose that some (many) terms have a core plain meaning relative to which contesting accounts of their meaning are inconsistent (or not reasonably susceptible) and therefore not admissible. Without such a conception, there is no limit in principle on the meanings that might be assigned to terms, and thus no firm meanings on which parties can rely.

HMT v. Sunshine Biscuit, excerpted in ***Note 2 on page 692***, deals with the issue of whether actual knowledge of usage of trade is necessary for it to be part of the contract. In that case, HMT claimed that its negotiator did not have knowledge of the usage of trade that made quantity terms in processing potato contracts estimates. The court held that regardless of actual knowledge, HMT was deemed to have constructive knowledge. First, one of its employees (who signed the contract) was knowledgeable of the business and aware of the trade custom. Second persons carrying on a particular trade are deemed to be aware of prominent customs in that trade. The questions following this excerpt in Note 2 are designed to highlight again the difficulties that come with the UCC's liberal, contextualist regime. This is perhaps the best example of how such a regime can thwart the will of the parties before the court. However, it also will make students consider the power courts have to influence the behavior of future parties who are similarly situated. Again, the merits of this depend on whether the liberal use of extrinsic evidence produces enough efficiency to overcome the harm done by thwarting the parties' will and the increased possibility of misinterpretation.

Note 3 on page 694 provides two more examples: one court following *Columbia Nitrogen*, the other following *Southern Concrete*. It then provides an excerpt from a law review article that suggests a middle ground. That is, if it is reasonable to construe a written term consistently with the commercial practice, that should be done. However, if it is unreasonable, the court should take the written term as expressing the parties' intent. According to the author of the article, some trades consistently ignore clauses that are variance with custom. Thus, a trade might regard trade usage as consistent with an express term because the usage is not a contradiction but only an occasional but definite exception to the term. In such a case, the court should interpret the contract according to the usage.

In fact, the court appears to believe the writing is *not* integrated with respect to the condition when it concludes, under UCC § 2-202, com. 3, that the parties would not have certainly included the condition in their writing.

CHAPTER 7

DEFINING THE TERMS OF PERFORMANCE

A. Introduction

As we suggest in the Introduction to this chapter, we find it helpful to introduce this material by separating the various default rules governing the performance of contractual obligations into "procedural" and "substantive" categories. By the "procedural" rules governing performance, we mean the various "traffic" rules that regulate the sequence of performances and dictate when and to what extent performance is due. Students find it helpful if you explain that the reason why these "traffic" rules are necessary is a function of reciprocity– the fact that each party is both a promisor and a promisee. As a promisor I have a duty to perform. As a promisee I have a right to receive your return performance. Thus the key question is: What is the relationship between my duty to perform and my right to receive a return performance?

The so-called "substantive" rules governing performance are of two kinds. The first category, the law of warranty, specifies the default understandings regarding the quality standards that any given performance must meet. And, more specifically, warranty law directs which party bears the risks of exogenous events that may affect the quality of that performance. Here we focus on the express and implied warranties for the sale of goods in Article 2 as exemplars of these quality standards. The second category of substantive rules deals with the question of how to measure compliance with those standards of quality. How much deviation from the legal default (or the express contract specs) is tolerated. This returns us to the comparison between substantial performance under the common law and perfect tender (and cure) under the Code that we began in Chapter 1 with the analysis in *Jacob & Youngs v. Kent*.

B. Conditions
Implied Conditions

We begin the chapter with the "traffic" rules governing performance– the law of constructive conditions of exchange. We find it useful to teach this material as an exercise in contract drafting. The attorney who is drafting a contract is, in essence, charged with the responsibility of writing a "private constitution" for the little "society" of a buyer and a seller. This constitution is not written on a blank slate, however. Rather, the parties start with a set of background rules that will govern unless they elect to draft a more apt alternative provision. It follows that before a lawyer can sensibly begin the task of drafting specific provisions for a client, she must first understand what the defaults are in order to make an intelligent choice between whether to accept them or to draft an alternative arrangement.

Implied or constructive conditions of exchange respond to the central problem of reciprocal performances. A promise to perform is implicitly conditioned on the receipt of a return performance. But if that is so, then how is one to solve the problem of who goes first? The answer is found in a set of defaults. The first presumption is that performances that can be provided (relatively)

177

simultaneously are concurrent conditions of each other. Where one performance extends over time, the additional default rules, such as "work before pay" and the divisibility principle come into play.

Bell v. Elder *(Page 699)*. Elder contracted to sell undeveloped land to Bell. In the contract, seller promised to provide water and other utility hook-ups before 10/15/80, or else the contract was void. The water hook-ups were not provided by the time specified and buyer sought rescission. Defense: the buyer has never applied for a building permit to build on the property. The trial court held that the seller had no duty to perform until the buyer required the performance and could benefit from it. It was sufficient that seller was ready to provide water once buyer sought a building permit.

The appellate court affirmed. The key to reciprocal performances is the *ability* to perform, not the actual performance per se. Thus, the sequence of performance is key. Who goes first? The answer in this class of cases is the general default principle that, in the absence of an express agreement to the contrary, the implied conditions of exchange are concurrent. Thus, neither can claim a breach until one tenders and the other fails to do so. The principle of concurrent conditions is intuitively sensible. The value of my performance is a function of the value of your performance. Thus, if the value of your performance declines, I am protected against strategic breach by being able to withhold my (now more valuable) performance.

Stewart v. Newbury *(Page 703)*. *Stewart* is an old "chestnut" that articulates one of the major qualifications to the general principle that implied or constructive conditions are concurrent conditions. In this case, the parties entered into a contract in which the plaintiff contractor agreed to do the concrete work on a building that the defendant company was constructing. The agreement specified the prices for each part of the job, but said nothing about when payment would be tendered. The plaintiff claimed that the industry custom was to pay 85% every thirty days, with the remaining 15% to be retained until the work was completed. After working for a few months, he submitted a bill for the completed work, which the defendants refused to pay. As a result, plaintiff discontinued his work on the building and sued to recover his costs plus damages for breach. The court held that, in the absence of an agreement to the contrary, the contract must be substantially performed before any payment can be demanded. In other words, if you don't opt out, the default rule will govern the contract, and "work before pay" is the default.

The "work before pay" rule is a solution to the problem of how to structure reciprocal performances where one party's performance extends over a period of time, while the other's can be performed in a moment (such as by the payment of a sum of money). Under these conditions, it is impractical if not impossible for the performances to be tendered concurrently. But that doesn't really answer the hard question. Why not "pay before work"? After all, as a distributional matter the worker is likely to be the party with the weaker bargaining position and thus more vulnerable to hold up.

One rationale for the rule is that it is designed to induce the parties to solve an apportionment problem that the law is ill suited to solve on its own. Money is fungible but a performance of services is not. There is no a priori reason to apportion services according to any particular criterion such as relative degree of efforts or amount of time invested to date relative to the time to be invested in the entire project. Only the parties know how to apportion the value of a performance that extends over time. Moreover, the provider of the services has the comparative advantage in proposing a sensible apportionment. The contractor building my house knows better than I at what point his work has progressed to the stage where progress payments are appropriate. The work before pay rule thus can be seen as an information forcing default rule, inducing the party with the informational advantage to opt out of the default rule and propose an appropriate apportionment scheme.

c. Divisibility

John v. United Advertising, Inc. *(Page 706)*. One way to get around the "work before pay" problem is to find that the contract is divisible. That is, where the parties themselves have indicated that the performance of the service provided can be apportioned in some manner, and that payment is made in proportion to each component part, then the court should give effect to the parties' manifest intentions. The problems arise where the scheme of apportionment is not clearly articulated but must be inferred from the structure of the contract itself. Such a case is *United Advertising*. Here the contract broke out the rental payments for seven billboards into a per billboard rate. The contract also provided that the modification or termination of a part of the contract did not effect the whole of the agreement. The defendant failed to provide 2 of 7 signs. Plaintiff meanwhile had paid for all seven. The question is how much money should the plaintiff get back in return– the entire rental payment or only the proportion attributable to the two signs that were not installed properly?

We often ask the students to argue this case for either side. The plaintiff's argument is that this is a package deal. The signs were designed to lead the viewer right to the door of the motel. (Thus, they were interrelated, much like the Burma Shave signs that readers as old as Scott will remember from their childhood.) The defendant responds, to the contrary, that not only is the rent apportioned on a per sign basis but each sign is independent in text of any other. In short, the Burma Shave analogy is inapt. The court agrees.

Note 3 (Page 710). We find it very helpful to explicitly call the students' attention to Note 3. A partial performance by a breaching party of an entire contract that is indivisible seems to provide the promisee with a windfall equal to the value of that part performance. But as we will see in Chapter 10, ordinarily the breacher can recover in restitution for the value of the benefit conferred on the nonbreacher. This rule reduces the incentives to engage in strategic inducements to breach.

Express Conditions
a. Promises v. Conditions
We find that students often have difficulty appreciating the doctrinal distinctions between promises and conditions. This is because the concepts are hard to understand without context. Thus, we begin by providing some background context. Why would a lawyer ever draft a contract clause in which a performance or obligation is structured as a condition rather than as a promise (or vice versa)? The answer to the question requires the students to review what they learned in Chapter 1 regarding the doctrine of substantial performance. Assume the obligation is a promise (as in the

Kent's promise to pay $77,000 (including a $3,000 final payment) for the construction of a summer house with Reading pipe). Then, as per *Jacob & Youngs,* that promise is impliedly conditioned on the performance by the construction firm in building the house according to the specifications. But if the contractors "substantially perform" their promise (and offer any compensating damages to make up the difference) then the return performance of the Kents is properly owed, even though most of the house has Cohoes pipe rather than Reading pipe. On the other hand, assume the Kents' lawyer writes the contract so that the contractor's exact compliance with all the specifications is an express condition of the Kents obligation to pay the contract price. Then the Kents can, at least in theory, escape the doctrine of substantial performance and insist on a "perfect tender," i.e., a precise compliance with the express condition.

Thus, express conditions allow the drafting attorney to escape the doctrine of substantial performance and to protect any non-market or idiosyncratic values that a client might have (for Reading pipe or anything else). How might the Kents realistically have opted out of the default of implied conditions and protected themselves in this way? An answer that is common in construction projects is to require a third party approval (such as an architect's certificate) as an express condition of the owner's duty to make the final payment. But wait a minute. Isn't that exactly what the Kents did in *Jacob & Youngs*? The answer is Yes! That is exactly what they did and Cardozo simply choose to ignore the express condition.

This is an important point. It explains why courts police express conditions so aggressively and why we have rules of thumb such as "the law abhors a forfeiture." The default rules are created, for the most part, by the common law courts based on their intuition about how most "reasonable" people would arrange their affairs. The very same courts also interpret the attempts by individual parties to opt out of these defaults by writing express conditions into their contracts. It is a common human failing, however, that what one believes is reasonable, one also believes is fair and proper. Thus, it is hard to imagine that any sensible person would agree to a different arrangement. Opt outs thus are viewed with suspicion since most decent people would not pay to arrange their affairs that way. There is a very important drafting lesson for young lawyers imbedded in all this: The attorney must draft express conditions clearly and conspicuously in order to overcome any inference that the parties didn't really "mean" what they appeared to say in the contract.

Howard v. FCIC *(Page 710).* Howard claimed against his insurance policy for rain damage to his tobacco crop. He properly filed proof of claims as per clause 5(b), but then disked and tilled the soil before FCIC inspected the rain damaged stalks. FCIC denied his claim on the basis of clause 5(f), which provided that the farmer must preserve the damaged crop until inspection. Issue: Is the "nondestruction" clause a promise or an express condition?

In analyzing these cases, courts begin with the presumption that when in doubt the clause is interpreted as a promise and not a condition ("The law abhors a forfeiture"). We often ask the students to argue this case for each side. The farmer argues the *text*. The contract doesn't use the words "condition precedent" in clause 5(f) although it was used elsewhere (i.e., in the clause providing for the filing of proof of claims). Therefore, "expressio unis" applies– the expression of one, implies the deliberate exclusion of the other. The insurer then must argue the *context*. Putting the contract in its context, it is obvious that key requirements designed to guard against fraudulent claims and stale evidence are those that require prompt filings of proof of loss and the right to inspect the damaged crops. Since they protect against fraudulent or stale claims they are strictly necessary and must be interpreted as conditions.

In finding for the farmer, the court focuses on the way the obligations were structured in the contract. Clause 5(f) focuses on something to be done – preserve the stalks – and not on something *not* to be done– i.e., the insurance will not be payable if evidence is not preserved until inspection. One wonders how important this distinction really is, but once again there is a key drafting tip for lawyers. Express conditions must articulate the consequences of the failure of the conditions– the return performance will be withheld.

Inman v. Clyde Hall Drilling Co. *(Page 714).* In *Inman,* a derrickman was fired by the drilling company for which he worked. He filed a claim against the company alleging that he had been terminated without cause. This, he claimed, was a breach of his employment contract, and he sought damages accordingly. The employment contract, however, specified that for any claim arising out of the employment contract, the employee was required to give written notice of the claim within thirty days and not to sue for six months. This requirement was expressly provided to be a condition precedent to any recovery against the employer. Plaintiff claimed he was wrongfully discharged and brought suit within thirty days but gave no written notice. The question here is not whether this provision was an express condition, but whether it violates public policy. In other words are the content of express conditions regulated more strictly than other contract provisions?

The court held that the clause in question is not "unfair, unreasonable or unconscionable." The express condition had a legitimate purpose: to preclude stale claims, to give the employer opportunity to promptly correct errors, etc. Moreover, the general duty to read rule applies here. The whole idea of an express condition is to require exact compliance as the promisor specifies, thus the filing of suit within thirty days is not a compliance with the terms of the condition. Filing suit is not an effective substitute since notice serves other purposes than merely alerting the promisor to the existence of a dispute.

Note 2 (Page 719). A contemporary example of the inability of courts to accept the fact that sometimes people will pay to opt out of the default rule is *Printz Services.* The Supreme Court of Colorado held in that case that a standard "pay if paid" clause, which provides that payment to the subcontractor is conditional on the general contractor being paid by the owner, was sufficiently ambiguous that it should be construed as a promise and not a condition. The court placed much emphasis on the fact that, as a general matter, the sub looks solely to the general contractor for payment and does not need to worry about the solvency of the owner.

The court's understanding of the standard practice is correct. But is the standard practice relevant? The whole idea of express conditions is to escape the standard practice and have an atypical practice be interpreted with the same dignity as the typical one. It may be true that ordinarily the sub is not dependant on the solvency of the owner, but that does not mean that such is never the case.

Note 3 (Page 719). In *River Brand Mills,* cited in the note, the court held that the two week requirement for giving notice of a shipment was a condition and not a promise. December delivery, the court held, was the essence of the contract. December is a time of peak activity for rice growers, and the court argued that both parties wanted the protection of a specific delivery period when the contract was made. The plaintiff wanted to guarantee supply so that it could meet its obligations to a third party buyer, and the defendant wanted to be able to establish a production and delivery schedule for this busy period. That the plaintiff wanted December delivery is supported by the fact that the letter of credit was only payable for December deliveries. Both parties, then, sought to ensure that all deliveries under the contract would be made before the end of December. In order for this to happen, the court found, the buyer needed to provide the two weeks notice. The rice was to be delivered free alongside ship, and the seller could not make such deliveries without the name and location of the ship, information that was to be included in the two weeks notice. Because the court ruled that notice was a condition, the defendant was within its rights when it rescinded the contract on December 18th and was not liable for breach.

b. Conditions Precedent and Conditions Subsequent
Gray v. Gardner *(Page 721).* *Gray* is another famous "chestnut." In exchange for plaintiff's sale of oil at a fixed price, defendant promised in a note to pay the plaintiff @ $6,000 on condition that if more oil arrived in Nantucket before October 1 this year than did the previous year, the note was void. In essence, then, the note with its condition was a primitive form of price indexing against future market shifts in the volatile whale oil market where changes in supply had a significant price effect. The key question in *Gray* was who had the burden of proof since it was unclear whether the *Lady Adams* had arrived in Nantucket harbor before midnight on the first of October. If the clause is construed as a condition precedent, then the plaintiff would have the burden of proving that the condition was satisfied. But if it is a condition subsequent, then the defendant has the burden of showing that the obligation was extinguished by the occurrence of the condition. The court held that the plain language construction of the phrase controls this issue and thus this is a condition subsequent and plaintiff prevails.

Because the difference between conditions precedent and subsequent turn on sentence construction and not on substance, the reporters of the Second Restatement sought to eliminate the distinction and treat what were formerly classified as conditions subsequent under the general framework of discharge. But *Note 2 on page 723* demonstrates a modern application of conditions subsequent in the common use of "Attorney Approval" clauses in residential home sales contracts. Most courts interpret these provisions as conditions subsequent. Thus the contract is binding unless and until the attorney fails to approve. This suggests that careful drafting remains important for the attorney who is creating conditional obligations.

c. Modification, Waiver, Election and Estoppel of Conditions.
The most significant issues surrounding promises and conditions arise in the context of waiver and modification. The distinctions are often confusing to students. We begin, therefore, with a rule of thumb that helps to sort many, but not all, of the questions. In general, promises are

modified and conditions are waived.   Moreover, there is a clear doctrinal distinction between a modification – which requires a subsequent agreement between the parties – and a waiver – which is a unilateral act or conduct on the part of the promisee and does not, in theory, require any consent of the promisor (except perhaps reliance in some instances). A good example of these distinctions comes in the first case.

Clark v. West *(Page 725).* Students are amused by a case involving an alcoholic law professor (although we are not sure whether Clark taught or not). In any case, the contract provided that Clark would write a series of law books for West, and West would pay him $2 per page and, if he abstained from alcohol, an additional $4 per page. Clark did not abstain but submitted Clark on Corporations in any event. West continued to accept pages of the manuscript even though they knew he was still imbibing. Clark claims the abstinence clause was an express condition and that it was waived by West's conduct. West, on the other hand, argues that these are simply alternative promises: $2 per page for work done drunk and $6 per page for work done sober. Thus, West argues the $4 is the consideration for abstinence.

The case thus shows the continuing relevance of the distinctions between promises and conditions. Conditions, after all, can be waived by a unilateral action, but promises can only be modified by a mutual agreement. Here the court interprets the abstinence obligation as a condition. This was a contract to write a book for $6 per page with a $2 per page advance and the balance payable on completion of the book on condition of abstinence. Here West elected to accept the manuscript notwithstanding their knowledge that Clark was drinking. Thus, they elected to take the product without abstinence and the condition precedent to the $4 per page balance was waived. The case contains a nice discussion of the distinction between waiver by election and waiver by estoppel. The former doesn't require proof of any action in reliance by the promisor.

Wisconsin Knife Works v. National Metal Crafters *(Page 728).* This case, involving dueling analyses by two of the smartest judges writing today, is worth some time because it allows students to see the merit in careful reasoning as well as teaching them about statutory construction in general and UCC § 2-209 in particular.

Buyer purchased spade bit blanks from seller via several purchase orders and acknowledgments. The PO said (in essence): "No modification without a signed writing." The relevant delivery dates were written in on the PO's after they had been specified by the seller in the acknowledgment. Seller missed the delivery dates; Buyer did not terminate but issued new PO's. One year later, Buyer terminated when only 144 thousand of 281 thousand bits had been delivered and sued for breach. The 7th circuit (Posner) held the "no modification except by writing" clause was valid and enforceable under the Code and it was error for the trial court to instruct the jury that it could find a modification of the contract by oral agreement or conduct.

But was this harmless error? Possibly yes, since under § 2-209(4) an attempted oral modification may still operate as a waiver. Posner thus asks whether the trial court's instruction can be understood as an instruction on waiver. He holds that the answer is no because § 2-209(4) has an implicit reliance requirement. Posner reaches this point because he reasons that if § 2-209(4) is interpreted as it reads, then § 2-209(2) disappears and that cannot be what the drafters intended since they were trying to make such no modification agreements enforceable. By focusing on the language "it *can* operate as a waiver," Posner reads a reliance requirement into § 2-209(4). But what about § 2-209(5), which explicitly states that a party who has made a waiver my retract it *"unless the retraction would be unjust in view of a material change of position in reliance on the waiver"*? Surely, § 2-209(5) implies that the category of waivers in subsection (4) is broader than those waivers on which the plaintiff relied, else subsection (5) makes no sense. There is no inconsistency, Posner states, because § 2-209(5) (with its express reliance language) applies to any waivers, including a written one, while subsection (4) applies only to oral waivers.. Thus, it was error for the trial court to instruct on waiver without requiring proof of reliance.

In dissent, Frank Easterbrook disagrees and argues that reliance is not an essential element of a waiver in § 2-209(4). Easterbrook argues that Posner simply does not attend adequately to § 2-209(5), which treats waiver and reliance as two different concepts. If it is a "mere" waiver it can be retracted unless there is reliance. Posner's error, therefore, was that he finds the two sections have different domains, that (4) applies to a subset of (5). But that is exactly backwards. In fact they have the same domains. Subsection (4) says it may be a waiver and (5) qualifies the effectiveness of that waiver without reliance. Thus, the correct interpretation, according to Easterbrook, is that all attempted modifications that fail may operate as waivers. But they are subject to retraction unless there is reliance.

In our view, Easterbrook clearly has the better argument. After all, as per *Clark v. West,* not all waivers require reliance (e.g., waiver by election). There is no reason to believe that the drafters wanted to change that very respected rule without any commentary whatsoever. Indeed, § 2-209(2) is not designed (as Posner suggests) to police strategic behavior by promisors. Rather it is designed to constrain agents and to preserve evidence (as a complement to the statue of frauds).

Note 1 (Page 736). We think the apparent contradiction in contract law between "easy" waiver and the rigid rules governing modification at common law is a function of the tension between promises and conditions and the continuing judicial hostility to the idiosyncratic bargainer. Courts don't like express conditions. As we have reminded the students numerous times (with apologies to Neil Sedaka): "Opting out is hard to do."

Note 4 (Page 737). This note gives the students our take on the conditions/forfeiture/waiver set of issues. For reasons that contract law fails to acknowledge, its theory of enforcement, which is premised on both the efficiency and the autonomy of choice ("more choice is better than less" ceteris paribus), is not fully implemented in practice. Courts pay less attention to the language of contracts than they should and this causes them to undermine the efforts of atypical parties to change the default settings of contract law. For us, the key to accommodating the tension between the legitimate interests of atypical parties and the risk of strategic claims if special requirements are literally interpreted is to look to the market for substitute performances. In relatively competitive markets, courts will (and should) worry less about the risk of harsh conditions that deprive a promisee of the benefits of her bargains because in such a setting the market checks the strategic behavior of the promisor. The promisee cannot easily be exploited because the value of the promisor's performance can always be tested on the market. But where the performance is specialized or contract-specific, then there are reasons for courts to police conditions to ensure that the promisor isn't engaging in hold up.

C. Performance Standards
Warranties
We turn now to the so-called "substantive" default rules governing performance of a contract. The first category of these substantive rules are the rules providing the standard of quality that the promisor's performance must meet. The paradigmatic examples are the express and implied warranties for the sale of goods under the Code. The questions we pose to students are these: First, can you identify precisely what are the default rules regarding quality? Second, does it matter that they are in the form of broad standards rather than bright line rules (i.e., are they useful in that form?)? For example, what should we make of the fact that commercial parties routinely opt out of the Code warranties in their contracts in lieu of detailed specifications and standard form repair and replacement provisions that displace the Code defaults?

a. Express Warranties.
Express warranties are something of a misnomer. To be sure, a seller can expressly guarantee the quality of goods sold and will be liable for failure to meet that quality as with any contractual obligation. But the law of "express warranty" actually deals with a different problem. What inferences are properly to be drawn about liability and risk from seller statements that are clear about seller's belief as to their truth content, but unclear as to whether seller is *also assuming the risk of liability* if the statements turn out to be untrue without the knowledge or carelessness of the seller? The challenge then is to distinguish innocent representations that allocate to the seller the risk of their falsity and those that do not. Section 2-313 seeks to draw this distinction. The question is whether it does so successfully.

Sessa v. Riegle *(Page 740)*. Buyer sent a trusted agent to look at a horse he was interested in purchasing. The agent was satisfied, but, in addition, the seller got on the phone with the buyer and said, inter alia, "The horse is sound." Both parties were experienced horse owners. A week after delivery, the horse went lame with a condition that may have pre-dated the sale. The seller sued for breach of express warranty of affirmation of fact under § 2-313(1)(a). The court held that the statement was not an affirmation within § 2-313(1)(a) but rather was a statement of "opinion" falling under § 2-313(2) and thus did not create a warranty. Important to the court was the fact, as per the custom among horse traders, that experienced parties did not take such statements as guarantees but merely a matter of honest opinion because horses were so fragile. Only where the buyer was inexperienced and relying completely on the seller are statements as to soundness regarded as more than expressions of opinion. Moreover, the second prong of the § 2-313(1) test, that the statement is part of the "basis of the bargain," is not satisfied where, as here, the buyer was relying so completely on the judgment of a trusted agent.

Note 2 *(Page 746)*. The question is: What generalizations can be made from this case that offer a rule to guide future parties as to when seller statements are warranties? We believe that the focus of the common law courts on the relative experience or inexperience of the parties is the key factor. Where the seller is experienced and the buyer is not, statements such as "these chinchillas are proven breeders" are affirmations that create warranties (see *Note 1 on page 745*). But where, as here, both parties are equally experienced, the very same statement is likely to be held to be only a matter of opinion. Thus, it is not the words used but the context in which they are used that creates the inference of guarantee. Why does experience matter? We suggest that it is because experienced buyers commonly understand that matters of quality are not susceptible to precise proof and thus statements by the seller are understood to be a question of honest judgment. Inexperienced buyers, on the other hand, are more likely to believe that sellers stand behind their products and are more likely to take such representations as guarantees in the absence of a disclaimer. Moreover, the relative experience factor operates as an information-forcing default, inducing the party with the greater information–the experienced seller–to disclose more explicitly that the statement is just opinion and not a guarantee.

b. Implied Warranties

From our discussion of so-called "express warranties," it is clear that default risk allocations regarding unknown quality defects are inferred by courts from various contextual factors. As we have seen, one such factor is the relative experience of the parties in understanding the meaning of innocent representations. We now consider two other contextual factors under the rubric of "implied warranties." The first, the implied warranty of merchantability, concerns the status of the seller as a merchant (§ 2-314), and the second, the implied warranty of fitness for a particular purpose, arises because of the peculiar needs and circumstances of the buyer which are made known to the seller (§ 2-315).

Flippo v. Mode O'Day Frock Shops of Hollywood *(Page 748).* Gladys Flippo tried on two pairs of pants at the Mode O'Day clothing store. When she put on the second pair, she felt a burning sensation on her thigh. She immediately removed the pants, shook them, and a spider fell out onto the floor. As a result of the spider bite, Flippo was hospitalized for 30 days. Flippo sued Mode O'Day for, among other things, breach of an implied warranty that the pants were fit for the purpose for which they were purchased, and the presence of the spider, she alleged, made them unfit for that purpose.

Flippo is an easy case at one level. Where the spider was inside the pants, but not in any sense a part of the product, the goods were not "defective" in any meaningful sense and thus they were "fit for the ordinary purposes for which goods are used." But the case is, nonetheless a good vehicle for examining what really counts in § 2-314 claims. To give this warranty the seller must be a merchant. But why exactly does that status matter? One answer, we believe, is that a merchant (as defined in § 2-104) has experience with the goods. This experience gives the merchant a comparative advantage in comparing the quality of the goods offered for sale with the quality standards of similar goods in the market. Thus, the merchantability warranty is simply that these goods will function as similar goods in the market function. That factor explains why Flippo is so easy. The retail clothier may be experienced with regard to women's slacks, but there is no reason to believe it has any comparative advantage in guarding against the rare circumstance of a brown recluse spider being inside the garment.

The relevance of experience also gives some purchase to the standard defense of "misuse," which is often raised by sellers in merchantability cases. In essence, by alleging misuse, the seller is claiming that the buyer's use of the goods does not fall with in the seller's range of experience because it is a nonstandard use.

Note 6 (Page 753). We have the students read § 2-315 and use an hypothetical to illustrate the operation of the implied warranty of fitness for a particular purpose. An easy example is given in Comment 2. Imagine an inexperienced hiker who wishes to buy a pair of hiking boots to climb Mt. Denali. Then imagine that the hiker explains to the seller that she has never climbed any mountains before and thus is entirely dependent on the seller's judgment in selecting appropriate boots. If the seller recommends a pair that is inadequate to prevent frostbite in extremely cold environments, and does not disclaim any superior knowledge, the seller is liable for the fitness of the goods for the buyer's unique needs. Section 2-315 is a further example of an information-forcing default rule. It indues the party with the superior knowledge to inform the buyer of the limitations of his experience or risk the imposition of liability for whatever the buyer's special needs require.

c. Warranty Disclaimers.
The most important difference between warranty liability under the Code and strict liability in tort is that Code warranties are only default rules. Thus, with some qualifications, Code warranties can be completely disclaimed. Section 2-316 explains how to accomplish this purpose and also outlines the limitations on disclaimers (*see* §2-316(1)). But, unlike other default rules in the Code and the common law, here the methods of opting out are strictly regulated (*see* § 2-316(2),(3)).

Pelc v. Simmons *(Page 755).* Simmons, the defendant, placed his used 1978 Sunbird for sale on a used car lot to increase exposure. Posted on the car was a "sold as is" sign. The plaintiff's uncle, at her request, looked the car over and asked Simmons about the motor. Simmons told him that he had rebuilt the motor himself because the timing chain had gone out and that the only problem with the car was that the air conditioner compressor needed a charge. Plaintiff purchased the car for $1,500, but several days later began experiencing serious problems. Because of the problems, plaintiff's uncle estimated that the car was worth only about $200 for parts. Plaintiff sued for breach of warranty. Defense: all warranties were disclaimed by the sign, "sold as is."

Pelc is an interesting case for several reasons. First, it demonstrates one method of opting out that is regulated by § 2-316(3). If the context of the sale is such that it invokes commonly understood customs that in certain kinds of sales the buyer bears all risks then no warranties arise. The salient examples given by the Code are sales that are advertized as "As Is" or "With all Faults." Thus, on its face, the (apparently conspicuous) sign on the car, "Sold As Is," would qualify under § 2-316(3).

But there is a further complication. The seller (and defendant) in this case was not the owner of the used car lot, but an airplane mechanic who was allowed to place his car on the lot to attract potential buyers. If that is so, then it seems clear that the defendant is not "a merchant with respect to goods of this kind" under § 2-314(1) and § 2-104(1) (*see, e.g.* §2-314, Comment 3). Thus, no implied warranty of merchantability was created by this sale. Neither was there any evidence sufficient to raise a claim under § 2-315. If that is so, since no implied warranties arose in the first place, there was nothing to disclaim under § 2-316(3). There was an express warranty of description – a 1978 Sunbird – and there is a possible claim under § 2-313(1)(a) that the statement, "the only thing that's wrong with the car is the air conditioning," is an affirmation of fact. But § 2-316(3) only operates to disclaim implied warranties. By its terms it has no effect on express warranties. And, if an express warranty arose that is inconsistent with any disclaimer, the express warranty controls as per § 2-316(1).

        Note 2 (Page 758). The *Parke-Bernet* case cited in the note is a good example of the limits on the use of "as is" disclaimers. There the textual statement, "As Is," as part of the "Conditions of Sale" in an 80-page catalogue for an auction was insufficiently conspicuous to disclaim the implied warranty of merchantability for a painting attributed to Raoul Dufy. The courts have in general created two separate categories for the application of disclaimers under § 2-316(2) and § 2-316(3): "As Is" disclaimers under subsection (3) are those where the *context* "makes it plain" that there are no warranties. On the other hand, if a seller wishes explicitly to disclaim warranty liability as part of a standard form written text, then the appropriate language is prescribed in § 2-316(2). Under that subsection, the disclaimer must be conspicuous and, in the case of § 2-314, must mention the magic word, "MERCHANTABILITY." We discuss the purposes behind the recitation of magic words of disclaimer in *Note 3 on page 759.*

        There is a final question we ask students concerning the Code warranties: How useful are these defaults? In order to cover such a broad range of contexts and heterogeneous parties, the defaults are framed as broad standards rather than bright line rules. But, at least in commercial cases, parties need precision in determining their contractual obligations (and lawyers certainly need it as well) in order to assess risks and price them accordingly ex ante. This perhaps explains why most commercial buyers and sellers choose to opt out of the Code warranties entirely in their contracts. Instead, a typical commercial sales contract will contain very elaborate description of the goods as part of an express warranty. But then a disclaimer of all the Code warranties will be followed by a standard repair and replacement clause that will share risks between buyer and seller. The seller will bear loss of bargain risks from defective products and the buyer will bear the risks of consequential damages.

Measuring Compliance

        Once we know what quality benchmarks we use to measure the performance of the promisor, we turn to the final question: By what standard do we measure compliance with the quality benchmarks? This returns us once again to the fundamental choice between substantial performance and perfect tender.

        O.W. Grun Roofing & Construction Co. v. Cope *(Page 760). Cope* offers an opportunity to determine when the aesthetic preferences of the promisee are relevant in determining whether performance has been "substantial." Here the roof that defendant installed was substantial and fit, but because the tiles were not arranged properly, the color was not uniform but "streaky." The court considers several "tests" for measuring compliance–the extent of the non-performance or the ratio of the value of tendered performance and promised performance–but none are very helpful for a case such as this. The idea, of course, is to determine whether the "essence"of the "general plan" has been tendered. But what is the general plan in this case? Is it a substantial roof? Or a substantial roof of uniform color? The court uses ordinary intuition to determine that people place aesthetic value on their homes and thus taste or personal preference is important. Indeed, if these preference are generally held, it is not just an idiosyncratic preference but one that would likely be reflected in market value as well.

Haymore v. Levinson *(Page 763)*. The relevance of market reactions to matters of taste and aesthetics is made clear in *Haymore*. Here the buyers of a new home refused to give the final payment because the contractor had not satisfactorily performed on the second set of "punch list" items. The defendants argued that the term "satisfactory completion" is to be construed subjectively. That is, until they personally are satisfied with the work, they are under no obligation to pay the balance due. The plaintiff, on the other hand, claimed that "satisfactory completion" is an objective term and that he had met his obligations under it. The court agreed that the test of satisfaction in this case was objective and not subjective. Thus, unlike the production of items of personal taste and fancy – such as a portrait of the promisee – or other items of purely aesthetic value, building contracts are generally grouped in the category of performances which are measured by objective – that is, market – measures of satisfaction.

Does this imply that the two cases are inconsistent? Not necessarily. They would be inconsistent if the court in *Cope* had rejected evidence that the streaky roof was inconsequential to other prospective buyers of the house and thus had no effect on the market value of the home.

b. *Perfect Tender and Cure*

We use this section to provide a sharper contrast between the substantial performance and perfect tender doctrines. Why is it that substantial performance is universally applied in construction and other services contracts but perfect tender remains the norm in sales cases? One answer that we explored in Chapter 1 is that construction contracts produce a much greater risk of strategic hold up by the promisee-owner. Since the contractor has made a sunk cost investment on the owner's land, the value of that investment is not redeployable on the market. If the home owner "rejects" the house, as in *Haymore*, the contractor cannot simply offer the house to another buyer and recoup its investment. Since the promisor's investment in the contract is specialized to the contract, there is a greater hold up risk. The substantial performance doctrine responds to that risk by permitting the contractor to recover the return performance if it has substantially performed and can make up the deficiency with an objective, market based monetary settlement.

But why then does the perfect tender rule govern in sales cases? One answer is that the risk of hold up is reduced so long as the underlying market conditions have not changed between contract and performance. And what if the market conditions have shifted? That is the circumstance in which the seller can properly invoke the right of cure under § 2-508(2).

T.W. Oil, Inc. v. Consolodated Edison Co. *(Page 769).* Plaintiff T.W. Oil purchased a shipment of oil whose sulphur content was represented as no greater than 1%. While the oil was still en route, its sulphur content was, in fact, certified at .52%. T.W.Oil then contracted to sell the oil to Con Ed, describing it as containing .5% sulphur, but when the oil arrived, testing revealed that the actual sulphur content was .92%. Con Ed rejected the oil in a timely manner in compliance with UCC § 2-602, even though it was authorized to buy and burn oil with a sulphur content of up to 1%. Con Ed, though it could use the oil, insisted on paying only the current market price which had fallen 25% below the contract price. Plaintiff then offered to cure the defect with a substitute shipment of oil to arrive later, but Con Ed rejected that proposal too. Plaintiff then sold both shipments to third parties at a price considerably lower than the contract price.

The precise question in *TW Oil* is: Can a seller properly invoke § 2-508(2) where the seller was, in fact, ignorant of the defect at the time of tender? The court answers in the affirmative notwithstanding the language of § 2-508(2), which allows cure if the "seller *had* reasonable grounds to believe that the tender would be acceptable with or without money allowance." (In other words, the court reads the language of the Code as allowing cure if the "seller *would have* had reasonable grounds....")

This case is precisely the context in which the cure rule is properly invoked to prevent a strategic rejection by the buyer. Here the sulphur content was slightly higher than buyer had warranted, but within the buyer's general requirements, and the seller is able to produce a conforming tender in short order. Seller rejected because the market price for oil has dropped 25% since the time of contracting and the seller could now do much better on the open market. The case thus gives some meaning to the otherwise vague standard of "reasonable grounds" in § 2-508(2). Under this interpretation, the buyer has "reasonable grounds" to believe the seller would accept the goods whenever a seller would find the substitute perfectly acceptable but for the motivation to behave strategically. Reasonable grounds is thus an assumption that a seller acting in good faith would find the substitute tender indistinguishable from the contract specs.

Ramirez v. Autosport *(Page 773).* In *Ramirez*, consumer buyers rejected a van which had minor defects. The sellers offered to cure, but despite the fact that the buyers phoned and came by several times, the sellers failed to do so within a reasonable time. In fact, at the time the suit was initiated – nearly four months after the contract was signed – the defects were still not cured. Since the seller failed to comply with § 2-508(2), the buyers were entitled to rely on § 2-601 and cancel the contract and recover damages.

Ramirez illustrates the important point that the right of cure is not a right to tender a "substantial performance." In that regard it differs from the substantial performance standard. Rather, the right of cure is the right to substitute a (perfectly) conforming tender within a reasonable time after the date of performance. In other words, it gives the seller some more time to attain perfection, but it does not require the buyer to accept anything less. If the seller is unable to substitute perfectly conforming goods within a reasonable time, the buyer, as in *Ramirez,* is within his rights in rejecting under § 2-601 even for minor or nonmaterial defects.

CHAPTER 8

MISTAKE AND EXCUSE

A. Introduction

By presenting the law of mistake and excuse in its own chapter, contracts casebooks reinforce the impression that this law constitutes a new and independent theoretical territory not covered in the preceding chapters. This is consistent with the rhetoric courts use when applying these doctrines. The language of judicial opinions applying mistake and excuse suggests that these doctrines are vehicles for setting aside, or overriding, the parties' agreement. This is especially clear with the law of excuse. The very concept of excuse implies that one party will be relieved of her contractual duties under certain circumstances. Similarly, the law of mistake operates to nullify an agreement by establishing that an agreement never in fact came into existence because one or both parties lacked the requisite intent. Both doctrines therefore present themselves as "acontractual"– they demonstrate that the parties' obligations at issue were never (mistake), or are no longer (excuse), governed by contract.

We believe this view of the law of mistake and excuse is, for the most part, fundamentally wrong. As the *Introductory Essay on page 785* indicates, most questions of mistake and excuse are resolved by interpreting whether and how a particular risk was allocated by contract, rather than how it should be allocated outside of contract. That one or both parties were mistaken about a material fact at the time of formation, or that they failed to anticipate an improbable event subsequent to formation, does not establish that they did not allocate the risk of the mistake or event, respectively. Risks are allocated in contract law by three kinds of terms: express, implied by context and imputed by default. Courts typically respect express risk allocations, even of improbable mistakes or future events. Context can also provide persuasive reasons for treating a risk as implicitly allocated by agreement. But when there are neither express nor implied terms allocating certain risks, the doctrines of mistake and excuse constitute contract default rules to allocate these risks constructively. Once in place, these default rules make the allocation of such risks part of contract law, even though the parties by hypothesis did not allocate them by their actual agreement.

The classic illustration of such constructive risk allocation is the remote risk grounding excuse. Some scholars characterize such risks as unallocated by contract, and thus view excuse as a vehicle for setting aside, or restricting the scope of, the agreement on the ground that the parties did not, or could not, anticipate the risk. It is, on this view, a fiction that the parties' agreement governs the risk in question. Although we agree that these risks are not allocated by terms the parties consciously considered, terms imputed by default rules are nonetheless part of the parties' agreement according to contract law. Moreover, while the risks governed by mistake and excuse are, by hypothesis, not anticipated or considered by the parties, they almost always can be described as falling within a general category of risks that were. Thus, although parties might not be able to anticipate every particular mistake or future event that could materially affect their agreement, they can anticipate that unanticipated mistakes or future events might arise. Thus, while the risks covered by the rules of mistake or excuse might be best described as allocated constructively, such risks can also plausibly be characterized as implicitly allocated by the parties, since the parties often do, at least implicitly, consider the general risk of unanticipated mistakes and future events.

The doctrinal challenge of this chapter is to provide a coherent explication of the rules of mistake and excuse as unified mechanisms for allocating unanticipated risks. The theoretical challenge is to provide a rationale for allocating risks the parties failed to anticipate. The default rules allocating these risks will not, by hypothesis, affect the future behavior of others because these rules allocate only those risks that parties fail to anticipate. If parties fail to anticipate a risk, the default rules governing those risks will have no effect, such as precaution-taking, on the behavior of future parties. The true mistake or excuse case thus presents the most compelling context for justifying fairness or sharing rules. One of the theoretical challenges, therefore, is to explain why common law courts have been reluctant to develop sharing rules for these contexts. Instead, the rules governing excuse and mistake are binary, placing all the risk on one party or the other. Of course, sharing rules have no place if, in fact, the parties expressly allocated the risk of unanticipated events. This is precisely what parties attempt to accomplish by using the broad language and concepts typically included in *force majeure* clauses. It may be, therefore, that the excuse and mistake default rules are designed to encourage just this sort of express risk allocation by the parties themselves. In that sense, thinking of these rules as a form of information-forcing default may provide the most traction on a concededly difficult topic.

B. Mistaken Beliefs About Facts that Exist at the Time of Agreement
Excuse Based on Mistake

Sherwood v. Walker *(Page 789)*. In this classic chestnut, the court concluded that the evidence demonstrated that *both* parties at the time of the agreement believed the cow, Rose 2d of Aberlone, to be barren: One of the defendants claimed it was "probably barren," but the defendants "introduced evidence tending to show that at the time of the alleged sale it was believed by both the plaintiff and [the defendants] that the cow was barren and would not breed." The dissent, however, claims that the record shows that "from what the plaintiff had been told by defendants . . . he believed the cow was farrow, but still thought she could be made to breed. Given that the majority believed that both parties mistakenly believed the cow was barren, the court turns to the question of whether such mutual mistake constitutes grounds for rescinding the agreement. The court held that a mutual mistake about a material fact is grounds for rescission. Material facts, according to the court, include "the subject-matter of the sale, the price, or some collateral fact materially inducing the agreement." As to the subject-matter of the sale, the court further distinguished between "the substance of the thing bargained for" (also referred to as "the root of the matter") and "a difference in some quality or accident, even though the mistake may have been the actuating motive to the purchaser or seller, or both of them" (also referred to as "an error as to which does not affect the substance of the whole consideration.") Applying this distinction to the facts of the case, the court held that the parties' mistaken belief that the cow was barren constituted a mistake as to "the whole substance of the agreement"– it was "not of the mere quality of the animal, but went to the very nature of the thing." The court concludes the mistake goes to the substance of the agreement because (1) the mistake dramatically affected the value of the good (the price of a breeder would be $750 while the price if barren was $80) and (2) the mistake affected the character of the animal for all time.

Given the dissent's view that the buyer was speculating that, contrary to seller's belief, the cow was fertile, the dissent argues that the sellers "sold the cow for what they believed her to be, and the plaintiff bought her as he believed she was, after the statements made by the defendants. . . . "[B]oth parties were equally ignorant, and as to this each party took his chances." The dissent thus holds, in the terms of the majority's opinion, that the mistake went to the *quality*, rather than substance, of the thing bargained for. When parties buy or sell a good knowing that they are not certain about some of its properties, they are not excused from their agreement if their guesses about those properties turn out to be wrong. To allow rescission under these circumstances would be to, as the dissent puts it, "interpolate" a condition into the parties' contract where none exists.

Anderson Brothers v. O'Meara (*Page 795*). Anderson Brothers (appellant) sold O'Meara (appellee) a dredge that was designed for digging trenches, not "sweep" dredging (creating canals), which is the use for which appellee purchased it. The appellee's agent inspected the dredge but, since he was an expert on engines but not dredges, he reported back to appellee only on the condition of the dredge engines. He did not report that the dredge was incapable of performing sweep dredging, presumably because he lacked the knowledge to determine that fact. The appellee's claims of fraud and breach of express and implied warranties were rejected by the trial court, but its claim of mutual mistake was granted. The appeals court reversed this decision on the grounds that the mistake was not mutual, that is, appellant was aware of the type of work of which the dredge in question was capable. Only the appellee was unaware, and that was only because of its failure to use any diligence whatsoever (which prevents the appellee from claiming that enforcement given its unilateral mistake would be unconscionable). Moreover, the district court's finding that the appellant did not know of the appellee's intended use was not clearly erroneous. Therefore, the appellee is not entitled to relief under the doctrine that knowledge by one party that the other is laboring under a mistake makes the contract voidable by the mistaken party (*see* R2d 153(b)).

Pedagogy on **Sherwood** *and* **O'Meara.** The law of mutual mistake is on its firmest ground in *Raffles v. Wichelhaus on page 789*. Recall that their contract called for the delivery of cotton by way of a ship named "Peerless" sailing from Bombay to Liverpool, when in fact there turned out to be two ships named "Peerless" sailing from Bombay to Liverpool within three months of each other. Here, the parties weren't mistaken as to which ship the term "Peerless" referred. Rather, each party was mistaken in his belief that the other party understood the term "Peerless" to refer to the same ship to which he intended it to refer. That mistake, in turn, was a product of both parties' implicit, mistaken belief that there was only one ship named "Peerless" sailing from Bombay to Liverpool that year. Of course, if the parties had intended the term "Peerless" to refer to the same ship, the term would not have been ambiguous despite the existence of a second ship named "Peerless" because the parties' mutual intentions would have determined the reference of that term in their agreement. But when the parties have divergent intentions about the reference of a term, the reference of the term is ambiguous; the term in fact does not uniquely refer to one ship or the other. Thus, *Raffles* is the clearest case of a mutual mistake that grounds rescission because the parties' mutual mistake clearly prevented formation of their agreement– the parties erroneously believed they had explicitly agreed on which ship would carry the cotton, and thus on when delivery of the cotton was due, when in fact they had not so agreed.

In *Sherwood*, the court faces a much harder question. There was no ambiguity underlying the reference of the terms of their agreement (both intended "Rose 2d of Aberlone" to refer to the same cow). However, according to the majority, both parties were mistaken about the physical characteristics of that cow: They both believed the cow was barren. Even assuming these facts, however, the question is whether the parties considered and allocated the risk that their belief might be wrong. If both parties assumed it to be true, without recognizing that it might be false, then the court's analysis seems persuasive. Whether a cow is fertile or barren has a dramatic effect on its value and the purpose to which it can be put. Thus, the assumption that the cow is barren is a basic one on which the agreement was based. We can therefore fairly conclude that had the parties realized they might be mistaken about their assumption, they would not have made the bargain they did. In particular, the seller would have a charged an additional premium reflecting the risk that the cow turns out to be fertile (let alone with calf). (Note that the seller would not have charged the price of a cow he *knew* to be fertile at the time of sale, but rather the price reflecting the probability that the cow turns out to be fertile). In contrast, even assuming the parties believed the cow was probably, or even almost surely, barren, if they nonetheless recognized that they might be mistaken about this belief then the majority opinion is unpersuasive. On this view, the seller charged a premium reflecting the risk that he might be wrong, and so should not be entitled to rescind when the cow turns out to be fertile. Despite the existence of a mutual mistake about a material fact, no recovery should be allowed if the risk of that mistake has been allocated by the parties' agreement. This rule is reflected in R2d § 152(1), which provides that a mutual mistake regarding a basic assumption about a material fact makes a contract voidable by the adversely affected party *unless he bears the risk of the mistake* under the rule stated in R2d § 154. R2d §154(a) provides that "a party bears the risk of a mistake *when the risk is allocated to him by agreement* of the parties."

Thus, the majority is right that rescission for mutual mistake requires a mutual mistake about a material fact, but it is wrong that more is not required. In particular, the court must determine whether the parties allocated the risk of that mistake by contract. At bottom, this is the dissent's point. The dissent insists that the buyer believed the cow was fertile. If true, that would eliminate a claim based on mutual mistake, since only one of the parties would have been mistaken about the cow's fertility. But if we assume, contrary to the dissent's factual conclusion, that the buyer did not believe the cow was fertile (but, say, merely hoped against the odds that she was), then the parties would have made a mutual mistake about a basic assumption regarding a material fact.

But the dissent would still rightly argue that rescission is justified only if the parties did not allocate the risk of that mutual mistake by agreement. Recall that in the dissent's view on the question of whether the cow was fertile was that "each party took his chances." In short, the dissent believes that both parties understood that the cow might turn out to be fertile, had different estimates of that probability and bargained in light of that risk. If true, even if both parties believed the cow was barren, rescission should be denied under R2d § 154(a). The hard question is how to determine whether the risk was presumed not to exist or allocated by agreement. As a doctrinal matter, the question is whether or not the belief constituted a "basic assumption" under R2d 152. A belief constitutes a basic assumption only if neither party realized the belief might be false. Otherwise, it is a belief the parties realized might be false, and we can reasonably presume the contract allocated that risk (i.e., one party was paid to take it).

The dissent doesn't reach that question because under his factual assumptions the answer is clear in this case: The buyer in fact believed the cow *was* fertile, so there was no mutual mistake. (And although the issue is moot under this factual assumption for lack of a mutual mistake, certainly the risk that the cow turns out to be fertile or barren would be allocated by the agreement). Only context can determine whether a belief constituted a basic assumption. As we've noted above, the best objective evidence on the question would be an otherwise inexplicable price premium in the agreement (by comparison with other agreements in which the parties *do* know the cow is barren–e.g., the vet performed a hysterectomy).

Although *Anderson* is presented as a mutual mistake case, the court decides there was no mutual mistake and treats the case instead as raising the defense of unilateral mistake. We begin by noting that whether or not a mistake is mutual may turn on somewhat arbitrary characterizations of the parties' beliefs. In rejecting the existence of a mutual mistake, the court acknowledges that both the buyer and seller had mistaken beliefs at the time of formation, but finds that each had a different mistaken belief. The buyer's mistake was "in believing that the dredge was capable, without modification, of performing sweep dredging," while the seller's mistake was "in assuming that the [buyer] intended to use the dredge within its designed capabilities." Using this logic, one could argue that there was no mutual mistake in *Raffles*: One party believed "Peerless" referred to a ship departing Bombay in October, while the other party believed "Peerless" referred to a ship departing Bombay in December. Thus, because the parties did not share the same mistaken belief, there was no mutual mistake. But as we've said above, these beliefs were mistaken because the term "Peerless" in fact has no unique reference when the two parties agreeing on the term intend it to refer to different ships. We can therefore identify one mistaken belief the parties shared– viz, that each of them intends the term "Peerless" to refer to the same ship. Similarly, in *Anderson*, we can identify one mistaken belief the parties share– viz, that the dredge is suitable for buyer's purposes (cf., the district court's conclusion that the parties shared a mistaken belief "with respect to the capabilities of the subject dredge"). The issue then becomes whether this shared belief constituted a basic assumption or instead was allocated to one party by the contract. See R2d 152, com. b.

The threshold issue, then, is whether the parties realized that they might be mistaken that the dredge would not suit buyer's purpose. In our view, the facts suggest that this belief was a basic assumption for the buyer but not the seller. While seller certainly knew that its dredge was suitable for some dredging purposes but not others, it is not clear that buyer was aware that different dredging purposes required different dredges (or perhaps even that there were different dredging purposes). As the court notes, according to the buyer's own testimony, he was "conscious of his own lack of knowledge concerning dredges, he took no steps, prior to purchase, to learn if the dredge which he saw pictured and described . . . , was suited to his purposes. Admittedly he did not even inquire as to the use the appellant had made or intended to make of the dredge." It's hard to explain this conduct unless the buyer was so ignorant of dredges that he did not know that he needed to send a dredge expert, instead of or in addition to an expert on dredge engines, to inspect the dredge. If the buyer simply assumed that dredges were all-purpose, or that dredges had only one purpose, this would explain his failure to disclose his intended use (it went without saying– namely, the only use to which dredges can be put), his failure to ask the seller's intended purpose for the dredge, and his failure to send an expert dredge inspector to assess the dredge's suitability for his purposes. This is precisely the kind of assumption that grounds rescission based on mutual mistake if it is a basic assumption for the seller as well.

However, even if the seller shared buyer's belief that the dredge would be suitable for buyer's purposes, it is clear that seller did not share buyer's *reasons* for that belief. Clearly, seller knew the difference between sweep and trench dredges. Thus, seller also must have realized that buyer could be wrong about its belief that the dredge is suitable for his purposes. Because seller knew his belief might be wrong, it was not a basic assumption for seller. We conclude, then, that there was no mutual mistake in this case, not because the parties did not share a mistaken belief about a material fact (contrary to the court's analysis), but because their shared belief constituted "a basic assumption on which the contract was made" only for the buyer but not the seller. Under R2d 152(1), the belief must constitute a basic assumption for both parties, not just one.

The court, then, rightly focuses it's analysis on whether buyer can avoid the contract based on the doctrine of unilateral mistake (under R2d § 153). Clearly, the contract is not voidable under R2d § 153(b) because the seller neither had no reason to know of the mistake nor caused buyer's mistaken belief. Indeed, the court finds that the buyer failed even to "disclose to the appellant the use he intended to make of the dredge." The core of the court's analysis takes place under R2d §153(a) where it responds to the claim that enforcement of the contract, given buyer's unilateral mistake, would be unconscionable. The court here, however, avoids reaching the question of what would ground an unconscionability claim based on unilateral mistake. In its view, equitable principles bar a defense based on unconscionability from a buyer who failed to exercise due diligence by failing to make a reasonable inspection. But given our view that the buyer's belief about the dredge's suitability for buyer's purposes was a basic assumption, rather than a calculated risk, his failure to make an adequate inspection is understandable. Thus, if a substantive unconscionability defense would otherwise apply, the court's reason for denying it here is not obvious. On the other hand, the court's decision might be justified in order to maximize incentives to take efficient precautions. But this objective presumes that incentives can induce people to make fewer unreasonable assumptions. In the end, perhaps the decision is justified on distributive grounds: Between reasonable and unreasonable people, we believe reasonable people are inherently more deserving.

Problems (Page 805). a. After rejecting claims of express warranty and implied warranty (the latter on the ground that the plaintiffs were not justified in relying on any representations by the defendant), the *Backus* court also rejected the claim of mutual mistake. That doctrine requires that the party seeking rescission did not bear the risk with regard to the mistaken fact. The court found that because the plaintiff knew there was doubt as to whether the bull was sterile, it could not void the contract because it was disappointed after the resolution of that doubt. *See also* 154(b).

b. In *Winkelman*, the court found for the Winkelmans. It based its decision on the rule that a contract can be rescinded at the request of a party when that party entered into an agreement based on a mistake about a material fact and the party was not negligent with regard to ascertaining that fact. Here, it was material because it related to the identity of the subject matter of the contract. Also, the plaintiffs were not negligent in accepting as the boundaries of the land what was regarded in the neighborhood as such.

c. In *Denton*, the court found that the release agreement should be voided. It asserted a distinction in the law of mistake between mistake of a fact and mistake of prophecy or opinion; the former will justify rescission, but the latter will not. In this case, the plaintiff knew of no injuries at the time he signed the release, and there was no discussion (much less bargaining) about injuries. Accordingly, the court rejected the argument that in signing the release the plaintiff understood that he was waiving all claims as to any injuries that might develop.

The court seemed to drift (in extensive dicta) among issues of mistake, fraud, contract theory, and, finally, contractual interpretation (i.e., it would be unreasonable, in the court's view, to say that the plaintiff agreed to a release from all injury claims). In the end, however, the opinion can be understood as either a finding of mistake (mutual or unilateral) that justified reformation, or of contractual interpretation (under both the objective and subjective theories, the court would find no agreement as to the waiver of all injury claims).

d. In *Jeselsohn v. Park Trust*, the court rescinded the contract on the ground that all parties were mistaken in their belief that the lot purchased by the plaintiff had a building on it and the plaintiff was not negligent in failing to discover the mistake. Under such circumstances, it would inequitable to hold the plaintiff to the contract.

e. In *Shoreline Communications*, the court rejected Norwich's argument for rescission. Norwich made a unilateral mistake about the suitability of the tower equipment for its needs. Furthermore, it could have discovered the problem with a reasonable inspection. Since Norwich was aware of the possibility that the equipment would not suit its needs and nonetheless entered into the agreement, it assumed the risk that the doubt would be resolved against it. Rescinding the contract would put that risk on Shoreline, which had no reason to consider or compensate for it (it did not have knowledge of Norwich's expectations about the equipment).

The court rejected Norwich's claim that enforcement would be unconscionable for several reasons. First, R2d § 153's reference to unconscionability applies only in the absence of an assumption of risk by the party seeking rescission. Also, the court found no precedent for invoking unconscionability without a showing of some kind of misconduct by the party seeking enforcement. Further, it rejected the gross-disparity-in-values-exchanged argument in part because the tower space was not defective or valueless, even if not suitable for Norwich's needs.

Mutual Mistake and Reformation

Alcoa v. Essex Group *(Page 807).* ALCOA and Esssex entered into a long term contract that contained an elaborate price indexing system, which Alcoa expended significant costs in developing (including hiring not-yet Chairman of the Federal Reserve, Alan Greenspan). At Essex's insistence, the index related to Alcoa's costs included a circuit breaker if the index rose too fast relative to the underlying market price. But Alcoa did not require a corresponding "booster" if the index moved too slowly. Thus, the index had a ceiling but not a floor. Unfortunately for Alcoa, the index moved too slowly relative to the actual market owing to the under-representation of energy costs in the basket of inputs that comprise the wholesale price index for industrial costs relative to the costs of converting alumina into aluminum.

The court granted Alcoa relief in the form of reformation because of mutual mistake, commercial impracticability and frustration of purpose. In its mutual mistake analysis, the court concluded that there was a mistake as to a fact– the belief that the index would work as the parties expected. It also found that this mistake was mutual because mutuality is a question of understanding, not motivation (it thus rejected Essex's argument that the mistake was not mutual since Essex was not concerned about keeping Alcoa's cost in check). The court claimed that Essex conceded that the parties assumed the price indicator would function properly within narrow limits and that the price indicator's function was material to the contract.

Finally, the court found that Alcoa did not assume the risk through any of the four ways one can do so. First, the court rejected the argument that, by not including a floor in the price term, Alcoa expressly or implicitly agreed to bear the risk. Rather, the court said, Alcoa merely thought the possibility that a floor would be necessary was too remote to put into the contract. The court also rejected Essex's argument that the contract should be interpreted against its drafter (Alcoa) because, according to the court, that is only appropriate when there is ambiguity or a policy concern, neither of which were present in the instant case. As to assuming risk by conscious ignorance of the risk, the court said that the measure is not whether they were aware at some level that uncertainty existed, but rather whether they believed the uncertainty was limited (which Alcoa did). Finally, the court found that there was no reason for court allocation of the risk to Alcoa, and that customary dealing did not call for Alcoa to assume the risk.

The court also considered impracticability and frustration, which have the same basic doctrinal requirements as mistake, but focus on the hardship. It found for Alcoa on both of these grounds based on its 60 million dollar loss, which resulted from the failure of the index. (*See page 860 for that portion of the court's opinion.*)

Pedagogy on Alcoa. We begin by reinforcing our previous doctrinal analysis of mutual mistake, which identifies a basic assumption as a belief that the parties did not realize might be false. The court in *Aloca* reminds us that the mistake doctrine applies to a mistaken belief about a particular fact only if, as Corbin argues, a court decides "the parties made a definite assumption that it existed and made their agreement in the belief that *there was no risk with respect to it.*" The alleged mutual mistake in *Alcoa* is the parties' belief in "the suitability of the WPI-IC as an index to accomplish the purposes of the parties."   The court finds that "each [party] assumed the Index was adequate to fulfill its purpose. This mistaken assumption was essentially a present actuarial error."

Because the court finds the doctrine of mutual mistake applicable to this case, it would seem to follow that it believes the parties "made their agreement in the belief that there was no risk" that the price index would fail to reflect ALCOA'S actual costs. This is precisely the claim Essex denies. As the court notes, "Essex first asserts that ALCOA expressly or implicitly assumed the risk that the WPI-IC would not track ALCOA's non-labor production cots. Essex asserts that ALCOA drafted the index provision . . . and that ALCOA's officials knew of the inherent risk that the index would not reflect cost changes." The court's response is to demonstrate that the parties "plainly sought to limit the risks of their undertaking."   Chief among the pieces of evidence the court cites to demonstrate the parties' efforts to limit risk under their agreement is the fact that ALCOA hired Dr. Alan Greenspan to advise it on the drafting of the objective price index. As to why ALCOA did not include a price floor, just as Essex included a price ceiling, the court responds: "the absence of an express floor limitation can only be understood to imply that the parties deemed the risk too remote and their meaning too clear to trifle with additional negotiation and drafting." Finally, the court argues that "the proper question is not simply whether the parties to a contract were conscious of uncertainty with respect to a vital fact, but whether they believed that uncertainty was effectively limited within a designated range so that they would deem outcomes beyond that range to be highly unlikely. . . . Both consciously undertook a closely calculated risk rather than a limitless one." Thus, the court moves from Corbin's requirement that the parties believe there is *no risk* that they are wrong about their shared factual belief, to a more liberal requirement that the parties believe it is *highly unlikely* that their shared factual belief is wrong.

In our view, the case for rescission or reformation based on mutual mistake is clearest when the mistaken (material) belief fits Corbin's criterion– the parties did not even realize they might be wrong because they unconsciously assumed it to be true; that is, it simply never occurred to them that their factual belief would be wrong. In such a case, by hypothesis, the risk that the assumption turns out to be false is not allocated by agreement, so the scope of the parties' agreement is limited to the set of circumstances in which this factual assumption turns out to be true. Put simply, there is no agreement between the parties about their obligations in the event that fact turns out to be false. At least rescission, if not reformation, is justified in these circumstances.

But when the parties are conscious of a particular risk, and yet form a belief that the risk has been reduced or eliminated, it is no longer plausible to argue that it did not occur to them that their belief might be wrong. In such a case, it is far more difficult to conclude that the parties failed to allocate this risk. The court argues that the parties' demonstrable efforts to reduce the risk show that they failed to allocate the reduced risk. In its view, the parties considered that risk so remote that is was not worth allocating. Hence, ALCOA's failure to bother with drafting a floor to protect it against the remote risk that their price index would not function as it anticipated. This is certainly possible, but it is highly improbable. Even if both parties – perhaps because of Greenspan's role in drafting the index – believed the probability that the price index would malfunction was extremely low, it does not follow that ALCOA, let alone Essex, understood the contract to be subject to the condition that the index function as the parties anticipated it would. Indeed, if both parties believed the contract was, in effect, conditional on the price index functioning to limit the range of price variation to no more than three cents per pound, it is difficult to explain why Essex insisted on a price ceiling (or circuit breaker) on the index. And given that Essex did include a price ceiling, it is difficult to explain how ALCOA could reasonably conclude that Essex believed the contract was conditional on the price index working as predicted.

Suppose, however, that inclusion of the price ceiling could be reconciled with ALCOA's claim that the contract was conditional on the price index functioning as predicted. We still believe that the court fails properly to engage the fundamental question of whether the risk of the index malfunctioning was allocated by the agreement. Again, when the parties have failed even to realize they were making an assumption that might be false, it is clear that the risk of such an assumption being false is not allocated by the agreement. But in a case like *Alcoa*, where both parties were clearly aware of the risk, the fundamental question is whether the parties conditioned the contract on the risk not materializing, or whether they allocated the risk between them. The court argues that the parties' significant efforts to reduce the risk is evidence that they conditioned their agreement on the risk not materializing. The court relies on these efforts to demonstrate that the parties were motivated, and intended, to reduce the risk of price fluctuations. But the issue is not whether the parties intended to reduce this risk; clearly, they did. That they intended to, and in fact did, reduce the price risk does not, by itself, provide any evidence of their intent to condition their agreement on the residual risk not materializing.

To see this point, it is helpful to distinguish between two kinds of contractual intent, which we might call the parties' "intended contractual means" and "intended contractual ends." The court is correct that the parties intended to greatly reduce the risk of price fluctuations. This was the parties' intended contractual *end* (i.e., goal or objective). But the question before the court concerns the parties' intended contractual *means*: How did the parties intend to achieve their goal of reducing the risk of price fluctuations? There are two basic approaches to reducing the risk of price fluctuations in an agreement. The first is to include at most a presumptive price term in the agreement, but to make clear that the parties do not wish to be bound unless that price term functions to achieve the parties' particular objective (e.g., reflects the current market price of the contract good, tracks the costs of producing that good, etc.). In the extreme, parties can omit any express price term at all, thereby leaving it to a court *ex post* to impute a reasonable price at the time and place of delivery (*see e.g.*, UCC § 2-305). Or they could instruct a court to determine a price that achieves their objective for the price. We call this approach the "standard-based strategy" because it has all the advantages and disadvantages of regulation by use of standards. Its advantages are that it is inexpensive to draft *ex ante* and it holds out the prospect of custom-tailoring contract terms to the parties' objectives in light of actual circumstances determined *ex post* rather than predictions of circumstances made *ex ante*.

The standard-based approach, however, has three principal disadvantages. First, such a drafting strategy subjects the parties' agreement to the risk of misinterpretation by a court. A court might misinterpret the parties contractual objective (e.g., whether they intended the price to track retail or wholesale prices or costs, whether or not the parties intended to share the risk of price fluctuations equally, etc.) and the relevant market circumstances obtaining at the time adjudication (e.g., what the parties' relevant costs and market prices are in a given industry, etc.). Second, because such adjudication is factually expansive and subjective, it is costly for both the parties and courts. Third, given the potentially costly and subjective nature of such adjudication, parties can use the threat of litigating such a price term (in bad faith) as a strategy for extracting concessions from each other. Thus, the existence of such terms potentially undermines the reliability of the contract's initial distributive allocations.

The second basic approach to reducing the risk of price fluctuations in an agreement is to include a precise and conclusive price term. Such price terms will achieve the contractual objective of reducing price volatility only if they are carefully drafted to track the cost indicators in the relevant markets. We call this approach the "rule-based strategy" because it has all the advantages and disadvantages of regulation by use of rules. Like a rule, this strategy requires parties to incur *ex ante* the bulk of their costs of determining the price of their contract. Its chief advantage is that, by making proof of the price term trivial, it reduces the expected costs of adjudication, and the concomitant prospect of strategic (and thus inefficient) threat of adjudication,. The chief disadvantage is that it might not achieve the objective the parties intend it to achieve. Like all rules, a precise price term, no matter how sophisticated, is likely to be over- or under-inclusive over a large range of possible future circumstances. The best rule is one that provides an expected price that meets the parties' objective subject to an acceptable risk of volatility. But unlike the standards approach, the parties anticipate having no recourse to a court *ex post* in the event the precise price term does not function as predicted because unlikely future events materialize.

Thus, in drafting their agreements, parties face the familiar trade-offs of standards versus rules. Should they draft a general or vague price term and leave it to courts *ex post* to fix a more precise term for them, or should they draft a precise and conclusive price term knowing that it may not function as predicted? Under both approaches, the parties might fail to achieve their contractual objective of reducing price volatility. Under the standard-based approach, courts might misinterpret their agreement, thereby undermining the parties' objectives. Under the rule-based approach, the price term might fail to function as predicted. The best approach is one that is most likely to achieve the parties' contractual objective (e.g., of reducing volatility) at least cost. Rules are costly to create (if they are to be designed to function as the parties desire), but cheap to adjudicate (indeed, if drafted clearly enough, they will deter adjudication entirely). Standards are cheap to create, but costly to adjudicate.

Returning to *ALCOA*, we can now focus on the central question in the case: What was the parties' intended contractual means for achieving this objective? Our fundamental point is that *both approaches are consistent with the parties' intended contractual objective of reducing price volatility*. So the question is simply which strategy – rule-based or standard-based – did the parties, in fact, adopt? We believe the evidence strongly suggests that Alcoa and Essex both understood that they were using the rule-based approach– viz, that the parties intended the price term to be conclusive. The rule-based approach requires parties to incur substantial drafting costs *ex ante*. Such costs are rational to incur only if they create off-setting savings in the form of reduced expected costs of adjudication (and the inefficient strategic consequences attending a significant risk of costly adjudication). If the parties intended an *ex post* adjudicatory determination of their contract's price term (based on a court's attempt to achieve their contractual objective of reduced volatility), ALCOA's major *ex ante* investment in drafting a price term does not seem cost-effective. ALCOA should have drafted a vague standard (i.e., "the price shall be a reasonable price that guarantees ALCOA a profit of not less than $.01 nor more than .$03 per pound . . .") and made it clear that the term was only a presumptive binding effort to reduce price volatility and subject to judicial determination *ex post*. Instead, ALCOA's efforts seem clearly designed to achieve the benefits, and incur the costs, of a rule-based approach: heavy *ex ante* investment in drafting a precise term likely to achieve, by its own lights, the contractual objective of reduced volatility. Absent compelling evidence to the contrary, a court should presume that ALCOA (and Essex) chose the contractual means of a rule-based approach to achieve their contractual end of reducing price volatility.

Finally, we contrast *ALCOA* with ***Eastern Airlines v. Gulf Oil on page 326***, in which the contract price term was both inexpensive and clear: Platts Oilgram. In that case, the price index malfunctioned by failing report the price of released (unregulated) oil. We believe this case presents a clear example of a mutual mistake about a basic material assumption: that Platts would continue accurately and fully to report the market prices of oil. Clearly, this was not a risk the parties considered but deemed too remote to address: Neither party considered the possibility that oil would be deregulated *and* that Platts would not report that unregulated price. This risk simply never occurred to them. Because the price index was neither complex nor expensive to create, there is less reason than in *ALCOA* to believe the parties' intended contractual means for preventing price volatility was a conclusive price term. Admittedly, the price index is clear and precise, like a rule. This argues against excusing performance based on mistake or reforming the agreement. But given that it was inexpensive to draft, the cause of its malfunction was not even remotely contemplated by the parties, and reformation of the term to conform with the parties' contractual objectives is straightforward (simply include the price of unregulated oil in the price index), we believe the case for mutual mistake and reformation is far stronger in *Eastern Airlines* than in *ALCOA*. Ironically, the court rejects mutual mistake in *Eastern Airlines* but accepts it in *ALCOA*.

Atlas Corporation v. United States *(Page 824).* Atlas and other companies sued the U.S. government for reformation of contracts between the government and those corporations for the mining of uranium and thorium. They claimed that the parties were mutually mistaken as to whether the tailings (a sand-like residue produced in the mining operations) piles posed a significant health risk and would require decontamination expenditures. The court rejected this claim because the existence of the fact in question was not known at the time of contract formation, which means the parties could not have had a (mistaken) belief of that fact. The distinction between the *existence* of a fact being unknown and the *outcome* of a fact being unknown was of great importance to the court. It used it to distinguish *Sherwood*, which it said was about a fact the existence of which was known, but the outcome of which was not. In such a case, there can be a mistake as to that fact. In a case such as *Atlas*, where the very existence of a fact is unknown, the court said, there can be no mistake.

Pedagogy on Atlas. The *Atlas* court begins with the point that reformation must be based on the parties' agreement. The clearest case for reformation is a scrivener's error. In that case, there is no question what term the parties intended and no question that the writing failed to reflect that intent. Reformation is possible by revising the writing to reflect the term the parties intended, but failed, to include in the writing. Similarly, the *Atlas* court argues, reformation is possible in other cases only when the term the parties intended but failed to include in their agreement is clear. In *Atlas*, however, the court argues that parties did not intend any term to govern tailings expenses. Thus, reformation is impossible: The agreement cannot be formed to reflect the actual intent of the parties because the parties had no term intended to govern tailings expenses.

Assuming that this argument is compelling, shouldn't it undermine *Alcoa*? The court says no: "[E]ven though the *outcome* of a fact is unknowable, the parties can make a mistake concerning that fact. But where the *existence* of a fact is unknowable, the parties cannot have a belief concerning that fact, and they cannot make a mistake about it." The court, then, claims that in *Alcoa* the parties knew that the price index might function as intended, but they didn't know *whether* it would or not. They could, therefore, form a belief about whether it would function as intended. In *Atlas*, the court claims, the parties didn't even know there *were* tailings expenses, let alone what they would be. Thus, they could not form a belief of who would bear the cost of the tailings expenses.

In our view, this kind of analysis is deeply problematic because it relies on an arbitrary description of the relevant belief. We could argue that the parties in *Alcoa* had no belief about the probability that both an OPEC embargo and significant increases in pollution control costs would cause the WPI-IC price indicator clause to underestimate ALCOA's electricity costs by 500%. Just as it would have been *possible* for the parties in *Alcoa* to contemplate this risk even though they did not, it would also have been possible for the parties in *Atlas* to contemplate the costs of tailings containment even though they did not. It is true that the parties in *Alcoa* clearly *did* contemplate the more general prospect that the price indicator would not function properly. But it is also clear that the parties in *Atlas* contemplated the prospect that the private companies would not recover their costs plus a reasonable profit. In both cases, the parties sought to eliminate these risks: in *Alcoa* by adopting a complex price escalator; in *Atlas* by including "pricing provisions designed so that the private companies could recover their costs, plus a reasonable profit." That the parties in *Atlas* did not anticipate the existence of tailings costs seems no more relevant than that the parties in *Alcoa* failed to anticipate the OPEC embargo and pollution control cost increases.

In short, in both cases the parties included terms in their agreements designed to achieve an undisputed contractual objective, and in both cases the term failed to achieve that objective. In neither case did the parties form an intention with respect to the particular risk that materialized. But in both cases, the parties' contractual objectives were undermined by the effect of unanticipated events on the functioning of their chosen price term. *Note 2 on page 831* encourages students to make the argument that *Atlas* is on no less firm ground for reformation than *Alcoa*. As to whether mutual mistake and reformation are appropriate, we believe the answer depends on whether context indicates the parties chose a rule or standard-based approach as their contractual means for achieving their contractual ends. *See* the discussion of *Alcoa* above for elaboration on this thesis.

C. Impossibility and Commercial Impracticability

The Traditional Impossibility Doctrine: Agreements Concerning Particular Property, Goods, or Services

Howell v. Coupland *(Page 836)*. The defendant agreed to sell the plaintiff "200 tons of regent potatoes grown on land belonging to the said Robert Coupland in Whaplode." Most of the potatoes were killed by a disease that could not have been prevented and from which they could not have been saved. Thus, when the time came for delivery, the defendant had less than half the amount called for in the contract. The plaintiff sued for breach, and the defendant claimed excuse based on impossibility. The court held in favor of the defendant, finding an implied condition that the potatoes, which were to be grown at a specific place, be in existence when the time came for performance. Since they were not, performance was excused.

Carroll v. Bowersock *(Page 837)*. The plaintiff contracted with the owner of a warehouse to construct a reinforced concrete floor in the warehouse. When part of the work had been done, the warehouse was destroyed by fire through no fault of either party. The defendant had insured the building in its pre-improvement condition and had collected on that insurance. The defendant refused to build again, thereby rendering further performance by plaintiff impossible. The court found that performance of the contract was tied to the particular warehouse, and defendant had no obligation to rebuild the warehouse. However, the court also held that the defendant was entitled to compensation for the benefit he conferred, as measured by the amount of the contract work done which, but for the destruction, would have inured to the defendant as contemplated in the contract. This included work removing the old floor and the completed concrete footings; however, the plaintiff should not recover for temporary structures and devices.

Seitz v. Mark-O-Lite Sign Contractors *(Page 841)*. The plaintiff, under its contract to renovate a theater, hired the defendant to replace the neon sign marquee. The day after the agreement was signed, the defendant's sheet metal worker, who was the only of the defendant's employees capable of doing the work, was hospitalized due to diabetes. The defendant informed the plaintiff that it would be unable to perform and the plaintiff hired another subcontractor at a higher price. The plaintiff sued the defendant for the difference in price.

The defendant claimed that its performance was excused under a *force majeure* clause in the contract. It argued that the hospitalization of its employee fell under the clause's language, "other conditions or contingencies beyond [defendant's] control." The court rejected this argument, construing the clause narrowly under the rule of *ejusdem generis*. That rule requires courts to interpret the broad language to which defendant appealed as contemplating only those things of the same general nature as those specifically enumerated. The court ruled that the hospitalization of the employee due to a chronic disease is not of the same general nature as the events or things enumerated in the clause. The court also considered whether the defendant was entitled to relief under the impossibility doctrine. In the court's view, this question turned on whether the duty in question can only be performed by a particular person. Since the agreement was silent as to whether the defendant's hospitalized employee was the only person who could perform the duty as understood by the parties, the court considered all of the circumstances. The question, then, becomes whether the duty is delegable. The court found that it could be was performed by another and nothing indicated that only the defendant's employee could do the work. That the defendant contacted other sign contractors to determine whether it could cover is strong evidence of that fact. The court entered judgment for the plaintiff.

Canadian Industrial Alcohol v. Dunbar Molasses Co. *(Page 845)*. The defendant agreed to supply the plaintiff with 1,500,000 gallons of molasses from the usual run of a particular refinery. The run of that refinery was insufficient for the defendant to meet its obligations, and it delivered only approximately 350,000 gallons. The defendant claimed impossibility based on the unusually low production by the specified refinery (it only produced about 485,000 gallons). The court rejected this claim. The court suggested that an implied presupposition that the refinery would not be destroyed, etc., might be reasonable. However, the court argued, it would be unreasonable to read the agreement as containing an implied presupposition that a reduction in production by the refinery, without any effort by the defendant to ensure full production, would excuse performance. The court viewed the contract as imposing upon the defendant the burden of ensuring that the refinery would produce the required quantity. Otherwise, the plaintiff would have dealt directly with the refinery. Thus, the court held in favor of the plaintiff.

Pedagogy on Impossibility. The impossibility doctrine can usefully be conceived as extending the principle underlying mutual mistake to facts and circumstances not in existence at the time of formation (and thus to facts about which the parties could not have been mutually mistaken at the time of formation). Both doctrines in effect hold that the parties' contractual obligations are valid only within a limited domain of circumstances. Mutual mistake doctrine holds that an agreement is valid only if material circumstances assumed to exist by both parties at the time of formation in fact obtained at that time, unless the parties realized and allocated the risk that their assumption might be false. Such circumstances can be characterized as constituting a condition precedent to either party's liability under their agreement. Similarly, the impossibility doctrine holds that an agreement does not bind the parties if the parties' contract was, explicitly or implicitly, conditioned on performance by the promisor remaining possible during the performance period. When faced with contracts for unique goods, services that require the continued existence of a structure or the services of a particular individual, courts must decide whether the parties allocated the risk that the performance becomes impossible or instead implicitly conditioned the parties obligation on performance remaining possible throughout the performance period.

Howell v. Coupland nicely illustrates the analysis of the doctrine of impossibility as resting on a default interpretation of an implied condition in contracts for unique goods or services. The court there holds that the parties' agreement "was not an absolute contract of delivery under all circumstances, but a contract to deliver so many potatoes, of a particular kind, grown on a specific place, *if deliverable from that place.* On the facts the condition did arise and the performance was excused." The *Coupland* court takes the specification of particular goods to ground the inference that the parties' contract was subject to an implied condition that performance remain possible. Similarly, R2d § 261, quoted in *Seitz* holds that performance is excused "by the occurrence of an event the non-occurrence of which was a basic assumption on which the contract was made . . . unless the language or the circumstances indicate the contrary." We suggest analyzing this "basic assumption" condition just as we analyzed the "basic assumption" requirement for mutual mistake in R2d 152: as an implied condition of the agreement. The key point in *Seitz* is that the judicial determination of whether the contract is for a unique good or service will depend on the *buyer's perspective.* Here, the contract is not transformed into an agreement for a unique service simply because the seller intended to perform by using a particular person (Jorgenson). The buyer was indifferent to whether Jorgenson or another person (or indeed another company entirely) performed the sheet metal work on its sign. The buyer never indicated a desire to purchase unique goods or services and would be (in fact was) content with a market substitute.

Finally, *Dunbar Molasses* also takes the impossibility doctrine to require a finding that, as the defendant argued, "by an implied term of the contract, the duty to deliver was conditioned upon the production by the National Sugar Refinery at Yonkers of molasses sufficient quantity to fill the plaintiff's order." Interestingly, the court declines to find such a condition even though the contract specified a unique good (i.e., the molasses from a particular refinery, not just any equivalent molasses available on the market). The court instead reasoned that a buyer that contracts for a unique good with a middleman, rather than directly with the refinery, does not intend to assume the risk of non-delivery due to underproduction: "The defendant asks us to assume that a manufacturer, having made a contract with a middleman for a stock of molasses to be procured from a particular refiner, would expect the contract to lapse whenever the refiner chose to diminish his production, and this in the face of the middleman's omission to do anything to charge the refiner with a duty to continue." The court's argument is that the very purpose of the buyer's contract was to transfer this risk to the middleman (i.e., to pay the middleman to take whatever measures are necessary to insure delivery of an adequate supply from that refinery). Otherwise, the buyer "very likely would have preferred to deal with the refinery directly, instead of dealing with a middleman."

Carroll v. Bowersock, however, most closely treats the impossibility doctrine on analogy with the mutual mistake doctrine. The court holds that the parties' agreement is valid only under the basic assumption that the warehouse continued to exist throughout the performance period. Because the parties never contemplated the destruction of the warehouse (they unconsciously assumed its continued existence: "Impossibility of performance because of destruction of the building was not contemplated by either party"), the agreement simply does not specify what should happen in the event of the warehouse's destruction. Thus, the allocation of that risk cannot, as a matter of law, be settled by contract doctrine. Instead, the court retreats to the law of restitution, finding that "to the extent the owner has been benefitted the law may properly consider him as resting under a duty to pay. The benefit which the owner has received may or may not be equivalent to the detriment which the contractor has suffered. The only basis on which the law can raise an obligation on the part of the owner is the consideration he has received by way of benefit, advantage, or value to him." In other words, the contract provides no basis for the contractor's recovery because it does not apply when its basic assumption about the future turns out to be false. Only restitution can ground his recovery.

As a theoretical matter, why would parties be inclined to condition liability on the continued possibility of performance? As we note in the opening *Essay* to this section (*page 833*), liability is easily and routinely imposed by requiring payment of damages when performance becomes impossible. So when would parties want to excuse performance rather than require payment of damages when performance becomes impossible? As we suggested in our discussion of *Taylor v. Caldwell on page 89* (*see Essay, Page 93*) the impossibility doctrine might be justified as a crude information-forcing rule. If a party contracts for a unique good or performance, he is presumably signaling that he values that good or performance differently than any possible market substitute. But unless he stipulates liquidated damages, his contracting partner would be unable to determine the buyer's subjective valuation of performance, and thus would be unable to price the contract to reflect the buyer's true expectancy. The impossibility excuse, therefore, excuses the seller when performance becomes impossible in order to motivate the buyer to disclose his subjective valuation at the time of formation. If the buyer indicates his subjective value by including a liquidated damages clause, then courts will not excuse performance when it becomes impossible because the parties have agreed to payment for lack of performance.

Unfortunately, this explanation is unsatisfying unless it is limited to cases involving unique goods or performances being exchanged in a "thin" market. In such a case, the problem courts would face in awarding expectancy damages, rather than granting excuse, is the lack of a market measure with which to determine expectancy with reasonable certainty. In a thin market there is no reliable measure of lost expectancy, and the absence of substitutes explains why courts are reluctant to award damages rather than to excuse performance. In such a market, therefore, the deep explanation for an excuse rule is not that it induces disclosure by buyers that enables sellers to take efficient precautions, but rather that courts are unable to specify an expectancy default that would so motivate the buyer. Thus, granting excuse where a specialized performance is impossible can be seen as a per se application of the general rule that speculative damages are not recoverable.

Assume, however, that the market for substitutes is thick (i.e., the potatoes under contract in *Howell v. Coupland*). Here, the information-forcing rationale is subject to two criticisms. First, it is over-broad as an information-forcing default rule. Rather than excusing the performance entirely, a default rule that limited the buyer's recovery to market -based expectancy would be sufficient to motivate the buyer to reveal his subjective valuation. Indeed, an expectancy default would provide an optimal incentive for the buyer to reveal his subjective valuation. Unsurprisingly, this is precisely the how the classic case of an information-forcing rule – *Hadley v. Baxendale, page 118* – works in the context of consequential damages (*See*

Chapter 1, *Page 125, note 9*): Consequential damages are limited to foreseeable damages, thus barring recovery for damages the breacher had no way of anticipating at the time of formation (or performance). But the breacher is not excused from performance entirely. The breacher is excused only from paying those damages it caused but had no way of anticipating at the time of formation given the promisee's failure to reveal its idiosyncratic risks. Thus, by excusing performance entirely, rather than limiting recovery to market damages, the impossibility doctrine provides an inefficiently strong incentive to reveal information.

Second, unlike the *Hadley* rule, this information-forcing account fails to explain why parties would continue to contract for unique goods or services in a thick market without specifying liquidated damages. Under the *Hadley* explanation, it is easy to explain why some parties continue to write contracts that entitle them only to ordinary, foreseeable damages that don't allow compensation for idiosyncratic consequential damages: Presumably, the parties that fail to reveal idiosyncratic risks will be the parties who have no idiosyncratic risks. But parties that contract for unique goods or services in a thick market by hypothesis value the contracted-for unique performance above the market value of equivalents. Thus, on this account, it remains a mystery why any such parties, given the existence of the impossibility doctrine, would fail to specify liquidated damages.

If the information-forcing explanation for the impossibility doctrine fails in the case of a contract for goods that are otherwise traded in a thick market, then the doctrine remains something of a mystery in this context. Wouldn't most parties to such contracts prefer market damages to no damages in the event performance becomes impossible? We think so. We can only suggest risk sharing as the motivation for the parties in cases such as *Howell v. Coupland*. The farmer, by contracting to deliver potatoes on designated land, is shifting the risk of adverse conditions – such as severe drought or flooding – that would increase the expected price of cover if damages were the default. Shifting this risk to the buyer would be optimal if, for example, the framer were a risk averse individual and the buyer were a risk neutral cooperative. But explanations based on risk aversion are often too facile. Thus, that leaves us without a satisfactory explanation of the impossibility doctrine as applied to contracts for a particularized performance in a thick market. Perhaps all that can be said is that the doctrine is an ancient one not appropriately tailored to the informational purposes it was (at best implicitly) designed to serve.

Problem (Page 848). The most important facts you would need to know to apply *Dunbar Molasses* to this case is whether Murray had a contract with GM and whether the contingencies were reasonably foreseeable. The agreement between Murray and GM bound GM only upon release of products to production, gave GM discretion in distribution and was contingent on other factors that might affect availability of the products. Therefore, in the case between Murray and the School Board, the court found that the risk of the manufacturer's cancellation was reasonably foreseeable. In addition, there was no clause in the contract conditioning performance on GM's delivery of the goods. These two facts combine to deny the defense of commercial impracticability to Murray. The court also rejected excuse based on the government regulations on the ground that intervening regulations do not excuse performance where the non-performing party has assumed the risk of such a regulation. In this case, the agreement provided that Murray keep abreast of government regulations.

The Modern Excuse of Commercial Impracticability

Transatlantic Financing Corp v. United States *(Page 849).* Transatlantic agreed to ship goods from Texas to Iran. Shortly before the agreement was reached, Egypt took over the Suez Canal. Later, Israel and other countries attacked Egypt in an effort to free the Canal from that country's control. This resulted in Egypt blocking the Canal with sunk ships. This closure occurred while the Transatlantic ship was en route. As a result, the ship was forced to go around the Cape of Good Hope to deliver the goods, and thus incurred extra costs. The price of the contract was approximately $350,000 and the additional costs were approximately $40,000. After delivering the goods, Transatlantic recovered the contract price and sought additional money to cover the added expenses. When the U.S. refused, they sued in *quantum meruit* for the additional $40,000 expense. Transatlantic argued that it was entitled to the $40,000 because its unanticipated trip around the Cape constituted a conferral of a benefit on the United States.

The court walked through the plaintiff's argument and rejected it. Since the contract did not specify a route for the delivery of the goods, the court agreed with the plaintiff that custom and the doctrine of deviation anticipated that delivery would be by the "usual and customary" route. The court then considered whether that physical impossibility made performance of the contract impracticable. Since the contract was negotiated with awareness of the developments regarding the Suez Canal, the court found that the plaintiff agreed to assume abnormal risks, even though it did not assume the risk of closure of the Canal. For this reason, the court considered the impracticability question with greater strictness than usual.

In considering that question, the court first asserted that the plaintiff was in a better position to insure against the risk of closure (because gauging such risks is part of the plaintiff's business). Here, the court seems to be reconsidering the question of whether the risk was/should be allocated to the plaintiff and not whether performance was impracticable. The court then compared the cost of the deviation to the contract price. It concluded that the cost of the deviation was not significant enough to warrant a finding that performance was commercially impracticable. The court also noted that Transatlantic's theory of recovery was inconsistent with a finding of impossibility or impracticability: These doctrines render the contract void, and thus leave Transatlantic no right to the price under the contract. Instead, Transatlantic would be entitled to recover on *quantum meruit* for its entire performance (conferral of benefit). But Transatlantic already accepted the price and was suing "off the contract" (in *quantum meruit*) for the additional expense of going around the Cape. The court held that these theories of recovery were inconsistent, and implied that Transatlantic, by accepting the price, rejected its own theory of impossibility or impracticability.

***Pedagogy on* Transatlantic.** *Transatlantic* introduces students to UCC § 2-615. The core of the provision extends the common law impossibility doctrine's test based on a "basic assumption" to excuse based on impracticability, rather than impossibility. It excuses performance "if performance as agreed has been made impracticable by the occurrence of a contingency the non-occurrence of which was a basic assumption on which the contract was made." The circumstance making performance impracticable must be an "unforeseen supervening circumstance not within the contemplation of the parties at the time of contracting." UCC § 2-615, com. 1. The *Transatlantic* court emphasizes that it rejects the "implied term" test for impracticability. Instead, it believes that parties can be excused not only when a court finds the non-occurrence of an event that occurred to be an implied (from context) condition of their agreement, but also if the court is prepared to "construct a condition of performance based on the changed circumstances."

The construction of such a condition, in our view, is equivalent to a finding that the non-occurrence of the condition was a basic assumption of the agreement. Because such assumptions are not conscious, occurrent beliefs, the parties do not allocate the risk that their assumption is false. Thus, we agree with the court that excuse doctrine (as well as mistake doctrine) does not require a finding of an actual, implied term– i.e., a term to which the parties actually agreed, though did not express orally or in writing. Nonetheless, we follow other courts and commentators who do not carefully distinguish between implied and constructive (or default) terms, and instead use the term "implied" to cover both cases. Thus, when we analyze mistake doctrine as requiring a finding of an implied condition precedent, the implication of such a term can be based on the parties' actual intent *or* on the fact that the parties never contemplated the issue in question.

The challenge in *Transatlantic* is the same as in the excuse and impossibility cases we have already covered. The court must first ask if the parties anticipated the event that occurred. Here, as we have seen (e.g., in *Atlas*), the trick is that the event can be described at different levels of generality to reach opposite conclusions. For example, the parties certainly did not contemplate that Egypt would deliberately sink ships in the Suez Canal, yet arguably at least Transatlantic anticipated some risk that the Suez Canal might not be available due to political volatility in the region. Which description should control the excuse analysis? If the event was anticipated, the court must determine if the risk of that event was allocated. As the court argues, "foreseeability or even recognition of a risk does not necessarily prove its allocation. . . . Parties to a contract are not always able to provide for all the possibilities of which they are aware, sometimes because they cannot agree, often simply because they are too busy." Thus, if the parties failed to anticipate an event, or anticipated it but failed to allocate the risk of its occurrence, the contract does not resolve the question of allocating the losses occasioned by its occurrence. Just as the *Bowersock* court turned to the off-contract doctrine of restitution, the court here argues that *quantum meruit* would apply to allow the contractor to recover. But, of course, the court determines that Transatlantic assumed the risk of abnormal events (even though it did not specifically assume the risk of Egypt's actions). It apparently reasons that when an experienced party such as Transatlantic contracts against the background of the geopolitics of the time, it is necessarily assuming abnormal risks (or perhaps, the normal risks of that abnormal time). Given its superior knowledge of the implications of these risks for its costs of performance, the court argues it is the superior insurer against such risks. Thus, the court concludes that the parties (constructively) agreed that Transatlantic would bear that risk.

It's not clear, however, whether the court believes Transatlantic implicitly or constructively agreed to assume this risk. If the argument is that Transatlantic's comparative advantage in assuming the risk is grounds for believing it implicitly assumed the risk, then the decision is supportable (though certainly subject to reasonable disagreement on the facts of the matter). But if the argument is that Transatlantic should bear the risk according to a general default rule that places such risks on the party best able to bear it, even if that party did not implicitly assume the risk, the argument cannot be sustained. As we argue in the *Essay on page 867*, comparative advantage in risk bearing does not apply in the pure case of an genuinely unforeseeable risk. Thus, the default rules governing unforeseeable events cannot be justified by their incentive effects because, by hypothesis, the risk in question is one the parties never did or would have considered. Hence, neither party could have taken precautions against it. Whether one party would have been better able to bear the risk had they been able to anticipate it, under these circumstances, is irrelevant.

Problems (Page 855). *a.* According to *United States v. Wegematic Corp*, Larry has breached the contract. In that case, the court held that a manufacturer who agrees to provide a product bears the risk of such engineering difficulties. If the manufacturer does not want to bear this risk, she must bargain for her contracting party to bear that risk. Otherwise, the court says, those in the business of developing technology would have a wide degree of latitude with respect to performance while holding an option to make the buyer pay if the "gamble should pan out."

b. In order to decide this case, one would need to know more about the labor dispute. Importantly, one must know whether the non-occurrence of a labor-dispute was a basic assumption of the contract. If labor disputes were extremely common for the plaintiff, or if for some other reason the parties expected or should have expected a dispute, the defense of impracticability would not be available. Also, one would need to know the extent to which the dispute frustrated the ability of the defendant to perform (i.e., enough to make performance impracticable?).

c. The first place to look for Schmitz's rights against Dale is the agreement– how did the parties deal with the issue of approval from the Association? Since this approval was usually a formality, they were unlikely to provide for their respective obligations once this contingency occurred. Therefore, we must decide based on the common law (this is mostly a contract for services, not sale of goods, so the UCC doesn't apply) whether Schmitz's declaration that Dale must stop work constituted a breach. If so, Schmitz has no rights against Dale. If not, Schmitz may have some rights.

The question of whether Schmitz breached the contract turns on whether he bore the risk of the denial by the Association. That question requires a determination of how the parties would have allocated that risk had they considered it. Dale will argue that since Schmitz was the member of the Association, he is the better risk bearer. He presumably knows the people involved and the procedures required for obtaining approval. Meanwhile, Schmitz will argue that Dale is the better risk bearer because of his experience as a contractor. That experience will presumably have exposed him to the processes involved and the likelihood of success. This argument will be more persuasive if Dale has done extensive work with this Association or ones similar to it. Assuming these issues are resolved in favor of Schmitz, the court will consider whether Dale can insist on an increase in price. Since the court will have already allocated the risk of the denial by the Association to him, Dale's only option will be to argue impracticability. Because his costs haven't increased by much, he is unlikely to be successful with that argument. Thus, if the risk of denial by the Association is allocated to Dale, Schmitz will be able to enforce the contract at its original price.

Eastern Air Lines v. Gulf Oil Corp. *(Page 857).* This is the second part of the *Eastern Airlines* opinion which is excerpted in Chapter 4. In this portion of the opinion, the court rejects Gulf's argument of commercial impracticability. According to the court, excuse by failure of presupposed condition requires an unforeseeable failure of an underlying assumption, the risk of which was not specifically allocated to the complaining party. The court rejected Gulf's argument that the combination of the oil embargo and deregulation was unforeseeable. The court pointed first to the fact that OPEC had made threats before, and second, to the fact that Gulf lobbied for the deregulation. Because the failure of the underlying assumption was not unforeseeable, the court did not need to consider the question of risk.

Alcoa v. Essex Group *(Page 860).* This is the last portion of the *ALCOA* opinion excerpted earlier in this Chapter. In addition to finding in favor of Alcoa on mutual mistake, the court held in favor of Alcoa on the grounds of impracticability and frustration of purpose. This excerpt focuses on the impracticability claim. The court applies its findings on the mistake issue to the impracticability issue, finding that the non-occurrence of the event (and the non-existence of the fact) that caused the impracticability was a basic assumption on which the contract was made. Also, the court found there was no assumption of risk by Alcoa. The difficulty envisioned in the impracticability doctrine, according to the court, must be extreme and unreasonable; a change in degree is not sufficient, unless it is well beyond the normal range. In this case, the loss was so significant in absolute size and proportion to the value of the contract ($60 million) that it altered the essential nature of performance (it was beyond the limit on the risk of market change that was part of the purpose of the contract).

Pedagogy on **Eastern** *and* **Alcoa.** As we noted in our discussion of the mistake doctrine, it is something of a mystery why Gulf failed to argue mutual mistake. We have little doubt that had Judge Teitelbaum decided *Eastern Airlines*, he would have been amenable, at the very least, to the mutual mistake claim. Instead, Gulf's lawyers chose to argue that Eastern failed to act in good faith (by fuel freighting– *see* Chapter 4) and that Gulf should be excused because subsequent events caused performance to become commercially impracticable. In our view, the latter tries to fit a square peg in a round hole. Even if, as the court holds, the OPEC embargo and the deregulation of oil were foreseeable, it was surely unforeseeable that Platts Oilgram would not report the price of deregulated (new and released) as well as regulated (old) oil. But for that unforeseeable (indeed bizarre) fact, neither the embargo nor deregulation would have affected the price Eastern paid for Gulf fuel under the contract. Just as we believe the parties' bargain was based on the basic, material assumption that Platts would accurately report the market price of oil, and thus grounds relief based on mutual mistake, we believe one could plausibly argue that their bargain was made on the basic assumption of the non-occurrence of Platt's failure to report the price of deregulated oil.

The failure of Platts to report the price of deregulated oil is an unforeseeable event that would ground relief based on commercial impracticability provided it caused undue hardship to Gulf. Given precedents holding that even a doubling of costs need not constitute undue hardship, Gulf would have to prove it suffered extraordinary losses owing to the difference between the contract's price of fuel, based on the $5/barrel market price of regulated oil, and the $11/barrel market price of deregulated oil. (See the Chapter 4 excerpt for these figures). Since Gulf focused on litigating the fuel freighting claim, it apparently did not set out a compelling case demonstrating its actual losses. Such an effort would require it to demonstrate the extent of its losses over the course of the entire contract and to compare those losses with typical variances in other similar contracts in the industry. Though Gulf may have lost even with good lawyering, it had no chance given the arguments it advanced.

This portion of the *Alcoa* opinion is most noteworthy for its express view that the doctrines of mutual mistake, commercial impracticability and frustration of purpose amount to virtually the same thing. The traditional distinction between mutual mistake and the latter two doctrines is that a mutual mistake must be about an endogenous event; that is, a fact in existence at the time of agreement, while impracticability (and impossibility) and frustration of purpose are based on exogenous events occurring subsequent to formation. Essex had argued that the change in the price of electricity was a future, exogenous event and therefore could not form the basis of a mutual mistake. The court responded that the parties' mutual mistake was in believing the price index (and endogenous fact) would function as predicted. Such reasoning allows the court to transform a mistaken prediction about a future event into a present mistake of fact. Unsurprisingly, therefore, the court finds the traditional distinction between these doctrines meaningless. Instead, it focuses on the undue hardship requirement unique to impracticability. We believe that although the distinction between mistake and impracticability is sometimes difficult to discern, the distinction between mistaken assumptions about facts in existence at the time of formation and mistaken assumptions about future events is conceptually tenable as a doctrinal matter. Doctrinally, the distinction matters not only because it determines whether the undue hardship element applies, but also because mutual mistakes are not explicitly subject to a foreseeability test. But other than these sometimes important doctrinal distinctions, we agree with the *Alcoa* court that the doctrines serve largely the same purposes.

When we teach the mistake and impracticability (and impossibility) doctrines, our chief objective is to identify possible policy objectives these excuses might serve. As we noted in the **Essay on page 867**, if the parties to an agreement make a mistake as to a basic assumption (whether about a material fact at the time of formation or about the non-occurrence of an unforseeable event), then they did not consider, let alone allocate, the risk of the assumption being wrong. Since default rules here will by hypothesis have no effect on future parties in similar circumstances, an analysis of the incentive effects of alternative default rules would seem irrelevant to explaining and justifying this doctrine. Hence, a number of scholars have argued that the law should seek "just, equitable, or fair" divisions of the losses these errors occasion.

But note that all the errors that otherwise qualify as grounding excuse based on mutual mistake or impracticability can also be described at a suitable level of generality to qualify them as "basic conscious beliefs" rather than "basic assumptions," which are therefore allocated by agreement. Thus, to review, even if the reasons for the WPI-IC were unforseeable, the parties certainly knew that, in general, there was a risk that it would malfunction. The same can be said for the malfunctioning escalator term in *Eastern Airlines*, and as *Transatlantic* argues, the general prospect of war and embargoes in turbulent times and places (even if not the particular manifestations they might take). Indeed, *force majeure* clauses reflect parties' efforts to signal to courts that although the parties may have failed entirely to consider particular events that affect their burdens under their agreement, they have considered and allocated the general risk that such events might take place. *See Note 2 (Page 864)*. Once we accept that all risk can be subsumed under the general rubric of a term covering "unanticipated material events," there are no events that cannot be anticipated by the parties' agreement. An analysis based on comparative advantage can proceed, therefore, by justifying the defaults as assigning these general risks to the party that can bear them at least cost.

D. Frustration of Purpose

Krell v. Henry *(Page 870)*. The defendant agreed to rent the plaintiff's flat for the purpose of viewing the processions associated with the coronation of the new King of England. Before the balance of the payment was due, it was announced that the processions would not be held because of the ill health of the King. The defendant refused to pay the balance and the plaintiff sued. The defendant counter-claimed for the return of his deposit, but that claim was apparently withdrawn on appeal.

The court held in favor of the defendant. According to the court, a contract is not binding if a contingency that was at the foundation of a contract was of such a character as could not be reasonably said to have been in the contemplation of the parties at the date of the contract, and the non-occurrence of the contingency prevented performance of the contract. The court rejects the notion that either party ought to have guarded against the non-occurrence of the event, since neither party contemplated that non-occurrence. Finally, the court asserts that it is not essential to the application of the *Taylor v. Caldwell* principle that the "direct subject" of the contract be the thing that is destroyed or does not occur.

Lloyd v. Murphy *(Page 873)*. The defendant leased property in Beverly Hills from the plaintiff for the purpose of selling new cars, fuel and occasionally, used cars. Subsequently, the federal government, because of the increased demands of the military on production capacity arising from engagement in World War II, restricted the sale of new cars. The plaintiffs offered to lower defendant's rent and allow him to sublease the premises (not permitted in the lease without written permission). The defendant instead vacated the premises and repudiated the contract. The plaintiffs quickly leased the property in order to mitigate damages and then sued the defendant.

The court found in favor of the plaintiff, rejecting the defendant's impossibility and frustration of purpose arguments. First, the court found that the risk of restriction on production was reasonably foreseeable at the time of the contract. The Congress had already passed a statute allowing the President to allocate materials and mobilize industry for national defense. Also, automobile sales were soaring because of consumer expectation that production would be restricted. Thus, the court asserted that this risk must have been contemplated, and, as it was not expressly allocated, the court concluded it was assumed by the defendant.

The court then found that the value of the lease had not been destroyed and its purpose had not been frustrated. That the property was easily sublet was strong evidence that the value of the lease was not destroyed, especially since the defendant had received permission to sublease. Also, the plaintiffs gave the defendant permission to use the property for other purposes, for which the property clearly had value (as evidenced, again, by the quick subletting). Further, the fact that sales of new cars were not prohibited, but merely restricted, meant that the purpose was not frustrated. The defendant failed to demonstrate, according to the court, that it faced the extreme level of hardship required for the frustration of purpose defense. Indeed, the defendant admitted that he continued to sell new cars elsewhere in the same county. This left the defendant a long way from meeting his burden in the view of the court.

Pedagogy on Krell and Lloyd. Like impracticability, frustration is another variant on impossibility that excuses performance when unanticipated supervening events fall short of making performance impossible, but nonetheless materially affect the contract. Frustration applies when performance is made pointless, rather than impossible, by intervening events. As always, the most critical element is that the risk of the intervening event was not contemplated (and allocated) by the parties. But, in addition, a frustration defense requires a showing that there was a clear, mutually understood, predominant purpose of the agreement, and that the unanticipated event so utterly undermines that purpose from being achieved that the non-occurrence of that event must have been a basic assumption of the agreement. The point, of course, is not that had they realized that their assumption might be mistaken the parties would not have contracted, but rather that they would have instead allocated that risk to the promisee (the party seeking to enforce the contract after the event occurs). As we point out in *Note 4 on page 879*, the frustration doctrine excuses performance only when a *joint* purpose had been defeated by intervening events, not a purpose of one party only. It is often not easy, however, to identify the joint purpose of a contract.

Krell is the classic frustration case, representing a host of "coronation" cases. The court views the case as a variant of *Taylor v. Caldwell*. Here, in order to explain why the frustration doctrine excuses the lessee, we must first identify a shared purpose that was defeated by intervening events. The shared purpose is ostensibly "the letting of a room for the purpose of viewing the coronation." Of course, viewing the coronation is the purpose the lessee achieves, not the lessor. But it is nonetheless the purpose for which both parties agreed to rent the room.

Contrast this to the purpose in *Lloyd*. Clearly, the lessee intended to sell new cars, but the lessor was simply leasing commercial property. At most, he anticipated that the lessor would sell or service cars, but it cannot be said that the parties' *joint* purpose was to rent the property to sell new cars. (More important, in *Lloyd* the court finds that the parties *did* anticipate the prospect of intervening government regulation of new car sales. Thus, the court treats the risk as implicitly allocated to the lessee).

In *Krell*, why should the court allocate the risk of the coronation cancellation to the lessor? Attending to the particular facts of the case, we could argue that the lessor will not be harmed, since he will be able to re-let the premises should the coronation be rescheduled. Thus, even if the lessee were liable, damages likely would be fully mitigated by the lessor. The liability rule wouldn't matter. But if we suppose the coronation is never rescheduled, then presumably the lessor will not be able to re-let the room, at the same rate, for a period of two days only. So viewed, the contract is for a good tied to a unique event– if the event is canceled, there is no market substitute for the lessor. Although the apartment is not unique (there are other apartments with a view of the scheduled procession), the contract price is tied exclusively to a unique event. What would the parties have agreed to had they expressly dickered over this risk? Would the lessor have insisted on payment even in the event of cancellation, or would the lessee have insisted the contract be made conditional on the non-cancellation of the coronation? Unless we postulate asymmetric risk-aversion, there is no way to say whether the lessor would have done the former (and thus charged less) or that the lessee would have demanded the latter (and agreed to pay a higher price). Perhaps the landlord has the comparative advantage in bearing the risk of cancellation because he could, in principle, arrange a back-up lease (albeit at a normal rate reflecting the apartment's ordinary rental value) to reduce his losses in the event the coronation is canceled. For example, he might rent the apartment on an annual basis before the coronation is scheduled, but reserve in the lease his right to rent out the apartment on whatever days the coronation takes place. But the landlord would have the incentive to take this, and other, precautions whether or not the short-term lease for viewing the coronation procession is conditional on non-cancellation of the proceedings.

Since neither party has a comparative advantage in bearing the risk of cancellation, any clear default rule for allocating this risk (in the absence of the parties' agreement to the contrary) will maximize the joint value of such contracts by deterring litigation over the issue. (Contrast *Lloyd*: it seems clear that the lessee has the comparative advantage in bearing the risk of arguably foreseeable governmental regulations governing his line of business). Unfortunately, since the kinds of issues raised in *Krell* (and all successful frustration cases) are ones the parties did not contemplate at the time of formation, the party assigned the risk by the default rule will not charge the cost of bearing such risks. Thus, in true frustration cases the concern for *ex post* fairness argues for a risk-splitting default rule. No harm is done to *ex ante* efficiency or fairness since issues grounding a frustration defense are, by hypothesis, ones the parties failed to anticipate. The fact that common law courts stubbornly declined to develop such sharing rules and instead adopted a default that places the losses where they would fall in the absence of contract may explain why subsequent courts have only infrequently granted excuse for any of the reasons discussed in this Chapter.

Problem (Page 880). In *Alabama Football v. Wright*, Wright's response was that he had already given adequate consideration for the bonus payment, and that Alabama Football bore the risk of the failure of its team and the World Football League. The court sided with Wright on the first claim, but rejected the second. It found that, in the context of football contracts, the bonus payment was properly understood as compensation for the signing of the contract. Furthermore, Alabama Football received the additional benefit of being able to use Wright's name in promoting its team. Also, Wright gave up the possibility of contracting with another team when he signed the contract.

The court rejected Wright's claim for damages for Alabama Football's failure to perform on the remainder of the contract on the grounds of impossibility. It first found that the provisions of the contract were separable (there were five components, each a separate financial agreement). It then found that the financial failure that caused the impossibility of actual performance could not have reasonably been expected by either party. Next, the court asserted that the risk of this contingency was not expressly or impliedly allocated to either party. And finally, it pointed to the undisputed fact that the contingency (the dissolution of the team and the league) made performance impossible. Thus, it found that both parties were excused from further performance.

CHAPTER 9

CONDUCT CONSTITUTING BREACH

A. Introduction

The doctrine of anticipatory repudiation presents a number of challenges. Initially, the pedagogical objective is to explain why anticipatory repudiation matters. The simple answer is that it triggers the non-breacher's duty to mitigate. Mitigation is an anti-waste doctrine. Of course, even if the doctrine of anticipatory repudiation did not exist, the mitigation doctrine would still require mitigation when breach occurs at the time of performance. Anticipatory repudiation simply extends the reach of the mitigation doctrine to cost-effective waste-reducing measures *before* the time for performance has expired, but after one party has indicated an unwillingness or inability to perform. The justification for the anticipatory repudiation doctrine, then, ultimately turns on whether it in fact reduces costs by preventing waste before the time for performance has expired. Certainly, the goal of extending the mitigation requirement before the time for performance is laudable. As we explain in this introductory essay, in an ideal world, in every contract, both parties would have the duty to adjust optimally to new circumstances. The party with the comparative advantage in taking precautions against an undesirable event materializing (i.e., reducing its probability and costs) would be under an obligation to do so throughout the term of the contract. But the significant costs resulting from the opportunities for evasion and opportunism such a general duty would create, in all likelihood, outweigh its potential benefits from cost savings (see p. 885).

The doctrine of anticipatory repudiation represents a compromise between a comprehensive duty to adjust and a duty of mitigation that can be triggered only after the time for performance has expired. Instead of importing wholesale a duty to adjust throughout the term of a contract, anticipatory repudiation allows a party to breach, or trigger a breach, before the time for performance has expired. While anticipatory repudiation, like a general duty to adjust, can be triggered at any time before the time for performance has expired, the duty to mitigate is not triggered until anticipatory repudiation occurs. And therefore, unlike the general duty to adjust, a party can trigger his contractual partner's duty to mitigate before the time for performance has expired only by repudiating the agreement and thereby forfeiting his right to his partner's performance (see p. 886). This means that repudiation will be worthwhile only when the cost-savings to the repudiating party from the other party's mitigation outweigh the repudiating party's loss of expectancy. Thus, the doctrine of anticipatory repudiation responds to the strategic costs undermining a general duty to adjust by limiting the duty to mitigate to cases in which the potential cost savings are so significant (because they exceed the value of the repudiating party's expectancy) that they will outweigh any strategic costs the doctrine itself creates. In addition, the doctrine of anticipatory repudiation is elaborated with a number of subsidiary doctrines (such as the "clear repudiation" rules and the right to adequate assurances of performances) that are designed to reduce the prospect of the strategic abuse of anticipatory repudiation. Whether the doctrine delivers on its promise to net parties cost savings is an empirical matter. Throughout this chapter, we examine the precise contours of the anticipatory repudiation doctrines and ask whether they create a regime that reduces net costs by requiring mitigation or increases net costs by facilitating strategic abuse.

B. Anticipatory Breach

Hochester v. De La Tour *(Page 888)*. Plaintiff, a courier, was hired by the defendant to accompany the latter on a tour of a Europe. The two entered into the agreement in April, 1852, and the tour was set to commence on June 1st of the same year. On May 11th, however, the defendant informed the plaintiff that he had changed his mind and no longer required his services. After the defendant refused any payment in light of this action, the plaintiff filed suit. The plaintiff also obtained, before June 1st, similar employment on similar terms, but not to commence until July 4th of that year.

The defendant claimed that there could be no breach of the contract before June 1st. Therefore, the plaintiff, if he wished to maintain the contract, was bound to be ready to perform on that date, and no cause of action for breach by the defendant would accrue until that date. The court rejected this argument, reasoning that their agreement contained an implied promise by the defendant not to renounce his intention to perform. The court rejected the defendant's contention that the plaintiff has a cause of action only if he treats the contract as in force until the date of performance, asserting that it is in the best interests of both parties for the plaintiff to consider the contract breached and seek out alternative employment (which would mitigate his damages). The court then held that "it seems reasonable to allow an option to the injured party, either to sue immediately, or to wait till the time when the act was to be done, still holding it as prospectively binding for the exercise of this option, which may be advantageous to the innocent party, and cannot be prejudicial to the wrongdoer."

Pedagogy on **Hochster.** *Hochster* is generally regarded as the font of anticipatory repudiation in American law. We use it to illustrate the initial, now resolved, conceptual problems confronting the doctrine, as well as to introduce (but not resolve) some of the central problems that continue to plague the doctrine today. The initial conceptual problem, as presented in *Hochster*, is that it seemed to be impossible to breach a contract before the time for performance elapsed. After all, how can one be in breach when performance is not yet due? The doctrinal solution to this problem in *Hochster* is to imply into every agreement a promise not to repudiate the agreement. Hence, repudiation itself constitutes a breach of this subsidiary promise, even though there remains time to perform the principal promise. (This is the same strategy the court uses in *Marchiondo v. Scheck* (p. 269) for explaining why unilateral offers are not revocable until a reasonable time after the offeree has commenced performance– the court implies a subsidiary promise by the offeror not to revoke the unilateral offer, supported by the consideration of the offeree's commencing performance).

But the more important question is why the court should struggle to find conceptual space to allow pre-performance breach. In this case, the court's rationale is to permit the promisee to mitigate his damages by avoiding the expense of preparing for the trip the promisor no longer intends to take and by booking an alternative tour. The court states that it is "surely more rational, and more for the benefit of both parties, that, after the renunciation of the agreement by the defendant, the plaintiff should be at liberty to consider himself absolved from any future performance of it, retaining his right to sue for any damages he has suffered from the breach of it. Thus, instead of remaining idle and laying out money in preparations which must be useless, he is at liberty to seek service under another employer, which would go in mitigation of the damages to which he would otherwise be entitled for a breach of the contract." The court here is mystified why the repudiating promisor would begrudge the promisee the right to mitigate, when the effect of that right is to minimize the damages the repudiator must pay. But the right of anticipatory repudiation creates both potential advantages and disadvantages for both parties.

The potential advantage of anticipatory repudiation for the repudiator is that it might reduce the damages he must pay to the non-breacher. It might do this by allowing the repudiator to force the non-breacher to mitigate at the time of repudiation rather than waiting until the time of performance. (But note that the *Hochster* court would allow the non-breacher, at his option, to wait until the time of performance to mitigate). In *Hochster*, the non-breacher did mitigate sooner, and this presumably decreased the repudiator's damages (for example, had the non-breacher waited until the time of performance, he might have been unable to book an alternative tour, and thus lost his entire expectancy). The potential disadvantage to the repudiator is to deprive him of the option to perform. Anticipatory repudiation doctrine can allow the non-breacher to force the repudiator to repudiate even though he would prefer to keep the option of performance open. This occurs under the doctrine of adequate assurances when the repudiator has caused the non-breacher to become insecure about performance, the insecure party demands adequate assurance of performance, and the repudiator is unable to give this assurance. But under other circumstances, it might turn out that if the non-breacher had waited until the time of performance to mitigate, the repudiator's damages would be lower (for example, because the cover market price fell between the time of repudiation and the time of performance).

The potential advantage of anticipatory repudiation for the non-breacher is that it allows him to reduce his risk of under-compensation. It does this by allowing him to mitigate his damages sooner rather than later. (If damages were fully compensatory – including attorney's fees, speculative damages and pre-judgment interest rates – the non-breacher would not benefit from mitigation.) Of course, early mitigation is advantageous to the non-breacher only if it costs less than later mitigation. Thus, the potential disadvantage to the non-breacher is that the breacher might be able to force him to mitigate early (if a court rejects the *Hochster* rule allowing the non-breacher to wait until the time for performance before mitigating), even though it turns out that the cost of mitigation would have been lower had the non-breacher waited until the time of performance.

So one answer to the *Hochster* court's question of why the repudiator would object to the non-breacher's right to mitigate at the time of repudiation, rather than waiting until the time of performance, is that such early mitigation (1) treats the contract as breached before the time of performance and so deprives the repudiator of the right to perform, should he be able and willing, at the time of performance, and therefore not sacrifice his expectancy before it is absolutely necessary, and (2) might cost more, in retrospect, than later mitigation (mitigation at the time of performance). If, however, it is clear that the repudiator will not be able to perform in any event, and that early mitigation reduces the non-breacher's damages, there would be no legitimate reason for the repudiator to object to early mitigation.

Other answers are plausible as well. Since this is apparently a case of first impression, the repudiator might object to the non-breacher's right to treat the contract as breached before the time of performance, solely on conceptual grounds, to escape liability in this one instance. He might simply be taking advantage of the non-breacher's novel act of treating a contract as breached before the time of performance has expired. Or, while he might have repudiated early in order to induce early mitigation, he might have regretted that decision either because he decided he wanted to perform or discovered that mitigation would be cheaper at the time of performance, contrary to his prior expectation. All these reasons are purely *ex post* grounds for objecting to the right of anticipatory repudiation and early mitigation. They fail to provide good reasons why parties would object to that right *ex ante*.

On the other hand, all the *ex ante* reasons articulated above for having anticipatory repudiation (e.g., reduce the cost of breach to the breacher – by reducing damages he must pay – and to the non-breacher – by reducing his damages and therefore his exposure to the risk of under-compensation) are compelling only if the parties would have reason, *ex ante*, to expect that mitigation would either generally, or in a specific instance, be less costly when done before the time of performance. As we will note in later cases, there is no such thing as an *ex ante* rising market (i.e., a market that a party *knows* is rising in advance of its rise). In general, at any given time, there will be a symmetrical risk of a cover market rise or fall. So we are left with the puzzle of why anyone would want to repudiate, or force the other party to repudiate, an agreement before the time for performance. One explanation is that one or both parties are risk averse. But in the absence of risk aversion – as is typically thought to be the case with contracts between corporations – why would any parties value the option to mitigate before the time of performance? Indeed, unless parties are risk averse, why do they contract at all? Why not wait until the time for performance and make a purchase or sale at the price prevailing on the spot market at that time?

There are two reasons why even risk-neutral parties might value contracting, and thus the right of anticipatory repudiation and pre-performance mitigation. First, parties – even risk-neutral corporations – face an asymmetrical risk from market fluctuations. Although their expected payments remain stable over time, the peaks and valleys can require payments of large sums of cash at times when the corporations lack liquidity. If they are unable to pay a bill when it becomes due, they may be forced to close operations or declare bankruptcy. Thus, the potential upside, for a seller, of an equal risk of a market rise is outweighed by an equal risk of a market decline. This is because the expected loss from a downside risk might mean the death of a corporation, or the end of its management team. Thus, the upside risk required to compensate this downside risk must be a potential financial gain that is greater than the potential financial loss. In effect, the potential of a cash-flow problem makes a corporation's management team behave as if it were risk-averse with respect to risks large enough to trigger bankruptcy or extreme financial distress. Given that even corporations will behave as if risk-averse when facing significant financial disruption, they will value the right to mitigate early in order to limit possible losses to a level that does not risk incurring these disruption costs (including, in the extreme case, the risk of bankruptcy) even if there is a perfectly symmetrical probability of equally large gains be waiting until the time of performance to mitigate.

Second, risk-neutral parties might rationally desire to contract, and rationally value the right of anticipatory repudiation, in order to facilitate contract-specific investments. These investments can include the production of specialized goods, the development of human capital specific to a particular deal, or research to acquire information about future costs or prices. If the value of cooperation between partners requires one partner to incur reliance expenses recoverable only if the other party subsequently performs, the party making that initial investment might be subject to strategic hold-up and renegotiation by the other party. Contracts are rationally desirable in order to require the other party to perform, and thus to provide assurance to the investing party that he will not be subject to strategic hold-up. The right of anticipatory repudiation allows parties to a contract contemplating contract-specific investments to prevent their partner from making such investments, even after the contract has been formed, when the joint expected value of performance (taking into account the prospective contract-specific investments) is exceeded by its costs, that is, when the contract is no longer the parties' best option provided no future contract-specific investments are made. For more detailed elaboration of how anticipatory repudiation might be justified in contracts contemplating contract-specific investments, *see* Jody S. Kraus and George G. Triantis, Reconsidering Anticipatory Repudiation (forthcoming).

Taylor v. Johnston *(Page 890)*. Plaintiff contracted with defendant to breed two of plaintiff's mares with defendant's stallion, for a fee of $3,500 per mare. The contract guaranteed a live foal (the definition of a live foal being one that stands and nurses without assistance); if no live foal was produced, the plaintiff was entitled to a return breeding the following year at no additional charge. The contract was entered into in 1965, and the breeding was to take place in 1966. Later in 1965, the defendant sold the stallion to Dr. Pessin, who then syndicated the sire by selling shares. Each share entitled its holder to breed one mare each season to the stallion.

After the sale, the defendant notified the plaintiff of the sale and "released" the plaintiff from his "reservation" to breed with the stallion. Plaintiff objected, and, after plaintiff threatened suit, defendant arranged for plaintiff's mares to be bred with the stallion at the new owners' farm. Plaintiff later learned the mares could not be boarded at the new owners' farm so he arranged with a Mr. Frazier to board them nearby and take care of the breeding.

Frazier repeatedly tried to arrange breeding for one of the mares with the stallion but was turned away by Dr. Pessin's agent, due to shareholder reservations during each of the times that the mare was in heat. Eventually, in June of 1966 he abandoned efforts to breed the mare with the stallion and bred it with a Kentucky Derby winner for a fee of $10,000. After being turned away for the same reason after one attempt to arrange breeding with the other mare, Frazier bred it also with the Derby winner. Both of the mares became pregnant with twins and had to be aborted (twins are dangerous for the mare and not regarded as good for racing). Plaintiff did not have to pay the breeding fee since no live foal was produced.

Defendants appealed the trial court's verdict for the plaintiff, claiming there was no evidence in the record to support a claim of anticipatory or actual breach. The appellate court held that, since the time for performance (either the calendar year or the end of the breeding season) had not expired when the mares were bred with the Derby winner, there could have been no actual breach.

Anticipatory breach, the court said, can result from both express and implied repudiation. According to the court, "An express repudiation is a clear, positive, unequivocal refusal to perform; an implied repudiation results from conduct where the promisor puts it out of his power to perform so as to make substantial performance of his promise impossible." In response to repudiation, the injured party can either treat the repudiation as anticipatory breach and seek damages, thereby terminating the contract; or it can wait until the time of performance and seek damages if the other party fails to perform. If, however, during that time the repudiation is revoked, the repudiation is nullified.

The court considered two separate actions that were the basis of potential claims of repudiation of the contract. The first was an express repudiation which occurred when the stallion was sold and the defendants informed the plaintiff that he was "released." This repudiation was retracted, according to the court, when the defendant arranged for the contract to be honored by Dr. Pessin. As to the second alleged repudiation, the facts, at best, supported a repudiation implied by the actions of Pessin's agent, which the trial court held justified the plaintiff in thinking that the contract was not going to be performed. However, the appellate court held that this action was not sufficient to constitute an implied repudiation, because a repudiation can be implied only when the promisor makes his own performance impossible. Since at least one more heat for each mare remained in the breeding season at the time plaintiffs bred the mares to another stud, the defendants' delays had not yet made their performance impossible. Thus, there was no anticipatory breach, and the trial court's judgment was reversed.

Truman L. Flatt & Sons Co., Inc. v. Sara Lee Schupf *(Page 896)*. The plaintiff entered into a contract to buy a parcel of land from the defendant. That contract was contingent upon the plaintiff obtaining a zoning change to allow for the construction of an asphalt plant. If rezoning was not obtained within 120 days, the contract was voidable at the buyer's option. When it became apparent to the plaintiff that it would not obtain rezoning of the parcel, the plaintiff wrote the defendant on May 21, that it had withdrawn its request for rezoning but was still interested in the property, only now at a lower price (reflecting the value to the plaintiff under the current zoning). On June 9, the defendant rejected the offer at a lower price. On June 14, the plaintiff wrote, stating that it wished to proceed with the purchase at the contract price and requesting the scheduling of a closing date. On July 8, the defendant replied that it regarded plaintiff's failure to proceed under the contract at the time rezoning was denied by waiving the rezoning requirement, coupled with plaintiff's offer to buy at a lower price, as voiding the contract.

Plaintiff sued for specific performance, and defendant filed a motion for summary judgment based on a claim that the plaintiff repudiated the contract. During discovery, the defendant admitted not having engaged in discussions with any third party regarding a sale of the property. The trial court granted summary judgment for the defendant.

On appeal, the court stated that anticipatory breach requires an unequivocal manifestation of intention not to perform the contract. The court rejected the defendant's claim that the plaintiff's May 21 letter constituted such a manifestation. At most, the court said, the letter was ambiguous as to whether a repudiation had occurred, an interpretation conceded by the defendant in oral argument. However, the court held, even if that letter constituted repudiation, such repudiation was effectively retracted. The court cited the Restatement (Second) and the UCC in support of the rule that repudiation can be retracted as long as the other party has not materially altered its position or informed the repudiator that it considers the repudiation final. Since the defendant did not materially alter its position, as evidenced by it's admissions in response to discovery interrogatories, or notify the plaintiff that it regarded the contract as repudiated before the plaintiff's June 14 letter, the June 14 letter constituted an effective retraction.

Pedagogy on Taylor *and* Truman. Together these cases provide a thick context for introducing students both to the details of the repudiation and retraction doctrines and the fine-grained texture of the application of these doctrines to complex real-world settings. *Taylor* shows how the common law evolves to provide precise definitions to otherwise vague concepts, such as "repudiation." It clarifies that repudiations can be express or implied, requires express repudiations to be unequivocal, and implied repudiations to be acts that make performance impossible. *Note 2 on page 904* illustrates how other common law courts have liberalized the impossibility requirement for implied repudiations. *Taylor* and *Truman* also demonstrate how conduct falling short of express repudiation can nonetheless cause parties significant insecurity and often lead them to believe their partner has repudiated (e.g., a letter "releasing" Taylor from his obligation to breed with Fleet Nasrullah for $3,500 per mare, excessive delays in scheduling breeding appointments within the performance period of the contract, a letter proposing a reduced price for real estate sold by completed contract subject to condition for a higher price because the condition was not satisfied, etc). These cases illustrate how difficult it is to put into practice the general concepts on which the doctrine of anticipatory repudiation relies. It is one thing to allege a repudiation, it is another to prove it. Likewise, it is difficult to prove whether a repudiation has been accepted, thus eliminating the possibility of retraction, whether the aggrieved party has changed position in reliance on the repudiation (*See e.g.*, UCC § 2-611(1)), or whether the repudiator has retracted their repudiation (e.g., by agreeing to schedule a breeding session after repudiating the initial breeding agreement, or by agreeing to purchase real estate at the contract price after having implied in a letter an unwillingness to go through with the purchase without a price reduction). All of these elements of the doctrine of anticipatory repudiation open contractual relationships to litigation based on misunderstandings and mis-communication, as well as strategic litigation exploiting the doctrinal and factual vagueness in the doctrine's application.

As a classroom strategy, we suggest using a hypothetical in which repudiation, acceptance of repudiation, and retraction are raised on partial analogy to both cases. Have students marshal arguments using the main and note cases to support each side. We also introduce the question of whether repudiations based on good faith but erroneous contractual interpretations should be effective (*see Note 3 on page 906*) and whether insolvency constitutes an implied repudiation (*see Note 5 on page 908*). In all, these cases provide an excellent opportunity for in-class practice in making a legal argument based on precedent interpreting the contours of anticipatory repudiation. It provides the opportunity for a welcome doctrinal, practice-oriented exercise in what otherwise is mostly a theoretically challenging chapter, as the essays throughout the chapter make clear.

C. Measuring Damages for Anticipatory Repudiation

Cosden Oil & Chemical Co. v. Karl O. Helm Aktiengesellschaft *(Page 914).* In January of 1979, Helm contracted with Cosden to purchase 1250 metric tons of high impact polystyrene at $.2825 per pound and 250 metric tons of general purpose polystyrene at $.265 per pound. Delivery on these orders was to be made during January or February of 1979, in one or more shipments, and at Helm's instance. Included in the bargain for these purchases was an option for Helm to buy an additional 1000 metric tons of high impact and a similar option to purchase an additional 500 metric tons of general purpose, both for delivery during February and March. These options expired on January 31 of that year, and Helm informed Cosden of its decision to exercise them on January 23.

After making the first (partial) shipment, Cosden sent Helm an invoice that, by its terms, was subject to a *force majeure* provision. Helm paid the invoice in accordance with the agreement. Soon, Cosden began experiencing problems at its plants due to abnormal weather conditions and equipment problems. On February 6, Cosden informed Helm that it was canceling the general purpose order and both orders made pursuant to the options. An internal memo revealed that Helm's strategy in response to Cosden's cancellation would be to urge continued performance of the first high impact order and offset the amount it would owe Cosden from that order against the damages to which it would be entitled from Cosden's non-delivery of the rest. In addition, Helm requested a copy of the *force majeure* clause. Cosden made one more delivery under the first high impact order but then informed Helm that no further deliveries were possible.

Cosden sued Helm to recover damages from Helm's failure to pay for the delivered polystyrene, and Helm counter-claimed for Cosden's failure to perform. The jury found that Cosden anticipatorily repudiated the last three orders and that its cancellation of the first before Helm's failure to pay for the second delivery also constituted an anticipatory repudiation. It also made findings as to the market prices for the polystyrene at three different times: when Helm learned of the cancellation, at a commercially reasonable time thereafter and at the time for delivery. The district court set damages according to the market price at a commercially reasonable time after the repudiation. It also found that Cosden was entitled to a set-off against those damages for polystyrene delivered but not paid for.

The problem of determining which market price should be used to measure damages comes from the phrase in UCC § 2-713, "market price at the time when the buyer *learned of the breach.*" The court interprets this to mean a commercially reasonable time after learning of the repudiation because § 2-610 allows a party to wait a commercially reasonable time after learning of an anticipatory repudiation before resorting to his remedies of cover or damages. Interpreting § 2-713 to mean market price at the time the party learns of the repudiation would undercut the time allowed in § 2-610 to await performance. In addition, parts of § 2-610 (waiting a commercially reasonable time) and § 2-712 (act without reasonable delay) lose their meaning, according to the court, if damages are to be measured according to market price at time of performance.

In addition, since this question will normally arise in a rising market, the court says it is necessary to consider the incentives the possible rules will have on the parties. If the rule is that damages are measured at the time of repudiation, the seller has an ability to "fix buyer's damages," which will give him an incentive to repudiate. Meanwhile, if the rule is that damages are measured at time of performance, the buyer will have an incentive to wait until the time of performance "in hopes the market price will continue upward." Allowing the buyer a commercially reasonable time, the court says, provides her an opportunity to investigate the cover possibilities without fear that, if he is unsuccessful in obtaining cover, her damages will be measured according to the lower market price which was available at the time of repudiation.

Finally, the court asserts that it is not possible to interpret § 2-713 in a way that harmonizes it with all of the sections of the UCC. The court says its interpretation is out of step with part of § 2-713(a), but that section has "limited applicability" and that its comment states that it is not intended to exclude the use of any other reasonable means of determining market price or measuring damages.

Pedagogy on Cosden Oil. *Cosden Oil* picks up the measurement issue raised in *Hochster*: can the non-breacher wait until the time for performance to cover. The answer to that question will determine whether damages are measured at the time of repudiation or later (i.e., a reasonable time after repudiation, at the time the non-breacher covers, or at the time of performance). As we've already seen, if the point of the anticipatory repudiation doctrine is to trigger the non-breacher's duty to mitigate, the purpose of the doctrine would be defeated by allowing the non-breacher to wait until the time for performance to mitigate. (This is the point of the majority Judge in the hypothetical contained in the ***Essay: Measuring Damages After Repudiation on page 921***). This rationale, therefore, is consistent with either requiring mitigation at the time of repudiation or a reasonable time after repudiation. But as we say in ***Note 1 on page 920***, even if the rule requires mitigation at the time of repudiation, the standard mitigation doctrine would allow the non-breacher a reasonable time to mitigate after repudiation. These two apparently different mitigation rules, therefore, are really one in the same. Thus, if we assume the sole purpose of anticipatory repudiation is to allow the breacher to compel the non-breacher to mitigate early, the doctrine should require mitigation at the time of repudiation.

However, as we explain in the ***Introductory Essay to Part C on page 912 (Measuring Damages for Anticipatory Repudiation)***, the doctrinal mechanisms of anticipatory repudiation expose the non-breacher to potential strategic abuse by his contractual partner. Given that damages are systematically under-compensatory, the sole or primary purpose of anticipatory repudiation might instead be to minimize the non-breacher's exposure to under-compensation. On this approach, anticipatory repudiation allows the non-breacher to trigger his partner's repudiation by demanding adequate assurances of performance when his partner gives him good reason to doubt performance will be forthcoming. In order to minimize his damage bill, and thus reduce the impact of under-compensation, the non-breacher can mitigate early by ceasing any contract-specific investments and making alternative plans. On this rationale for the doctrine, there is no reason to require the non-breacher to mitigate at the time of repudiation. If the non-breacher triggered the repudiation himself though use of the adequate assurances doctrine, he should presumably be given the discretion (subject to a reasonableness constraint) to cover at the time he believes will be most likely to reduce his damage bill. Moreover, given that ambiguous repudiation signals expose the non-breacher to the "breacher status" problem (interpreting his partner's action as a repudiation, responding by covering, and having a court hold that because the partner's actions did not constitute repudiation his cover itself constituted breach), allowing the non-breacher to wait until the time of performance eliminates the risk that he will feel compelled to cover and risk the breacher status problem when a repudiation signal is ambiguous. (This is the point of the dissenting Judge in the *Essay on page 921*).

Of course, anticipatory repudiation is probably best viewed as serving both purposes (allowing the breacher to compel early mitigation to avoid wasteful reliance, and allowing the non-breacher to avoid exacerbating his risk of under-compensation by mitigating early). The former favors a rule requiring mitigation immediately upon repudiation, while the latter supports a rule giving the non-breacher reasonable discretion to mitigate any time from the time of repudiation through the time for performance. The rule requiring the non-breacher to mitigate within a reasonable time after repudiation (the ordinary mitigation doctrine applied to the time of repudiation) seems a sensible compromise that both protects the non-breacher from strategic use of ambiguous repudiation signals and yet allows the repudiator to minimize the costs of breach.

Cosden Oil grapples with this measurement problem by struggling to reconcile the language of the relevant Code provisions. Along the way, however, the court appears to evidence a rather profound misunderstanding of the context in which parties make performance decisions. In *Note 2 on page 920*, we consider the court's claim that the parties were in the midst of a rising market. Unfortunately, many courts reason as if the parties in such cases made decisions against the backdrop of a market *known* to be rising at the time of their decisions (*see e.g.*, *Ralston Purina v. McNabb*, 381 F. Supp. 181(1974)). In hindsight, it is clear the market was rising. But in our view, neither party could have known that at the time. Each was taking a gamble. The court is right that a repudiating party is likely, *ex post*, to advance a claim that the non-breacher covered too late when it turns out that the market cover price rose. The court then claims that a rule requiring mitigation at the time of repudiation encourages repudiation (because it gives the "seller the ability to fix buyer's damages"). The court implies that this would be bad. But of course, as long as the buyer is fully compensated, why would this be bad? And, as we've already said, requiring cover at the time of repudiation potentially reduces damages, lowers expected under-compensation, and facilitates efficient breach. In this Note, we ask whether seller would benefit from repudiating. If the seller is risk-averse, or because of the risk of severe disruption from adverse market movements acts as if it were, then repudiation does benefit the seller, just as the initial contract does (i.e., by reducing the sellers downside exposure– its risk of a decline in the price of the goods it is selling). If the seller is risk-neutral, the only benefit of repudiation is to prevent buyer from making any further contract-specific investments once the seller's expected value from performance becomes so low that seller no longer expects to perform. Otherwise, seller would be indifferent to repudiating or waiting until the time for performance to breach.

The court also claims that "measuring buyer's damages at the time of performance will tend to dissuade the buyer from covering, in hopes that the market price will continue upward until performance time." We ask: Wouldn't a buyer be indifferent between covering at the lower market price at the time of repudiation and covering at the higher market price at the time of performance, given that he is reimbursed for the difference between the contract price and the cover price either way? The answer is yes, unless the buyer secretly covers at the time of repudiation, then covers again at the time of performance, and sues the seller for the difference between the contract price and market price at the time for performance. If the market rose from the time of repudiation to the time for performance, buyer could then use the goods he purchased in one cover transaction as he originally intended, and then resell the other goods to gain the difference between the market price at the time for performance and the contract price, less the difference between the market price at the time of repudiation (when he secretly covered) and the contract price (i.e., the cost of this gambit is eating the loss from covering at the time of repudiation since buyer forgoes the right to compensation for this additional cost).

On the other hand, if buyer undertakes this gambit, he risks the possibility that the market price will decrease between the time of repudiation (when he secretly covers) and the time for performance (when the market price is lower). If the price falls below the contract price, the seller will retract his repudiation if he can. The seller cannot retract if buyer has expressly accepted the initial repudiation or changed position in reliance on seller's repudiation. Since buyer's initial cover is secret, he may not be able to prove reliance. If buyer can prove reliance or expressly accepted the seller's repudiation, however, then buyer cannot be held to the contract. But if the market price is below the contract price at the time for performance, he will have no damages for covering at that time, even though he secretly covered at the time of repudiation. If he can prove that he (secretly) covered at the time of repudiation, though, he would be entitled to reimbursement for the cover price/contract price differential at that time, even though the market price is below the contract price at the time for performance. This is, then, the ideal buyer's gambit: (1) secretly cover at the time of repudiation but retain proof of cover, (2) wait until time for performance and cover again, (3) if the market has risen, sue for the differential at the time for performance and resell the covered goods for a profit, (4) if the market has fallen, sue for the first or second cover differential, whichever is largest. The strategy depends crucially on the buyer's ability to secretly cover but prove cover if necessary (when the market declines after repudiation).

Roye Realty & Developing, Inc. v. Arkla, Inc. *(Page 925).* Arkla (through one of its divisions) entered into a contract with Gulf Oil Corporation, which provided for the sale by Gulf to Arkla of all of the gas Gulf acquired from certain leases and wells for a period of fifteen years. Six years after the execution of the contract, Roye Realty purchased Gulf's rights under the contract. The contract further required Roye Realty to hold the gas exclusively for Arkla, and required Arkla to take and pay for a certain quantity of gas. That quantity was calculated by first conducting deliverability tests, which determine the "daily deliverability" of a well, then dividing the daily deliverability figure in half, which determines the "average daily volume." The average daily volumes are added together to get the "contract annual volume," which is the minimum amount that Arkla would be required to "take-or-pay" for that year.

Roye Realty claims that Arkla repudiated the contract. It also claims that damages should be measured by the "pay" alternative in the contract and calculated according to Arkla's minimum obligation through the end of the contract term. Arkla claims had it honored its obligations, the amount taken and paid for would have been less than the amount required under the "pay" alternative. It also argues that its minimum obligation should be fixed not as of the date of the alleged repudiation, but based upon the physical ability of the wells to produce in the future.

The District court certified the following question to the Oklahoma Supreme Court: "What is the measure of damages under a take-or-pay gas purchase contract where the seller alleges an anticipatory repudiation by the buyer and the buyer alleges that had it elected to 'take' gas, seller could not have physically delivered gas over the entire term of the contract?" The court finds the question governed by the UCC, particularly § 2-708. In a previous case, *Golsen*, the Oklahoma Court said that §§ 2-706 and 2-708 did not support the theory that inability to sell gas at a profit excuses performance under the contract, and that § 2-708 reflected the policy toward damages in such situations. After discussing that case, the court noted that the comment to § 2-708 does not require the seller to resell upon repudiation, but that if the seller does resell, damages are measured by § 2-708. Applying § 2-708, as well as § 2-706 and § 2-723, to take-or-pay gas purchase contracts, the court held that the damages for repudiation of both the take and the pay obligations is the difference between market price at the time the aggrieved party learned of the repudiation and the unpaid contract price.

The court then discussed *Manchester Pipeline v. Peoples Natural Gas*, which reached the same conclusion on this issue based on the same provisions and the "virtue of certainty" that they provide (this "certainty" is in contrast to the speculation required by Williston's rule that damages are based on market price at the date of performance). It also discussed *Dyco v. ANR Pipeline*, in which the court rejected the argument that the obligation to pay money was separate from the sale of goods and therefore not governed by the UCC. The court in that case held that the obligation was governed by the UCC because it was an integral part of the contract for sale. That court also held that the take-or-pay obligation is a provision for alternative performance and not a measure of damages after the breach. This meant, according to the court, that using the deficiency payment obligation as the proper measure of damages was equivalent to granting specific performance, which the court viewed as inappropriate.

Roye Realty agreed that the UCC applied to this case but argued that the provisions allowing for liberal administration of the remedies provided by the UCC require the remedy to be based on the "pay" alternative. It reasoned that the contract provided for alternative obligations – to take and pay or to make a deficiency payment – and Arkla's decision not to perform the first of these alternatives meant that it was required to perform the second. This is because, under Oklahoma law, if the party making alternative promises does not elect which alternative he will perform before defaulting, the promisee may choose which alternative to accept.

The court, in rejecting Roye Realty's argument, first pointed out that the deficiency payment obligation is not a remedy for breach nor a clause which alters or limits the measure of damages. Thus, it does not come under § 2-719. Also, the court held that because there was an alternative available to Arkla, its failure to take and pay for gas is not a repudiation. Repudiation does not occur, said the court, until Arkla refused to make the required deficiency payments. The court then quotes from Corbin that once the promisor fails to perform the first obligation (in this case, once the period has passed for Arkla to take and pay and it hasn't done so), the obligation becomes "single" and is no longer alternative. The court then cites Corbin's argument that it is incorrect to determine damages according to the pay money alternative. Rather, the more appropriate measure, according to Corbin and the court, is the less valuable of the two alternatives, which is usually the market value of the "take" alternative.

The court also rejected Roye Realty's risk-allocation argument for damages measured by the "pay" alternative. The court agreed that take-or-pay contracts allocate the risk of market decline to the buyer, but did not agree that this is determinative of the measure of damages for anticipatory repudiation of such contracts. The court viewed the "pay" alternative as compensation for the seller's promise to take its gas off the market and sell it exclusively to the buyer. Refusal to make this payment is merely reneging on a promise to compensate and does not require measuring damages according to that promise.

Finally, the court held that, once the buyer repudiates its obligation to take or pay, the seller's inability to deliver the gas is irrelevant for measuring damages. The court again quoted Corbin, stating that, while the aggrieved party is not entitled to a remedy for repudiation if it could not or would not have performed, the ability to perform must only exist at the time of repudiation and need not be maintained. Moreover, following a repudiation, § 2-610 relieves the aggrieved party of the obligation to perform. The court found support for its holding in *Panhandle Pipeline*. There, the court held that the inability of the seller to make assurances that it would be able to cover the future requirements of the buyer and the makeup requirements (to which the buyer would be entitled after making deficiency payments) did not excuse the buyer from making deficiency payments. This is because an experienced buyer is deemed to have known the risk that it might not be able to recoup deficiency payments by taking makeup gas.

Thus, the court held in the present case that both the language of the contract and Oklahoma law support a finding that the measure of damages in a repudiation case is unaffected by the seller's future inability to deliver gas. All that is required is that the seller be able to perform on the date of breach.

Pedagogy on* Roye Realty.** We focus on the issues raised in ***Note 1 on page 934. The first fundamental issue raised in *Roye Realty* is how to measure the expectancy when an alternative performance is specified in the contract. Is it the value of the highest, the lowest, the average of the two alternatives, or (as Corbin suggests under certain circumstances) the last performance option remaining open before breach? Note that this question arises when measuring damages for breach generally, and not just damages for repudiation. As a normative matter, our view is that the *theoretically* ideal measure of damages is what we have called "theoretical reliance" (*see Expectation Damages as a Substitute for Performance on pages 970-971*, and Charles J. Goetz & Robert E. Scott, *Enforcing Promises: An Examination of the Basis of Contract*, 89 Yale L.J. 1261, 1281-1286 (1980)). Theoretical reliance is the amount of damages necessary to put the non-breacher in the position he would have been had he chosen his next best contractual option (i.e., legal reliance plus their true opportunity cost). By hypothesis, to induce a promisee to enter into a contract, the promisor's offer must have an expected value that exceeds that of the promisee's next best opportunity. The expected value of a promise to a promisee is a function of the value of performance to the promisee and the damages for breach (we here idealize and assume that damages for breach are always paid in full and adjudication costs are zero). Theoretical reliance damages guarantee the promisee damages for breach equal to the expected value of the promisee's next best alternative. Assuming that the value of performance to the promisee exceeds the value of the promisee's next best alternative, this damage award guarantees that, by accepting the promisor's offer, the promisee will do no worse, and might do better, than he would do if he accepted his next best alternative. Theoretical reliance is therefore the maximum damage payment the promisor would need to offer the promisee to induce the promisee to accept his offer.[1] It is also the most the promisee would be willing to pay for because any higher damages would be unnecessary to make the contract strictly preferable to the promisee's next best alternative.

Courts, however, routinely award expectation damages (measured by the value of performance to the promisee) rather than reliance because of the ease of proof provided by the expectation default rule. In any case, since the contract in *Roye* is presumably a highly competitive one (i.e., a "thick" market), the seller's next best alternative is likely to be precisely the same contractual arrangement with a different buyer, and thus theoretical reliance and expectancy are identical. Therefore, the ex ante expectancy of the seller, should the buyer breach, is to receive the value of the least valuable of the alternatives in the contract. This is because under this alternative contract the seller would receive one of two alternatives, and so could only rely on the least valuable alternative.

D. Insecurity and the Right to Demand Assurances

National Farmers Organization v. Bartlett & Co., Grain *(Page 938)*. The National Farmers Organization (seller) entered into numerous contracts to sell wheat and corn to Bartlett & Co. (buyer). The seller made late deliveries on numerous contracts, which were accepted by the buyer, and failed to complete performance on numerous contracts. After giving notice to the seller that complete delivery had not been made, the buyer withheld some of the purchase price of grain actually delivered as protection against realized or potential loss caused by the seller's failure to fully perform (this took place in December, 1972, and January, 1973). Shortly thereafter (January 26), the seller notified the buyer that it "was not going to deliver . . . on any of the 14 outstanding contracts . . . unless and until [buyer] paid [seller] a substantial amount of money due . . . ." The buyer treated this as an anticipatory repudiation of the contracts not yet due and informed the seller that it was "bringing all outstanding contracts . . . to current market price." It then (January 30 or 31) sent the seller a memo reflecting the balance due to the seller for deliveries made (the payments it had been withholding) and claiming a setoff on thirteen of the fourteen contracts resulting from the seller's anticipatory repudiation of those contracts. The buyer then paid the seller for the difference. The seller agreed that the setoffs were proper as to the contracts with last delivery dates

---

[1] If the probability of performance is sufficiently high, this damage measure will itself be higher than optimal– the expected value of the promisor's offer would exceed the expected value of the promisee's next best alternative even with damages set equal to an amount that is less than the expected value of the promisee's next best alternative.

prior to the date on which the buyer sent the memo to the seller, but argued against the propriety of setoffs on contracts having last delivery dates subsequent to that date.

According to the court, the resolution of this issue turns on whether the seller's statement on January 26 constituted an anticipatory repudiation. The court called this a "difficult and close" question, ultimately resolved by UCC § 2-610. Noting that neither the Code nor case law provides a clear and definite answer, the court first considered what the seller could have done on January 26 under § 2-609 and what it could not have done under § 2-612. Section 2-609 clearly applies to the instant case (the seller had reasonable grounds for insecurity), and thus the seller could have made, but did not make, a written demand for adequate assurance and withheld performance until receiving such assurance. The court also found that, on January 26, the seller could not have, pursuant to § 2-612, canceled the contracts on which payments had not been withheld because the value of those contracts was not substantially impaired as a whole on that date.

The court found that the seller repudiated on January 26 by imposing a condition precedent that went beyond each of the contracts not yet due. Since the breach by the buyer was on independent contracts, that breach did not allow the seller to refuse performance on other contracts. In holding for the buyer, the court rejected the seller's argument that this rule creates a commercially unacceptable result. The seller argued that the buyer did not have the right under the UCC to withhold payment on some contracts to cover losses on others. While the court found merit in the seller's argument, it found that suspending delivery under all contracts was not justified. The court relied on 7 critical facts: (1) time was not of the essence under the contracts, (2) seller had no reason to believe buyer's ability to pay was impaired, (3) seller could have taken actions short of suspending delivery, (4) seller could have but did not use § 2-609 to demand adequate assurances, (5) the contracts were treated separately by both parties throughout the performance period, (6) seller was the first party actually to breach– by failing to deliver amounts due under contract No. 996, and (7) seller failed to tender grain for any of the contracts with delivery dates after January 27, even though it had received and accepted substantial payment for them by February 9.

Norcon Power Partners v. Niagara Mohawk Power Corp *(Page 945).* Niagara, a public utility provider, contracted to purchase electricity from Norcon, an independent power producer, over a period of 25 years. The contract contained three periods, in each of which a different mechanism was to be used in determining the price to be paid by Niagara. The first was a fixed amount. The second and third based the price on Niagara's "avoided cost," which is the cost Niagara would pay to produce the electricity itself or purchase it on the market. In the second period, the price was subject to a ceiling and floor. In the third period, the ceiling and floor were removed and the price was based solely on the avoided cost. An "adjustment account" kept track of the difference between the actual payments made by Niagara and the amount required by the avoided cost calculation. Any difference at the end of the second period was to be made up by the favored party in the third period; any difference at the end of the third period was to be paid by the favored party within 30 days of the termination of that period.

The dispute arose as a result of Niagara's demand for adequate assurances from Norcon that Norcon would be able to satisfy and would satisfy its obligation to pay the balance owing to Niagara in the adjustment account at the end of the second period. Niagara's analysis predicted that this amount would reach over $610 million by the end of that period. Norcon sought a declaratory judgment from the district court that Niagara had no right to demand assurances beyond the provisions in the contract. Niagara counter-claimed for a declaration that it had properly invoked its right to demand adequate assurances.

The district court held in favor of Norcon. It reasoned that there were only two instances in which a party had a right to demand adequate assurances under New York law, and that neither applied to this case. The first is when the promisor becomes insolvent, which was not the case here. The second is when UCC § 2-609 governs, which it does not in this case. The Second Circuit certified the following question to the NY Court of Appeals: "Does a party have the right to demand adequate assurance . . . where the other party is solvent and the contract is not governed by the UCC?"

The NY court first discussed the evolution of the doctrine of adequate assurances. When a party's actions might constitute a repudiation but are not so unequivocal as to give the aggrieved party clear grounds for terminating its performance, the aggrieved party faces a dilemma: mitigate and risk a subsequent determination that the performing party did not repudiate, thus transforming mitigation itself into breach, or don't mitigate and risk a subsequent determination that the performing party did repudiate, thus forfeiting a claim for damages that could have been mitigated following repudiation. The demand for adequate assurances is a response to this dilemma. Under the UCC, when reasonable grounds for insecurity exist and a party demands adequate assurance of future performance, the failure of the other party to give such assurance allows the aggrieved party to act as though a repudiation has occurred. Restatement (Second) § 251 is modeled on § 2-609.

The New York court declined to make a "wholesale" adoption of R2d § 251 because such a sweeping change would "clash" with what it called its "customary incremental common-law developmental process. . . ." But the court was "persuaded that the policies underlying the UCC § 2-609 counterpart should apply" to this kind of controversy– namely, a "long-term commercial contract between corporate entities . . . which is complex and not reasonably susceptible of all security features being anticipated, bargained for and incorporated into the original contract."

Pedagogy on Bartlett and Norcon. We have several objectives when we teach the doctrine of adequate assurances. The first is to provide the students an opportunity to use the case method to argue both sides of a dispute in which the doctrine must be applied. This forces them to grapple with the difficulties of identifying the conditions under which a party will be deemed to have "reasonable grounds" for insecurity, as well as determining what constitutes "adequate assurances." A well-chosen hypothetical should allow students to marshal the Code, the common law (R2d § 251), *Bartlett* and *Norcon*, as well the caselaw summarized in **Note 4A. on page 952** to argue both sides. The second objective is to examine the particular approaches taken in *Bartlett* and *Norcon* in applying this doctrine. We try to tip our hand in the Notes directed at the cases.

Note 2 (Page 951). Our point here is that several of the factors on which the court relies in its determination of whether seller's January 26 letter constituted a repudiation would seem to be strictly irrelevant to how that letter could fairly be interpreted by the buyer. And this is the question the court should be asking– how would a reasonable person interpret the meaning of that letter? Certainly, it's difficult to see how seller's conduct two weeks after sending the letter bears on how a reasonable person would interpret the letter at the time it was sent. A second point of emphasis, brought out in *Note 1 on page 951*, is that the court here implicitly holds that the elements of UCC § 2-609 are mandatory rather than permissive. In determining that the seller's letter constitutes a repudiation, the court found it relevant that the seller failed to avail itself of its rights under UCC § 2-609. This suggests that insecure parties do not have the right to threaten non-performance unless they first seek adequate assurances as provided in § 2-609. This view is controversial, as the split case law in *Note 1* illustrates. A third point is that the court adopts the "separate contract" rule, which holds that neither party to a contract has the right "to refuse performance because the other has breached a separate contract between them." This contrasts with the rule under UCC § 2-612(3) which allows cancellation of future contracts if a breach with respect to a prior installment under a contract "substantially impairs the value of the whole contract. If only the seller's security in regard to future installments is impaired, he has the right to demand adequate assurances of proper future performance but has not an immediate right to cancel the entire contract." The court holds this provision inapplicable because "the present case involves not one but a number of installment contracts."

    Note 3 (Page 952). The *Norcon* court appears to have expanded New York's common law right to demand adequate assurances far beyond that allowed in the Code and other common law jurisdictions, despite the court's expressed goal of conservatism. This is because the court failed to add the requirement that Niagara Mohawk must have good grounds for its insecurity. It simply took the large sum at stake to be *per se* good grounds. But given the size of these corporations, more would be needed under the Code before Niagara Mohawk would have the right to demand adequate assurances. Some objective evidence of Norcon's prospective inability to pay must be present. The court does limit this new right in New York to long-term commercial contracts, which does make the right more qualified than under the Code. But the court offers no grounds for this seemingly arbitrary limitation. The rationale for the doctrine, which the court rehearses well, applies across the board to all kinds of contracts. Thus, it would have done better than apply the doctrine across the board to all contracts in New York, but to limit the right, as it is limited in the UCC, to parties who can prove objectively reasonable grounds for insecurity.

    Our third objective is to ask whether the right to demand adequate assurances of performance ameliorates or exacerbates the costs of strategic post-formation behavior between contractual partners. As we explain in the *Introduction on page 938*, the justification for the rule is its promise to reduce the parties' vulnerability to the breacher status problem, described in the *Essay on page 908*. But given the difficulty in defining the terms "reasonable grounds for insecurity" and "adequate assurances of performance," it's not clear whether the doctrine achieves this goal. Moreover, when it is interpreted as a mandatory rule, requiring a demand for adequate assurances before cancellation, it clearly exacerbates the aggrieved party's exposure to the breacher status problem, as *Bartlett* illustrates.

E. Installment Contracts

Pakas v. Hollingshead *(Page 958).* In 1898, Pakas contracted with Hollingshead to buy from the latter 50,000 pairs of bicycle pedals, to be delivered and paid for in installments. The defendant delivered only 2,608 pairs of pedals. In 1899, the plaintiff sued for breach of the contract based on the defendant's failure to make full delivery on the installment due in March of that year. Judgment was entered for the plaintiff and paid by the defendant.

Then, in 1900, the plaintiff commenced another action against the defendant, this time for damages from failure to deliver the balance of the goods (those owed on the subsequent installments). The plaintiff asserted that the judgment from its previous suit provides conclusive evidence in its favor, while the defendant asserted that the judgment was a bar to the second action. The plaintiff argued that it had the right to elect to sue for damages for failure to deliver one installment, but nonetheless to keep the contract in force going forward. Thus, plaintiff would retain the right to bring successive actions for damages for each future installment that was not delivered. In rejecting this argument, the court asserted that an installment contract is a single contract and the defendant's refusal to deliver on any of the installments was a breach of the entire contract. Since there was a "total breach" of the contract, the plaintiff must recover all of its damages in one suit. That suit estops plaintiff from bringing any subsequent actions on the same contract.

The dissent argued that the plaintiff was not obliged to rescind the entire contract after the defendant's default on the first installment, citing cases involving obligations to make payments of money in installments where the promisee was required to sue for the installments as they became due. Finding that the question is not settled by the authority, the dissent turned to "principle." He argued that a party should not be able to transmute its obligations over a long term contract, the obligations of which are easily severable, into a damage claim against it. Where damages are damages for failure to make future installments are speculative, this rule defeats the point of the contract. In installment contracts, "it is by no means improbable that [the buyer] has paid more than the present market price solely by reason of the uncertainty of the market price in the future. Under the decision about to be made he must either sue at the time of the first breach, when his damages will necessarily be speculative, a speculation it was the very object of the contract to avoid, or perhaps wait till the time for the last delivery has passed, when it may be that under the doctrine now declared his cause of action would be barred by the statute of limitations." (p. 962) The aggrieved party should be able to elect whether or not to keep the contract in force (and sue for damages with each failure to perform) or cancel it (and sue for current and future damages).

Cherwell-Ralli, Inc. v. Rytman Grain Co. *(Page 962).* Cherwell-Ralli contracted to sell certain goods to Rytman Grain in installments, with payment due within ten days after delivery. The buyer quickly fell behind in its payments and the seller repeatedly called these arrearages to the buyer's attention. The seller continued to make deliveries, but after several months the buyer became concerned that the seller might not complete performance. By telephone, the buyer expressed his concerned and the seller assured the buyer that it would perform if the buyer made the payments it owed on deliveries already made. Shortly after the buyer sent a check to the seller in satisfaction of those obligations, the buyer was told by a truck driver, not employed by the seller, that the present shipment would be his last. In response, the buyer stopped payment on the check. The buyer then made a written demand for assurances, and the seller again demanded payment. Thereafter, no shipments were requested or made.

The court concluded that the buyer was in breach and rejected its claim for damages arising out of the plaintiff's refusal to deliver the remaining installments under the contract. The first conclusion was based on a finding that the buyer's refusal to pay substantially impaired the value of the whole contract, so as to constitute a breach of the whole contract, as required under § 2-612(3). The court affirmed the trial court's ruling on that issue as one of fact, amply supported by the record. The court rejected the buyer's argument that a seller in an installment contract cannot cancel the contract without following the procedures required by § 2-609. If the buyer's conduct is sufficiently egregious such conduct will by itself constitute substantial impairment of the value of the whole contract, and thus a present breach of the contract. Upon breach of the whole contract, § 2-703 permits a seller to cancel the remainder of the contract. This remedy is not canceled by a suit seeking recovery for payments due. Section 2-613 states that a contract is reinstated by such a suit, but not, according to the court, when it is clear to the buyer that the seller intended to cancel the contract.

The court's second conclusion was a rejection of the buyer's argument that the seller was obligated to provide assurance of its further performance. In rejecting that argument, the court found that the buyer did not have reasonable grounds for insecurity. A party cannot suspend performance for which it has already received the agreed return. In this case, the performance the buyer was withholding was payment for goods it had already received. Also, the buyer did not show, or explain why it did not show, the damages it suffered as a result of the seller's non-delivery.

Pedagogy on **Pakas** *and* **Cherwell-Ralli**. We begin by asking: When is it appropriate to treat a sale of goods transaction as an installment contract? Section 2-612(1) defines an installment contract as "one which requires or authorizes the delivery of goods in separate lots to be separately accepted, even though the contract contains a clause 'each delivery is a separate contract' or its equivalent." Section 2-612, com. 1 adds that installment contracts include "installment deliveries tacitly authorized by the circumstances or by the option of either party." Since this definition is designed to turn on substance rather than form, it cannot be applied without an understanding of the justification for the special rules that apply to installment contracts. The first special rule, laid out in § 2-612(2), is that the buyer's right of rejection is limited to defective tenders that "substantially impair" the value of the installment, and which seller cannot cure or for which seller fails to give adequate assurances of cure. Under the perfect tender rule in § 2-601, buyers in non-installment contracts have the right to reject any defective tender, subject to the more limited right to cure in § 2-508. However, if the "non-conformity or default with respect to one or more installments substantially impairs the value of the whole contract, the whole contract is breached." § 2-612(3). The second special rule applies to this last case: "the aggrieved party reinstates the contract if he accepts a non-conforming installment without giving notice of cancellation, or if he brings an action with respect only to past installments or demands performance as to future." This last rule reverses the *Pakas* rule, which effectively prevents an aggrieved party from suing for past non-conforming tenders without canceling the remainder of the contract. The *Pakas* court rejected the claim that a plaintiff who had sued and recovered damages for seller's failure to deliver the required number of shoes due on one of the initial installment deliveries under their agreement, nonetheless "had the right to elect to waive or disregard the breach, keep the contract in force and maintain successive actions for damages from time to time as the installments of goods were to be delivered." Section 2-612(3) instead adopts the dissent's view that the aggrieved party "should have the option to treat the contract as still continuing in force and, therefore, assert his right to recover damages for each default as it might occur."

The first special rule treats installment contracts as appropriate contexts for giving the seller of goods *more* flexibility and constraining the buyer's right of rejection. We believe this more fluid performance standard reflects the commercial realities unique to relational contracts. Since the parties to an installment contract have chosen an on-going relationship, rather than entering into discrete transactions, they are more likely to expect each other to cooperate by allowing cure or making price adjustments for non-conforming tenders throughout the course of performance. Their main concern is not whether any particular installment conforms, but whether the totality of installments delivered is sufficient to accomplish their purposes for entering into their relationship. Particularly when the individual installments are not resalable on a competitive market, subjecting each installment to the perfect tender rule would invite strategic behavior by the buyer. The substantial performance rule in installment contracts has, therefore, the same justification it has in construction contracts: it replaces the perfect tender rule, which would invite fly-specking to extort price reductions by buyers. The benefits of the additional right to reject any non-conforming individual installment is outweighed by the strategic opportunities it creates.

On the other hand, the second special rule for installment contracts recognizes that while the buyer has little at stake in any single installment, its true stake is in the performance of the whole contract. Thus, § 2-612(3) protects buyer's interests by providing it not only the right to cancel once any single non-conforming installment, or the cumulative effect of all non-conforming installments, substantially impairs the value of the whole contract, but also to sue for damages for past non-conforming deliveries without canceling the remainder of the contract. As the dissent argues in *Pakas*, the chief value of the right is that the buyer's damages for seller's future non-performance may be speculative at the time seller's non-conforming tenders amount to a breach of the whole contract. But if the buyer waits to sue until the time for tendering all installments has passed, the statute of limitations may have run on the early non-conforming tenders. We would add that even if the formal statute has not run, problems of proof may nonetheless bar recovery for non-conforming tenders that took place long in the past. The Code rule protects the buyer's interests in suing when damages are ripe by allowing successive suits for each non-conforming installment once there have been sufficiently serious the non-conforming deliveries to constitute a breach of the whole contract.

Given that the rationale for the special installment contract rules relies on the repeat-play, or relational, character of the contract, one might think these rules should apply to any parties entering into successive yet independent contracts for different deliveries of the same or similar goods. Hence, the Code's insistence that even contracts that specify "each delivery is a separate contract" are governed by § 2-612. Yet, these rules are only default rules. While most parties in such relationships may well prefer the looser performance standard for sellers and the robust breach-response options for buyers, some parties may want to opt out. By writing explicitly that "each delivery is a separate contract," we would have thought the parties were signaling their intent to opt out of any special installment contract rules and treat each delivery under ordinary perfect tender regime. Like many of the Code's provisions, we suspect that the drafters have invited courts to treat § 2-612 as a preferred, if not mandatory, rule regime for repeat trade parties, even though the rule can be justified only as a default rule.

CHAPTER 10

REMEDIES

A. The Basic Standards.
Expectation Damages as a Substitute for Performance.

For those who covered the remedies material in Chapter 1, this introductory section should serve primarily as a review. We have found, however, that students do benefit from a review of the remedies discussion (which seems to many to have taken place "way back" at the beginning of the semester). We find the following the most important conceptual points to emphasize. First, contract remedies are default rules and, as with any defaults, parties are invited to opt out of them (in whole or in part). Thus, they are best evaluated from the ex ante perspective. By now students understand that, whatever their views of efficiency or autonomy as justifying contract rules, their own professional task as practicing lawyers is to decide whether to take the defaults or to change them, and this requires lawyers to consider the issue ex ante.

Second, viewed ex ante, the substitution principle creates efficient incentives for promisors in deciding whether to breach or perform and, in the main, creates efficient incentives for promisees to rely. To be sure, the literature over the past twenty years has shown that, as a theoretical matter, efficient investment is best achieved with a reliance rather than an expectation measure. (The notion is that expectation damages are a guarantee of the value of performance and, thus, the promisee will be motivated to over-rely and not to take into account the probability of exogenous events that alter the efficiency of the contract ex post.) But notwithstanding the risk of over-reliance, the primacy of expectation damages as a default rule is justified by its simple, verifiable characteristics. As a general matter, it is much easier for the promisee to verify the position she would have achieved had the promise been performed than to prove the position she would have occupied had the promise never been made in the first place. Parties will not, as a general matter, write contracts that condition on non-verifiable facts. Similarly, under either efficiency or autonomy criteria, the state's default rules ought to mimic what most parties would agree to. It follows that if the parties would not generally specify a reliance measure, the state should not create such a default. Thus, even in considering only the investment decision, expectation damages are the best proxy for a theoretically optimal reliance measure where the value of reliance is either unobservable or unverifiable or both.

Third, viewed from the perspective of the promisee, it is easy to see why neither nominal nor punitive damages are the majoritarian default rule (and thus why the substitution principle dominates). The promisee wants the promisor's promise to be reliable but not more reliable than it is worth (since she has to pay for reliability in her return promise). Thus, any two bargainers working out an acceptable contract term to cover the contingency of breach are likely to agree on some version of expectation damages (to the extent those damages can be verified). The promisor wants his promise to be sufficiently reliable to entice the promisee to make a return promise. The promisee, in turn, is willing to pay for reliability but only up to the value of that promise to her.

Measuring Expectancy: Cost of Completion or Diminution in Value.

From the foregoing, it should be clear that the critical point for the parties (and for courts interpreting their contracts) is to determine precisely how to measure the lost expectancy once the contract is breached. We illustrate this basic point by focusing on the choice between diminution in value and cost of completion in the so-called "land grading" cases.

American Standard, Inc. v. Schectman *and* Peevyhouse v. Garland Coal & Mining Co. *(Pages 974 & 977)*. These two cases are best considered in tandem. *American Standard* is a modern version of *Groves v. John Wunder* and reaches the same result. The defendant agreed to remove all foundations on a commercial property to a depth of at least one foot below a specified grade. The defendant breached this portion of the agreement. At trial, defendant attempted to show that the cost of completion would be $110,500 while the failure to grade diminished the market value of the land by only $3,000. On appeal, the court held that the evidence was properly excluded since the "diminished value" rule only applied to construction cases where there would be "economic waste" in requiring the promisor, as per *Jacobs & Youngs v. Kent*, to tear down the structure in order to perform the promise fully. There was no such "waste" in this case since no new construction had to be destroyed. The court rejected the more "liberal" economic benefit test applied in *Peevyhouse* which measures expectancy by diminished value whenever the cost of completion greatly exceeds the *economic benefits* of completion as determined by fair market valuation. Thus, in *American Standard,* the court applies the "cost of completion" rule to a contract between two business entities to convey a commercial parcel of land.

In *Peevyhouse,* on the other hand, the court (using the economic benefit test) applies the diminished value measure to a contract to regrade a family farm at the conclusion of a mining lease term. Here the diminished market value was $300 while the cost of completion was estimated to be $29,000. Since the economic benefit of regrading would be so greatly exceed by its cost, the court measured the expectancy by the lesser amount.

These cases seem difficult for students unless the issues are carefully framed. First, we find it useful to emphasize that the contract damages questions are independent of any environmental regulations that may or may not expose the landowner to superfund liability or the like. Clearly, if the owner/buyer is liable to a third party for the regrading, the cost of completion measure is the correct default in all cases. Thus, in order to reach the damages question one must assume that the choice to regrade or not lies entirely with the contracting parties in these cases.

Second, we find it helpful to use these cases to test the students understanding of damage measurement questions. The key question in measuring expectation damages is to determine two different economic states of the world. The first is easy: What is the economic position the promisee currently occupies with ungraded land? The second is the critical question: What precisely was the position the promisee expected to occupy had the contract been performed? This question can be rephrased as follows: In the contract, did the promisor promise to provide "graded value" land or, rather, did the promisor promise to "regrade regardless of the value of regrading"? In any given contract, the parties can resolve this question by an explicit clause that specifies the obligation of the promisor precisely. In the absence of such a clause, the court needs to provide a default that will govern unless parties opt out. Which default is best? Looking at both of these contracts, one can argue that both cases are wrongly decided. In *American Standard,* the most plausible default for a commercial sale of land between business firms is that the promisee's expectation is "graded value land." Since the land is being exchanged for its economic value, it is unlikely that non-economic factors, such as family heritage or other non-market considerations would have been paid for ex ante by the promisee. *Peevyhouse,* on the other hand, seems just the opposite. A family farm owned by native Americans (who may attach even greater non-market values to the land) is the most likely case where the promisee would pay for "regraded land regardless of the value of regrading." This conclusion is bolstered in *Peevyhouse* by the evidence that the Peevyhouses sought expressly to include the regrading provisions in the lease contract at the time it was written.

Specific Performance.

In Chapter 1, we considered *Klein v. Pepsico,* a case establishing the proposition that specific performance is not generally available so long as money damages are "adequate." We now consider the question in more depth. What explains the circumstances where specific performance will be granted? How can we explain or justify where we draw the line between damages and specific performance? And, why isn't specific performance generally available or at least available at the option of the contracting parties?

Sedmak v. Charlie's Chevrolet, Inc. *(Page 986).* Dr. and Mrs. Sedmak were automobile enthusiasts who owned six Corvettes. Upon reading that a limited edition Corvette would be produced to commemorate the selection of the Corvette as the pace car for the Indianapolis 500, the Sedmaks contacted Charlie's sales manager, Tom Kells, about ordering one. Mrs. Sedmak put down a deposit on the car, and, when Kells told her that the car would definitely be theirs, she requested certain changes to the stock model. Kells then told her that he could not quote a definite price for the car because he did not know how much the changes would cost, but the price, he said, would be the manufacturer's retail price. A few months later, the car arrived with the requested modifications, but Kells told the Sedmaks that they could not purchase the car for the manufacturer's retail price because high demand had inflated the car's value. He informed them further that they would have to bid on the car. The Sedmaks declined to submit a bid and instead filed suit seeking specific performance of the contract.

Sedmak applies UCC § 2-716. The promisee can get specific performance where the "goods are unique or in other proper circumstances." In this case, the evidence shows that other pace cars with the same features were available from other dealers. Just how many is not clear. 6,000 cars were made but only a "limited" number of those had the options ordered by the Sedmaks. Moreover, a number of those cars had undoubtedly been already sold to collectors and would be costly to track down. Nevertheless, the goods were not "unique" in any meaningful sense of that word. Thus, this case must be an example of "other proper circumstances." Comment 1 suggests that "inability to cover" is such a circumstance. But that statement cannot be taken literally. Rather, it must be interpreted to mean "inability to cover at an acceptable cost." When, then, is the cost of cover unacceptably high justifying an award of specific performance?

One way to think about this question is to ask: Given a default rule of expectation damages equal to the value of the broken contract to the promisee, why would anyone ever breach (except inadvertently)? [1] And yet, we observe advertent breach. There are two possible explanations for a promisor's decision to breach in the face of an expectation damages rule. The first is benign: the decision to breach is a "cry for help"– a request that the contracting partner adjust to the broken contract by covering (or reselling) on the market and submitting a "damages" bill to the promisor.[2] The alternative explanation is strategic: breach is motivated by the imperfections in the judicial system that systematically deny the promisee his contractual expectancy. Promisors who breach, under this conception, are able to exploit these imperfections to secure a favorable settlement of the disputed transaction. The challenge for contract theory is to predict when the benign scenario is more likely than the malign one (and vice versa). If the benign story is the more probable explanation for the promisor's breach, an efficient default rule would direct courts to award only a damages remedy to the promisee, thus encouraging the promisee to respond to the cry for help by acting appropriately on the market. On the other hand, if the malign scenario is the more probable in the particular case, the rule should direct the court to grant specific relief to the promisee, thus trumping the (presumptively) strategic request for assistance.

Under the Article 2 scheme, the nature of the market for substitute goods determines which of these explanations is more likely in any particular case.[3] Where the market is thin, the implicit assumption is that breach is more likely to be strategic and the promisee can trump the "cry for help"

---

[1] The efficient breach hypothesis — which holds that breach enables the promisor to take advantage of a better market opportunity while guaranteeing the promisee the value of its bargain — fails to explain breach in markets where substitute goods are available. In such a case, the promisor can always "perform" the contract by covering on the market from a third party and tendering the substitute "performance" in satisfaction of the contract, thereby freeing the promisor to purse any alternative market opportunity without having to suffer the reputational consequences of breaching a contract. Thus the question: In a market where goods are available in substitution for the contract, what explains why any party would advertently breach?

[2] The assumption here is that the promisor recognizes that it will suffer a loss on the contract and wishes to enlist the promisee's assistance in minimizing that loss. The decision to breach, on this view, is made after comparing the promisor's costs of acting on the market with the (presumably lower) salvage costs of the promisee (for example, a breaching seller presumably would incur greater costs in finding a substitute seller from whom to purchase conforming goods to tender to the buyer than would the buyer, who knows better the market for the goods that it requires).

[3] The Code's remedial scheme implicitly adopts an initial presumption that breach is a cry for help. Thus, specific performance (or an action for the price) is an extraordinary remedy (*see* §§ 2-703, 2-711). The promisee-buyer has an option of either covering on the market (§ 2-712) or establishing what a cover contract would have cost (§ 2-713). But, in either case, as long as there is a market for the goods, the buyer is presumed to have the comparative advantage in salvaging the broken contract and must act on the market and subsequently submit a damage claim to the seller. The same presumption holds for the promisee-seller, who must initially choose between resale (§ 2-706) or proof of what a resale would have yielded on the market (§ 2-708(1)). In either case, only when the promisee can show that the market for substitutes is thin does the Code presumption shift toward the malign story. In such a case, the promisee-buyer can secure specific performance (§ 2-716, Comment 2: "inability to cover is 'other proper circumstances'"), and the promisee-seller can recover the price (§ 2-709(1)(b): "unable after reasonable effort to resell").

by demanding either specific performance or the contract price (as the case may be).[4] Where there is an available market for the contract goods, however, the promisee is limited to market damages. This motivates the promisee to adjust efficiently to the breach by salvaging the broken contract on the market, either by resale or by cover (or, in the alternative, by relying on proof of what such an action on the market would have yielded).

In sum, the baseline assumption of the Code (and the common law) is that breach is benign. Thus, wherever there exists a market for the contract goods, damages are the norm. The idea is that the promisor will only beach after considering the option of covering himself on the market and supplying those goods to the promisee in satisfaction of the contract. When a promisor rejects that option and breaches (advertently), it must then be because the promisor has determined that the promisee can better salvage the broken contract by covering on the market. To permit the promisee to trump that request by requiring specific performance would be to require an inefficient and more costly salvage thus reducing the size of the contractual pie. On the other hand, the obligation of the promisee to cover will be considered unacceptably high when the market thins to the point where there the risk of strategic breach is more likely than not. Now the promisee is vulnerable to a strategic claim by the promisee that its cover action was unreasonable and thus cannot be the basis for a damage claim. When this risk arises, courts will award specific performance. Such was the case in *Sedmak*.

Reliance Damages

As a matter of theory, expectation damages are always *at least* equal to or greater than reliance damages. Once we have established expectation damages as the general default (for reasons of verifiability if not because it is the best default in theory), when, if ever, should courts use a reliance measure instead? And, if reliance is always available as an option to an injured promisee, when will it be preferred?

Sullivan v. O'Connor *(Page 995).* The plaintiff in this case, a professional entertainer, enlisted the services of the defendant plastic surgeon to improve the appearance of her nose. She alleged that she entered into a contract with the defendant in which he promised to enhance her beauty by performing two operations on her nose. However, the surgeries went badly, and the appearance of her nose worsened. The physician undertook a third operation to try and correct the damage, but to no avail. She sued both for breach of contract and medical malpractice seeking to recover damages for out-of-pocket expenses, damages resulting from the breach, including loss of employment, and pain and suffering damages.

Sullivan provides one answer to the first question posed above. Expectation damages dominate as the default rule because they motivate efficient decisions by the promisor to either breach or perform, and they are the best proxy for efficient decisions to rely by the promisee. If so, then under what circumstances would a court ever choose reliance as the default rule? This court's

---

[4] *See* UCC §§ 2-716, 2-709(1)(b). The argument is that, in a thin market, a promisee is unlikely to enjoy a comparative advantage over the promisor in covering on the market while, at the same time, the promisee is more vulnerable to strategic claims that the cover contract was unreasonable since market prices are more difficult to prove.

answer: when the contractual expectation (a pretty nose) is difficult to establish because there are no market values for comparing the ugly nose with the pretty one. Moreover, Justice Kaplan finds additional support from the fact that reliance is the lesser included remedy, and, given the uncertainty about using contract rather than tort in medical malpractice cases (did the physician really "promise" a beautiful nose or did he merely promise to use appropriate skill, leaving the outcome a matter of probabilities), the tort-based reliance measure is preferred on that ground as well. In any case, since the promisee abandoned her claim for expectation damages, the case doesn't really present the opportunity to create precedent on the choice between expectation and reliance as a default rule.

Note 1 (Page 1001). The court is skeptical of the plaintiff's contract claims despite the fact that claims made under similar circumstances have prevailed in Massachusetts courts. Any statements a doctor makes concerning the outcome of treatment, the court believes, cannot rightly be construed as firm promises. There are simply too many risks and variables in medical treatment for a doctor of even "average integrity" to make such promises. Hence, there is a presumption against contract formation in the context of medical treatment, and the plaintiff's burden of proof is automatically higher because she must rebut that presumption. Furthermore, the adoption of reliance damages makes the issue more or less moot. As noted in the discussion of the case, reliance damages are tort-based and choosing reliance as a default in "medical contract" cases precludes recovery based on the normal contract default rule of expectancy damages. Even if the presumption is effectively rebutted, the plaintiff will not be able to recover the difference between what she bargained for and what she got.

Note 2 (Page 1001). The difference between the pretty nose and the wheat is that there is a market value by which a court can measure the expectancy interest of the wheat buyer– namely, the difference between the contract price and the market price at the time of breach. As the Sullivan court notes, there is no such market value for the pretty nose.

In calculating her reliance interest, it is, practically speaking, irrelevant that she would have entered into the same contract with another doctor. To be sure, the goal of reliance damages is to put the injured party in the same position she would have occupied had the contract never been made, and that would theoretically require the defendant to compensate the plaintiff for opportunities lost as a result of the contract. However, courts do not include opportunity costs when calculating reliance damages, presumably because they would be impossible to calculate. To that extent, reliance damages suffer from the same difficulty that plagues expectancy damages in the medical contract setting: indefiniteness. Reliance damages are always under-compensatory. However, it is not as difficult to measure accurately the other aspects of reliance (the "out of pocket" costs incurred in time and money invested, for instance) and this is one of the reasons that reliance damages are superior to expectancy damages in such cases.

Kizas v. Webster *(Page 1001).* The plaintiffs in this case were clerical workers employed by the FBI. The court had previously granted their motion for summary judgment, arguing that the termination of a program giving FBI clerical workers preference when applying for jobs as special agents constituted a taking of private property without compensation. Having ruled in favor of the plaintiffs on the issue of liability, the court now must rule on the plaintiff's motion for summary judgment on damages.

Kizas answers the second question posed above. Promisees will seek reliance damages when expectation losses are too difficult to prove with certainty. In this case, the clerical workers were allowed to recover the difference between the wages they earned with the FBI and the (higher) market value of their clerical services together with the costs of moving to the FBI jobs. This recovery was the provable reliance damages for breach of the FBI promise that they would be eligible for special consideration for future appointment as FBI agents. Defendant argued that reliance could never exceed expectancy and that expectancy was zero in this case. While the proposition that reliance cannot exceed expectancy is valid in general (see *Note 2 on page 1006*), it does not apply to these plaintiffs since the lost opportunity to become FBI agents does have value to the promisee ex ante.

Problem (Page 1007). At first blush, Reed's argument makes intuitive sense: Anglia could not have relied on his services prior to contract formation. The counter-argument is that Anglia hired a director and made other investments in anticipation of finding a suitable leading man. Reed knew, therefore, that Anglia was relying on him to make these investments worthwhile. If he breached and Anglia was unable to mitigate (as was the case), those expenditures would be sunk costs. In making the contract, Reed therefore assumed the responsibility for these costs even though they were incurred prior to his agreement.

Restitution

Those teaching a four-credit course may find it useful to skip this section and the following section on punitive damages as the issues are relatively clear and straightforward and most lawyers can (and do) learn them on their own. For those teaching the entire book, note that restitution questions are of two sorts. First, how are we to measure the value of the "benefit conferred" in a claim for restitution? Second, under what circumstances can the breaching promisor recover in restitution for a partial performance?

United States v. Zara Contracting Co. *(Page 1008).* The plaintiffs subcontracted with Zara to perform construction work on an airport, including preparing the ground for the construction of landing strips. While performing this work, plaintiffs encountered unexpected soil conditions, including a great deal of clay material, that made progress difficult and caused their machinery to break down. After their demands for more money went unheard, plaintiffs ceased work on the airfield, and Zara took over using equipment furnished by the plaintiffs at the contract site. Plaintiffs sued, alleging that Zara had wrongfully terminated the contract and sought to recover damages for the work performed and the reasonable rental value of the equipment.

Zara answers the question of how to measure the value of the benefit conferred. The promisee, upon breach, has the option of foregoing a suit on the contract in lieu of a claim in restitution for the reasonable value of his performance. When a restitution claim is made, the plaintiff can prove the value of the benefit conferred on the defendant by showing the cost of its performance. The fact that the cost of performance exceeded the contract estimates is no bar, especially in construction cases where unit prices ex post often vary from ex ante estimates.

Britton v. Turner *(Page 1011).* In *Britton*, the plaintiff entered a contract to work for a period of one year in return for a salary of $120. The plaintiff breached the contract by ceasing performance before the year had expired and sought to recover damages for the work performed on the basis of quantum meruit.

Britton answers the second question posed above. It is the accepted default rule today that a breaching party can still recover in restitution for the value of his partial performance. In such a case, the measure of recovery is limited to the benefit conferred (and not the cost of performance) less, of course, any damages owed to the promisee for the breach. As the court in *Britton* makes clear, a restitutionary recovery for actual benefit conferred does not create any perverse incentives for promisors to breach. Indeed, the reverse is true. By permitting recovery for part performance by the breacher, the default rule reduces the risk of strategic claims of breach by the promisee who would otherwise be motivated to induce breach and capture the value of part performance by the promisee. It is useful, once again, to note for students that this rule is only a default. As the court indicates, parties are free (subject to limits imposed by the penalty doctrine) to withhold any payment until and unless full performance is provided by the promisor.

Note 5 (Page 1017). Under Restatement § 371, Dickey would be able to recover the reasonable value of his services to the movie studio. As we saw in *Zara,* that amount may exceed the contract price, as it would in this case. The analogy to the construction contract in Zara would seem to hold because the estimated profits from a film often vary from the actual profits, just as construction estimates often vary from actual construction costs. Hence, the actual value of an actor's services may be far greater (or far less) than the amount reflected in the contract.

Punitive Damages
Hibschman Pontiac, Inc. v. Batchelor *and* Miller Brewing Co. v. Best Beers of Bloomington, Inc. *(Pages 1017 & 1021).* We teach these two cases together. In tandem the two opinions of the Indiana Supreme Court, separated by only 16 years, are a useful illustration of the rise and fall of punitive damage claims for breach of contract in the United States. In *Hibschman,* the court sustained a jury award of punitive damages to a car purchaser who was poorly served by the service department of the dealership on the ground that the jury could have found the contract "mingled" with "fraud, gross negligence or oppression." Subsequently, in *Best Beers,* the same court limited *Hibschmen* to its facts by narrowly confining the award of punitive damages to those cases where the plaintiff was able to establish the elements of an independent tort for which punitive damages are routinely available, and not merely "tort-like conduct" in a breach of contract claim.

Note 2 and Note 4 (Pages 1028 & 1030). These notes are designed to provide a further opportunity to test the justification for punitive damages in contract cases. We find it useful to contrast Judge Kozinski's fears of the "tortification of contract law" with the argument of Professor Dodge in *Note 4.* Dodge argues that the systematic under compensation in contract damages – owing to limitations in prejudgment interest and the inability of plaintiffs to recover attorneys fees and court costs – encourages strategic breaches that can only be efficiently deterred by an appropriate award of punitive damages. Moreover, Dodge would extend the award of punitive damages to any advertent breach, even if there is no strategic motivation, on the grounds that punitive damages will function much like specific performance, to require renegotiation by the promisor to buy its way out of the contract with the promisee by sharing some of the gains from breach that it anticipates.

Dodge's argument assumes that there are no "benign" reasons why a promisor might advertently breach. Thus, he appears to deny the practical relevance of the mitigation principle in a breach/performance decision. Recall that the benign story is that breach is a "cry for help." By breaching, and (implicitly) promising to pay the promisee's damages bill once it is submitted to him, the promisor enlists the promisee's aid in salvaging a broken contract. Requiring this assistance (such as finding the cheapest cover contract available on the market) is justified on the grounds that the promisee has a comparative advantage in mitigating the cost of breach. Ex ante, both parties gain if expected breach costs can be minimized. Thus, Dodge appears to ignore the possibility of hold up– that the routine award of punitive damages will actually encourage strategic behavior by promisees, who will refuse to cooperate in mitigating the costs of contractual breakdown in order to require a renegotiation in which they get "paid" ex post for their cooperation.

B. Limitations on Compensation.
In Chapter 1, we examined the foreseeability limitation in *Hadley v. Baxendale*. This section is designed to explore the three principal limitation doctrines – certainty, foreseeability and mitigation – in depth.

The Certainty Limitation.
It is a commonplace that the plaintiff must prove its damages with reasonable certainty. The relevance of this limitation is most apparent in the case of the so-called new business rule, which restricts recovery of lost profits in the case of an enterprise that lacks an established track record.

Drews Company, Inc. v. Ledwith-Wolfe Associates, Inc. *(Page 1033).* Ledwith-Wolfe enlisted the services of Drews to convert a building it owned into a restaurant. From the start, the project was plagued by delays, work change orders, and disagreement between the contractor and the owner. Drews stopped work and filed a lien for labor and materials for the work it had performed. It then tried to foreclose on the lien. Ledwith counterclaimed that Drews had breached the contract and sued to recover damages for having to redo part of the work and for profits lost as a result of the delay in opening the restaurant. The court refused to apply the old common law rule that lost profits claimed by a "new business" are per se uncertain and speculative. Instead, the court held that the new business rule should be merely a presumption against lost profits claims for a new business, a presumption that the plaintiff could overcome in an appropriate case. Unfortunately for the plaintiff in this case, however, its evidence failed to meet the lower threshold established by the court.

Drews is an excellent case to illustrate the evolution of the "new business" rule from the strict common law rule to the more modern presumption. Some states continue to follow the older common law rule that a "new business" is absolutely precluded from recovering lost profits as a matter of law. The rule is based on the notion that future profits are an extrapolation of past profits. In the case of a new business, no such extrapolation is possible. Moreover, given the uncertainties associated with a new enterprise, it is simply unclear when or if profits will be earned. Thus, projections from a business or marketing plan or even evidence of profits earned by similar, established businesses are too speculative as a matter of law.

The problem with the per se rule, of course, is that it invites strategic behavior by the promisor. A promisor can enter an enforceable contract with a new business, secure in the knowledge that if future contingencies are unfavorable, breach will essentially be a zero cost option. This concern has prompted a growing number of courts to apply the rule only as a test of evidentiary sufficiency rather than as an automatic bar. Thus, market forecasts, comparable business analyses and expert testimony are all ways to potentially establish lost profits even in a new business context. As *Drews* demonstrates, however, evidence of gross profits, without corresponding evidence of overhead or operating costs, together with plaintiff's estimate that "one third" of the gross would be net profits, is insufficient to rebut the presumption.

Problem (Page 1038). The problem offers a chance to review some of the material covered earlier. Expectation damages – the value of the chance that Adam might win the prize with Lucy – are too speculative in this case. Adam, therefore, should be allowed to recover reliance damages. What is the value of the alternative activity he forewent to attempt to win the prize? This might allow Adam to at least recover the reasonable value of his "time" spent in pursuing the prize. Or, perhaps Adam can recover in restitution the reasonable value of the "benefit" conferred as measured by the "cost of his performance," which would, again, be the value of time spent at the pet store.

Foreseeability.

Those who covered *Hadley v. Baxendale* carefully in Chapter 1 might choose to omit this section. But for those with some time available, the cases are worth teaching.

Spang Industries v. Aetna Casualty and Surety Co. (*Page 1039*). Spang's Fort Pitt Bridge division contracted to deliver 240 tons of structural steel to Torrington Construction Co. to be used in the erection of a bridge. The original delivery date requested by Torrington was late June, 1970. Fort Pitt originally agreed to this date, but later notified Torrington that it could not make the deliveries until August of that year. The steel was finally shipped in late August and early September, but there was not enough steel at the job site to commence construction until September 16th. Because of the delay, Torrington was not able to pour concrete until October 28th. The temperature by that time had fallen below the 40 degrees normally required for the pouring of concrete, and Torrington had to get special permission from the supervising engineer to pour. Moreover, because freezing temperatures were imminent, the work had to be completed in a single day, forcing Torrington to incur extra costs in the form of overtime pay and special equipment to protect the concrete against freezing. In July of the following year, Fort Pitt sued Torrington's bonding agent, Aetna, to recover the unpaid balance on the subcontract, and Torrington then filed suit alleging that the delay in delivery amounted to breach of contract. The trial court ruled that Fort Pitt had breached and subtracted the amount of Torrington's damage claim from the balance remaining on the subcontract. On appeal, Fort Pitt argued that the ruling against it violated the foreseeability rule of *Hadley*.

Spang Industries thus raises the very interesting question of "*Hadley v. Baxendale* extended." Fort Pitt claims, in essence, that it could not have foreseen the special costs incurred in pouring concrete in cold temperatures at the time the contract was made, as the earlier date for delivery of the contract steel was not specified until *after* the contract was made. The court avoids the problem of extending the *Hadley* rule to the disclosure of special circumstances after the making of the contract but before performance is due by holding that the contract term specifying "delivery to be mutually agreed upon" served to incorporate as of the time of contacting the subsequent agreement of a June 1970 delivery date. Thus, Fort Pitt was constructively charged with notice of the importance of a June 1970 delivery as of the time the contract was made.

But why shouldn't the principle of *Hadley v. Baxendale* extend to information received by the promisor *after the contract but before performance is due* assuming that the promisor has sufficient opportunity to act upon it? Such a rule would require the promisor to adjust to subsequent information where she as able to do so (say, by adding workers sufficient to meet a delivery date once the knowledge of the extraordinary cost of delay became clear), and, in turn, require the promisee to "pay" for any such cost-effective adjustments. One answer, of course, is that the enhanced obligation of the promisor would not have been reflected in the initial contract price and the value of the subsequent precautions may be hard to prove.

But think of the problem in terms of mitigation and not as a question of foreseeable consequential damages. Under a robust mitigation principle, the parties would both agree at the time of contract that each would have an implied obligation to minimize the costs of a contractual breakdown when they were able to do so. A robust mitigation obligation would reduce expected breach costs and thus increase the size of the pie for both parties. Yet the doctrine of avoidable consequences only applies after one party has breached, but not prior to a breach. What explains the failure of contract law to impose a rule of pre-breach cost-effective mitigation? Surely such a principle would reduce expected contracting costs. One answer, of course, is that the information needed to trigger a pre-breach mitigation responsibility is likely to be unobservable or unverifiable to courts. If so, the familiar problem of coping with hidden information would explain why a theoretically attractive mitigation rule is not practical in real world contracting. For one view of this "cathedral," see Charles J. Goetz & Robert E. Scott, *The Mitigation Principle: Toward a General Theory of Contractual Obligation,* 69 Virginia L. Rev. 967, 1011-1018 (1983).

Cricket Alley Corp. v. Data Terminal Systems, Inc. *(Page 1043)*. *Cricket Alley* involves a claim for breach of an express warranty. The plaintiff, Cricket Alley, wanted to buy cash registers that could electronically send sales and inventory information from its individual stores to the main computer in its home office. After consulting with Wang, the manufacturer of the computer, and a cash register dealer, it purchased ten computerized cash registers manufactured by Data Terminal Systems (DTS). There were several bugs in the program, however, and the cash registers were never able to communicate with the main computer. Cricket Alley replaced the DTS registers with IBM registers and sued for its increased labor costs as consequential damages for breach of warranty. On appeal, the court affirmed the trial court's decision to permit the consequential damages claim to go to the jury even though the claimed damages for increased labor costs had not been made known to DTS at the time of contracting.

For those who want to pursue foreseeability even further, this case is a good example of a modern application of the *Hadley* rule and the use of the "common feature" test of general versus special circumstances. If the circumstances in question are a "common" rather than a "unique" feature of the contract performance, then the first prong of the *Hadley* rule applies and there is no requirement that the circumstances have been made known to the promisor. In this case, the increased labor costs were a "common" or "natural" consequence of a failure of the computer system to function properly.

Duty to Mitigate.

Rockingham County v. Luten Bridge Co. *and* **Parker v. Twentieth Century Fox** *(Pages 1050 &1053).* *Luten Bridge* involves a suit for breach of a construction contract. The plaintiff agreed to build a bridge in a remote part of the county, but the County Board of Commissioners rescinded the contract after a public outcry against the contract. The contractor had incurred $1,900 in construction costs to that point. Upon being notified of the Board's decision, plaintiff considered the contract breached but continued work on the bridge. Plaintiff then sued to recover damages for all of the work completed. The County argued, and the court agreed, that the plaintiff had exacerbated damages by continuing construction after the County rescinded, and thus should only be allowed to recover the $1,900 expended prior to rescission. *Luten Bridge* is one of the old "chestnuts" that states the common law doctrine of avoidable consequences. We ask the students to read the case, but reserve class discussion for *Parker*.

In *Parker*, Actress Shirley MacLaine entered a contract with Twentieth Century-Fox to play the lead in a musical called *Bloomer Girl*. The contract had a "play or pay" clause stipulating that Fox was not obligated to utilize her services in the film; rather, its only obligation was to pay her the compensation agreed upon. It also gave MacLaine the right to approve several aspects of the production. Fox later decided not to produce *Bloomer Girl* and offered MacLaine the lead in another picture, *Big Country, Big Man*. Due to time constraints, however, Fox did not offer her approval rights on the new film. MacLaine declined the offer and sued Fox for breach. Fox claimed summary judgment was wrongly granted as the alternative movie offer raised a triable issue of fact as to whether MacLaine had a duty to mitigate and accept the offer.

We ask the class to argue each side of *Parker*. The plaintiff's initial argument is that defendant breached the contract and owes compensatory damages. Fox argues, on the other hand, that MacLaine has a duty to mitigate or take reasonable steps to avoid damages as a condition to recovery. MacLaine's reply, which prevails in sustaining a summary judgment, is that this duty does not require her to take on substitute employment that is "different and inferior." As a factual matter, this argument is strengthened by the fact that *Bloomer Girl* was a film with a strong social context and quite different from the alternative western role Fox offered. But isn't this a factual question that should entitle Fox to avoid summary judgment and have a trial on the merits? After all, the test is "employment in the same general line" and determining whether the alternative role qualifies, or is "different and inferior," would seem to require a factual inquiry.

As Victor Goldberg has shown, however, (*see Note 2 on page 1059*) MacLaine had a much better (and easier) argument to make: The "play or pay" clause (footnote 58) establishes that not producing the movie is not a breach by Fox. Fox had a right not to produce *Bloomer Girl*. But whether they produced the movie or not, they still owed MacLaine $750,000. In essence, the studio purchased an option on MacLaine's time whether she performed for them or not. Thus, Fox owes her the money under the explicit terms of the contract, and the alternative offer in *Big Country* is irrelevant. This is simply a breach of a promise to pay $750,000 in exchange for the option on plaintiff's services and the damages are precisely measured by the option price.

Liquidated Damages.

California and Hawaiian Sugar Co. v. Sun Ship, Inc, *and* **Lake River v. Carborundum Co.** *(Pages 1062 &1068).* In *Sun Ship,* C&H's previous carrier withdrew its services and C&H resolved to commission the building of a large shipping vessel so that it could handle shipping itself. C&H decided on a hybrid ship, one consisting of a catamaran tug and a barge. Sun Ship agreed to build the barge, and Halter agreed to build the tug. The Sun Ship contract contained a liquidated damages clause. Neither builder met the delivery date, and C&H sued to recover the stipulated damages. Halter settled, but Sun Ship argued that the amount of liquidated damages was unenforceable because it amounted to a penalty. The Ninth Circuit rejected the penalty defense, holding, per Judge Noonan, that where anticipated damages are difficult to establish, even though actual damages turn out to be easily measured and/or minimal, Pennsylvania law favors enforcement of liquidated damages clauses.

In *Lake River,* the plaintiff, Lake River, agreed to distribute Carborundum's Ferro Carbo product, an abrasive powder used in making steel. Carborundum insisted that Lake River install a new bagging system in order to meet the demands of the contract, and Lake River, in turn, insisted on a minimum-quantity guarantee to ensure that it could cover the cost of the new system and still make a profit. If it failed to meet the minimum quantity, Carborundum agreed to pay liquidated damages. After the contract was signed, the market for domestic steel crashed, and demand for Ferro Carbo plummeted. Carborundum was therefore unable to deliver the minimum quantity and Lake River demanded payment according to the liquidated damages formula. Like Sun Ship, Carborundum argued that the minimum guarantee clause was an unenforceable penalty clause. The Seventh Circuit, per Judge Posner, found the "take or pay" clause void as a penalty on the grounds that, under Illinois law, a liquidated damages clause must be both reasonable and difficult to establish ex ante, at the time of contract, and ex post, at the time of breach. Thus, if damages are easily determined after the breach or the estimate exceeds any reasonable ex post calculation, the clause is void as a penalty. Here Posner finds the clause fails these principles because the amount of damages are invariant to the extent of the breach.

The continuing vitality of the penalty doctrine even as applied to contracts between two business firms, negotiated with the advice of counsel on both sides, remains a puzzle to us and to most academic commentators. *Sun Ship* and *Lake River* provide an opportunity both to analyze the subtle doctrinal differences among jurisdictions as well as to discuss the justifications for why courts reserve for special scrutiny stipulated damages terms that opt out of the damages default rules.

In *Sun Ship,* Judge Noonan, perhaps reflecting the academic consensus, argues for giving commercial entities great latitude in stipulating damages so long as there are ex ante uncertainties about the amount of loss that might result from a breach. Thus, even though the actual losses were negligible in this case, given the failure of Halter to deliver the tug, the stipulated damages were reasonable, viewed ex ante. In *Lake River,* Judge Posner finds that the "take or pay" clause is void as a penalty because it is invariant to the breach and thus can't be seen as a reasonable estimate notwithstanding the difficulty of estimating losses ex ante. In dictum, Posner clearly indicates that, as a matter of theory, the rule is difficult to defend. But when called upon to apply Illinois law, he faithfully follows the rather conservative approach of the Illinois courts in resolving doubts in favor of striking down the stipulated damages clause in question.

We find unpersuasive Posner's attempt to distinguish this "take or pay" clause from those more commonly found in the natural gas industry. The essential point is that fixed-cost investments expose the promisee to strategic breaches absent some assurance of a supply sufficient to amortize those costs. If this clause was so penal in character, why does Posner imagine that Carborundum and its lawyers would have agreed to it in the first place? Indeed, as Alan Schwartz has shown (*see Note 1 on page 1075*), there is no reason to believe that commercial parties would ever contract for supra-compensatory damages in the first place. Thus, the strongest inference is that the clause, negotiated between business firms with counsel on both sides, covers various anticipated costs that are either too speculative or otherwise noncompensable under the standard damages default rules. Both efficiency and autonomy arguments line up in favor of free enforcement of freely negotiated damages clauses that opt out of ill-fitting contract law defaults.

C. Sales of Goods

As we suggested in the introduction to this manual, one alternative to coverage of Parts A and B of this Chapter is to focus instead on a careful analysis of how the UCC incorporates the various default rules of contract damages into a coherent statutory scheme. One of us has used this approach with some success in a four credit course. Obviously, if many of the students are likely to elect a separate course in Sales or Commercial Law, it might be prudent to omit this Part.

Seller's Damages

If you are planning on teaching this Part, we recommend using the **hypothetical on page 1080** as the framework for analysis and then relying on the cases as illustrations of how the Code provisions apply in particular contexts. Thus, one might begin by asking the students to serve as the attorneys advising the aggrieved seller in this hypothetical case. Thus, following Buyer's refusal to take delivery of specially manufactured circuit boards, Seller consults with its attorneys. Seller's first question: Can I sue and recover the contract price from the breaching buyer? The second question: If not, what damages am I entitled to?

a. Recovery of the contract price

The answer to the first question is that generally the seller is not entitled to recover the contract price. The seller's action for the price is an extraordinary remedy that parallels the buyer's claim for specific performance and thus it is not generally available. Why not? One answer is that the default rules assume that breach is benign–a cry for help from the buyer, in essence, breach is a request of the seller to salvage the broken contract by reselling the goods on the market and then to send buyer the bill for damages. Given that presumption, § 2-709 specifies two separate circumstance where seller can sue for the price.

Industrial Molded Plastic Products, Inc. v. J. Gross & Sons, Inc. *(Page 1081)*. The first circumstance where a seller can recover the price is illustrated by *J. Gross & Sons*. In this case, the son of defendant's president negotiated a contract for the production of 5,000,000 plastic clothing clips, even though he was only authorized to order a much smaller amount as a trial run. The defendant planned to market the clips to retail clothing stores but had trouble selling them. Defendant took delivery of and paid for 772,000 clips. Despite repeated demands by the plaintiff, the defendant failed to pick up any more clips but they also failed to repudiate the contract. Plaintiff manufactured all 5,000,000 clips and warehoused the remaining 4,228,000. Plaintiff finally filed suit, seeking to recover the unpaid balance of the contract price. The court holds that, where the goods were made available to the buyer for about one year, the buyer has failed to reject within a reasonable time under § 2-602(1). Therefore, seller has "accepted" the goods and can recover the price under § 2-707(1)(a).

Assume, in the alternative, that the buyer repudiates prior to the time for delivery (so § 2-709(1)(a) is not applicable). The only other option open to the seller who wants to recover the full price is to seek recovery under § 2-709(1)(b) by showing that it is "unable to resell the goods with reasonable efforts at a reasonable price" (*see Emanuel Law Outlines*, **Note 2 on page 1083**). What does that mean? One answer is that the test of § 2-709(1)(b) is not the "reasonableness" of the resale price per se, but rather the relative risk that the seller faces if the buyer chooses subsequently to dispute the reasonableness of the seller's actions as a way of avoiding payment of damages. On this view, the question turns on the thickness of the market. If there are many buyers at a given price, then resale is reasonable because the seller can subsequently verify the reasonableness of its actions in market terms. But if the market is thin, the seller then risks strategic "foot dragging" by the buyer who may quibble about the seller's resale action ("that can't possibly be the best price"). In addition, in a thin market it is unlikely that seller enjoys any comparative advantage in locating the best available resale price.

b. Market-based damages

Assume now that Seller answers "yes" to the question: Is there an available market for the contract goods? In this case, Seller's attorney must advise him that an action for the price is unavailable (because the goods can be sold after reasonable effort for a reasonable price per § 2-709(1)(b)). This raises the next question Seller asks his attorneys: Assuming there is a market for the goods, must I resell now or can I put the goods back on the shelf and sell them later at my own convenience?

This question raises the choice between § 2-706 (the right of resale) and § 2-708(1) (contract/market damages). In theory, these two provisions are equivalent methods of measuring the market and Seller has the option of choosing the best alternative. Seller can, if he chooses, resell the goods following the guidelines of § 2-706, which require notice and a commercially reasonable auction or private resale. The benefit of a "supervised" resale is that it reduces the seller's proof problems in subsequent litigation. Seller can then use the difference between the contract price and the resale price to prove damages without having to rely on the potential difficulty of proving the relevant market price. Alternatively, Seller can return the goods to inventory, resell them without notifying Buyer, and subsequently prove damages under § 2-708(1) by establishing (through proof of market prices at the time and place of tender) what a sale on the market would hypothetically have brought. This option requires Seller to introduce competent testimony of the market price at the time and place for tender (*see* § 2-723).

Tesoro Petroleum Corp. v. Holborn Oil Co., Ltd. *(Page 1084).* The question, then, which is illustrated by *Tesoro,* is this: If the seller has an opportunity to resell the contract goods and does so, must he then in all events measure his damages by § 2-706? Or, can seller still use the § 2-708(1) measure assuming that the market price was less then the resale price and thus damages would be higher under the later formula?

In Tesoro, the plaintiff contracted to sell about 10 million gallons of gasoline to the defendant at $1.30 per gallon, having purchased it a few days earlier at $1.26. Plaintiff sent notice of the name of the vessel delivering the product, but was told by defendant that it would not be accepted because, in its opinion, no binding agreement had been formed. Tesoro then resold the gasoline to Esso Sapa for $1.10 per gallon. Plaintiff claimed, however, notwithstanding the sale to Esso Sapa, that a sharp drop in the market actually had reduced the value of the oil at the time of breach to $.80 per gallon. Plaintiff thus seeks damages of $.50 per gallon under § 2-708(1) based on the difference between the contract price and the market price at the time of breach. The *Tesoro* court holds that the seller is restricted to the § 2-706 formula, and can only recover damages of $.20 per gallon based on the difference between the contract price and the resale price to Esso Sapa. If the seller resells the goods, and the resale price is higher than the market price, then seller is limited to the lesser sum under § 1-106 which directs courts to interpret damages rules so as to put injured party in same position as performance would have done.

We ask students to argue for the seller in this case. Seller's best argument is that the Code scheme of free choice between §§ 2-706 and 2-708(1) should be preserved because the seller bears a risk of under-compensation as the mitigator of the breach. *Tesoro's* error, under this argument, is that it looks at the question ex post. Viewed ex ante, there is no reason to believe that seller can out-guess the market. Seller bears the downside risk; that is, if seller seeks contract/market damages based on § 2-713 but subsequently resells the goods at a price below the § 2-713 market, it is limited to the contract/market differential. If seller bears the downside risk of holding the goods and waiting for a resale opportunity down the road, then it should get the upside as well. We think this argument is convincing, at least in theory. After all, a fixed price contract is an option on the goods at the contract price and seller is entitled to the full value of the option. Nevertheless, most courts agree with *Tesoro*.

c. Lost volume sellers

Seller's final question in our hypothetical situation, then, is: When can I use § 2-708(2) and recover my lost profits on the broken contract? By its terms, § 2-708(2) applies when the "damages under subsection (1) are inadequate" to provide Seller its expectancy. The question is: When does this section properly apply? There is one clear case for the application of § 2-708(2). Assume there is no available market for the contract goods (because they are specially manufactured or custom goods) and buyer breaches prior to the time for performance, while the seller is still in the process of producing the custom order. In such a case, the seller has the option under § 2-704(2) to either complete performance and recover the contract price, or to salvage the broken contract by selling off the components. If a seller chooses the salvage option under § 2-704, there is no market and there are no goods. Thus, only a recovery of estimated profits under § 2-708(2) can make the seller whole.

The controversial case, however, is the applicability of a lost volume claim by sellers. The claim arises where a seller resells the contract goods and then claims that it could have made two sales (and two profits) but for the breach, and thus the breach has deprived the seller of its profit on the breached contract. To consider that question we have the students read the next two cases, *Diasonics* and *Rodriguez*.

R.E. Davis Chemical Corporation v. Diasonics, Inc. *(Page 1091).* In *Diasonics,* R.E. Davis had entered into a contract with two partners, Dobbin and Valvassori, to establish a medical facility. It then contracted to purchase a piece of medical diagnostic equipment from Diasonics for use at the facility. Pursuant to the contract, Davis paid Diasonics a $300,000 deposit. Davis' partners later breached, and as a result, Davis refused to take delivery of the equipment and pay the balance of the contract price. Diasonics subsequently resold the equipment to another buyer at the same price Davis had agreed to pay. Davis sued to recover the deposit, and Diasonics counterclaimed, alleging that it could have sold machines to both Davis and the second buyer had Davis not breached. Thus, it should be entitled to a lost profits under § 2-708(2) as compensation for the lost volume.

Diasonics makes the important point that the lost volume question does not turn, as some earlier cases had held, on the mere evidence that the seller had the *capacity* to make two sales. Rather, the question is whether, in addition to capacity, the seller can establish that it could have made both sales *profitably.* On that basis the court remanded to the trial court to calculate damages under § 2-708(2) if *Diasonics* is able to meet that threshold.

Rodriguez v. Learjet *(Page 1094).* *Rodriguez* illustrates a seller complying with the *Diasonics* test. The buyer in this case, Rodriguez, contracted to buy a jet with payment to be made in four installments. After paying the first installment of $250,000, Rodrguez's employer, for whom he was buying the plane, informed him that he no longer wanted it. Rodriguez, in turn, repudiated the contract and demanded the return of the $250,000. Learjet informed Rodriguez that it considered the contract terminated and that it would retain the money as liquidated damages. The jet was then sold to a third party for a greater profit than would have been realized under the Rodriguez contract. The court held that, per *Diasonics,* Learjet was a lost volume seller and was entitled to lost profits because it showed: a) that it had a 60% capacity; b) that it had the ability to produce more planes in any given year; and, c) that additional sales would be profitable (i.e., that marginal costs were less than marginal revenues).

Clearly, courts have become more sophisticated in analyzing lost volume claims, but the problem with the case law is that courts look at the question ex post rather than ex ante. One way to rethink the question from the ex ante perspective is to use the fishing model developed (independently) by Vic Goldberg and Bob Cooter and Mel Eisenberg (*see the Essay on page 1100*). Assume in *Rodriguez* that the seller "fishes" for 50 buyers with 50 Learjets. One buyer breaches. Seller has now lost part of its *expected volume*; that is, the opportunity to catch one more buyer. The key question is: What is the value of that lost opportunity? One answer is that the lost opportunity is represented by the fixed pre-breach *selling costs* incurred by the seller in fishing for 50 buyers when they only "caught" 49. Thus, the breacher needs to pay its share of those lost selling costs. These selling costs are not zero, but neither are they equal to the full expected profit that seller is claiming under § 2-708(2). Viewed in this light, the lost volume claim is really a claim about incidental damages. Unhappily, courts have been willing to award sellers only their *post-breach* expenses under § 2-710. Thus, how is a seller to recover it *pre-breach expenses*? Given how the doctrine has evolved, the practical choice a court faces today is between granting the seller full lost profits recovery under § 2-708(2), which is greater than the seller's pre-breach selling costs and thus over-compensates the seller, or awarding incidental damages under § 2-710 which, given the prevailing limited interpretation of incidental damages, under-compensates the seller.

Buyer's Damages

Since the students will already have covered many of these problems already in the course, this is a section that can be omitted without any significant loss of coverage or comprehension. The essential point of the section is that the buyer's remedies under the Code are parallel to the options available to an aggrieved seller. The first question, then, (as we have seen already) is the choice between specific performance and damages. Assuming that specific performance is unavailable under § 2-716, buyer then is limited to market-based damages. Here, the buyer, just as is the seller, is provided an initial option: Either the buyer can "cover" under § 2-712 (and then recover the contract price/cover price differential) or the buyer can recover the contract/market differential under § 2-713. The major issue that is litigated here is how to correctly interpret the "learned of the breach" language in § 2-713. This question arises in litigation over the proper measure of buyer's damages in the case of an anticipatory repudiation. This issue was covered in Chapter 9 in *Cosden Oil and Chemical Company v. Karl O. Helm* on page 914.

The unique feature of buyer's damages which does not parallel the scheme of seller's damages applies to cases where the buyer has *accepted the goods* even though they are defective, or the buyer learns of the defect after the goods have been accepted. Once goods are accepted by the buyer, market-based damages no longer are applicable. Instead, the accepting buyer's damages are measured by § 2-714.

Carlson v. Rysavy *(Page 1109).* *Carlson* illustrates the issues courts confront in applying the difference in "value" measure of damages of § 2-714. The Carlsons purchased a double-wide modular home from Rysavy that turned out to have several serious defects. Though some of the defects were apparent at the time of delivery, some of them caused problems that did not become apparent until later. The Carlsons sent a letter to Town and Country, the manufacturer of the home, listing 21 defects, but Town and Country largely ignored the complaint. The Carlsons then sued for breach of warranty.

The first requirement that a buyer must satisfy under § 2-714 is to give the seller notice of the defect within a reasonable time after the defect was or should have been discovered pursuant to § 2-607(3), which the Carlson's clearly did. Thereafter, buyers, such as the Carlsons, are free to prove losses under § 2-714(2). In theory, the best evidence of the difference between "value with the defect" and "value as warranted" is the cost of repair. But where, as here, repair is not feasible, courts will allow the buyer to recover under § 2-714 by showing the difference between the contract price (as a proxy for value as warranted) and the salvage value (value as is with the defect).

Chatlos v. National Cash Register *(Page 1113).* Chatlos purchased a computer system for $46,000 from NCR that did not function properly. Chatlos sued NCR for breach of warranty, and the district court found the defendant liable. Following a remand, the district court awarded Chatlos $201,826 in damages under § 2-714(2) based on the difference between the value of the system as warranted (which, based on plaintiff's expert's testimony the court determined was $207,826) and the value as accepted, which the court fixed at $6,000. NCR appealed arguing that the $46,000 purchase price should fix the outer limit of "value as warranted." The Third Circuit disagreed and affirmed the district court.

The plaintiff's expert had testified that the computer system was worth $207,000 as warranted. Defendant, in turn, did not rebut the expert testimony but rested its case on the evidence of the $46,000 contract price as the value as warranted. This was a big mistake. The court held that the expert testimony was a better measure of value as warranted than the contact price. To be sure, the court held, the contract price was evidence of "value as warranted," but it was only a proxy. In any given case, therefore, plaintiff is free to show that the value of the goods as warranted exceeded the contract price. The dissent points out in this case that "value as warranted" refers to the goods that the buyer actually selected and not hypothetical goods that buyer could have selected. On this point, we think the dissent is clearly right.

CHAPTER 11

THIRD-PARTY RIGHTS

A. Introduction

As we suggested in the Introduction to the manual, we find that third party issues are different in kind and more doctrinally complex than the standard contract law issues covered thus far in the course. Thus, this material does not work well when introduced at the end of a one- semester course of four or five credits. We believe that this Chapter is best taught in the spring semester as part of a more traditional six-credit, two-semester offering. In that context, it provides a useful introduction to issues of trusts, agency and commercial financing. The first question is: When can a third party who is affected by the making (or breaking) of a contract sue to enforce the rights of the promisee? As a general proposition, of course, the answer should be never. That is because to date we have assumed that the contract created a little "society" in which only the interests of the two parties to the contract were affected. This then permitted us to analyze the legal issues either in terms of the autonomy interests of the contracting parties or in terms of their shared goal of maximizing their welfare as determined by the size of the contractual pie.

Third party beneficiary law requires, therefore, that we relax the assumption that there are no external effects from making contracts. But if we were to relax that assumption completely, the costs of nonperformance to promisors would increase to the point where no promisee would ever be willing to pay the premium charged by the promisor for entering into a binding commitment. In other words, the problem is that so long as the promisee does not internalize the third party benefits, she will not be willing to pay the promisor to bear the increased costs of third party performance. The question, then, for this discussion of third party beneficiaries is: When, if ever, do promisees sufficiently internalize third party benefits from a contract to support a default rule that the third party can also enforce the contract against the promisor?

Lawrence v. Fox *(Page 1127).* Holly loaned Fox $300 in consideration for Fox's promise to repay the sum to Lawrence (to satisfy Holly's debt to Lawrence). Lawrence sues Fox (not Holly?) to recover the debt. The defense: There was no consideration for defendant's promise and, in any case, plaintiff is not in privity of contract with the defendant. The court rejects both claims. First, there was consideration running to defendant in the $300 loan from Holly. Second, the plaintiff is in privity of contract as the promise Fox made to Holly embodies an implied promise to Lawrence as well.

This case is one of the old "chestnuts" articulating the doctrinal justifications for the rule that a promise made for consideration to perform for a third party, which had traditionally been enforceable in cases of trust or agency, could be extended to any circumstance where the third party was a creditor of the promisee.

Note 2 (Page 1133). The excerpt from Mel Eisenberg's article shows why the third party beneficiary principle is carefully circumscribed. A general rule of third party recovery on the grounds that the third party "benefitted" from performance of the contract would increase significantly the contract price for the promisee. Ordinarily, the promisee will not be willing to pay the extra premium that a promisor will charge to cover the greater liability if third parties have rights of enforcement as well as the promisee. Thus, the key question: Under what circumstances would the promisee be willing to pay the premium to obtain third party enforcement rights? One answer, provided by *Lawrence* and its progeny, is that promisees will be willing to pay to permit their creditors to recover on their behalf and thereby extinguish an obligation owed by the promisee to the third party.

This focus on the interests of the promisee in "purchasing" additional third party rights explains the traditional focus of courts in this area on the *intent* of the contracting parties. In short, where the parties intend to create third party rights of enforcement, their intent will, in general, be honored. The difficult question in the cases, therefore, is how to discern intent where the parties have not signaled their intent explicitly one way or the other. We find it useful to have the students read Restatement § 302 at this point and focus on its test– a manifestation of intent *plus* either a) a promise to satisfy a debt owed by the promisee or b) a specific intent by the promisee to make a gift to the third party.

B. Intended and Incidental Beneficiaries
The "Donee Beneficiary" Cases.

Seaver v. Ransom *(Page 1135)*. *Seaver* is another of the "old chestnuts." Here the court sets out the classic doctrinal requirements for a third party "donee" beneficiary to recover on a contract made for his or her benefit. Judge Beman drew up a will for his wife as she lay dying. In accordance with her wishes, the will provided that her husband would receive a life estate in her house with the remainder to the ASPCA. After the will was read to her, Mrs. Beman said that she wanted instead to leave the house to her niece, the plaintiff. The judge offered to rewrite the will, but Mrs. Beman feared she would not live long enough to sign it. He then promised that if she would sign the existing will, he would leave the plaintiff enough in his will to make up the difference. Upon his death, however, it was discovered that no such provision had been made. The plaintiff brought suit to recover damages resulting from the judge's failure to keep his promise. The court found for the plaintiff, recognizing as an exception to the general requirement of privity of contract, the right of a third party beneficiary who has a close personal relationship with the promisee to sue on a contract that was *expressly* made for the benefit of the donee. In this case a favorite niece satisfies this "close relationship" test.

The straightforward donee beneficiary case, as this one, is easy to explain on internalization grounds. To the extent that there is a close family, or other personal, relationship between the promisee and the donee beneficiary, it is likely that the benefits to the donee are internalized by the promisee. Thus, it is plausible to assume that the promisee will bear both the costs and the benefits of having the right to extend enforcement to a third party and thus the value of third party enforcement will be "paid" for in the initial contract.

Drake v. Drake *(Page 1138)*. *Drake* begins to test how far the *Seaver* principle can be extended. In this case, the plaintiff's parents separated in 1963 and later divorced. According to the terms of the separation agreement, the father promised to pay periodic payments to the mother for the support of their five children. The amount of the payments was tied to the husband's earnings, and the agreement provided for escalated payments as his earnings increased. Payments were to continue until each child turned 21, died, became self-supporting, or married, and were to be reduced on a fixed schedule. The defendant made the scheduled payments, but he did not increase their amount as his income grew. When she was a senior in high school, the plaintiff – the last of the Drake children still at home – moved from her mother's house to the house of a friend and requested that her father send payments directly to her. Upon finding out that his daughter had left home, he assumed that she was self-supporting and ceased making payments. The plaintiff subsequently learned of the terms of the separation agreement and brought suit to recover the difference between the payments made and the escalated payments. She also sought an order compelling defendant to make payments directly to her.

Drake asks the question: Is a child of divorced parents entitled to enforce the support provisions of the parents separation agreement as a third party beneficiary? The court's answer is no. Here, the support payments were payable to the former spouse who had discretion as to the disposition of the funds. Children are not specifically intended beneficiaries of support provisions of their parents' divorce agreement although they can enforce other specific provisions clearly made for their benefit, such as a promise to pay college tuition or make the child a beneficiary of a life insurance policy.

We wonder whether the distinction advanced in *Drake* makes sense in terms of the internalization analysis offered earlier. Surely the promisee in such a case will internalize all of the benefits her children will receive by being entitled to enforce the agreement independently. If so, then we can be confident that the promisee will "pay" for the privilege to have third party enforcement rights as part of the contract. Perhaps one answer is that generic support payments are primarily directed at the divorced spouse and only incidently are designed to aid the children. Another answer may be that courts indulge in the assumption that parents are paternalistic and do not intend to give dependent children independent rights unless the context is crystal clear.

Detroit Institute of Arts v. Rose *(Page 1141)*. For aging baby boomers, at least, the "Howdy Doody" case conjures up great memories, if not interesting analysis. In this case, Rufus Rose, one of the show's puppeteers, contracts with NBC to, inter alia, give the Howdy Doody puppet to the Detroit Institute of Arts. Subsequently, Rose loaned Howdy Doody to Buffalo Bob, who was making public appearances in his role from the show, and he informed Buffalo Bob that he had agreed with NBC to donate the puppet to the DIA. Sometime later Buffalo Bob (in financial straights) and Rose's son seek to sell the puppet and pocket the proceeds. The Detroit Institute sues to enforce the original contract as a third party beneficiary. The Court holds for the plaintiffs, extending the "donee" beneficiary case beyond the context of a close personal relationship. The court based its decision on the clear intent of Rufus Rose and NBC to have the puppet placed in the

Museum.

As *Note 3 on page 1148* suggests, courts have extended the common law donee beneficiary cases to include any situation where the promisee clearly intends to make a gift, whether or not the beneficiary enjoys a close personal relationship with the promisee. The extension beyond personal relationships does mean that the court must place all the weight of the decision on the evidence of donative intent. Does the fact of donative intent alone imply that the promisee wishes as well to pay for the donee's right to sue independently as a third party beneficiary? One can argue, to the contrary, that the two issues are independent. I may well wish to make you a gift of my right to a return promise without, at the same time, wanting to give you a second gift, the right to independently enforce the promise of the promisor.

The "Creditor Beneficiary" Cases

Hamill v. Maryland Casualty Co. *(Page 1149).* Hamill contracts to finance 10% of Gunnell's construction contracts in return for 10% of the net profits, payable only after full performance and payment of all bills. Gunnell subsequently contracted to build a science lab and Maryland Casualty put up the performance bond on the strength of the financing contract between Hamill and Gunnell. After the construction was completed, Hamill recovered its profits from Gunnell prior to full payment of outstanding claims. Gunnell then failed to pay all the unpaid subcontractors and materialmen. Maryland Casualty, the surety, paid off the subs and sues Hamill as a third party creditor beneficiary of Hamill's promise to advance 10% of the contract price for the construction contract.

In permitting MC to recover, the court recognized that the primary motive of the contract was to benefit just the immediate parties Hamill and Gunnell. But, in order to accomplish that purpose, Hamill also had the intent to induce the surety to issue the performance bond. In order to secure that bond, Hamill had promised that, as a financer, it would be eligible for repayment only after completion of the project and the payment of all the bills. This promise necessarily implies a subsidiary promise to pay the expenses incident with performance to the extent of ten percent of the contract price. This promise was an asset of Gunnell on which the surety relied in issuing the performance bond.

Pierce Associates, Inc. v. Nemours Foundation *(Page 1152).* Contrast *Hamill,* which uses reliance as a test of intent to create third party rights, with *Pierce.* In *Pierce,* Gilbane, a general contractor, contracted to complete a hospital for Nemours. Subsequently, Gilbane subcontracted with Pierce for the HVAC work. Pierce walked away from the job following a dispute, and Nemours sued Pierce for damages as a third party beneficiary of the subcontract. The sub-contract incorporated by reference the American Institute of Architects' "General Conditions of the Contract for Construction" which contain a standard-form clause stating inter alia: "Nothing in the Contract Documents shall create any contractual relationship between the Owner and a subcontractor."

The court rejected the owner's third party beneficiary claim on the grounds that typically in construction contracts an owner has no relationship with the various subs. The owner thus ordinarily looks exclusively to the GC and not to the subs both for performance and for contract damages in the case of breach. Indeed, the performance is usually assured by a bond issued by the GC for which the owner is the obligee. This insulates the owner from subcontractors non-performance of their contract obligations and, in turn, from having any remedies directly against the sub if there is a default. The court found persuasive the incorporation by reference of the AIA General Conditions in the sub-contract as well as the general contract.

To be sure, this is merely a default rule. The parties are always free to provide explicitly that the owner shall have independent rights to enforce the sub-contract. But such an express opt out from the default rule must be evidenced by the explicit language of the sub-contract. In this case, the sub-contact shows, to the contrary, that Peirce was to be liable only to Gilbane, the GC, and not to the owner, Nemours. The fact that the owner was the ultimate beneficiary of the construction subcontract does not, without more, create a right in the owner to recover as a third party beneficiary.

Note 4 (Page 1164). As *Hamill* and *Pierce* demonstrate, the test of intention to create third party rights in the so-called creditor cases is often based on inferred intent rather than direct evidence of that intention (as would be the case if the parties had included an expressly negotiated "third party beneficiary clause" in the contract). But how is that intention to be inferred? *Hamill* uses reliance. *Pierce* suggests that, absent reliance, specific evidence of intent from the text of the contract may be required. It is not enough, as Mel Eisenberg suggests (*see Note 4*), that the contract evidence a general intent to benefit a third party. As we have seen in the donee cases, there are two kinds of external benefits that a third party might assert. The first is a general benefit that arises either from a gift or a satisfaction of a debt. The second is a specific intent to create a third party right to enforce that first benefit. In the donee cases, we used the notion of internalization to find this specific intent. What kind of evidence is appropriate in the creditor cases? Orna Paglin seems to suggest (*see Note 4*) that it would be better (clearer) to substitute a bright line presumption against third party enforcement rights in most creditor cases and let the parties then signal their desire to opt out of that default with a specific clause conferring third party rights.

C. Special Applications

This section explores other circumstances in which plaintiffs have sued on a third-party beneficiary theory, namely suits relating to insurance and government contracts.

Barrera v. State Farm Mutual Automobile Insurance Co. *(Page 1169).* The plaintiff was injured by the negligent driving of Sandra Alves who had taken out a policy with the defendant. State Farm argued that the policy was void because it was issued in reliance on a material misrepresentation made by Ms. Alves's husband. The trial court found that Mr. Alves had told a State Farm agent that his license had never been suspended when in fact his DMV report showed one suspension and two probation orders, and State Farm was therefore within its rights when it rescinded the contract. However, State Farm had failed to check Alves's DMV report until the accident occurred, 1½ years after Alves had taken out the policy. On appeal, the plaintiff contended that the failure to investigate Alves's driving record in a timely manner constituted negligence on

State Farm's part, and that they should therefore be estopped from rescinding the contract and denying coverage. He further argued that allowing rescission violated the public policy expressed in California's Financial Responsibility Law.

The appellate court agreed with the plaintiff and held that "an automobile liability insurer must undertake a reasonable investigation of the insured's insurability within a reasonable period of time . . . ." Public policy dictates that a person injured by the careless driving of others should have the ability to sue a financially responsible party, and insurance companies assume the risk of such suits when issuing automobile insurance policies. If insurance companies are allowed to wait until after a claim is filed to investigate the validity of information provided by the insured party, they can accept compensation in the form of premiums without accepting any risk. Injured parties would be the ones most harmed by such a rule because in many cases they would be left with no effective way to recover once the policy is rescinded. Hence, once an injured party obtains judgement against the tortfeasor and that judgement goes unsatisfied, she can proceed against the insurance company even though she was not a party to the insurance contract. If the insurance company has negligently failed to investigate the insured's insurability, it may not raise misrepresentation as a defense against the action.

H.R. Moch v. Rensselaer Water Co. *(Page 1175).* The defendant had contracted with the city of Rensselaer to provide water for, among other things, the city's fire hydrants. During the term of the contract, a fire erupted in a building near the plaintiff's warehouse. The water company was notified, but it failed to supply an adequate amount of water with sufficient pressure to extinguish the fire in accordance with the terms of the contract. The plaintiff alleged that this failure resulted in the fire spreading to his warehouse, which was destroyed along with its contents. The plaintiff sued on three separate theories: breach of contractual duty to a third-party beneficiary (citing *Lawrence v. Fox*), breach of a common-law tort duty, and breach of a statutory duty.

Cardozo rejected the third-party beneficiary theory. Because a city has no legal duty to protect its citizens against fire, a third-party cannot sue a company that has contracted with the city to provide water absent a manifestation of intent by the parties to make the company answerable to individuals as well as to the city. The terms of the contract, he argued, do not indicate such an intent. To construe the contract so as to make individuals intended beneficiaries of the contract would expose the company to almost unlimited liability, a proposition that it surely would have rejected at the time of contracting. Cardozo likewise found no cause of action under the other two theories and dismissed the plaintiff's claim.

Klamath Water Users Protective Association v. Patterson *(Page 1177).* This case involves a contract between the US Bureau of Reclamation and the California Oregon Power Company (Copco) for the construction and operation of a dam. The contract stipulated that Copco would construct the dam and then convey it to the US, but Copco would continue operating it. The Klamath Water Users Protective Association consisted of irrigators who used water released from the dam to supply their irrigation operations. When PacificCorp, Copco's successor in interest in the contract, agreed with Reclamation to modify the contract provisions relating to the amount of water to be released from the dam, the irrigators filed suit claiming that they were third party beneficiaries and that the modification violated the parties' contractual obligation to them.

The court recited the rule that third parties must demonstrate that the contract reflects the express or implied intention of the parties that the contract benefit the third party. The contract said that Copco could regulate the water level, but that the contracting officer could specify a higher minimum water level if necessary to protect irrigation requirements. It further stated that Copco could not use any water if it is required by the US or any irrigation district. The court said that, although this language indicates that the contract was meant in part to benefit the irrigators, it does not manifest an intention to give the irrigators the right to enforce the contract; rather, it simply gives the US the right to take control of dam operations if the need arises. The irrigators are incidental but not intended beneficiaries.

Problem 6 (Page 1185). The rule in such cases is that beneficiaries of a will can sue an attorney who fails to carry out the intent of the testator through negligent drafting as third party beneficiaries. Earlier cases had held that will beneficiaries could not sue due to a lack of privity, but the result of this rule was that drafting attorneys could not be held accountable for their negligence. The estate could sue, but the estate does not suffer harm in such cases and could therefore not recover more than nominal damages. The parties that do suffer harm – the intended beneficiaries – had no valid claim. Hence, there was no legal deterrent to negligent will drafting and no recourse for those harmed by it. Some courts, including the *Lucas* court, have predicated third-party beneficiary status upon the fact that harm to the beneficiary was highly foreseeable (*see also Simpson v. Calivas*, 650 A.2d 318), but the language of Restatement (Second) § 302 seems to make the issue of foreseeability irrelevant. The beneficiary of a will is clearly an intended beneficiary under this section and therefore has standing to sue in contract as a third party beneficiary.

D. Assignment and Delegation.

The common law rule is that contract rights and duties are generally assignable and delegable (Restatement (Second)§ 318) so long as performance does not involve unique personal services or impose greater burdens on the promisee. The principal exceptions to free delegation of duties relate to contacts for personal services and to contracts for the exercise of personal skill or discretion. In the absence of a contrary agreement, Restatement (Second) § 318(2) precludes delegation only where a substantial reason is shown why delegated performance is not as satisfactory as personal performance. This rule is also embodied in the UCC. Section 2-210(1) provides that a party may perform his duty through a delegate unless otherwise agreed or unless the other party has a substantial interest in having his original promisor perform or control the acts required by the contract. Comment 4 to § 2-210 explains that this provision was designed to clarify the freedom of parties to assign rights and delegate duties under output, requirements and exclusive dealings contracts.[1]

There are no formal requirements necessary to effect an assignment of rights. Rather, the common law only requires evidence that the obligee *manifest an intention* to transfer the rights in question. This manifestation need not take any particular form. It can be made to the other party or to a third party and, unless required by the contract or by statute, may be made orally or by a writing (Restatement (Second) § 324). Typically, an assignment of "all rights" under an agreement operates as both an assignment of rights and a delegation of duties. In any case, as with any contract, an assignment requires the acceptance of the contractual obligations by the assignee, but absent a provision in the contract, it does not require the assent of the obligor (Restatement (Second) §§ 317,318).

Crane Ice Cream Co. v. Terminal Freezing & Heating Co. *(Page 1187).* Crane and Frederick contracted for the delivery of ice to Frederick under a requirements contract. Frederick sold its business (and assigned the contract) to Terminal. Crane declined to perform for Terminal and Terminal sued to enforce. In finding for Crane, the court stated the general rule: 1) contract rights are assignable unless the contract requires a personal performance; 2) contract duties cannot be assigned without a novation; 3) but contract performance can be delegated, so long as performance is not personal. In that case, the assignor remains liable until performance is satisfied.

Applying those principles to a requirements contract, the court found that the essence of a requirements contract turns on the good faith performance and business stability of the requirements buyer. Thus, the character of the buyer is key. This necessarily implies that rights and duties under such a contract cannot be assigned by the buyer. To be sure, performance of contract duties can ordinarily be delegated, but not in a case such as this where the personal qualifications of the assignor are central to the inducements given to the requirements supplier to make the contract.

Note that courts under the Code have relaxed the strict standard of non-assignability of requirements contracts expressed in cases such as *Crane*. Under the UCC, delegation of performance under a contract is a normal and permissible incident of exclusive dealings and distribution contracts of the sort at issue in *Crane* (*see* § 2-210, Comment 4).

Evening News Association v. Peterson *(Page 1190).* In *Peterson,* the court faces the question of whether long-time Washington news anchor Gordon Peterson's employment contract with Channel 9 in D.C. was assignable when a new owner bought the station. Peterson claimed that his services were unique and that his assent to the contract was based on a the close, personal relationship he had with the news director and executive producer. The court rejected Peterson's

---

[1] UCC § 2-210, Comment 4 provides: "In the first place, the section on requirements and exclusive dealings removes from the construction of the original contract most of the 'personal discretion' element by substituting the reasonably objective standard of good faith operation of the plant or business to be supplied. Secondly, the section on insecurity and assurances . . . frees the other party from the doubts and uncertainty which may afflict him under an assignment of the character in question by permitting him to demand adequate assurance of due performance . . . ."

claim, holding that the contract was freely assignable to the new owner of the station. Key to the decision was the fact that Peterson's duties did not change, nor was his employment contract made contingent on his working with any particular news director or producer. It is true, of course, that personal service contracts such as this are not delegable. But that does not mean that the rights to receive the benefits of those services are not freely assignable.

Sally Beauty Company v. Nexxus Products Company *(Page 1196)*. Nexxus contracted with Best to give Best an exclusive license to distribute Nexxus' products in Texas. Best was subsequently acquired by Sally Beauty, a wholly-owned subsidiary of Alberto-Culver, which competed with Nexxus in the marketing and sale of beauty products. The 7th circuit rejected the trial court's holding that this was a contract for personal services and therefore unassignable. The appellate court did, however, affirm the trial court's grant of Nexxus' motion for summary judgment on the grounds that § 2-210 forbids, as a matter of law, an assignment of rights under an exclusive dealings contract to a subsidiary of a direct competitor of the exclusive dealings supplier. Under § 2-210(1), contract duties cannot be delegated if there is a reason why the non-assigning party would find performance by the delegate substantially different. The court found that this best efforts contract was just such a case.

In dissent, Judge Posner disagreed with the court's use of a per se rule. He pointed out that Sally was going to operate in Texas using the same personnel as Best. Moreover, Sally was a non-exclusive distributor, meaning that it handled multiple product lines. Thus, without more facts, he would deny summary judgment in this case. His argument rests on the belief that, as a profit maximizer, Sally (and Alberto-Culver) would want to promote Nexxus products to the extent that those products were superior on the market to Alberto-Culver's products. While it is difficult to disagree with Posner on the summary judgment point, his understanding of the dynamics of best efforts contracts is a bit naive. Best efforts contracts are notoriously difficult to enforce. Best efforts suppliers usually lose such cases except where there has been a clear failure to perform by the distributor. Given the hidden information problems that make enforcement of small scale chiseling and the like unenforceable in litigation, parties have every incentive to rely on social norms and other extra legal mechanisms to aid in enforcing the best efforts obligation. In such an environment, the identity of the best efforts distributor and the degree to which the distributor is responsive to social sanctions such as guilt and shaming becomes very relevant. Thus, the majority may well be correct in holding that, under these circumstances, an assignment to a direct competitor weakens those extra legal sanctions and thus imposes a greater burden on the best efforts supplier.

E. Novation

Rosenbergs v. Son, Inc. *(Page 1212)*. The Rosenbergs sold their Dairy Queen franchise, inventory, and equipment to Mary Pratt who later assigned her rights and delegated her duties to Son, Inc. This transaction was agreed to by the Rosenbergs in a consent clause contained in the assignment contract. Son subsequently assigned the contract to Merit Corp. without the Rosenberg's consent. Merit subsequently defaulted, and the Rosenbergs brought an action against Pratt and Son to collect the outstanding debt.

When assignments or delegations are made, the assignor remains liable to the promisee for the performance of the duty. If the assignee fails to perform, the promisee can enforce the promise against the assignor. The assignor can, however, escape liability for non-performance by executing a novation, but the language of the contract must clearly indicate that all parties involved intend liability for non-performance to shift from assignor to assignee. The court found that the Rosenbergs consented only to an assignment and not a novation when Pratt assigned the contract to Son. Furthermore, Son agreed to a clause promising to indemnify Pratt should Son fail to perform. This shows that Pratt intended to be ultimately liable for performance and sought to protect herself against the risks involved. However, changes in the contractual obligation that arose after the assignment and that prejudicially effected the assignor can effectively release the assignor from liability and create a new contractual relationship between the assignee and promisee. The court found that, given the subsequent transaction between Son and Merit, there is a question of fact regarding whether or not Pratt remained liable. The trial court's grant of summary judgement against the Rosenbergs was therefore inappropriate, and the trial court reversed and remanded.